Series: *Studies in Drama & Theatre*

1. D. Pietropaolo ed., *The Performance Text*
2. G. Sanguinetti Katz, V. Golini and D. Pietropaolo eds., *Theatre and the Visual Arts*

Cover: Compugraphics by Pierre Bertrand

Theatre and the Visual Arts

Edited by

Giuliana Sanguinetti Katz
Vera Golini and Domenico Pietropaolo

LEGAS

New York Ottawa Toronto

Canadian Cataloguing in Publication Data

Main entry under title:
Theatre and the visual arts

(Studies in drama & theatre ; 2)
Papers originally presented at a colloquium held Jan. 22-24, 1999 at the Graduate Centre for Study of Drama, University of Toronto.
Includes bibliographical references.
ISBN 1-894508-28-9

1. Theater—Philosophy—Congresses. 2. Theater in art—Congresses. 3. Theaters—Stage-setting and scenery—History—Congresses. I. Katz, Giuliana, 1938- II. Golini, Vera III. Pietropaolo, Domenico, 1949- IV.University of Toronto. Graduate Centre for Study of Drama V. Series.

PN1637.T48 2001 792'.01 C2001-903859-3

For further information and for orders:

LEGAS

P. O. Box 040328
Brooklyn, New York
USA 11204

3 Wood Aster Bay
Ottawa, Ontario
K2R 1B3

2908 Dufferin Street
Toronto, Ontario
M6B 3S8

Printed and bound in Canada

CONTENTS

Editors' Introduction 7

Eric Csapo
The First Artistic Representations of Theatre: Dramatic Illusion and Dramatic Performance in Attic and South Italian Art 17

Luba Eleen
The Three Kings in Drama and Visual Arts: The Chicken and the Egg 39

Konrad Eisenbichler
Depicting Theatre: Contemporary Evidence for Renaissance Theatre Sets in Renaissance Italy 51

Mary Alexandra Watt
Poliziano's Orfeo*: Italian Renaissance as Festival Decor* 65

Anna Migliarisi
De Sommi on Mise en Scène 85

Francesco Guardiani
Descrizioni liriche di temi teatrali nel poema epico del Marino 99

Salvatore Bancheri
Dalla botola sciasciana alle scene plastiche: elementi per una storia della messinscena del Riscatto d'Adamo 111

Nancy Copeland
Visualizing the Restoration: "Neo-baroque" Costuming at the Stratford Festival 127

Enzo Zappulla
La figlia di Iorio *di Gabriele d'Annunzio: un secolo di messe in scena* 139

Sarah Zappulla Muscarà
La figlia di Iorio *di Gabriele d'Annunzio fra lingua e dialetto* 161

Paolo Puppa
La figlia di Iorio *between Michetti and d'Annunzio* 177

Claude Evans
Visual Arts and Riders to the Sea 197

Anne Urbancic
Cinematographic Techniques and Stereotypes in the Stories of Annie Vivanti 209

Jennifer Hirsh
Staging the Self: Giorgio de Chirico and the Theatricality of Self-Portraiture 221

Luca Somigli
Theatre and Its 'Truth': A Reading of Alberto Savinio's Il suo nome 239

Deborah Tihanyi
Man, Man as Dancer, Art Figure: Oskar Sclemmer's Experiments on the Bauhaus Stage 257

Ilona Fried
Soft Dictatorship as Asylum. The Performance of The Persecution and Assassination of Jean-Paul Marat as Performed by the Inmates of the Asylum of Charenton under the Direction of the Marquis De Sade *by Peter Weiss, During the Last Decade of the Kádár Regime in Hungary* 271

Giuliana Sanguinetti Katz
Lepage's Psychoanalytic Interpretation of Schoenberg's Erwartung 281

List of Contributors 293

Theatre and the Visual Arts

Eds. Giuliana Sanguinetti Katz, Vera Golini

and Domenico Pietropaolo

At the present time theatre is thriving with unprecedented numbers of new scripts, and productions drawing on advanced technology. Thanks to new methods of research and re-evaluation of documents, long standing views on the origins of drama in Athens have been revised, as well as notions on playwriting and staging in medieval and later Europe. Recent scholarly studies have made it possible to analyze in greater detail the work of individual directors and designers at peak moments of theatre activity during the past 2000 years. Computerized research facilities and enhanced travel possibilities continue to afford audiences and scholars alike access to stages across the world and open greater vistas upon theatre as a visual cultural medium. These and other considerations inspired the colloquium on *Theatre and the Visual Arts* which was held on 22nd to 24th January 1999 at the Graduate Centre for Study of Drama at the University of Toronto and was sponsored by the Emilio Goggio Chair of Italian Studies at the University of Toronto, the Italian Cultural Institute in Toronto and the Graduate Centre for Study of Drama at the University of Toronto.

Through their deliberately wide scope, these studies, deriving from the colloquium, address many of the possible relationships between drama and the visual arts: portrayal of theatrical scenes in contemporary arts, illustrations of dramatic texts, designs of theatrical costumes and sets, special occasions and festivals for dramatic performances, staging and directing of plays and operas, and the influence of cinema on dramatic texts. In their very broad range and long reach, the studies here contained offer new considerations on a variety of texts and artistic products from Ancient Greece to a recent staging of a German opera by the Canadian Opera Company.

This collection demonstrates and invites the reader to consider the vast and often fascinating relationships extant among various types of visual, oral and written communication which have been traditionally compartmentalized. To this end the authors of the articles, who come from diverse disciplines, stress the interrelationship between drama, literature, history and the visual arts from different perspectives.

In "The First Artistic Representations of Theatre: Dramatic Illusion and Dramatic Performance in Attic and South Italian Art," Csapo examines the representation of dramatic performances in several Greek vases of the fifth and fourth centuries. Most of the designs described involve comic scenes from Aristophanes, and the portrayal of the chorus before entering the stage. After a careful description of several vases, Csapo comments insightfully on the scarcity of dramatic representations in Attic vases of the Classical period, where the subjects of dramatic performances were represented as stories of gods and heroes, in contrast with the South Italian vases which showed awareness of the actual performance occurring on stage. Csapo suggests that Classical spectators in Athens saw the play as portraying archetypal and mythic realities, not fiction. Only later on in Athens and especially in Southern Italy, with a new perception of the surface of reality rather than of its hidden meaning, theatrical performances were represented as such, especially where "the illusion was weakest, namely the chorus and comedy."

Eleen in "The Three Kings in Drama and Visual Art: The Chicken and the Egg" deals with the possible relations between the representation of the Adoration of the Magi on the Three Kings Shrine, the gold casket made to hold the relics of the Magi in the Cathedral of Cologne, and contemporary sacred drama of the arrival of the Three Kings, enacted by the clergy in church.

Eleen argues that the influence of contemporary drama on the Cologne representation might perhaps be traced in the costumes of the Magi. Moreover, the fact that the Virgin and Child portrayed on the Shrine are treated as sculptures, rather than human beings, and are crowned and placed on a throne, signifies that they are at the same time part of a particular narrative scene and that they are timeless and divine creatures. This emblematic representation is common in twelfth century monumental art and is present in contemporary drama, where the actors deposited their gifts in church not in front of other actors but in front of a cult statue of the type discussed above. Eleen concludes that, though it is impossible to establish a clear derivation of the Cologne

Magi from drama, since artists saw dramatic performances and playwrights saw public art, they probably influenced each other in many ways.

In "Depicting Theatre: Contemporary Evidence for Renaissance Theatre Sets in Renaissance Italy," Eisenbichler discusses what evidence we have of the sets and the special staging devices with which Renaissance plays were staged in their time. He maintains that the complex architectural sets sketched by Serlio represented ideal rather than real stage sets. The latter are probably more faithfully portrayed in the simple woodcuts that illustrated the title page of the publications of the *sacre rappresentazioni*, showing either a rudimentary stage with a series of low panels, or a free standing structure (a portico) and some ingenious levitating devices. Eisenbichler points out that in any case the scanty narrative and visual records the critics have examined so far should be correlated with the records left by the scribes and accountants of the various confraternities where the *sacre rappresentazioni* were performed. This would allow us in our time to reconstruct "the time-line, process, materials, support, networks, crew, and cast of premodern performances."

In her study "Poliziano's *Orfeo*: Italian Renaissance Drama as Festival Décor", Watt stresses the need to enhance a literary analysis with a socio-historical perspective when looking at Italian Renaissance drama. She points out that "Italian Renaissance drama, more than an erudite enterprise inviting literary criticism, might be better characterized as festival décor, an audio-visual nicety coordinated thematically with all of the other elements that combined to create the great *feste* of fifteenth- and sixteenth-century Italy." These festivals were spectacles of great visual splendour and were celebrated by the rulers of a city state in occasion of baptisms, weddings, and other social festivities, to obtain popular support and strengthen the prestige of the rulers. Using the description of festivals that took place towards the end of the fifteenth and the beginning of the sixteenth century, Watt reconstructs the festive occasion in which Poliziano's *Orfeo* may have been performed, as well as its sets, costumes and stage machinery.

In "De Sommi on *Mise en Scène*" Migliarisi studies the content of De Sommi's treatise on how to perform a play, *Quattro dialoghi in materia di rappresentazioni sceniche,* and observes that the work represents the author's "conscious attempt to codify theatrical representation from the point of view of the director." According to Migliarisi "the *Quattro dialoghi* are the first systematic account of the professional director in western theatre" because they are a "manual of practical instruction" dealing with all aspects of drama, rather than "an abstract theory for scholars and playwrights."

De Sommi's sections on costumes, lighting and stage settings, show his knowledge of stage techniques, his concern for realism and, in the case of settings, his desire to harmonize the 'ideal' with modern taste and conventions. Most of all, he insists that the various elements of the performance must be subordinated to the meaning of the text, so that the different parts of the *mise en scène* may create a harmonious whole. In conclusion, De Sommi's methodology "could be compared to the aesthetic principles of some of his professional counterparts in modern theatre."

Guardiani in "Descrizioni liriche di temi teatrali nel poema epico del Marino" ("Lyrical Descriptions of Theatrical Themes in Marino's Epic Poem") shows how Marino uses the metaphor of "the great theatre of the world" in his main work *L'Adone*. Marino stated that we all create ourselves and our roles in life like actors on the stage and thereby use our creative capacities. The author's unified view of the world can be seen also in the fact that in the *Adone* he fuses the three Aristotelian literary genres of drama, epic and lyric poetry, in contrast with the late Renaissance tendency to divide and classify literary themes in different genres.

This united view of the world is clear in the 5th canto, in the description of the theater of Venus, a square shape placed within the circle of the tower of "touch," which in turn is placed within a square corresponding to the other four senses. Each side of the theater is dedicated to one of the four elements, on its ceiling is represented the heavenly sphere and on the floor the underworld. The story of Diana and Actaeon is performed on the stage, but instead of bloodthirsty scenes and fateful recognitions, typical of Renaissance tragedy, we have a very peaceful performance with a ballet and a concert, described in lyrical terms. Finally, in the 20th canto, Venus with the help of all the forces of nature presides over the games that celebrate the death of Adonis and render him immortal. The pagan goddess, now become "Charitas,"celebrates the death of Adonis, become a Christ figure.

Bancheri in "Dalla botola sciasciana alle scene plastiche: elementi per una storia della messinscena del *Riscatto d'Adamo*" ("From Sciascia's Trapdoor to Tableaux Vivants: Elements for the History of the Staging of *Adam's Ransom*") examines the various performances of Filippo Orioles's mystery play "*Riscatto d'Adamo nella morte di Cristo,*" from the first half of the eighteenth century, when the play was written, up to the present time.

After mentioning the extraordinary popularity of the play and its frequent performances in Sicily and southern Italy, Bancheri devotes particular attention to the performances of the play that take place every Easter in Delia, a little town in Sicily. He shows the active participation of the whole town to the story of Christ's passion, which unfolds in front of their eyes, through the city streets. He also shows how the director manages to attract every year a vast public of visitors by updating the performance with the addition of tableaux vivants of the life of Christ and the creation of ingenious sets whose parts can be used in different combinations.

In "Visualizing the Restoration: 'Neo-baroque' Costuming at the Stratford Festival" Copeland reviews an array of costume designs used at Stratford for Restoration dramas in order to understand how they reflect different views of the plays. She identifies at first an elaborate and ornate style of costuming, influenced by British productions, that "portrayed a play-world that was self-consciously artificial, exaggerated, and fantastic." She traces the brief appearance in the 1960s of a new concept of Restoration drama, "one that stressed the social reality of the play, with a corresponding change from decorative to functional design." Finally she points out that since the 1970s there has been a return to the artificial and exaggerated style of the beginning. In particular a 'neo-baroque' style has developed in late-twentieth-century productions which, in postmodern fashion, mixes realism and artificiality, and stresses grotesque elements and spectacular effects. This recent style aims at entertaining the public and drawing large crowds but, unfortunately, disregards "historical specificity, social content and individual qualities of the play," thus reducing the Restoration to a "frivolous, decadent, but not particularly significant" period.

Enzo Zappulla and Sarah Zappulla Muscarà examine respectively the different *mise-en scènes* of d'Annunzio's masterpiece *La figlia di Iorio* and the difference between the Italian original of the play and its translation into various dialects.[1] Enzo Zappulla in " 'La figlia di Iorio' di Gabriele d'Annunzio: un secolo di messe in scena" ("Gabriele d'Annunzio's 'La figlia di Iorio': one century of *mise en scènes*") reconstructs the exciting preparations for the first performance of the

1. Both Enzo Zappulla and Sarah Zappulla Muscarà base their articles on their Introduction to Gabriele d'Annunzio, *'La figlia di Iorio' tra lingua e dialetti*. Catania: La Cantinella, 1997.

play in 1904 and the search for authentic costumes, furniture and convincing sets of Abruzzo's countryside so as to give the spectator a feeling of truth. He shows that the subsequent performances of the play oscillated between the passionate *verismo* of Sicilian actors, who played *La figlia di Iorio* in Sicilian, harking back to the tragic love stories portrayed by Verga and Capuana, the realistic performance of the play in 1927 in d'Annunzio's open air theatre at the Vittoriale, and Pirandello's mystical rendition of the play in a fairy-tale landscape, helped by de Chirico's metaphysical sets and costumes in 1934. Zappulla stresses the difficulty of combining the play's mythical and archaic themes with its precise cultural and historical references and observes that most post-war *mise-en-scènes* of *La figlia di Iorio* have tended to be either too realistic or too lyrical, thereby missing an important component of the play.

Sarah Zappulla Muscarà in " 'La figlia di Iorio' di Gabriele d'Annunzio fra lingua e dialetto" ("Gabriele d'Annunzio's 'La figlia di Iorio' between language and dialect") describes the performance of *'A figghia di Joriu,* a translation in Sicilian dialect of d'Annunzio's play, which took place shortly after the first performance of the play in Italian. The passionality and dramatic ability of the actors of the "Compagnia Drammatica Siciliana," combined with the force and immediacy of dialect, contributed to making a great success of the Sicilian version. Muscarà stresses the effectiveness of Borgese's Sicilian translation, which, though faithful to the original text, gives greater prominence to the play's environment, and to its characters and their primitive feelings. His use of metathesis, verbal tenses, diminutives, augmentatives and pejoratives, differing from the original version, bring to the sentence new feelings of tenderness or contempt.

Next to the Sicilian version of the play, we have also a version in Abruzzese dialect by De Titta, *La fijje di Iorie,* which is simple, and rough with a strong local colour. And we have also a Neapolitan parody of the play, *Il figlio di Iorio,* by Scarpetta, who was accused of copyright infringement and was compelled to withdraw his play by an irate d'Annunzio.

Puppa in his article "*La figlia di Iorio* betwen Michetti and d'Annunzio"[2] studies the similarities and the differences between Michetti's painting *La figlia di Iorio* and d'Annunzio's play on the same subject. Michetti's humble rural scene of a prostitute "walking among

---

2. This is a translation of Paolo Puppa's article "La figlia di Iorio tra Michetti e D'Annunzio," in Paolo Puppa, *La parola alta*. Bari: Laterza, 1993, 107-28.

sleeping reapers with the Maiella in the background" is "pervaded with a dream-like atmosphere that bears allegorical overtones." D'Annunzio stresses this dream-like quality, creates "an esoteric, magic and ancestral atmosphere," gives up Michetti's obsession with reproducing reality and projects on the stage an embodiment of his passionate feelings. Yet the author will always remain torn between the different elements of his play "swinging between truthful and recognizable pictures and oneiric oddity." He will accept with equal enthusiasm the realistic staging of his play in 1927 by Forzano and the stylized, unrealistic staging by Pirandello in 1934, with sets and costumes by de Chirico.

Another point in common between Michetti and d'Annunzio is their treatment of crowds: "It is also thanks to Michetti... that d'Annunzio's crowd becomes gradually more composed... finally becoming an allegory of people, of nationality, in which the hero, as a modern Anteo, rediscovers his true roots."

In "Visual Arts and *Riders to the Sea*" Evans examines how Synge was influenced by his visits to the Aran islands and how they inspired his work, especially his first play *Riders to the Sea*. The beautiful black and white photographs that Synge took of the islanders in their traditional costumes and of their primitive life and customs clearly stimulated his creativity as a dramatist. Evans shows the correspondence between the Aran islanders photographed by Synge with their homes, animals, tools and customs and the props, sets, costumes, and traditional Irish life portrayed by the dramatist in his renowned play. These correspondences range from the description of Maurya's cottage in the play, clearly based on a typical island dwelling, to the special Aran petticoats for the actresses and the pampooties-cowhide moccasins for the actors, to the tradition of rope-making and the particular way of mourning for the dead.

In concluding, Evans points out that it is indeed this superimposition of imagery, starting with Synge's photographs and "echoing themes of Celtic and Greek mythology and Medieval Christian tradition" that "gives *Riders to the Sea* its extraordinary density."

Urbancic in her article on "Cinematographic Techniques and Stereotypes in the Stories of Annie Vivanti" demonstrates how Vivanti "felt the influence of the [cinematic] genre and how she incorporated in her writing the attitudes, the stereotypes and the stylistics of the genre." In particular she analyzes two of Vivanti's short stories "Il cinematografo" and "The Beauty Contest" showing that these stories not only portray in a humorous way the world of movies, actors and scriptwriters, but are also written, at least in part, as screen-plays, with a quick series of scenes, a minimum of narrative and "the incorporation of cinematographic elements into narrative discourse." In "Il cinematografo," in each scene she describes, destined to be used by the scriptwriter of the story, Vivanti uses a visual language that is appropriate both for the film scene and satisfies the feelings of the frustrated scriptwriter. In the two stories she also uses film terminology, such as "in focus," to describe mental activities, and tells part of the stories in the present tense, rather than in the expected past tense, in order to "emphasize the cinematic characteristic of the short story."

Hirsh in "Staging the Self: Giorgio de Chirico and the Theatricality of Self-Portraiture" examines the massive body of self-portraits de Chirico painted throughout his life and in which he carefully "constructed his various identities and immortalized his image in paint." In his self-portraits that combine great figures and monuments from the past with personal items "de Chirico presents historical traces as though they are pieces of his own memory, thus fusing his personal profile with history that indeed, if only fleetingly, functioned as a memory of a now-past society that he reclaims as his own."

Hirsh concludes her article by noting that "de Chirico transcends representational limits to ensure the continual performance of his pictorial and verbal eulogy ... and underlines his immortality by problematizing what he defines as the monumental project of constructing his identity through his unique *pre-* rather than *post-mortem* memorial gestures."

Somigli in "Theatre and Its 'Truth': A Reading of Alberto Savinio's *Il suo nome*" discusses Alberto Savinio's views on theatre as the place of fantasy, dreams and a plurality of meanings rather than the representation of the solid, familiar and one-dimensional world advocated by *verismo*. Somigli analyzes Savinio's 1945 one-act play *Il suo nome*, as an example of the theories the writer had expressed in his journalistic writings. In this play Savinio "multiplies the levels of representation, making them collide with one another, and placing Lodovico [the main character] at the centre (as narrator) and on the margin (as character) of the representation."

The various events of Ludovico's life he narrates to the spectators are enacted on the stage in quick scenes, *scenarietti*, which serve "as doubles of the events that the protagonist relates and as the materializations of his psychic mechanisms." Moreover one *scenarietto*, with a woman waiting for the return of her beloved, appears to be connected with two previous paintings where Savinio makes fun of the well known theme of the faithful wife waiting for her husband by representing the woman as a bourgeois matron with a bird head. This reference, then, would make of the play another example of the theme of "sterile and deferred love" so common in Savinio's works.

In "Man, Man as Dancer, Art Figure: Oskar Schlemmer's Experiments on the Bauhaus Stage" Tihanyi examines how Oskar Schlemmer, head of the Bauhaus stage workshop, created several ballets in which he followed the Bauhaus endeavor to join the "artistic-ideal" with the "craftsmanlike-practical." Schlemmer was particularly influenced by the ideas of the nineteenth-century playwright Heinrich von Kleist and believed that only an intensive study of the elements of nature would lead him to a state of innocence. In his pursuit of the ideal, Schlemmer created ballets that "dealt with the relationship between man and space, and were inscribed by very strict, geometric construct." He was also inspired by the marionette theater and made dancers wear costumes compelling them to move like puppets, or created "dances where the actors were invisible and only the prop pieces could be seen, or used actual puppets on the stage." The costumes he used reduced the human form to "its most basic components — a series of cubes or of spheres and ellipses that transformed the actor into 'ambulant architecture… [or] the marionette'. "

In "Soft Dictatorship as Asylum" Fried studies the *mise en scène* of *The Persecution and Assassination of Jean-Paul Marat* by Peter Weiss, during the last decade of the Kádár regime in Hungary. The play was performed in the country town of Kaposvár for eight years and enjoyed an incredible success because "it had been adapted to mirror and comment on the political events of the time and allowed the Hungarian people to express their otherwise forbidden feelings towards the government." Since it was impossible to criticize the government in politics and in the newspapers, people found an outlet for their thoughts and feelings in literature and the performing arts, which used parables and grotesque imagery to represent current situations.

Since the *Marat-Sade* play portrays the conflict between individualism and social upheaval, as well as attempts at a revolution and its inevitable failure, "the Hungarian director Ács János uses the play to criticize the 'soft dictatorship' of the Kádár regime." Ács finishes the play "on a note of complete failure, with the Narrator mourning over the defeated revolt and lost ideals both for the oppressors and the oppressed."

Sanguinetti Katz in "Lepage's Psychoanalytic Interpretation of Schoenberg's *Erwartung*" examines the particular interpretation that Lepage gave of Schoenberg's *Erwartung* in his *mise en scène* of this opera that was performed by the Canadian Opera Company in 1993 and 1995. Lepage transforms Pappenheim's poetic and dreamlike libretto–about a woman who wanders in the woods in search of her lover and then discovers his body murdered by her in a fit of jealousy–into an analytic session between a patient held in a straightjacket and her psychiatrist in a mental hospital. The visionary quality of the woman's words is stressed by the surrealistic way in which people and props appear and disappear through or over a transversal wall, that functions both as enclosure of the mental hospital and as the wall of the woman's ego "through which break the dreams and memories of her unconscious."

In the course of the opera we have a portrayal of the woman torn by her ambivalent attitude towards the men in her life, seen alternatively as threatening, seductive, and controlling (the psychiatrist) or as tender, loving, and victims of the woman's jealousy (the lover). We also see her as completely trapped by society and the medical establishment, reduced to be the object of a psychiatric case history.

From its earliest origins theatre has sought to bridge disparate elements of human experience, to join old and new, and to celebrate its interplay with the arts upon the stage of life. Much work remains yet to be done in order to grasp more fully the signal and intricate role of the visual arts in the theatre. We hope that the present collection will give rise to further investigation.

ACKNOWLEDGMENTS

We gratefully acknowledge the assistance of the following for the present publication:

The Emilio Goggio Chair of Italian Studies, University of Toronto
The Dean of Arts and Science, University of Toronto
The Italian Cultural Institute in Toronto
Alitalia

We are also deeply grateful to Professor Corrado Federici, of Brock University, for his most helpful editorial suggestions.

The First Artistic Representations of Theatre: Dramatic Illusion and Dramatic Performance in Attic and South Italian Art

Eric Csapo

University of Toronto

Artistic representations of drama are nearly as old as theatre itself.[1] Drama became a subject for the (other) visual arts within two decades of the new Athenian democracy's creation of dramatic competitions. By the Hellenistic period illustrations of drama formed part of the standard repertoire of a large variety of artistic media (we know over 5,000 artworks showing figures from the ancient stage). But for all that, fifth-century Athenian artists reveal an astonishing reticence towards the representation of dramatic performance *as performance*. This reticence is not overcome until the fourth century, and less in Athenian than in South Italian art. Recent discoveries have enriched and radically changed our understanding of the relationship art bears to theatre in the Classical period. This study will characterize the evolving impact of drama on the visual arts in the first two centuries of theatre's existence, and make some recent discoveries available to general theatre- and art-historians.[2]

Athenian drama and painting from 490-390 are uniquely well-preserved: forty-four complete plays and some 100,000 vasepaintings. This hundred-year stretch happens to coincide with the canonical "great

1. All dates are BC except those referring to the nineteenth and twentieth centuries. Where possible, I will refer to artifacts by their museum inventory numbers and/or numbers in T. B. L Webster, *Monuments Illustrating Tragedy and Satyrplay*, A. D. Trendall, *Phlyax Vases*, and T. B. L. Webster and J. R. Green, *Monuments Illustrating Old and Middle Comedy*. For these works I use only the standard abbreviations *MTS, PhV* and *MMC* respectively. The details of illustrated artifacts appear in the captions to the plates.

2. For excellent summaries of various aspects of this relationship, see especially J. R. Green, "On Seeing and Depicting," and *Theatre in Ancient Greek Society;* O. Taplin, *Comic Angels*, and "The Pictorial Record."

age" of both genres. Attic red figure pottery is justly famous for the breadth of its repertoire, including contemporary subjects drawn from all facets of social life, even the most intimate, and in often highly realistic detail. It is therefore almost as puzzling as it is disappointing to learn how few Attic artifacts depict theatrical scenes.

One ought not to speculate that Athenian artists had little interest in theatre. On the contrary. Drama is a complex subject —it is itself a representation— and in representing the representation the artist may focus on the performance or on the story, or indeed allow his gaze to waver somewhere between the theatrical event and the dramatic illusion. Most Athenian artists succumbed to the illusion. *Mythological scenes* retelling stories enacted in drama appear on hundreds of Attic vasepaintings. But unless we know the plays, there is little to remind us of drama. In general Athenian artists, no matter how directly inspired by the theatre, drew not masks, but faces, not stages, but palaces or temples, not messengers narrating, but the concrete actions reported by their narratives. Not till close to the end of the fifth century did artists begin to pay closer attention to the dramatic medium, to represent the theatrical signs which had hitherto been transparent windows to the represented worlds of myth and fantasy.

An early fourth-century Attic vase may serve us as an example of the general practice (FIGURE 1). The subject depicted is an incident in the life of the mythological hero Telephus, an incident entirely invented by Euripides to serve as the climax of his *Telephus* performed in 438. According to myth, the first expedition of the Greeks to Troy went astray. They were not yet good sailors. They landed in Mysia and, thinking it Troy, began to lay waste to the territory, but were intercepted by the king of Mysia, Telephus. In the

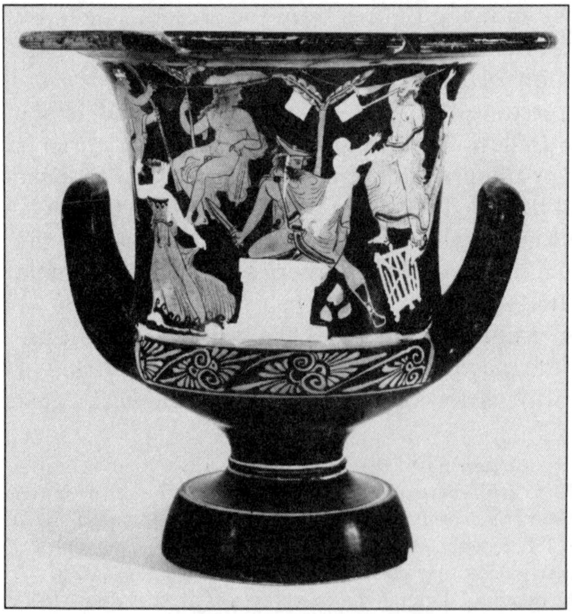

FIGURE 1. Attic calyx-krater, c. 400-375 BC. Berlin 3974. *MTS* p. 164. Courtesy, Antikensammlung, Staatliche Museen zu Berlin, Preussischer Kulturbesitz. Photo: G. Stenzel.

ensuing battle Telephus was wounded by Achilles, but the Greeks retreated and, realizing their mistake, returned home. Telephus's wound began to fester and the oracle of Apollo told him that "the wounder would heal." So Telephus went to Argos, where the Greek chiefs were discussing a second expedition to Troy. They interpreted the oracle to mean that rust from Achilles's spear would heal Telephus and in return Telephus agreed to guide the expedition to Troy. Aeschylus was the first to base a tragedy on the myth. In it he made Telephus' request for help more dramatic. Telephus performed a rare rite of supplication by sitting on an altar with Agamemnon's son, the baby Orestes, on his knee. Euripides sensationalized the tableau by turning it into a hostage-taking incident: Telephus infiltrated the war council disguised as a beggar, was exposed, and, grabbing Orestes, suddenly jumped on an altar, and held a knife to the baby's throat. It is this hostage taking that we see on FIGURE 1: Telephus, centre, kneels on the altar threatening his hostage; Agamemnon in the upper right reacts initially with ill-considered aggression. Other characters look on, adding a tone of theatricality to the composition: a woman to the left reacts emotionally, in contrast to the placid interest shown by the gods hovering above the action (upper left). Yet despite the image's total dependence upon the plot of Euripides's tragedy, and despite the dramatic tone of its own compositional style, this is an illustration not of tragedy, but of *myth*.

To postmodern eyes, this is an utterly naive way of seeing drama, yet the art shows that this was just how artists (and presumably the public) viewed drama until late in the fifth century. It is therefore difficult to generalize about art and theatre in Athens. For our study the subject might more effectively be approached through the exceptions, about a dozen vases which go much further in the direction of depicting dramatic performance in preference to dramatic narrative. These exceptions seem to confirm the rule.

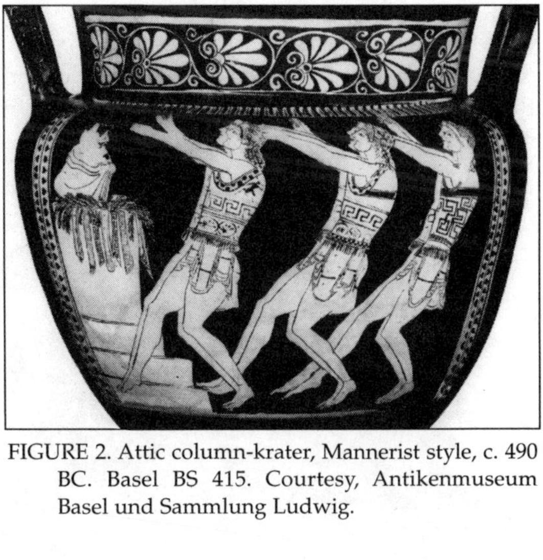

FIGURE 2. Attic column-krater, Mannerist style, c. 490 BC. Basel BS 415. Courtesy, Antikenmuseum Basel und Sammlung Ludwig.

Most are choral. As many as four vasepaintings, ranging in date from about 490-460, show tragic choruses in performance. FIGURE 2 shows three ranks and two files of young men in rectangular formation, a synecdoche for a full tragic chorus which in this period moves in four ranks and three files. They are costumed as soldiers but are not really soldiers: they wear diadems rather than helmets, dance rather than march, and carry no weapons. A series of Os emerge from their mouths in added red paint (not visible in the photograph) to show that they are singing. They approach the *orchestra's* central altar, behind which a diminutive actor rises. This is evidently one of the many "ghost-raising" scenes which were especially popular in early tragedy (as in Aeschylus's *Persae*). The faces of the choreuts are all alike: gaping mouths, jutting chins, and extended chin lines suggest masks. Nonetheless, they are not clearly masks rather than faces. Three additional vases, which probably portray a tragic chorus, show neither masks nor costumes. A black-figured lekythos in Munich (1871 inv. 6025) shows young men kneeling in a line with uniform gestures of lamentation. This alone makes us think of a tragic chorus. FIGURE 3 gives us no hint that the dancing maenad is a costumed choreut; the only sign of performance is the theatrical piper beside her. The piper is also the only theatrical signifier on the Corinthian hydria fragments showing a tragedy (Corinth T 1144, *MTS* AV 13), perhaps about Croesus.

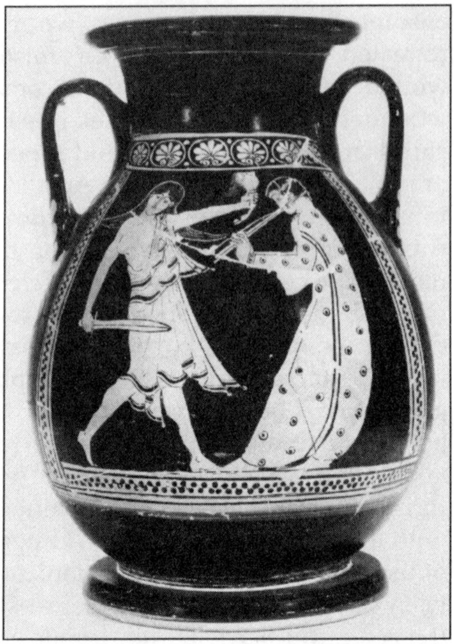

FIGURE 3. Attic pelike, Earlier Mannerist, c. 470 BC. Berlin 3223. *MTS* AV 15. Courtesy, Antikensammlung, Staatliche Museen zu Berlin, Preussischer Kulturbesitz.
Photo: Johannes Laurentius.

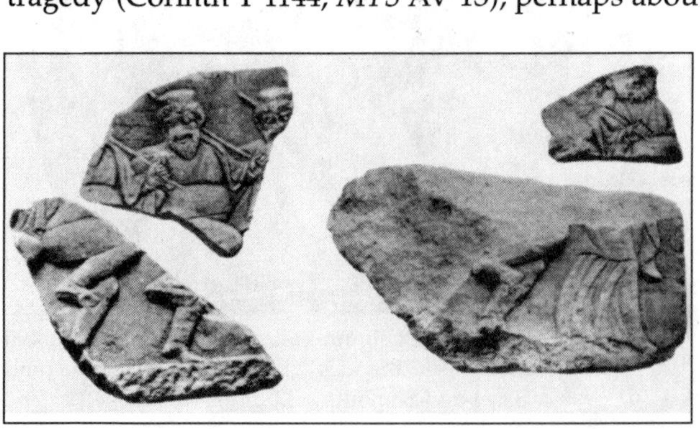

FIGURE 4. Fragments of marble relief, c. 350 BC. Athens, Agora S 1025 and 1586. *MMC* AS 3. Courtesy, American School of Classical Studies at Athens: Agora Excavations.

By contrast, three mid fourth-century illustrations of comic choruses in performance on two marble reliefs (FIGURE 4) and a winejug, show realistic details of costume, including mask and the typical belly-and-buttock padding of the comic costume. In each the comic chorus dances in formation; two have the remains of a piper leading the formation.[3]

It is much more difficult to identify scenes of satyrplay in performance. Satyrs have many mythical and ritual connections, and signs of performance such as costume, masks, or pipers may indicate a performance having nothing to do with drama, or they may simply appear as Dionysiac imagery. A best-case scenario for the representation of satyrdrama is provided by the Leningrad Painter (FIGURE 5), who also painted the "Croesus(?)-tragedy" just mentioned. Here several formal indices of performance make this a uniquely good candidate for an illustration of satyrplay: the presence of a piper, the costume (the usual loincloths with erect phalloi, called *perizomata*, and lines at the wrist and ankles indicating the body tights worn by all ancient actors), mask-like features (bug-eyes, double-lines marking the hair-line at the back of the three-quarter mask), even a certain amount of co-ordination in the satyrs' movements. But nothing permits us to insist that it shows a dramatic performance. Satyr costume was worn in other Dionysiac rituals, especially in parades at the beginning of Dionysiac festivals. Such contexts also require music and, in formal processions, a certain regimentation of

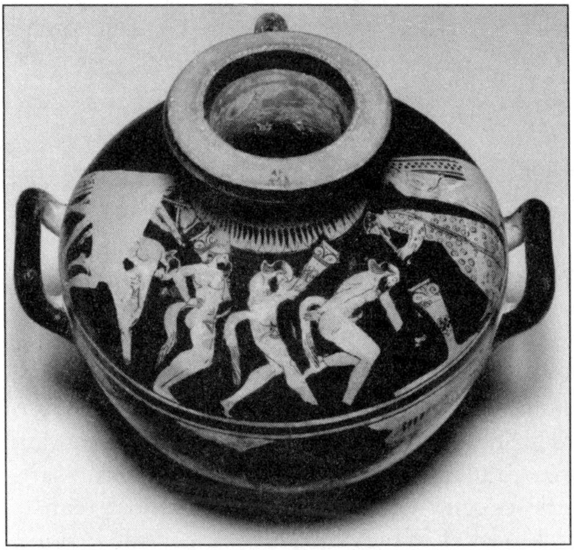

FIGURE 5. Attic hydria, Leningrad Painter, 475-450 BC. Boston MFA 03.788. *MTS* AV 14. Courtesy, Museum of Fine Arts, Boston. Reproduced with permission. ©1999 Museum of Fine Arts, Boston. All Rights Reserved.

3. The two not illustrated are: Athens, Agora S 2098S (*MMC* AS 4); Benaki 30890 and 30895 (see Pingiatoglou, Eine Komödiendarstellung). Something over twenty vases ranging in date from c. 560 - 480 are usually thought to depict early or proto-comic choral performances. They are clearly Dionysiac. But I do not believe they are directly related to comedy, and they are not included here. See J. R. Green, "A Representation of the *Birds.*"

movements, and narrative themes cannot be excluded. The dilemma is well illustrated by a vase showing three satyrs in procession playing lyres moving in step towards a piper: an inscription identifies them as "singers at the Panathenaia," a procession for Athena.[4] Even the Leningrad Painter, like his contemporaries, succumbs at least half-way to the illusion created by the mask: the mouths of the satyrs are closed, but choral masks need open mouths.

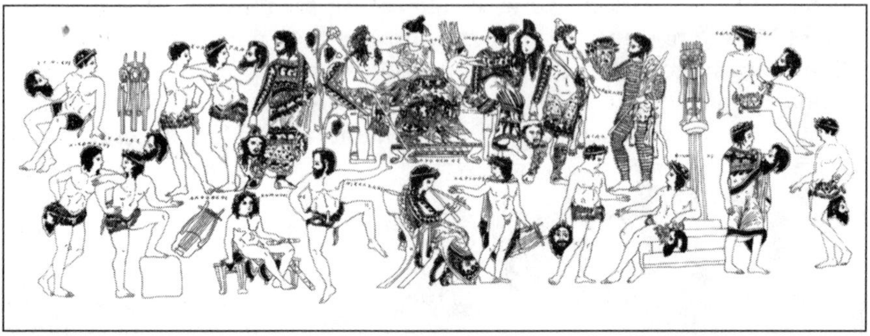

FIGURE 6. Attic volute-krater, Pronomos Painter, c. 400 BC. Naples, MN 3240. *MTS* AV 25. Drawing by E.R. Malyon.

Though they cannot be counted as scenes of drama in performance, eleven vases with theatrical "genre scenes" are closely associated with these paintings of performing choruses.[5] Genre-scenes depict tragic, comic and satyric choreuts, sometimes with pipers in the "dressing room," as it were, just before the performance, or in the sanctuary of Dionysus, just afterwards. The choreuts still wear their costume and normally hold their masks in their hands. Of all the fifth-century artifacts discussed so far, these genre-scenes give us the most realistic depictions of costume and mask, but they also sometimes show symptoms of seduction by the dramatic illusion. The most famous, the so-called Pronomos vase, produced around 400 (FIGURE 6), depicts the cast of a satyrplay celebrating a victory at the Dionysia in the sanctuary of Dionysus. In addition to the chorus, poet and piper, we see three actors immediately adjacent to the couch on which recline Dionysus and Ariadne (top centre). Unlike the chorus, who carry satyr masks but have individualized human faces, the actors' faces are identical to those of their masks. The actor, who holds a female mask and sits at the end of the couch, is even depicted as female (though all actors were male),

4. See the (optimistic) discussion by G. Hedreen, *Silens in Attic Black-Figure* 105-78, and (the much less hopeful) discussion by F. Lissarrague, "Why Satyrs are Good to Represent."

5. See A.W. Pickard-Cambridge, *Dramatic Festivals of Athens*, figs. 32-34, 49-53, 85; J. R. Green, "Dedications of Masks," figs. 1-4.

and the actor to the right of her is labeled "Heracles," after the part he plays. By contrast, the choreuts, poet, and piper are all labeled with their real names.

There is a good institutional reason for granting this kind of "production-realism" to depictions of choruses, even while actors continue to function as transparencies for the roles they play. In Classical Athens dramatic choruses and *choregoi,* the sponsors of dramatic choruses, were all citizen volunteers acting in the service of the god. Actors, on the other hand, were hirelings of the state. A successful *choregos* typically dedicated paintings or relief-sculptures in the temple of Dionysus to celebrate his victory, but also to commemorate his and his choruses' service to god and community. These paintings and reliefs typically depicted the chorus in performance, or preparing for the performance, or celebrating it. Vases are an unlikely medium for choregic dedications. However the vases just examined are likely to be copies of sculptures or easel paintings hanging in the sanctuary of Dionysus. Drinking and relaxing in celebration of one's achievements are also suitable themes for sympotic drinking vessels, which all these vases are, and, incidentally, for funerary grave goods. Most of these vases were only preserved because they were used as grave-gifts. The two fourth-century marble reliefs showing performing comic choruses (FIGURE 4) are themselves almost certainly fragments of choregic dedications, as are two marble reliefs which show genre scenes.

Nonetheless, not all Attic vasepaintings depicting dramatic performance depict choruses. There are perhaps five scenes of performing actors. All belong to the last two decades of the fifth century and all are comic. Not surprisingly, comic actors are the first to break through the dramatic illusion. The illusion is most fragile in Attic Old Comedy, to the point where many experts question the utility of the term. Something of the character of Dionysiac ritual survives in the fragility of Old Comedy's "fourth wall," and the ease with which the audience are drawn, as participants, into the performance. The earliest scene is on a winejug of about 420 (FIGURE 7). Perhaps the most interesting —certainly the most unusual— of all Attic representations of drama, it is also one of the most damaged and is here presented in a partly reconstructed

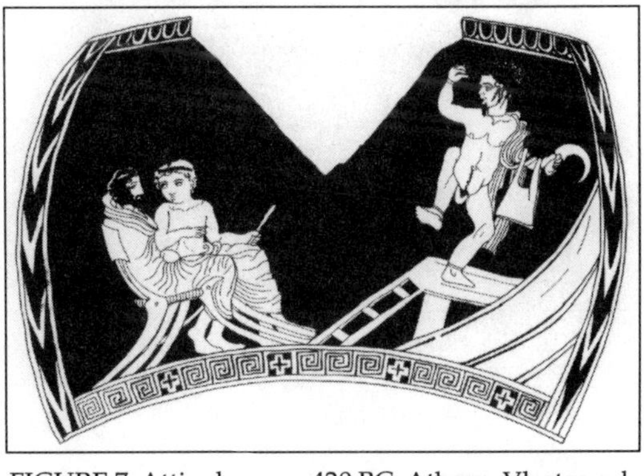

FIGURE 7. Attic chous, c. 420 BC. Athens, Vlastos collection. *MMC* AV 4. Drawing by E.R. Malyon.

drawing. An actor, wearing body tights (note the lines at wrists and ankles) and a phallus (both represent "stage-nakedness"), dances on a low stage and carries the sickle and magic bag which are the standard attributes of Perseus. The stage is represented nowhere else in Attic iconography, but is common on South Italian comic pots, as we will see. Also unique, not just in Attic, but in Greek iconography, is the representation of an audience, here a synecdoche of two figures in the front row. The artist has elided the *orchestra* between auditorium and stage, but included the steps leading from the stage down to *orchestra* level. Despite unmistakable signs that the artist is primarily concerned to represent performance, the absence of an obvious mask, and the apparent absence of the still more obvious artificial phallus (as represented, this actor's is too small for comedy) have caused some to doubt that this is an ordinary comic performance.[6] But as we have pointed out, the failure to distinguish masked and costumed actors from the mythical characters they represent is typical of fifth-century Attic representations. The same ambiguity between the world of myth and the world of theatre is revealed by an Attic vase of c. 410 (Louvre N 3408, *MMC* AV 6), which depicts a comic Heracles and a snub-nosed Victory together in a chariot pulled by centaurs. The hero's face is identical to that of the mask used for Heracles in the later tradition, and the torchbearer who leads the chariot has a full-sized comic phallus. Apart from these details, and the general tone of caricature, there is nothing to signify a comic production. On the contrary, the centaurs are real centaurs, not pantomime horse-men.

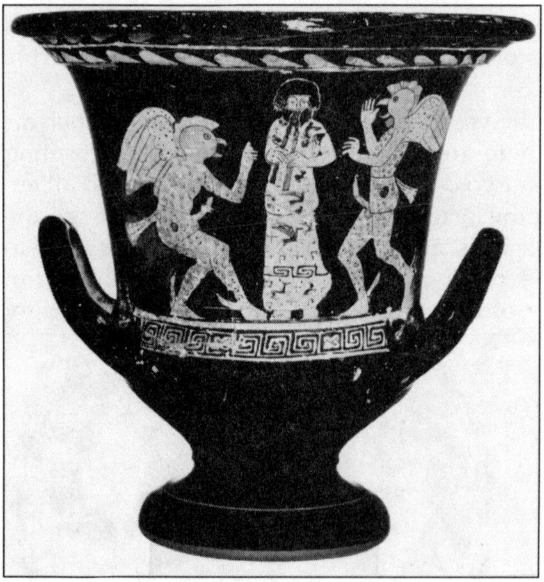

FIGURE 8. Attic calyx-krater, c. 415 BC. Malibu 82.AE.83. Courtesy, The J. Paul Getty Museum, Malibu, California.

Perhaps the only artifact showing performance with unambiguous theatre-realism is on an Attic calyx-krater of about 415 (FIGURE 8). A piper in full regalia pipes between two men

6. O. Taplin, *Comic Angels*, p. 9, suggests an uncostumed rehearsal; M. Schmidt, "Tes ges," denies any connection with drama.

costumed as fighting cocks. The first publication of the vase (1985) associated it with the chorus of Aristophanes's *Birds*, but since the scene shows a comic cockfight (and cocks do not appear in the chorus of *Birds*), a better link exists with the production of Aristophanes's *Clouds*. An ancient source informs us that the Greater and Lesser Arguments appeared dressed as fighting cocks in the original production. Production details are very clear in the costume. One can, for example, see the lines demarcating the "shorts" which hold the tail and phallus, or the details of the strings (note the left cock's right foot) which tie on the phallic spurs. The very best connection with a known comedy comes from crudely painted winejug fragments of c. 400, with two labelled figures in comic costume (FIGURE 9), Dionysus, left, and Phormio ("Phor-" is preserved), an Athenian general, seated right.[7] The two characters appeared together in a comedy by Aristophanes's contemporary, Eupolis. In *Taxiarchoi* Dionysus joined the navy and was given lessons in oarsmanship. The posture of Phormio is suited to that of someone plying oars, though the vase is too badly damaged to preserve helpful details. Enough of the figures survives to suggest the standard comic bodysuit with breast, belly and buttock padding. The large heads and gaping mouths hint at a mask, but in general, as the original publication notes, "an accurate portrayal of a comic actor does not seem to have been intended" (Crosby 81).

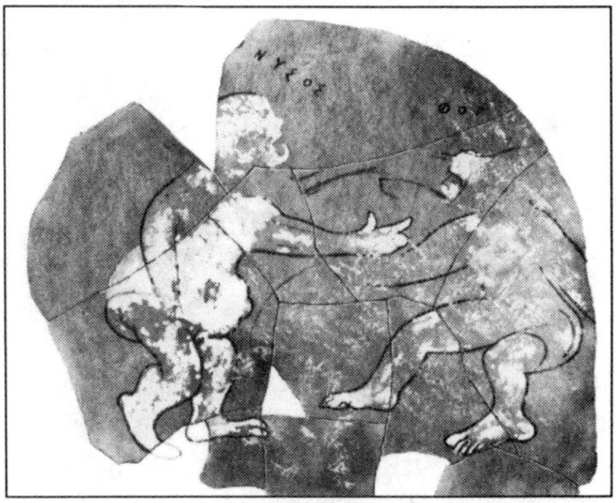

FIGURE 9. Attic chous, c. 400 BC. Athens, Agora P 23985. *MMC* AV 14. Courtesy, American School of Classical Studies at Athens: Agora Excavations. Drawing by Piet de Jong.

It is only in the fourth century and in the minor art of terracotta sculpture that we detect any serious interest in depicting dramatic performance. From the beginning to the end of the fourth century, Athens produced terracotta figurines showing comic actors or comic masks, of which about 150 survive. The figurines may originally have been sold as tourist-souvenirs at the Athenian Dionysia. They were copied or imitated all over the Greek world. Possibly the figures are extracts from lost paintings (this certainly happened from the third century), and could be bought in a set to

7. Four other winejugs from the same deposit are said to depict comedy, but two winejugs show Dionysiac ritual, not comedy (*MMC* AV 12-13), and one shows Dionysiac fantasy (*MMC* AV 10, a man rowing a fish). Only one other small fragment (*MMC* AV 11) probably depicts comedy.

recreate a scene from performed drama. But there is no good evidence for this, and they come to us only as isolated figures. For artistic representations of dramatic performance we have to look elsewhere.

Many Athenian vases (most whole ones) survive because they were exported to Italy where they served as grave gifts. By about 440 the Italiot Greeks began to produce imitations of Attic pottery and within a few decades they had their own distinctive local style and repertoire. The centres of production are in such diverse cities as Taranto, Metaponto, Syracuse, and Paestum. However, despite local variation, there is broad enough coherence that one can speak generically of fourth-century South Italian vasepainting. Both style and repertoire show the influence of drama far more than Athenian pottery. The influence of drama is greatest from 400 —just the time when Athenian vasepainters lose interest— and continues to the last decades of the fourth century.

As in Athens, it is comedy which receives the most realistic treatment. Comic actors are found on well over three hundred vases and the number is growing with legal and illegal excavations. Since the mid 1980s the market value of South Italian red figure has increased tenfold for ordinary wares, and more than a hundredfold for distinguished vases. Consequently, the activity of illegal excavators (the *tumbaroli)* in Southern Italy has also increased. Single actors or actors in non-theatrical contexts account for most of the corpus. One of them, Derkylos ("Bright-Eyes"), an ancient Maurice Chevalier, ogles the viewer of an Apulian calyx-krater (FIGURE 10). About sixty currently known vases show complete scenes of comic performance.

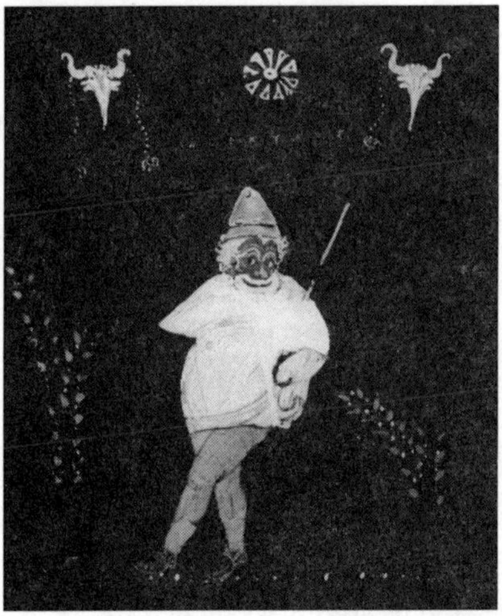

FIGURE 10. Apulian calyx-krater, 350-325 BC. Tampa 7.94.8. From the collection of William Knight Zewadski. Courtesy, Tampa Museum of Art.

The whole group of comic vases are usually referred to as "phlyakes" (singular, "phlyax"). The name comes from a local mummery, said to be native to Southern Italy, about which we know nothing more than the name. The connection between the South Italian vasepaintings and the otherwise unknown mummery was made with the first collection and study of the pottery in 1886 and reasserted as recently as three years ago in the third edition of the *Oxford Classical Dictionary*. But since the 1980s there has been every reason to think that the South Italian pots depict Attic comedy.

The argument is not new. As early as 1948, Webster ("South Italian Vases") pointed out that the "phlyax" costumes were identical to those of the Attic terracotta figurines of comic actors, that the paintings suggest plots not very different from those found in contemporary Attic comedy, and that Attic tragedy at least was well known in Southern Italy: it was a major source for the South Italian vasepainter's repertoire of myths. To these general arguments Webster added an important observation. Many pots are accompanied by inscriptions. These inscriptions are usually character labels (eg. FIGURES 10, 12, 14, 18). In one case (FIGURE 16) we have lines of dialogue. Although the centres of production for these vases were all cities that spoke the Doric dialect, the form of the names and words in the inscriptions are in Athenian dialect. Webster argued that this was because the comedy was Athenian. Webster's persuasive arguments were promptly ignored by the scholarly community.

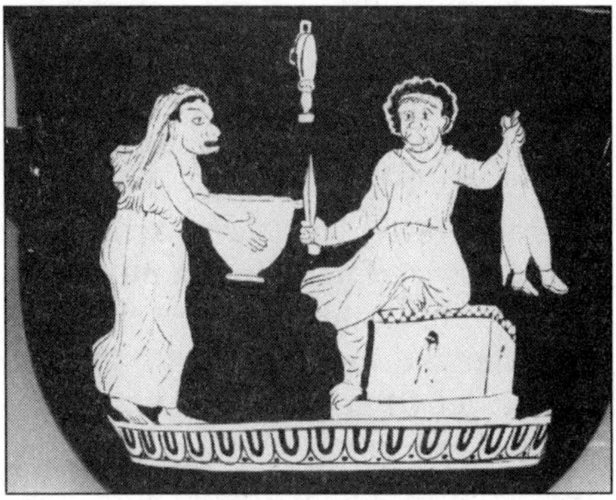

FIGURE 11. Apulian bell-krater, Schiller Painter, c. 370 BC. Würzburg H5697. Courtesy, Martin von Wagner Museum, University of Würzburg.

Webster is now vindicated by an Apulian bell-krater of about 370 acquired by the University of Würzburg in 1978 (FIGURE 11). It shows two comic actors atop a stage. One kneels astride an altar. His right hand holds a sword, his left a wineskin. The wineskin wears baby-booties. It is not entirely clear whether the actor is playing a male or female role. On the other vases and on figurines the comic costume for mature male characters normally includes a beard and a very short tunic. The tunic is designed not to cover but to reveal the most notorious feature of Classical Greek comic costume, namely the large dangling phallus of conspicuously bright red leather. But this character appears sexually indeterminate, indeed ambivalent: though beardless, he has what appears to be razor stubble around the mouth, and he wears a garment that is too long to be male but too short to be female. The only consistently feminine thing about him is the headband and the rather fluffy hairdo, which one can compare with the woman eating cake on FIGURE 12. The actor's stance on the altar is well known to iconographers as the "position agenouillée." It characterizes mythological scenes showing Telephus on the altar with Orestes, both in Attic (as in FIGURE 1) and South Italian iconography. As we know this incident was invented by Euripides, we can guess that the performance of

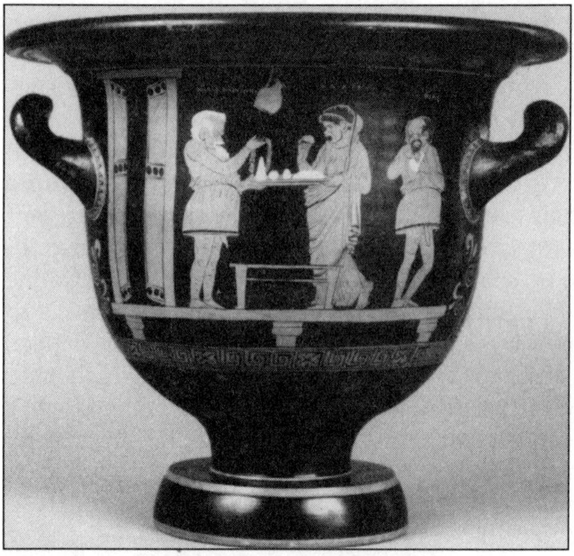

FIGURE 12. Apulian bell-krater, 400-380 BC. Milan AO.9.284. *PhV* 45. Courtesy, Civiche Raccolte Archeologiche e Numismatiche di Milano.

Telephus ultimately inspired the painters' kneeling position. The sexually ambivalent character here parodies the climactic moment of Euripides's play. On the left a female character rushes towards the altar with a bowl of the sort used for mixing wine. Just above the sword a mirror appears as if floating in the air.

We have two famous parodies of Euripides's *Telephus* in extant comedy. In Aristophanes's *Thesmophoriazusae* Euripides's "in-law" is shaved, and then disguised with an effeminate head-band and a woman's dress in order to infiltrate the Thesmophoria (an exclusively women's festival characterized by fasting and abstinence) where the women of Athens plan to debate collective action against Euripides for his alleged misogyny. At the women's "assembly," word comes that the meeting has been infiltrated by a man and suspicion falls upon the disguised in-law, who has just spoken in defense of Euripides. In desperation the in-law jumps upon the altar for asylum, but for added security grabs as hostage what appears to be the baby of one of the women and threatens it with a knife. Several women run in search of kindling to burn the in-law off the altar and away from his sanctuary. The following dialogue takes place in the *Thesmophoriazusae*:

> IN-LAW: *(to the women)* Go ahead, kindle! Burn! *(to the baby)* But you, off with this wrap right now! For your death, child, you have only your mother to blame. Hey, what's this? The girl has turned into a skin full of wine and wearing booties at that! O most flagrant women! O most bibulous of creatures, stopping at nothing to contrive an opportunity for a drink! … WOMAN: What have you done? You've stripped my chid naked, tiny as she is, you pervert! IN-LAW: Tiny! I'll say she's tiny!!... WOMAN: But give her back! IN-LAW: No, by Apollo! WOMAN: We'll set you on fire, then! IN-LAW: Go ahead! Burn! But this baby's going to get her throat cut, this instant! WOMAN: No! I beg you! Do whatever you like to me, but spare her! IN-LAW: I see you

> have a very maternal nature. But her throat will be cut nonetheless!
> WOMAN: Oh my child! Mania, give me the sacrificial bowl so that I can at least save the blood of my baby. (ll. 730-755)

A temporary truce is finally called between the women and the in-law and the wineskin is saved.

All the details fit perfectly: the *Telephus* parody on the altar, the wineskin with booties, the old woman rushing towards the threatened wineskin with a mixing bowl, the headband of the figure on the altar, the longish tunic which hides the actor's phallus, the beardless face and razor splotches. Even the floating mirror has a place in the shaving scene just before this episode. Perhaps we are to imagine it as a prop hung upon the wall of the stage building. The coincidence of detail could hardly appear in any drama otherwise distinguishable from Aristophanes's play. It is very clear that we have an illustration of the *Thesmophoriazusae*.

Once it was proven that the Würzburg krater showed a scene from Aristophanes, it was possible to look at other vases with a reasonable expectation of finding other scenes from Athenian comedies. The best example after the Würzburg krater is not a painted pot, but an Apulian mould-made oil can of about 330 (FIGURE 13). This comic actor's kneeling position is another parody of *Telephus*. It is in fact *the* other extant parody, the scene from Aristophanes's *Acharnians* where the hero, Dikaiopolis takes hostage and threatens to kill a coal-bucket which is notionally a friend and neighbour of the chorusmen from Acharnai (where charcoal burning was a major industry). Some scholars have said that the round object is a shield, not a bucket. They should look at it more closely. It is round and concave, far too small for a shield, and not held like any shield known to military science: the actor's fingers are wrapped around the rim.

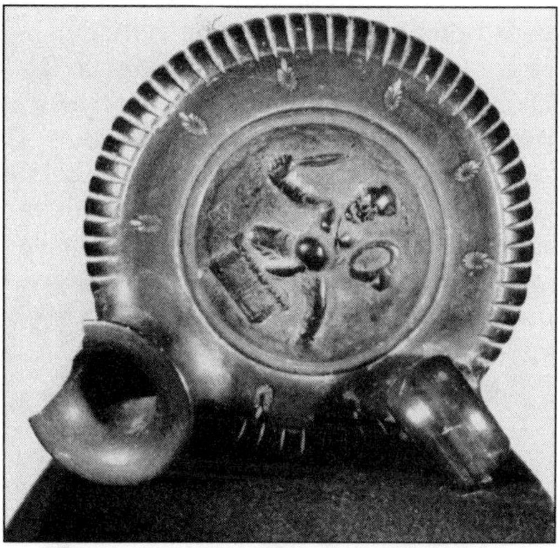

FIGURE 13. Apulian relief guttus, c. 330-320 BC. Naples MN Santangelo 368. Courtesy, Soprintendenza Archeologica di Napoli.

A Paestan bell-krater (FIGURE 14) shows two labeled characters, the lyric poet Phrynis and a "Pyronides," probably a deformation of the name of the old-fashioned Athenian general "Myronides." Both Phrynis

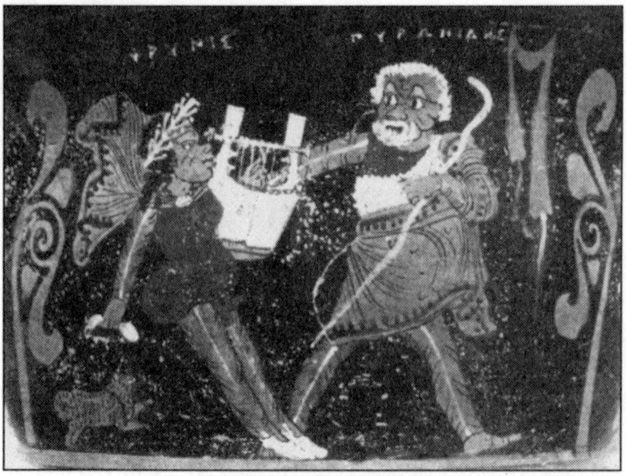

FIGURE 14. Paestan bell-krater, Asteas, c. 350 BC. Salerno, Museo Provinciale Pc 1812. *PhV* 58.

and Pyronides appear in Eupolis's *Demoi*. Another vase "disappeared" from the Berlin museum during the war. We know it only from an old photograph and drawing (FIGURE 15). At the beginning of Aristophanes's *Frogs*, Dionysus, disguised as Heracles with his lionskin and club, makes his way to Heracles' house to ask directions to the Underworld. Dionysus's slave sits on a donkey, but also carries a large pack upon his back. Here the only details that do not seem to fit are the face of the hero, which appears to be that of Heracles rather than Dionysus, and the fact that Dionysus is supposed to be wearing a diaphanous gown beneath his lionskin. This problem might perhaps be cleared up if we could locate the actual vase. The vase was in European collections since the early nineteenth century, when it was normal to refinish damaged antiquities. Any artist of the period seeing the club

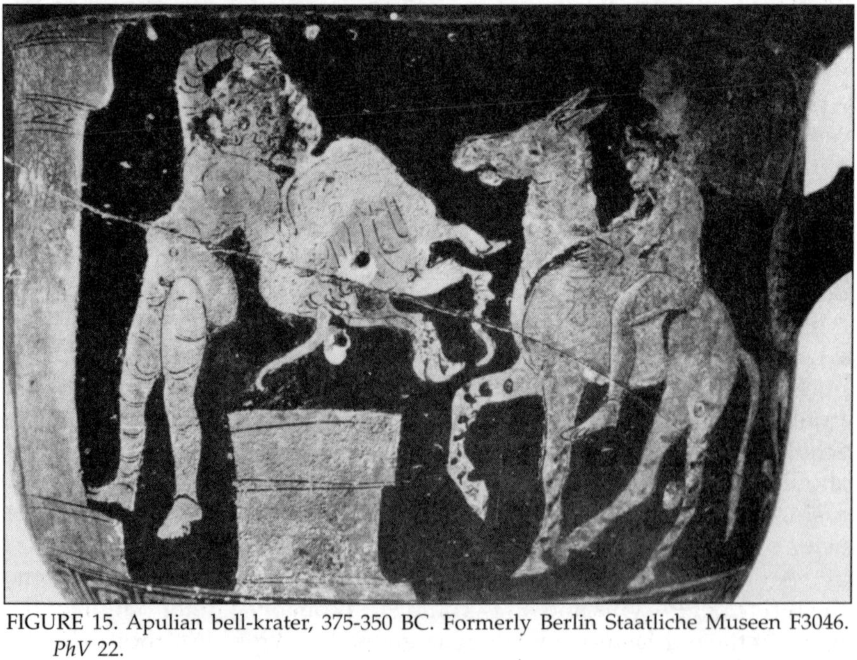

FIGURE 15. Apulian bell-krater, 375-350 BC. Formerly Berlin Staatliche Museen F3046. *PhV* 22.

and lionskin would assume it was Heracles and "restore" accordingly, erasing any traces of Dionysus beneath the disguise. But the problem may be more interesting. How is an artist to present an actor costumed as one character disguised as another? The South Italian vasepainters regularly prefer to depict the comic performance, not the illusion, but perhaps the performance within the performance proved too much even for this genre's relatively sophisticated theatre realism.

There are two things to stress about the South Italian pots. First, the details of many make little sense unless one knows the plays: they are not generic icons for comedy, but what Taplin calls "scene-specific" (*Comic Angels* 27-36). Second, pot-painting is not high art, but very much market-oriented, and South Italian pottery was not exported. The painter, then, apparently expected his customers, local Greeks of South Italy, to be able to recognize that *this* pot illustrates *this* scene from Aristophanes's *Thesmophoriazusae, Acharnians,* or other known work. Though some of these vases label characters, none gives the title of the comedy. They seem designed to challenge the viewer, like a problem from Trivial Pursuit. It is an impressive testimony to the degree of theatrical acculturation in Southern Italy in the early fourth century.

This leads to a new question. Where did the vasepainters find their models? It is conceivable that the painter formed an image from reading a text of the play, but less likely that imagination alone could supply an image which would be immediately recognizable to a consumer who also had only read the play. Besides, neither potpainters nor the average consumer were likely to be very bookish at this date. The book industry was in its infancy. It is even less likely that the image was drawn from an illustrated text. The earliest evidence for illustrated books is much later in date, and, before the use of parchment, illustrations were rarely more than very crude sketches. Moreover, if the vasepaintings are copies, we might expect to have duplicates of the more popular scenes, but this we never have. Each comic vase has an entirely unique scene. The easiest conclusion is that both artist and consumer knew the scene from local performance.

To these general arguments, I would add a few specific observations. We noted above that one comic vase actually makes the actors speak. An Apulian calyx-krater of about 400 shows three actors performing (FIGURE 16): an old woman on the stage to the right, and in the *orchestra* an old man with his hands raised in the air, approached by a thuggish young man with a stick. As in a modern cartoon, the words of each character emanate from their mouths. The old woman says "I hand him over to you," a legalistic formula of the sort one uses when offering a slave up for torture by a civic authority (the standard condition of accepting evidence from slaves in Athens). Something like this actually happens here, I suspect. The man in the centre of the *orchestra* on tiptoes with his hands raised says "he has tied up my hands." It was customary to suspend a slave before giving him lashes: this helps immobilize the target, tighten his skin and ensure the most damage with the least effort. The fellow behind him holding a switch is going to do the work. He is clean shaven to show that he is young. He says "Noraretteblo" which means as much in Greek as it does in English. In Athens Scythians were used as police, and his barbarism would seem to indicate that he is Scythian.

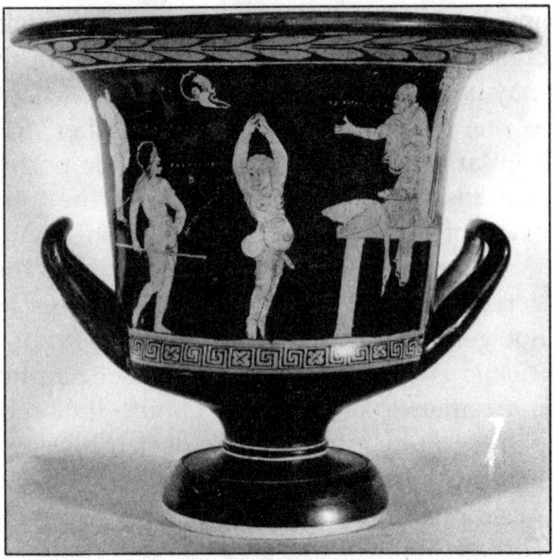

FIGURE 16. Apulian calyx-krater, Tarporley Painter, c. 400 BC. New York, 24.97.104. *PhV* 84. Courtesy, The Metropolitan Museum of Art, Fletcher Fund, 1924.

The appearance of these lines, all in Athenian dialect might seem to support the theory that books somehow played a role in the transmission or creation of the image. I maintain that it shows the opposite. For one thing, the lines are not in verse. Beazley tried to edit and arrange the lines so that they formed one and a half iambic trimeters, but I believe this was misguided. My guess is rather that they are not the exact words of the play, but words written to fit the moment in the drama that the artist is specifically remembering. Another feature of the inscription helps corroborate the view that this is memorywork. The dialect is Attic, because this is the language of the comedy, but the alphabet is the local alphabet of Taranto where the pot was produced. In other words it appears that the painter is not copying a text but sounding out the Attic dialect-words in his head and writing them down in a manner that comes naturally to him.

In 1970 two of the same characters came to light on an Apulian bell-krater, but by a different painter and painted some thirty years later than the krater just discussed (FIGURE 17). The thuggish young man still carries his stick, and the feisty old man oils himself because he is about to wrestle the thug. By focusing on the baskets at the lower right of each vase, we can see that each basket carries two goats and on each vase a goose stands or lies beside them.[8] This is not a standard prop in

8. The ears of a second goat on the calyx-krater (FIGURE 16), though normally overlooked, are visible on the right side of the basket.

Greek comedy, and it leaves little doubt that we are dealing with a different scene from the same comedy. The scene on FIGURE 17 is the earlier scene, if we can judge by the life-cycle of the goose, since the goose is still alive here but very dead on FIGURE 16. Here again, one might suppose that the similarity in costume and props indicates some kind of hardcopy transmission of the image, but there are some minor details which help to suggest a different conclusion. The basket here, for example, is a yoked double basket, but the basket on the earlier pot is a single one. This difference is unlikely to have occurred in any close copy of a single illustrated edition, and it is uneconomical — besides being unlikely— to suppose the existence of two illustrated editions of the same play thirty years apart. The general correspondence of masks, props and details of costume, taken together with some minor discrepancies of detail, is testimony, rather, to the continuance and conservatism of the performance tradition.

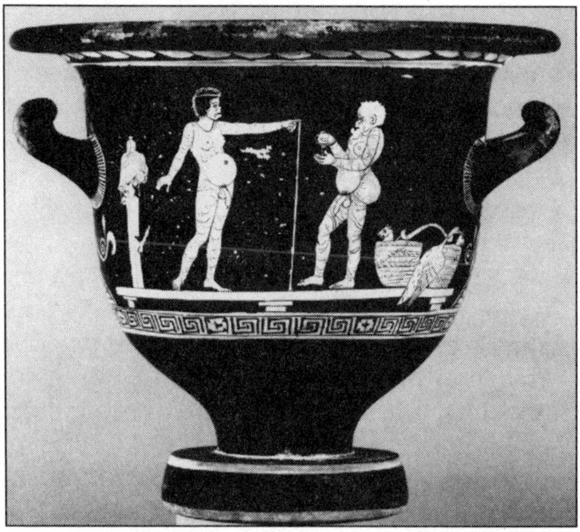

FIGURE 17. Apulian bell-krater, McDaniel Painter, c. 370 BC. Boston 69.951. Gift of Otis Norcross. Courtesy, Museum of Fine Arts, Boston. Reproduced with permission. © 1999 Museum of Fine Arts, Boston. All Rights Reserved.

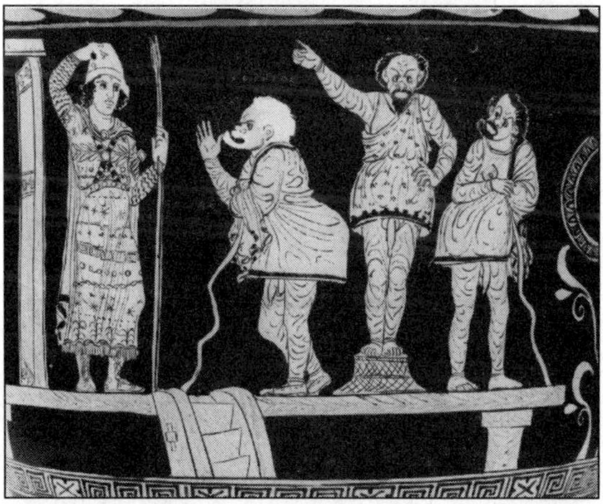

FIGURE 18. Apulian bell-krater, Choregos Painter, c. 380 BC. Malibu 96.AE.29. Courtesy, The J. Paul Getty Museum, Malibu, California. Photograph by Bruce White.

Not all the vases which show scenes are scene specific. Some vases simply show actors in the company of other members of Dionysus's retinue. Other vases appear to be comic distortions of mythical subjects based only on the artists' close familiarity with both idioms (Taplin 79-88). But most of the best paintings of the genre's creative period (c. 400-350) are scene specific, some so much so, that without knowledge of the comedy that they illustrate, the pictures are very puzzling, sometimes mind-boggling. The "Choregos vase" (FIGURE 18), for example, has given rise to much controversy since its publication in 1991. This Apulian bell-krater of c. 390 shows four characters on a typical comic stage. From left to right they are labeled Aegisthus, Choregos, Pyrrhia (sic), Choregos (again). The first and third are names: Aigisthus is of course the son of Thyestes and murderer of Agamemnon. Pyrrhias ("Red-head") is a standard comic slave name. The second and fourth labels designate the office of the sponsor or producer of tragedy and comedy. The word is in Attic dialect and the institution is known mainly from Athens at this time, and, in any case, not securely attested in the Greek West. This is clearly an Attic comedy, and the presence of *choregoi* suggests a metatheatrical plot. My guess, which relies heavily on Taplin's interpretation (*Comic Angels* 55-66), is that we have a debate between *choregoi* on the relative merits of comedy and tragedy. Comedy is championed by the typical comic slave Pyrrhias; tragedy is represented by Aegisthus (who looks puzzled to find himself arriving upon a comic stage). In the end the "Choregoi" will have to choose a winner (and will surely choose comedy). But the significant thing is that even with the help of the labels, this is little better than an educated guess. Nothing is self-evident. Appreciation of the painting depends on a good knowledge of comedy — in performance.

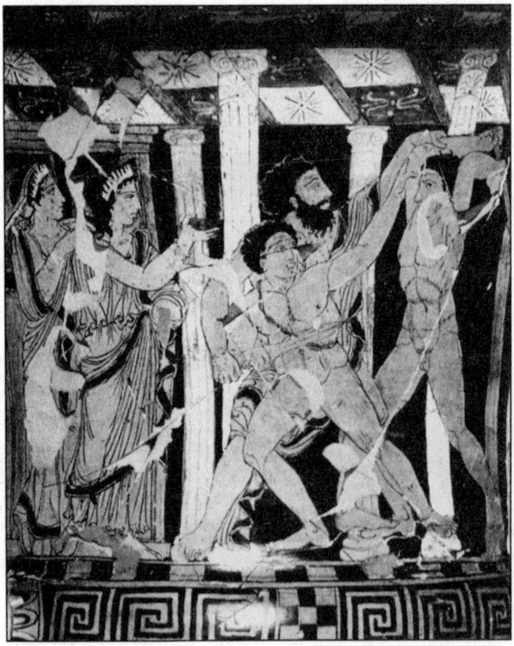

FIGURE 19. Sicilian calyx-krater, Adrastos Group, c. 340 BC. Lipari 10647.

There is one more very interesting detail on this vase. South Italian vases influenced by tragedy do not show performance. Nonetheless the style is often no less tragic in inspiration than the contents. The "tragic style" can be shown: by dramatic subjects (usually domestic violence or moments of recognition); by loud gestures and dramatic poses; by "stagey" or elaborate backgrounds, especially raised floors, multiple columns, or detailed ceilings and backdrops; by ornate costumes; or by the addition of characters marginal to the central action, usually women registering emotional reaction (like a chorus) and sometimes by placid gods hovering above as if from the machine. Some of these "tragic" features (domestic violence, loud poses, raised floor, elaborate columns, ceilings and costume, marginal women) are exemplified by a Sicilian kalyx-crater depicting Adrastus intervening in a fight between his sons-in-law, Tydeus and Polynices (FIGURE 19). The interesting thing about the Choregos vase (FIGURE 18) is that Aegisthus is represented as half actor and half mythological character: he wears no mask, as do all the comic characters (their mouths all gape open), but one can see the sleeves of his bodysuit. Mythological figures may wear ornate sleeved chitons or the oriental kandys. Here patterned actors' sleeves emerge from his chiton which ends, as is normal, at the shoulder. The artist, even in a comic medium, fails to illustrate the tragic character as a performing actor, but succumbs to the tragic illusion, half-drawing the mythological character, even when drawing a tragic actor in a comic context.

In fact, from the Classical period there is only one extant vase which gives a nearly realistic representation of tragic actors on stage (FIGURE 20). It is also Sicilian and very late in the Classical period (c. 330). The fragment depicts the climactic messenger scene from Sophocles's *Oedipus the King*. Uniquely, the igures are placed on a stage of the sort familiar from the comic vases. The actor to the left is the messenger. Though he speaks to Oedipus and Jocasta, the two adult figures to the right, he acts "up-front," looking towards the audience, and only gestures with his left hand towards the characters he notionally addresses. His arms clearly show the actor's tights

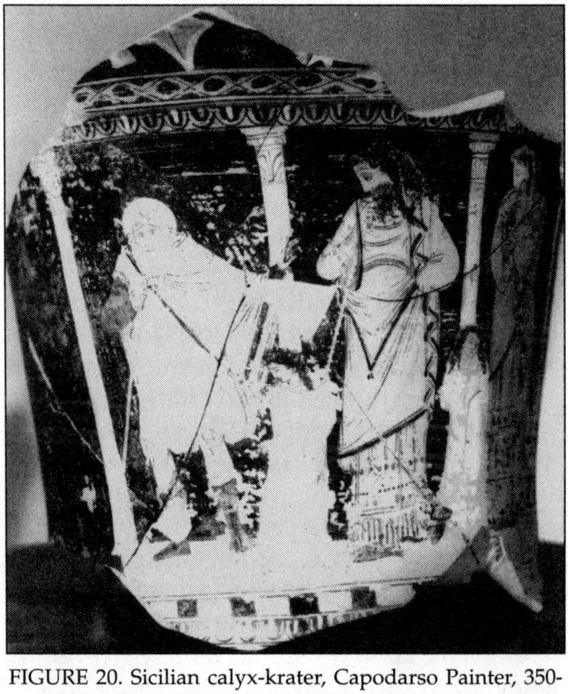

FIGURE 20. Sicilian calyx-krater, Capodarso Painter, 350-325 BC. Syracuse 66557. Courtesy, Museo Archeologico Regionale "Paolo Orsi" di Siracusa, by permission of the Assessorato Beni Culturali ed Ambientali della Regione Sicilia.

emerging from underneath his cloak (compare also Oedipus's right arm). There is a stiffness and angularity about the faces which suggests a mask (particularly emphasized by the messenger's frontality), and a codified conventionality about the gesture made by Jocasta to express her shock— she has just realized who Oedipus is. Even so, the mouths of the actors are not quite as open as we expect from a tragic mask. Moreover, the stage-realism is compromised, paradoxically, by some of the standard forms of theatrical "rhetoric" one finds on the mythological vases: Oedipus's daughters Antigone and Ismene are added for pathos, even though they are not part of this scene in Sophocles's play; a servant woman (not visible in the photograph) just behind Jocasta, turns away with a gesture of alarm, like the ubiquitous running women on South Italian mythological scenes.

In posing the question why Attic pottery avoids theatrical subjects, Taplin observes that Attic vasepainters generally avoided subjects dealing with the public and political life of Athens, such as depictions of the Assembly, Council, or lawcourts ("Pictorial Record" 88-90). This may well be so, though it is still hard to see just why such avoidances existed, or why drama was categorized with political life rather than the realm of Dionysiac subjects so favoured by vasepainters. In Taplin's view, South Italian art more readily accepted the theatre as a subject because its political aspects were not much recognized outside the original Athenian context.

But the problem strikes me as less one of avoidance than one of "seeing," as Green characterizes it ("On Seeing and Depicting the Theatre"), while the contrast between the practice of Attic and South Italian painters, though large, is in my view not as stark as Taplin describes it. In this study I have argued that the relationship between theatre and the visual arts is less characterized by reluctance to depict theatrical subjects, than by reluctance to see and depict performance *as performance*, and that this reluctance, though it dissolves with time and space, is present even in the South Italian wares. Theatre is a dynamic subject —itself a representation— and the artist wavered between drawing its signs or its referents. Except in special cases (the choral scenes) it took several generations before artists chose to draw drama in performance in preference to the myths or fantasies narrated by a performance. It is not easy to see why this is so, but it appears to be a practice existing even outside of Athens and a result of reasons more complex than a distaste for introducing politics into the symposium. Perhaps we should see it as a lingering remnant of the archaic cultural tendency to seek archetypal and mythic realities beneath the surface of events, and its feeling that the actor, like the poet, is merely a conduit for the Muse. It was precisely in the late fifth and especially in the fourth century that performers became a significant part of Greek society, and the whole notion of performance took hold of Greek consciousness. That is the time when actors, musicians, and orators first became culture heroes, and when, as Aristotle records, the actors became more important than the poets, just as the rhetorical delivery of a political speech became more important than its contents (*Rhetoric* 1403b, 31-35). Over the course of the fifth and fourth century, "reality," for most Greeks, rose closer to the surface of things and events: unlike his Archaic ancestor the Classical Greek was more inclined to contemplate the phenomenal world than to look through and beyond it. Perhaps for this reason the first realistic illustrations of dramatic performance affected precisely those parts of drama where the illusion was weakest, namely the chorus, and comedy, and perhaps for this reason the realistic depiction of theatrical performance was so much more successful outside of Athens, far away from drama's original performance context. At Athens the weight of native tradition, myths, rituals, and indeed politics made the dramatic referents more conspicuous and interesting than the play of theatrical signs.

WORKS CITED

Beazley, John D. "The New York 'Phlyax-Vase'." *American Journal of Archaeology*. Vol 56. 193-195.

Crosby, Margaret. "Five Comic Scenes from Athens." *Hesperia*. Vol 24. 76-84.

Green, J. Richard. "Dedications of Masks." *Revue Archéologique*. Vol 2. 237-248.

__. "A Representation of the *Birds* of Aristophanes." *Greek Vases in the J. Paul Getty Museum*. Vol 2. 95-118.

__. "On Seeing and Depicting the Theatre in Classical Athens." *Greek, Roman, and Byzantine Studies*. Vol 32. 15-50.

__. *Theatre in Ancient Greek Society*. London and New York: Routledge, 1994.

Pingiatoglou, Semeli. "Eine Komödiendarstellung auf einer Choenkanne des Benaki-Museums." *Kotinos*. Heide Fröning *et al.*, eds. Mainz: von Zabern, 1992. 292-300.

Hedreen, Guy. *Silens in Attic Black-figure Vase-painting*. Ann Arbor: University of Michigan Press, 1992.

Lissarrague, François. "Why Satyrs are Good to Represent." *Nothing to do with Dionysos?* J. J. Winkler and F. I. Zeitlin, eds. Princeton: Princeton UP, 1990. 228-236.

Pickard-Cambridge, Arthur W. *The Dramatic Festivals of Athens*. 2nd ed. Revised with supplement by John Gould and David M. Lewis. Oxford: Clarendon Press, 1988.

Schmidt, Margot. "Tes ges oukh haptomenos: Nochmals zur Choenkanne Vlastos aus Anavyssos." *Museum Helveticum*. Vol 52. 65-70.

Taplin, Oliver. *Comic Angels*. Oxford: Clarendon Press, 1993.

__. "The Pictorial Record." *The Cambridge Companion to Greek Tragedy*. Patricia Easterling, ed. Cambridge: Cambridge UP, 1997. 69-90.

Trendall, Arthur Dale. *Phlyax Vases*. 2nd Ed. Bulletin of the Institute of Classical Studies Supplement 19. London: Institute of Classical Studies, 1967. = *PhV*.

Webster, T. B. L. "South Italian Vases and Attic Drama." *Classical Quarterly*. Vol 42. 15-27.

__. *Monuments Illustrating Tragedy and Satyrplay*. 2nd ed. Bulletin of the Institute of Classical Studies Supplement 20. London: Institute of Classical Studies, 1967. = *MTS*.

__. *Monuments Illustrating Old and Middle Comedy*. 3rd ed. Revised and enlarged by J. Richard Green. Bulletin of the Institute of Classical Studies Supplement 39. London: Institute of Classical Studies, 1978. = *MMC*.

The Three Kings in Drama and the Visual Arts: The Chicken and the Egg

Luba Eleen

University of Toronto

On July 23, 1164, Rainald von Dassel, Archbishop of Cologne and Chancellor of the Holy Roman Emperor, Frederick Barbarossa, entered Cologne in a solemn procession. He was carrying the relics of the three Magi,[1] the wise men who, according to the Gospel of Matthew, were the first of the Gentiles to recognize and venerate the newborn Christ-child. Rainald had been given the relics two years previously by Barbarossa, who had seized them as spoils after his sacking of Milan. (According to the Milanese legend, they had been kept for seven hundred years in the church of Sant'Eustorgio.[2]) This translation and the continued possession of the relics were to become central themes in the mythology of Cologne, giving rise to a cult of the Magi[3] —by then referred to as the "Three Kings"— the patrons of the city, whose biblical deeds were enacted in a liturgical play,[4] whose translation from Milan and arrival in Cologne was preserved in a chronicle, the *Relacio de tribus Magis*[5], and whose images were depicted throughout the city, in windows, paintings, miniatures, even pastries.

The most reknowned of these pictorial representations was that on the Three Kings Shrine, the precious casket made to contain the relics of the

1. *Die heiligen drei Königen: Darstellung und Veherung*, catalogue of an exhibition (Cologne, 1982).
2. H. Hoffmann, *Die heiligen drei Könige. Zur heiligenverehrung im Kirchlichen gesellschaftlichen und politischen Leben des Mittelalters* (Bonn, 1975) 75-80.
3. J. Torsy, "800 Jahre Dreikönigenverehren in Köln," *Kölner Domblatt* (1964): 15-162.
4. Torsy 39; N. King, "Ein Magierspiel in kölner Dom?", *Kölner Domblatt* 43 (1964): 412-540, esp. n. 2.
5. Torsy 74.

Magi,[6] and still one of the major adornments of the Cathedral in Cologne (Fig. 1). This splendid shrine,[7] ornamented with precious stones and covered with figures of pure gold, created by one of the leading artists of the day,[8] was not completed until two generations after the arrival of the relics in 1164.[9] Apparently begun as early as 1180, the project was able to go forward partly through gifts from the newly-crowned king, Otto IV: in 1200 he donated the crowns worn by the skeletons when they were exposed on feast days, and several years later gave the gold and gems required to complete the façade of the shrine, with its representation of the Adoration of the Magi (Fig.2).[10] On the left hand side of the lower level, the three Magi are led by the eldest, the bearded Melchior, who is moving into a kneeling pose in front of the Virgin and Child, followed by the beardless

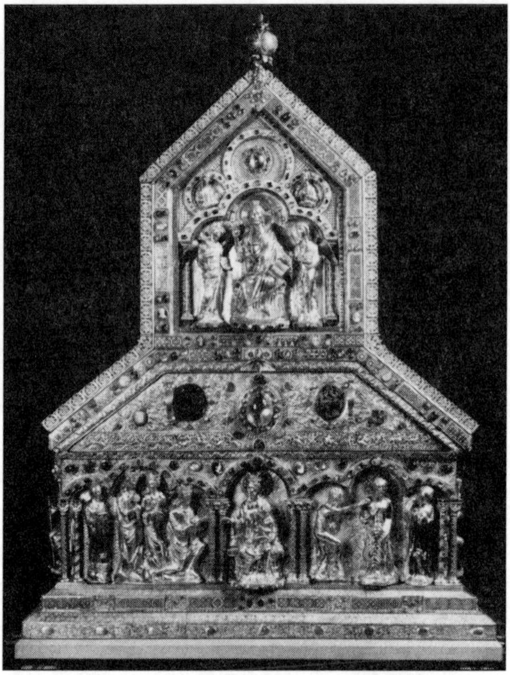

Fig. 1: Three Kings Shrine. Cologne Cathedral.

6. Accompanied by the bones of the soldier saints Felix and Nabor (also looted from Milan), and eventually Gregory of Spoleto.
7. *Ornamenta Ecclesia: Kunst und Künstler der Romanik,* catalogue of an exhibition of the Schnütgen Museum in the Josef-Haubrich Kunsthalle (Cologne, 1985) II, 216-226, no. E18.
8. The prophets on the sides and the design and some of the figures on the façade are usually atributed to the Mosan artist Nicholas of Verdun and his workshop; see, e.g., H. Schnitzler and P. Bloch, *Der Meister der Dreikönigenschreins,* catalogue of an exhibition in the Diözesan-Museum in Cologne, 11 July-23 Aug., 1964, published as a issue of *Kölner Domblatt* 43 (1964): 412-540, no. 1.
9. P.E. Schramm and F. Mütherich, *Denkmale der deutschen Könige und Kaiser* (Munich, 1981) I, no. 191; recently, Renata Kroos has disputed these dates, an issue not of relevance here. R. Kroos, "Zur datierung des Dreikönigenschreins," Kunstchronik 38 (1985): 290-298.
10. The Adoration of the Magi is balanced by the Baptism of Christ on the right, the Virgin and Child occupying the centre, under the figure of Christ of the Second Coming on the upper register; he is accompanied by two angels bearing the instruments of the passion and busts of three archangels. Between the two levels is a trapeze-shaped plaque that can be removed on feast days, to expose the bones of the Kings wearing the crowns donated by Otto IV.

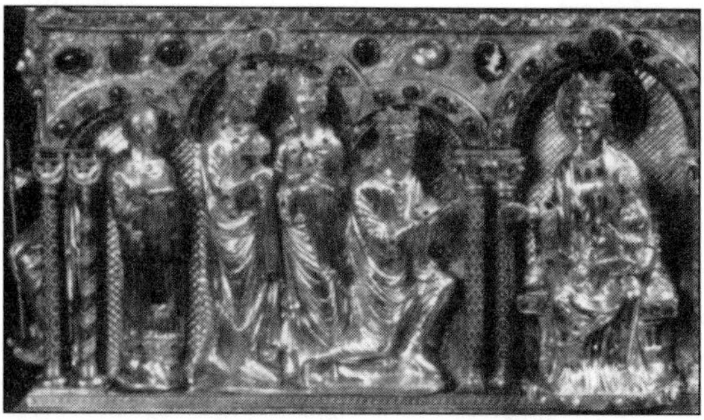

Fig. 2: The Adoration of the Magi. Detail of Fig. 1.

youth, Caspar, turning back to address the middle-aged, bearded Balthazar.[11] A fourth Magus has been added to the traditional three: he represents Otto IV, the patron of the shrine and the symbol of the continuing attempts to identify the Hohenstauffen kings with scriptural and sacred forbears.[12] For several generations after Otto's donation, as long as they remained a power in Germany, the Hohenstauffens proceeded from their coronations in Aachen directly to Cologne to venerate the relics.[13]

The casket and its figural decoration have given rise to an enormous literature and much speculation. In 1909, for example, Hugo Kehrer suggested in his work on the three kings in literature and art[14] that the iconography of the Adoration of the Magi on the shrine was an example of what he called the "French drama type", and that it derived from the actions of the participants in the dramatic enactments that in many localities formed part of the liturgy celebrating Epiphany, or the Feast of the Magi, on January 6. Kehrer's argument runs as follows: In the second half of the twelfth century it became common for the first Magus to be depicted kneeling, or moving into a kneeling position; this pose originates in the *genuflexio* described in the stage directions of most of the Magi plays, as does the gesture of the second Magus, who points to the star that has led them to Bethlehem. According to Kehrer, the imagery made its way first into the monumental sculpture of church façades in France, and subsequently into the minor arts (Fig. 9), as exemplified by the shrine in Cologne (Fig. 2).[15]

---

11. The names go back to the 6th c., and were cited by Bede (ca 673-735) in the *Collectanea et flores* (Basel, 1563) 649, who also specifies their ages and the arrangement with the youngest in the centre. In the majority of medieval depictions of the Adoration, the Magi move in order of age, the eldest first.

12. H.P. Hilger, "Sacrum Imperium, Insignien und Denkmale" *Ornamenta Ecclesia* III, 185-192.

13. Kehrer 185 (see following note).

14. H. Kehrer, *Die heiligen drei Könige in Literatur und Kunst*, 2 vols. (Leipzig, 1908-9).

15. Kehrer II, 129-158. Fig. 9, the Ingeborg Psalter, Chantilly, Musée Condé, cod. 1695, made in northeast France around 1200, is representative of the majority of examples of this type, where the second Magus points to the star; see F. Deuchler, *Der Ingeborgpsalter* (Berlin 1967).

Such an interpretation of the relationship between the arts is not surprising in a book making its appearance in 1909; it was a common judgment of its time, culminating in Émile Mâle's celebrated work on the iconography of the sculptures adorning French churches.[16] Mâle's observations regarding the similarities between the visual representations and the texts and stage directions of the plays are indeed compelling, and, in the first half of this century many scholars emulated his reasoning. (Mâle himself had supported Kehrer's hypothesis in 1910 in an article-cum-review in which he criticized some of Kehrer's details as "naive", but agreed with his theory.[17]) More recently, however, it has been increasingly accepted that Christian imagery in the Middle Ages has its own history transmitted through a tradition of copying, going back to the earliest period, and that similarities often can be explained by common sources in scripture and exegesis: relatively few pictorial expressions can be accepted unreservedly as having been inspired by the dramas.

It would be wrong, however, to reject all such interpretations of similarities between images and drama. Otto Pächt has pointed out that where Mâle's examples rely on depictions in art of costumes and actions that are not included in the scriptural and exegetical texts, but are components of the stage directions for plays, a strong case can be made for the influence of the latter on the former.[18] Pächt himself made an impressive contribution to the literature in his analysis of the Emmäus scenes in a group of manuscripts produced in the twelfth century in England, which he convincingly demonstrated were influenced by the stage directions for the Peregrinus plays. According to Pächt, not only the details of costumes and actions derive from the plays, but ".... it is the pictorial invention, the very style of the narrative [i.e., such modes of presentation as continuous narrative], which has been activated under the influence of the drama".[19] Another observation of Pächt's has more immediate relevance to the question of the Magi dramas and their significance for imagery: that there can be "a problem in pictorial representation to give solemnity and an aura of liturgical significance to a wide range of narrative matter", and that the experience of seeing staged dramas might have helped artists solve this problem.[20] This question will be re-visited later in this article.

In order to evaluate the importance of the Magi plays to the Three Kings Shrine in Cologne, it is necessary to look in greater detail at what

16. E. Mâle, *L'Art religieux du XIIe siècle en France* (Paris, 1922).

17. E Mâle, "Les Rois mages et le drame liturgique", *Gazette des beaux-arts* 52 (1910): 261-270.

18. O. Pächt, *The Rise of Pictorial Narrative in Twelfth-Century England* (Oxford, 1962) 33-35.

19. Pächt 41.

20. Pächt 51.

has been depicted there, and to compare it with the earlier iconography of the same scene, and with the Magi plays.

First, a summary of the text of Matthew 2:1-12: Wise men come from the East following a star. At the court of Herod in Jerusalem they are interrogated, and then directed to Bethlehem. Still following the star, they arrive at and enter a house in Bethlehem, where they fall down and adore the child, and deposit their gifts of gold, frankincense and myrrh. Then they fall asleep, and, following the advice given by an angel in a dream, go back to their homelands by a different route.

The Adoration of the Magi[21] was one of the first New Testament figural subjects to be employed by Christians, as opposed to Old Testament themes interpreted symbolically. It is to be found in wall paintings in catacombs and on sarcophagi as early as the beginning of the fourth century (Fig. 3). Both the depiction of the act of homage in an attitude of obeisance and the portrayal of the wise men as foreigners dressed in oriental-style garments —leggings and phrygian caps— probably derive from Roman imperial iconography, in which the defeated, foreign foemen offer tribute to the conquering Roman emperor Fig. 4).[22] Beginning with these images incised and painted on the walls of catacombs and carved on sarcophagi in the fourth, fifth and sixth centuries, the iconography for this subject became standardized: the three Magi move in single file in attitudes of reverence, carrying gifts for the Christ-child resting in the arms of his mother. From the earliest

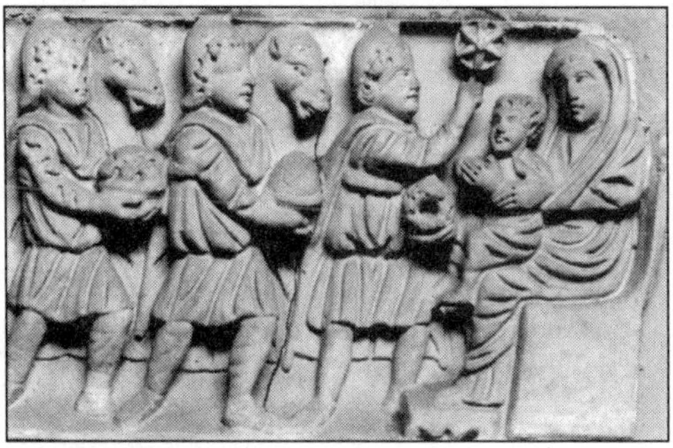

Fig. 3: The Adoration of the Magi. Sarcophagus, Vatican, Museo Cristiano, no.21.

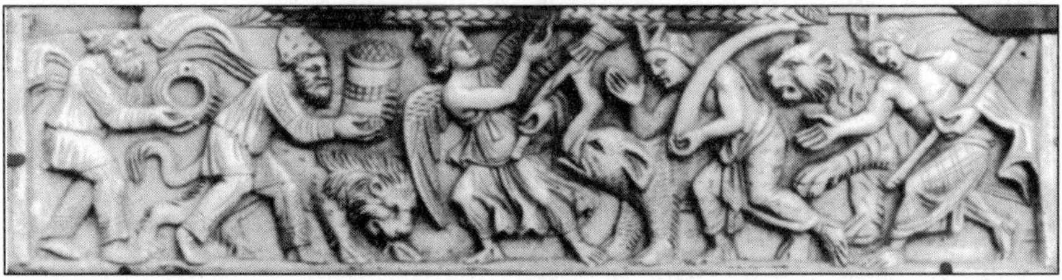

Fig. 4: Foreign prisoners offer gifts to the Roman Emperor Louvre, Barbarini diptych, detail.

21. G. Schiller, *Iconography of Christian Art* (Greenwich, Conn., 1971) I, 94-109.

22. A. Grabar, *Christian Iconography. A Study of Its Origins* (London, 1969) 44-45.

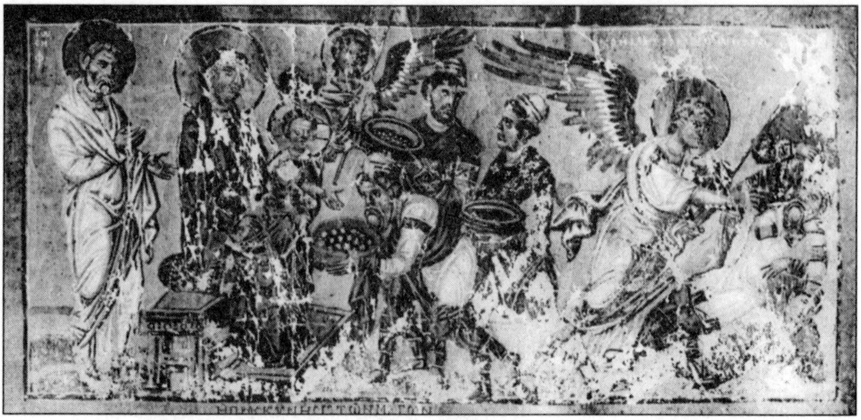

Fig. 5: The Adoration of the Magi. Paris, Bibliothèque nationale, cod. gr, 510 (the Homilies of Gregory of Nazianzus), fol. 137.

times, there were minor variations in gesture, with one of the Magi turning back, for example, or the foremost kneeling; the star may or may not be present, and one of the Magi may or may not point to it. From the late tenth century in western Europe, the Magi begin to be depicted as crowned kings.[23]

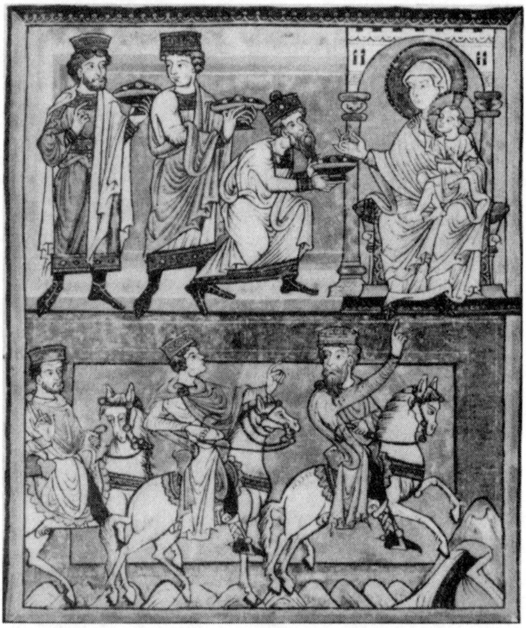

Fig. 6: The Adoration of the Magi; the Magi Follow the Star Karlsruhe, Badische Landesbibliothek, cod. Bruchsal 1, fol. 11.

What about the so-called "French drama type", like the representation on the Cologne shrine? It was not invented in the twelfth century, as claimed by Kehrer, but can also be seen in Byzantine art,[24] so important as a source of religious iconography for medieval artists, from at least the sixth

23. R. Deshman, "Christus rex et magi reges: Kingship and Christology in Ottonian and Anglo Saxon Art," *Frühmittelalterlichen Studien* 10 (1976): 367-405, esp. 377-381.

24. E..g., in souvenir ampullae from the Holy Land; see A. Grabar, *Ampoules de Terre Sainte, Monzo-Bobbio* (Milan, 1958) no. 1; and in a wall painting executed by a Greek painter in the church of Sta Maria Antica in Rome in the early 8th c.

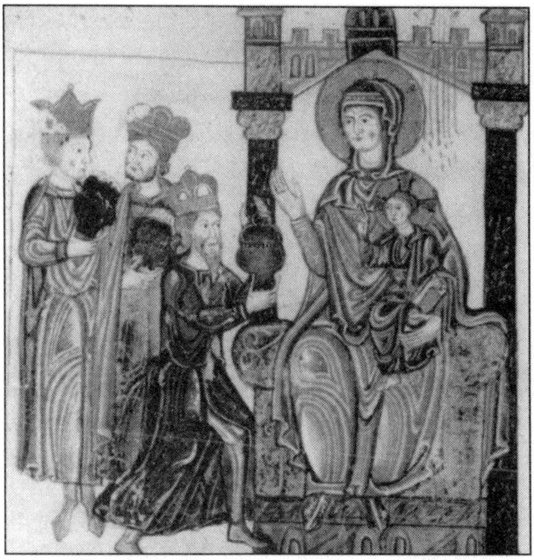

Fig. 7: The Adoration of the Magi. New Testament, Vatican Library, cod. Chigi. A IV 74, fol. 11.

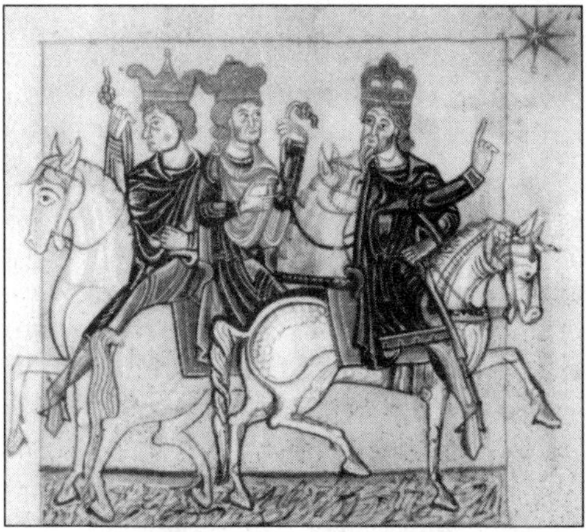

Fig. 8: The Magi Follow the Star. As in Fig. 9, fol. 11v.

century, and again in the Middle Byzantine period, as in the copy of the Homilies of Gregory of Nianza made in Constantinople around 880 (Fig. 5).[25] In these eastern examples the foremost Magus kneels and the second, who does not point to a star, turns back to converse with the third. This imagery can also be found in the West in the twelfth century. It was nowhere more popular than in works of art produced in the Rhineland around Cologne, and in the closely related school of Alsace, further up the Rhine (Figs. 6, 7). This holds true for sculpture, manuscripts and works of the minor arts produced in the later twelfth century, even before the creation of the image on the front of the Cologne shrine, but especially for those made later in the thirteenth century: its imagery must have exerted a powerful influence on the arts of the subsequent period.

If we return now to the shrine and compare it with a late twelfth-century Rhenish manuscript from Koblenz slightly earlier than the shrine, (Fig. 6),[26] and with another produced by a Rhenish artist working in Verona in the second quarter of the thirteenth century —thirty to forty years after the completion of the shrine (Figs. 7, 8)[27]— we see that they have many

25. Paris, Bn, MS grec 510, fol. 137; *Byzance. L'art byzantin dans les collections publiques françaises*, Catalogue of an exhibition held at the Musée du Louvre, Paris, from 3 Nov. 1992 to 1 Feb. 1993, no. 258, 346-348. As is common in Byzantine art, the scene in this example includes Joseph, standing behind Mary, and an angel introducing the Magi.

26. Karlsruhe, Badische Landesbibliothek, cod. Bruchsal 1, fol. 11; see below, n. 34.

27. Vatican Library, cod. Chigi. A IV 74, fols. 11, 11v; see below, n. 35.

features in common. The Magi, now kings, are dressed in costly, ornate garments, the first kneeling, the second turning back to speak to the third.[28] None of them, however, points to a star, although in two of these versions there is a star hovering above (it is probable that the Cologne shrine also included a star in its earliest designs). This rendering is actually more accurate in respect to the text than are those in the majority of medieval depictions (Fig. 9), since one would expect the Magi to have ceased pointing at the star once they have entered the house.

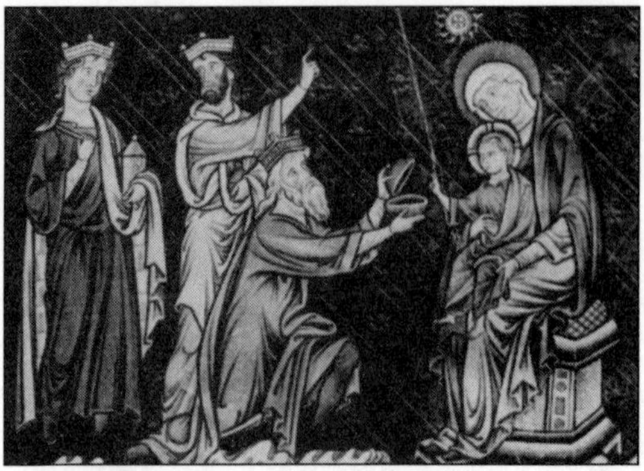

Fig. 9: The Adoration of the Magi. Ingeborg Psalter, Chantilly, Musée Condé, cod. 1695, fol. 11.

These observations lead us now to the *Officium Stellae*, the Magi drama, which was enacted in churches all over Europe from the eleventh century onwards, as part of the liturgy for Epiphany, the feast of the Magi.[29] The transformation of the Magi into kings was complete by this time, so that we must now refer to these dramas as the Three Kings plays. It is known that Cologne had a Three Kings play,[30] but unfortunately it has not survived, so that we are forced to rely on a general impression based on dramas from other locations. I propose to concentrate on the simplest of these dramas, with the fewest protagonists, since they are closer to the pictorial imagery we have seen, as opposed to the complex representations involving retinues of retainers accompanying the kings, a considerable entourage for Herod, and elaborate dialogue.

Two of the extant plays fit into this category, one from Limoges, the other from Besançon, both of uncertain date.[31] They are enacted inside the church, as part of the liturgy, and they require that certain areas of the church function as sites in the geography of the Holy Land. Both specify that three of the clergy of the church, bearing gifts and dressed in colourful silk garments and crowns, enter, either together or separately, point to the star and follow it, as it is made to move by some apparatus in the choir. Engaging in dialogue taken mainly from the text

28. The kings in the shrine and in the Koblenz version are in the order described by Bede (see above, n.11), a very unusual motif in the Middle Ages.

29. K. Young, *The Drama of the Medieval Church* (Oxford, 1933, 2nd ed. 1962) II, 29-58.

30. Torsy 39.

31. Young II, 34-42.

of Matthew, and singing antiphonally with the chorus, they stop at a location in the choir meant to stand for Jerusalem, then proceed to another place in the church symbolizing Bethlehem, where they make obeisance before the Virgin and Child on the high altar (the manger), and place their gifts. In both versions they leave by another door (in the Limoges play after being warned by an angel).

The kings actually take part in only two actions: they move from one place to another, guided by the star, and they bow in veneration and deposit gifts before the Virgin and Child. It is widely agreed that these latter roles were not portrayed by actors,[32] but represented by cult statues of the Virgin and Child of a type that had, during the Romanesque period, played an important role in observations in honour of the Virgin.[33]

There is no need for the Magi to point at the star once they have reached their destination. The pictorial depictions that we have seen earlier, where the Magi simultaneously perform their act of adoration and point to the star (Fig. 9), are actually conflating two moments into a single picture, a common approach of medieval artists in dealing with the passage of time. The Rhenish examples introduced here, on the other hand, depict only the moment of adoration, omitting the gesture towards the star. As already noted, this rendering is actually more accurate in respect to the text than those in the majority of medieval depictions. Does this precision with regard to time reflect an experience an artist has had in viewing a play?

The two examples of Rhenish illumination we have looked at already go farther in their attention to the details of narrative: they include separate scenes showing the kings on horseback on their way to Bethlehem, pointing at the star. One of these is from Koblenz of ca 1200,[34] and the second made by a Rhenish artist in Verona in Italy in the 1230's.[35] Before we jump to the conclusion that the imagery was inspired by the Three Kings plays, we should consider whether it also has a history in art. There are indeed examples of this two-part narrative scheme in earlier western art, but it is in Byzantium where this configuration has a

32. Young; Kehrer 57.

33. I.H. Forsyth, *The Throne of Wisdom. Wood Sculptures of the Madonna in Romanesque France* (Princeton, 1972) 49-59.

34. Karlsruhe, Badische Landesbibliothek, cod. Bruchsal 1, fol. 11; this MS actually has a cycle of 4 Magi scenes, on fols. 11 and 11v: the Magi on horse, pointing at the star; the Adoration; the sleeping Magi warned by an angel; and the Magi returning to their homelands in a boat; see K. Preisendanz and O. Homburger, *Das Evangeliar des Speyrer Doms* (Leipzig, 1930).

35. Vatican Library, cod. Chigi A IV 74, fols 11, 11v see L. Eleen, "New Testament Manuscripts and their Lay Owners in Verona in the Thirteenth Century," *Scriptorium* 41 (1987): 211-236.

long-standing tradition, as does that of extended cycles of all, or most, of the details in the text of Matthew. In representations of the Magi following the star in Byzantine art they are inevitably represented on horseback; this is true as well of almost all of the previous occurences of this event in western art, in contrast to the literary evidence of the way in which the plays were performed, with the Magi on foot.

The two-part narrative might not have been the only aspect of the imagery to have come from the East. As we have seen earlier, There are precedents as well for the so-called "French drama type" depicting the moment of the adoration itself in Byzantine art, going back to the sixth century. In all of these, the first Magus kneels, the second turns back towards the third, who is depicted in profile, in the manner of presentation in the Rhenish versions; all of them bear gifts. During the High Middle Ages, Byzantine models were much sought after in the West, as conveying a greater realism and greater range of emotion than was available in their own tradition, so that it is not impossible that this type of imagery for the Adoration, as well as the idea for the two-part narrative, has its source in an importation from the East. We know that fresh Byzantine models were available in the Rhineland in the later twelfth century.[36] The iconography of the Adoration in which the Magi do not point at the star might be of Byzantine derivation, and it might also be a survivor of a two- or multi-scene cycle.

What does this demonstration tell us about the Rhenish imagery we have been looking at? Did the artists get their inspiration from their experience of the Three Kings plays? They share with the plays the close attention to the precision of the narrative, but this comes from the Gospel text itself, and it is also to be found in Byzantine and occasionally in earlier western art. The evidence for the narrative iconography as a whole, therefore, is inconclusive, although a case could be made for the costumes, which may possibly reflect actual performance practice.

Aside from the narrative, there is another sense in which the two art forms resound against one another: the use of the sculptural group of the Virgin and Child introduces deeper levels of meaning in both. I have already alluded to the practice of having these sculptures function as the sacred figures in the dramas. Their iconography was of a special type, in which the Virgin represented the Throne of Wisdom.[37] Popular in the late eleventh and during the twelfth centuries, as the cult of the Virgin was capturing the popular imagination, these statues, sometimes holding precious relics, were brought out on special ceremonial occasions, to be placed on altars and carried in processions. They were

36. E. Kitzinger, "Norman Sicily as a Source of Byzantine Influence on Western Art of the Twelfth Century," *Byzantine Art an European Art* (Athens, 1966) 127-147, esp. p.135.

37. Forsyth 24.

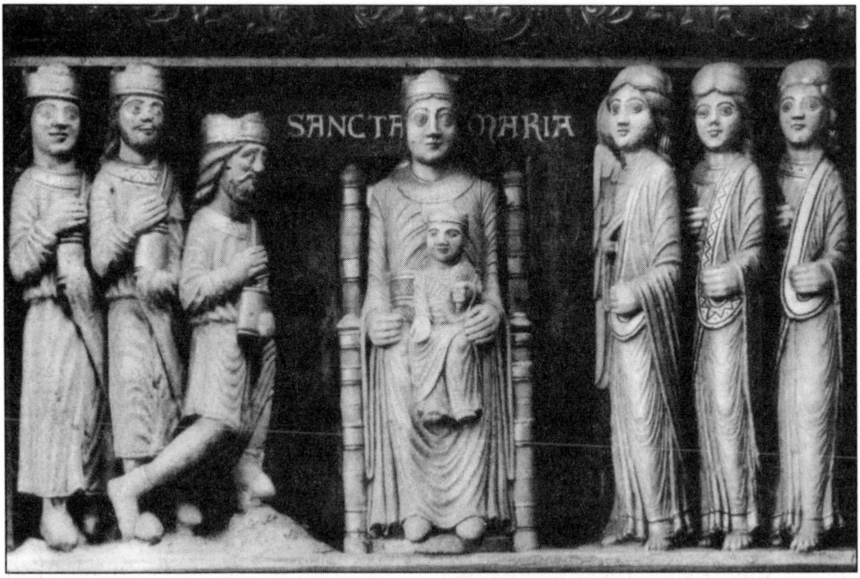

Fig. 10: The Adoration of the Magi. Retable, Oberpleis, St. Pankratius.

usually rigidly symmetrical, with the Child placed squarely in the lap of the Virgin, both facing forward. According to Ilene Forsyth, they functioned as "agencies of access", allowing the onlooker to form a spiritual connection with the prototype by means of the image.[38]

During the twelfth century, when the narrative subject of the Adoration of the Magi began to be used in a monumental context on the façades of churches, two problems presented themselves. One was purely compositional: how to fit an assymetrical scene depicting movement into the strict structure, with its central emphasis, of a tympanum, lintel or retable. The solution was to place the Virgin and Child in the centre, the Magi to the left, and with another scene, often related, on the other side. This central position also provided the response to the second problem, which was to communicate a spiritual message, in this case regarding the timeless, hieratic role of the Virgin, as *Theotokos*, or "God-bearer", by the visual means of placement and allusion. The earliest façade sculptures adapted the Throne of Wisdom to this end, depicting the central group in strict frontality, some of the sculptures actually imitating local cult statues.[39] A Rhenish example from the church of St. Pankratius at Oberpleis shows that the phenomenon was not limited to France (Fig. 10).[40]

38. Forsyth 38-45.

39. Forsyth 51.

40. F. Rademacher, *Die Regina Anglorum in der Kunst des frühen Mittalalters*. Die Kunstdenkmäler des Rheinlandes, Beiheft 17 (Düsseldorf 1972) 9-19.

Towards the end of the twelfth century, The Virgin began to be depicted as crowned, as she is at Oberpleis. This was in response to a long-standing notion that not only was she *Theotokos*, she was also Queen of Heaven.[41] This concept was expressed in art in the Early Christian period, but did not appear again until the middle of the twelfth century, when it made its appearance in monumental art, and she began to be depicted wearing a crown. In these centralized compositions, the Virgin and Child participate on the one hand in a narrative of the childhood of Christ, albeit one with theological and liturgical overtones; on the other hand they simultaneously signify the belief in the timeless reality of Mary as Mother of God and Queen of Heaven. Mary never wears a crown in purely narrative renditions of the scene: this symbolic attribute is reserved solely for those places where the image functions as an agency of access.[42]

This development in monumental art provided the background to the façade of the Three Kings Shrine in Cologne. Although it was an object of the minor arts, its meaning far surpassed its size. Constructed as a miniature basilica, its façades set forth comprehensive theological statements. The front face was a declaration of a three-fold Epiphany ("manifestation"): to the Jews, in the depiction of the Baptism of Christ on the right; to the Gentiles, in the Adoration of the Magi; and in the future, represented by Christ of the Second Coming in the top register. The hieratic and iconic role of the Virgin is emphasized by her placement on the central axis, immediately below the figure of Christ.[43] Unlike some of the earlier versions of the Virgin in Majesty, this one does not observe the rule of strict frontality, following the artistic tradition instead, but the meaning of the placement is unmistakeable.

In the dramas, although we have no literary confirmation, the onlooker's experience would have been coloured by the presence of the sculptural group of the Throne of Wisdom on the altar, so charged with meaning for contemporaries. We cannot know if the artists or the playwrights were the first to borrow the symbolic image to give "solemnity and an aura of liturgical significance" to the narrative, but there can be no doubt that playwrights observed public art, and artists were present at publicly performed plays, so that the influence of the one on the other was reciprocal and multi- stranded.

---

41. G. Schiller, *Ikonographie der christlichen Kunst* (Gütersloh 1980) IV,2, 181-183.

42. In the Karlsschrein in Aachen, a near contemporary of the Cologne shrine, Mary is not crowned in the Adoration scene, forming one of a series in a narrative cycle, but she is crowned in the scene on the façade, in which she is given a gift by Charlemagne

43. A. von Euw, "Darstellungen der Hl. Drei Könige im kölner Dom und ihre ikonographische Herleitung," *Kölner Domblatt* 43 (1964): 293-340, esp. 313.

Depicting Theatre: Contemporary Evidence for Renaissance Theatre Sets in Renaissance Italy

Konrad Eisenbichler

University of Toronto

When trying to visualize the staging of plays in Renaissance Italy, scholars often refer to stage sets sketched by contemporary artists. The three sets for comedy, tragedy, and the pastoral drawn by the architect Sebastiano Serlio (1475-1554) are probably the best known examples of contemporary depictions of stage sets. As such, they are often used in classroom situations and in published works as examples of Renaissance Italian stage sets (figures 1-3).

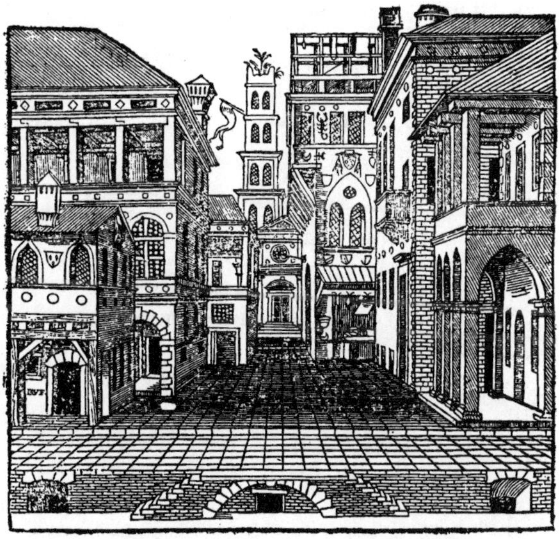

Figure 1: Sebastiano Serlio "Scena comica" (1619)

When examining Serlio's drawings, however, one should always bear in mind that they were "ideal" or "proposed" stage sets, not depictions of sets actually used in plays at the time. Admittedly, they may have inspired later sets, such as the one used for Leonardo Salviati's comedy *Il granchio* (1566) or for Cornelio Lanci's much later *La vedova*.[1] In this second case, the set

1. Cornelio Lanci published his works between 1583 and 1591. A native of Urbino, very little is known about him and he rarely appears in studies on Italian Renaissance comedy.

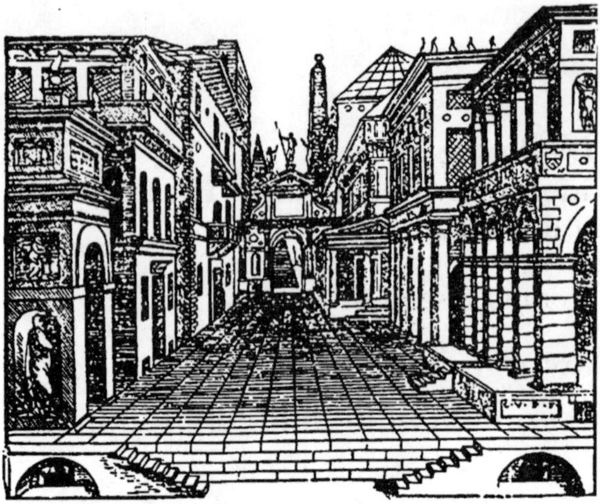

Fig. 2: Sebastiano Serlio "Scena tragica" (1619)

depicted not a generic street scene, as in Serlio's drawing, but contemporary downtown Florence, with Brunelleschi's dome and the Palazzo della Signoria clearly identifiable in the background. Similar visual references to well known landmarks of the city in which the play was set must have graced the stages— or, at least, the backdrops —of many a play in mid and later sixteenth-century Italy. On several occasions Giovan Maria Cecchi (1518-1587), the most prolific dramatist of his time, had the Prologo of his plays set the scene by pointing out well-known landmarks. In his 1548 comedy *Gl'incantesimi*, for example, the Prologo reveals that

> you know that this scene is in Florence; for the Cardo and the Cupola and the Piazza that are here represent it very clearly for you.[2]

At times, the recognizable, realistic elements of a stage set could provide the dramatist with occasion for humour, as Cecchi found in his *La romanesca* (1585); here, in this otherwise morally sober and uplifting work, the Prologo titillates the audience with an obscene *double-entendre*:

> The scene for this farce today is laid in Rome,
> And to prove that that's true, look there
> How she shows you her Colosseum uncovered.[3]

References such as these, however, are relatively late in Italian Renaissance theatre history and should be seen as such. Serlio's drawings of ideal stage sets, though relevant for later productions, must be used with caution when speaking about theatre before the mid-century.

---

2. "voi conoscete che questo proscenio è in Firenze; che 'l Cardo e la Cupola e la Piazza che è qui, ve la figurano assai chiara." Giovan Maria Cecchi, *Gl'incantesimi* in *Commedie* (1883), p. 129. Cecchi provides similar indications for Florence in *Il corredo* (1545), *Lo spirito* (1549), *Il donzello* (1550), *Il martello* (1561); for Genova in *La stiava* (1546); for Siena in *Gli sciamiti* (after 1557); and so forth.

3. "La scena della farsa è oggi Roma / E ch'e' sia 'l vero, eccovi che colà / La vi mostra scoperto il Culiseo." Cecchi, *La romanesca* (1880), p. 10. The speaker is punning on *culo suo* ("its bum") to suggest that Rome "is exposing her bum to you."

One should also remember that Serlio's sketches were devised by an architect as illustrations in a book on architecture, a sizeable work that runs the gamut from domestic to public, from civic to ecclesiastical buildings. Even though his suggested sets may have influenced mid- or late-sixteenth-century stage design, they do not reflect how the majority of sets were in fact constructed during most of the Italian Renaissance.

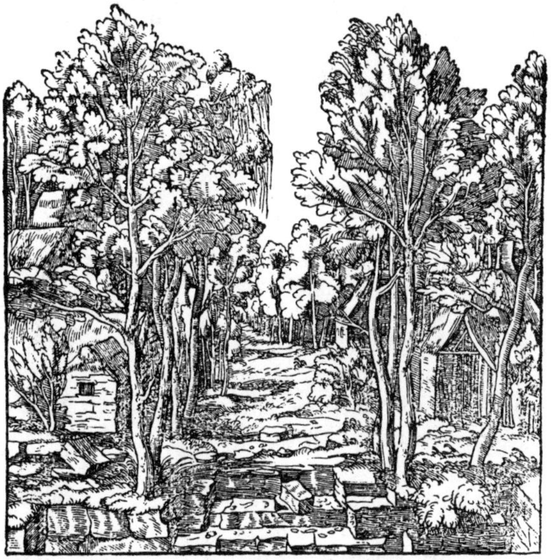

Fig. 3: Sebastiano Serlio "Scena satirica" (1619)

A third consideration to keep in mind is that not every acting troupe could afford to build a stage as fancy as Serlio proposed. Certainly, for important celebrations or entertainments the sponsoring agencies (state, court, or patrons) did demand an elaborate and visually stunning stage set, and picked up the bill for it. For the most part, however, in Renaissance Italy plays were performed on less formal occasions and for less exalted audiences — generally speaking, they were mounted as carnival and summertime entertainments at informal gatherings of friends or at convent or confraternal meetings for members of the group. Budgets, in these cases, were small and a generous amount of imagination and goodwill always supplemented the shortcomings of the production and of the actors.

With these considerations in mind, it becomes evident that Serlio's proposed sets, though wonderful to look at, are not necessarily a good starting point for a discussion on the stage sets generally used in Renaissance Italy. Direct evidence for such a discussion, however, is not as self-evident or as easily identifiable as Serlio's drawings. Contemporary artists did not consciously set out to depict a stage set. What extant sources survive are limited and, usually, somewhat obscured by other representational interests. In attempting to determine what was the usual stage set used in Renaissance Italy, therefore, we are obliged to identify first what kind of theatre was being performed and then how this theatre might be evidenced in contemporary sources, both visual and written.

In the case of Florence, the most popular form of theatre in the fifteenth century and in the first half of the sixteenth was the *sacra rappresentazione*. This was a genre of sacred plays that drew its plot lines from biblical, hagiographical or legendary sources. Using the vernacular, *sacre rappresentazioni* were written in poetic form; their standard verse was the hendecasyllable gathered into octaves rhymed ABABABCC (though occasionally other verse forms were temporarily used for specific purposes). Their authors were either the very prolific, but elusive Anonymous or a handful of more or less erudite individuals gravitating around the Medici circle — writers such as the dramatist Feo Belcari (1410-1484), the poet Bernardo Pulci (1438-1488), his wife the devout Antonia Pulci (1452-1501), the learned professor Castellan de' Castellani (1461-1519), or the elegant and versatile Lorenzo de' Medici himself (1449-1492).

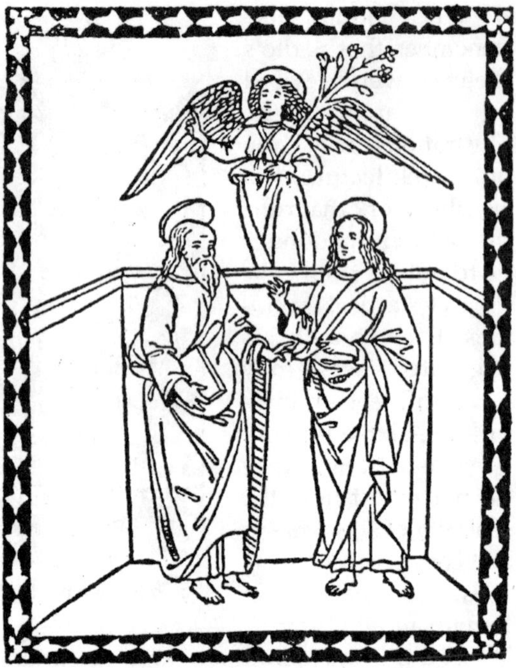

Fig. 4: Lorenzo de' Medici, *La rappresentazione di San Giovanni e Paolo* [c.1498]

The usual venues for such plays were the city's convents and confraternities. In both cases it was the younger members of the group, novices in the case of convents and teenaged boys in the case of confraternities, who performed in them. Both the convents and the confraternities staged *sacre rappresentazioni* usually as a carnival entertainment, when they sought to do something to treat themselves, their families or friends, not without, however, gathering some profit from the experience. In fact, the Horatian maxim of *delectare et docere*, to please and to teach, was often used in the prologues to these plays to explain the reason for mounting the event.

The *sacre rappresentazioni* were highly popular in their time, so much so that they were published in great numbers in low-cost, popular editions for general consumption.[4] These slender volumes often

4. See De Batines, *Bibliografia delle antiche rappresentazioni italiane sacre e profane* (1852); Cioni, *Bibliografia delle sacre rappresentazioni* (1961); *Inventario delle Sacre Rappresentazioni manoscritte e a stampa* (1988).

bore a simple woodcut illustration on the title page. Although often artistically crude, the title page woodcuts of these early editions offer us an insight into the variety and format of stage sets used in the production of *sacre rappresentazioni*.

The title page woodcut for a late fifteenth-century edition of *La rappresentazione di San Giovanni e Paolo* by Lorenzo de' Medici (1449-1492) shows the two titular saints, John and Paul, engaged in conversation in front of a low, three-panels wall, while an angel stands, or "floats" above them somewhere behind the wall (fig. 4).[5] The woodcut is simple, though not necessarily naïf, and suggests a stage set that was elementary at best: a series of three low panels, apparently about five or six feet tall, that served to delineate a performance space and provide a generic backdrop to it. Since one of the characteristics of the *sacra rappresentazione* was a multiplicity of acting spaces, or mansions, we can easily imagine how several such three-panels constructions could be laid out strategically in a larger space to represent various sites ranging from a private room to a banquet hall, from an urban street scene to a port town as required by the play's narrative. The angel standing behind the central panel could easily have been standing on a ladder or on a raised platform not visible to the audience so as to give the impression, in the simplest of ways, of being somehow suspended or floating in mid-air behind the other performers. The stage set this woodcut suggests is, therefore, not only absolutely simple, inexpensive to build, and easy to assemble, but also versatile and reusable, that is, it could serve its purpose in this or in a variety of other plays.

Ironically, the actual stage set for the première performance of Lorenzo de' Medici's *La rappresentazione di San Giovanni e Paolo* was not at all as simple or as inexpensive as the woodcut from its published version would suggest. The coppersmith Bartolomeo Masi, a young member of the confraternity of San Giovanni Evangelista that first performed the work on 17 February 1491, was an eye-witness to the event, and entered a description of it in his memoirs:

> "I recall how, on 21 December 1490, Piero my brother, and I, Bartolomeo, made our entry in the youth confraternity of San Giovanni Evangelista, which is located between [the churches of] Santo Barnaba and Santa Maria Madre. Among the twelve of us youths who made our entry on that day there was, for one, the shoemaker Giovanbatista d'Andrea, who was and is still our neighbour. The Guardian of the confraternity was then and is still now Cristofano di Miniato, a brass-worker [with a shop] near the archiepiscopal palace in Florence. The following Carnival, Giuliano di

5. Medici, *La rappresentazione di San Giovanni e Paolo* [c.1498]. For the dating of this edition to c.1498 see Rhodes, *Gli annali tipografici* (1988), p. 80. The woodcut is reproduced in Kristeller (1968), p. 25.

Lorenzo di Piero di Cosimo de' Medici was master of festivities in the confraternity. He organized three wonderful meals for all the youths in the confraternity, with so many baked goods, cream-filled cornets, round cakes and *trebbiano* wine that it was a wonderful thing. And then he organized a play in the confraternity's garden, with a stage that extended along the entire length of the loggia and reached as far out as the mound, with a stage set that was as beautiful as could be. The play was performed the second day of Lent that year. It was performed on that day because the stage-set was not ready beforehand, such a wonderful thing it was. And the play was the *Representation of Saints John and Paul*. Lorenzo de' Medici, father of the above-mentioned master of festivities, came to see the play, as well as many other eminent men, and so many other people that it was a wonderful thing. And all the youths of the confraternity stood on the stage, especially those who were wearing a gown and Piero and I, Bartolomeo, were among these."[6]

There are many noteworthy points in this description, but for our purposes we need to underline only that the play was staged outdoors, in the confraternity garden, and that the stage set was "as beautiful as could be", so much so that its construction delayed its performance by at least two days, moving the entire Carnival festivity into Lent and thereby raising its own set of problems with the ecclesiastical authorities.[7] One of the admirable aspects of this stage set was its size: it ran the entire length of the loggia, and out "as far as the mound." Cesare Molinari has suggested that it probably measured 15 metres in length.[8]

6. "Ricordo fo come, a' dì XXJ di dicenbre MCCCCLXXXX, Piero mio fratello ed io Bartolomeo faciemo l'entrata, questo dì sopradetto, nella conpagnia de' fanciugli di santo Giovanni evangelista; la quale è tra santo Barnaba e santa Maria Madre. Et in detto dì fumo a fare l'entrata circa di dodici fanciugli, tra' quali v'era, per uno, Giovanbatista d'Andrea calzolaio, el quale era, al presente, nostro vicino, et era guardiano di detta conpagnia, et ancora n'è Cristofano di Miniato, ottonaio sotto l'Arcivescovado di Firenze. El carnesciale seguente fu messere di detta conpagnia Giuliano di Lorenzo di Piero di Cosimo de' Medici; e fecie fare tre belle colizione a tutti e fanciugli di detta Conpagnia, con tante confezione e cialdoncini e berlingozzi e trebiano, che fu una cosa maravigliosa. E dipoi fecie fare una festa nell'orto di detta conpagnia, con un palco che teneva tutta la loggia e dava la volta per insino al monte, con un parato tanto bello quanto fu possibile fare; e feciesi detta festa el secondo di quaresima, di detto anno. Feciesi in detto dì perch'el parato non fu fatto prima, per la bella cosa ch'egli era. E la sopradetta festa fu la rappresentazione di santo Giovanni e Pagolo. Eravi a vedere detta festa Lorenzo de' Medici, padre del sopradetto messere, e di molti altri uomini da bene, e tanto popolo che era una cosa maravigliosa. E tutti e fanciugli della conpagnia istettono in sul palco, massimamente quegli che avevano indosso veste di drappo: che Piero e io Bartolomeo fumo di quegli a starvi." Masi, *Ricordanze* (1906), pp. 15-16.

7. For a discussion of this performance and its social context, see Eisenbichler, "Confraternities and Carnival."

8. Molinari, *Spettacoli fiorentini* (1961), p. 85.

This would make it similar in size to the stage erected on the same site for the 1589 production of Giovan Maria Cecchi's *L'esaltazione della Croce*, described in great detail by the dramatist's son, Bartolomeo Cecchi.[9] In order to accommodate the number and diversity of acting spaces required for Lorenzo's play, the large number of actors necessary for the performance, and the confraternity youths who viewed the event from on-stage, this 1491 stage must have been also several metres deep.

Aside from size, the stage set must have been impressive also because of its decorations — size alone does not make something "as beautiful as could be." Unfortunately, however, the young Bartolomeo Masi was much more impressed by the Medici sponsorship of the event, by the food and wine laid out for the boys and their guests, and by the presence of notable Florentines in the audience, than he was by the specific details of the stage, its construction, size and decorations, none of which he mentions. And neither was anyone else interested in recording these details, either in writing or in a sketch. Masi's description is the only one that seems ever to have been made.

For a hint of what the stage might have looked like, or what the confraternity could mount, we can jump ninety-eight years later and look at Bartolomeo Cecchi's description of the 1589 stage set for the performance of his father's *L'esaltazione della Croce*. As in the case of Lorenzo de' Medici's play, this one, too, was staged by the confraternity of San Giovanni Evangelista in its garden. On this occasion, aside from a very sizeable stage, an enormous tent had also been erected to cover both the stage and the audience, and large paintings, allegorical emblems, and heraldic crests had been commissioned and hung both around the walls of the tent and above the proscenium according to an elaborate and specific iconographical program in praise both of the Medici and of God.[10] Admittedly, this 1589 performance was elaborate because the confraternity wished to celebrate the wedding of Grand Duke Ferdinando I and Christine of Lorraine and, undoubtedly, also because the developing sense of Mannerist extravagance and splendour had clearly begun to influence both the decoration and the scale of the event.[11]

---

9. Bartolomeo Cecchi, "Descrizione dell'apparato e de gl'intermedj fatti per la storia dell'Esaltazione della Croce rappresentata in Firenze da' giovani della Compagnia di S. Giovanni Evangelista con l'occasione delle nozze delle Altezze Serenissime di Toscana nell'anno 1589" in *Sacre rappresentazioni del XIV, XV, e XVI secolo* (1872), vol. 3, pp. 121-138. For a study of this staging, as described by Bartolomeo Cecchi, see Eisenbichler, "Spazi e luoghi" (1987); see also Ferraro, "*L'esaltazione della Croce* (1986).

10. See Eisenbichler, "Spazi e luoghi" (1987).

11. For a discussion of seventeenth-century stage sets and performances in youth confraternities such as that of San Giovanni Evangelista, see Eisenbichler, *The Boys of the Archangel Raphael* (1998), pp. 218-235.

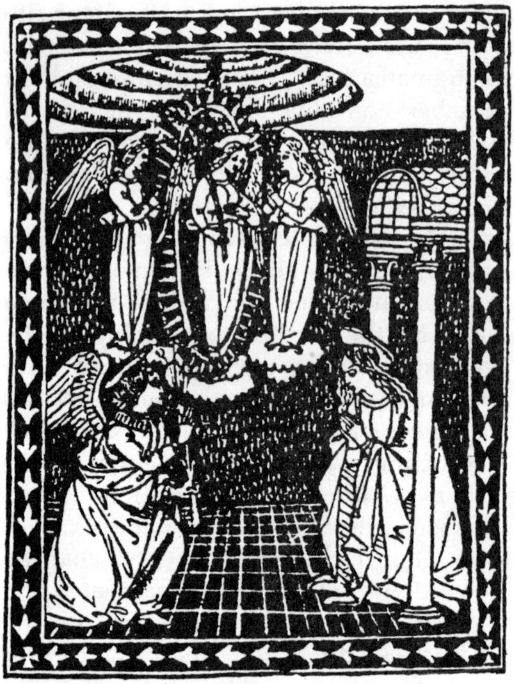

Fig. 5: Feo Belcari, *La festa dell'Annunciazione di Nostra Donna* [pre-1515]

Although generally similar, there are a number of variants in title-page woodcuts for early editions of *sacre rappresentazioni*. These variants provide insights into other and different staging techniques in use at that time.

The woodcut for an edition of the anonymous *Festa dell'Annunciazione di Nostra Donna,* published in Florence before 1515 (fig. 5), shows two different moments in the staging of an Annunciation play.[12] In the upper section, the Archangel Gabriel is seen in the company of two angels as the three descend from the heavens inside a resplendent mandorla, their feet resting on clouds. In the lower section the Archangel is seen kneeling on the left, making his announcement to the Virgin kneeling under a portico on the right. A tiled floor is laid out in perspective, suggesting not only horizontal depth, but also chronological movement from the scene in the background, where the figures appear smaller, to the scene in the foreground, where they appear larger and, therefore, more immediate. A black backdrop suggests a back wall probably nine to ten feet high.

This pre-1515 woodcut reveals a technically more elaborate set than the one suggested by the title-page woodcut in the 1498 edition of Lorenzo de' Medici's *La rappresentazione di San Giovanni e Paolo*. It reveals the presence of a free-standing architectural structure (the portico), the use of an ingenious levitating device (the mandorla), and the strategic placement of lights to achieve an effect (the flames on the perimeter of the mandorla). The angels are clearly not standing on a

12. Feo Belcari, *La festa dell'Annunciazione di Nostra Donna* (Firenze: Francesco di Giovanni Benvenuto, n.d. but before 1515). Benvenuto re-used this woodcut in several later editions. More recently, it has been reproduced in, among others, Kristeller (1968), ill. 53; *Le temps revient* (1992), p. 215; Newbigin, *Feste d'Oltrarno* (1996), p. 15.

ladder out of sight of the audience, but inside a cage that floats in mid-air and can be lowered and raised between the rafters and the ground. This device, in turn, is connected to a larger structure fixed to the ceiling that, by virtue of its shape as an inverted hemisphere, represents the *volta celeste*, that is, the inverted dome of the heavens or, perhaps, even the Empyrian. This simple woodcut, therefore, is not unlike Sandro Botticelli's much more elegant and refined painting of the *Mystical Nativity* which shows, in fact, a free-standing architectural structure (the portico of the manger), a circle of angels floating above it in mid-air, and an open heaven depicted as an inverted hemisphere from which angels appear to be descending in a joyous circular dance. Botticelli may have imagined the scene all on his own, or he may have been inspired to represent it in this manner by an actual stage set and dramatic performance he might have seen in Florence.[13]

In fact, in Florence Botticelli would have had on many occasions the opportunity to see such a stage device in action during the performance of the play of the Annunciation, staged on a regular basis at the church of San Felice in Piazza by the confraternity of Santa Maria delle Laudi e dell'Annunziata.[14] The Russian visitor Abraham, Bishop of Suzdal (in Florence for the meetings of the Ecumenical Council of 1439-1440) attended the play fifty years before Botticelli's time and described it in his journal, not without a sense of wonder and amazement, but, unlike the young coppersmith Bartolomeo Masi, also with a careful eye to size, measurements, and technology.[15] His description is so detailed that in 1975 two Italian theatre historians and an architect were able to construct a scale model of that 1439-40 stage using the measurements given by the visiting Russian bishop.[16]

A second, and much later description of the stage machinery for the Annunciation play in San Felice in Piazza was published in 1568 by the art historian Giorgio Vasari in his life of the architect Filippo

---

13. For a discussion of how artists may have been influenced by the theatrical performances and stage sets they saw, see Nerida Newbigin, "Art and Drama" (1996).

14. For a study of this play and its staging, see Newbigin, *Feste d'Oltrarno* (1996), pp. 1-43.

15. For the Russian original and the Latin translation see *Acta Slavica Concilii Florentini* (1976), pp. 112-124. Newbigin provided a new English translation based on this critical edition in her *Feste d'Oltrarno* (1996), vol. 1, pp. 3-7, and then she discussed it at length in the rest of her chapter on the Annunciation play at San Felice in Piazza (pp. 7-43). The earlier Italian translation by Alessandro D'Ancona in his *Origini del teatro italiano* (1891), vol. 1, pp. 246-253 is not reliable because it was done from a German translation of a seventeenth-century edition of the Russian original.

16. The model was built by the architect Cesare Lisi with scholarly assistance from Ludovico Zorzi and Annamaria Biancalani. Using a scale of 1:12.5, the model stands 147 cm. in height and is 189 cm. long and 125 cm. wide. Photographs of the model were published in *Le temps revient* (1992), p. 218.

Brunelleschi. In these well-known pages, Vasari attributes to Brunelleschi the invention of the intricate machinery that allowed the confraternity to build a heaven that opened and closed, with angels that descended, ascended, and floated in mid-air, and with a multitude of lights that illuminated the entire set with truly heavenly splendour.[17]

These descriptions of theatrical performances drawn from contemporary visual and narrative records should, of course, be correlated with other contemporary records, such as account books and log books. Recent archival research on the confraternities of Florence has revealed that important information on the staging of early theatre can be gleaned from the records of these lay religious organizations. One will not necessarily discover long-lost plays (though that can sometimes happen),[18] but one will find in them important information on how the majority of theatre was staged in Renaissance Florence, by whom, where, when, and why. Admittedly, the records vary significantly not only from confraternity to confraternity, but also within the same confraternity from scribe to scribe. Some scribes, in fact, were keenly interested in theatre and carefully recorded every occasion when a full fledged play, a brief dramatic interlude, or even a short madrigal sung in costume were performed at the confraternity. Others, instead, ignored theatre completely and did not record even the more extensive and engaging performances that took place within their confraternity's walls.

When scribes fail us, accountants can come to our aid. Thanks to their careful recording of expenses incurred in mounting an event, they often provide us with valuable information on the production of plays. Besides the usual weekly disbursals for candle wax, lamp oil, staff salaries, and other mundane necessities of Renaissance life, these records occasionally include payments to carpenters for the construction of sets, to various merchants for materials purchased, to professional musicians for music performed, to porters for the carting of props from one place to another, and so forth. Sometimes they also include donations received from members and friends of the confraternity to offset the costs of production. From this variety of information patient scholars can reconstruct, at least in part, the time-line, process, materials, support networks, crew, and cast of premodern

17. Vasari, *Le vite* (1966), vol. 3, pp. 188-191. Translated by Newbigin in *Feste d'Oltrarno* (1996), vol. 1, pp. 22-24.

18. The manuscripts of a previously unknown play by Giovan Maria Cecchi and of a play by Giovanni Nardi (1585-1654), a celebrated medical practitioner who enjoyed the friendship and respect of William Harvey, were both recently discovered in documents associated with the Florentine confraternities of the Purificazione and of the Arcangelo Raffaello respectively. For a preliminary study of these plays, see Eisenbichler, "Two Unknown Italian Plays" (1999).

performances. Undoubtedly because of the special skills needed to read, analyze, and correlate these financial records, the vast resources for early Italian theatre history present in account books have not yet been fully utilized.

Lastly, confraternity inventories occasionally reveal the presence of complete or partial stage sets in the organization's store rooms. The 1583 inventory of the youth confraternity of the Arcangelo Raffaello, for example, lists four pieces of "prospettiva."[19] A much later inventory (1690) lists a variety of stage set items including sixteen backdrops representing a woodland scene, seven representing a city view, one representing a forum, four pieces of proscenium, two pieces of sky, and two screens to block out the confraternity's windows.[20] These lists not only tell us that confraternities owned stage sets and, one assumes, that they periodically used them (otherwise there would be no point in keeping them), but they also reveal to us what type of plays the confraternity was inclined to perform — city views would suggest comedies, forums may indicate tragedies, woodland scenes pastoral plays.

Primary evidence for Renaissance stage sets in Italy is clearly not lacking. It is not to be found, however, in the obvious medium of direct visual records of contemporary stages or performances. Scholars searching for the premodern Italian stage set must, instead, turn their attention to more unassuming documents — title page woodcuts, diaries, chronicles, log books, account ledgers, and other such sources. Like the proverbial blind men trying to see the elephant, they cannot do justice to the topic by limiting themselves to a single point of contact. Instead, they must approach it from several directions, consider data from a variety of sources, and correlate the diversity they discover into a fuller, more comprehensive image of Renaissance theatre in Italy.

19. "4 pezzi di prospettiva" "Inventario ... 1583", Archivio di Stato di Firenze, Compagnie Religiose Soppresse da Pietro Leopoldo filza 155, fasc. 1.B, doc. 13, f. n.n.

20. "Sedici pezzi di scena, che rappresentano bosco. Quattro pezzi di proscenio, consistenti in quattro tele sopra suoi telai, dipintevi pietre. Sette pezzi di scena, che rappresentano civile. Un foro civile. Due pezzi di cielo aggangherati insieme. Due telai sopra i quali vi è tirata una tela ingessata per dipignerla, fatti fare per mettere alle finestre maggiori di Compagnia in occasione di feste, acciò vi sia meno lume, et anco per maggiore ornamento." "Inventario ... 1690" Archivio di Stato di Firenze, Compagnie Religiose Soppresse da Pietro Leopoldo, 164.

CITED TEXTS. MANUSCRIPT SOURCES

Archivio di Stato di Firenze, Compagnie Religiose Soppresse da Pietro Leopoldo, filze 155 and 164.

CITED TEXTS. PRINTED SOURCES

Acta Slavica Concilii Florentini. Narrationes et Documenta, ed. Joannes Krajcar. Concilium Florentinum Documenta et Scriptores, vol. 11. Roma: Pontificium Institutum Orientalium Studiorum, 1976.

Belcari, Feo. *La festa dell'Annunciazione di Nostra Donna*. Firenze: Francesco di Giovanni Benvenuto, n.d. [but before 1515].

Cecchi, Giovan Maria. *Commedie*, ed. Olindo Guerrini. Milano: Edoardo Sonzogno Editore, 1883.

Cecchi, Giovan Maria. *La romanesca*. Livorno: Tipografia P. Vannini e figlio. Casa Pia del Refugio, 1880.

Cioni, Alfredo. *Bibliografia delle sacre rappresentazioni*. Firenze: Sansoni, 1961.

D'Ancona, Alessandro. *Origini del teatro italiano*, 2nd ed. Torino: Loescher, 1891. 2 vols.

De Batines, Colomb. *Bibliografia delle antiche rappresentazioni italiane sacre e profane stampate nei secoli XV e XVI*. Firenze: Per la Società Tipografica, 1852.

Eisenbichler, Konrad "Spazi e luoghi nel teatro fiorentino del Cinquecento" *Yearbook of Italian Studies*. Ed. Pamela Stewart. 6 (1987): 51-62.

Eisenbichler, Konrad. "Confraternities and Carnival: The Context of Lorenzo de' Medici's *Rappresentazione di Giovanni e Paolo*" *Comparative Drama* 27:1 (1993): 128-139; reprinted in *Medieval Drama on the Continent of Europe*, ed. Clifford Davidson and John H. Stroupe. Kalamazoo, Mich.: Medieval Institute Publications, Western Michigan University, 1993. pp. 128-139.

Eisenbichler, Konrad. *The Boys of the Archangel Raphael. A Youth Confraternity in Florence, 1411-1785*. Toronto: University of Toronto Press, 1998.

Eisenbichler, Konrad. "Two Unknown Italian Plays at the Beinecke Library: Giovan Maria Cecchi's *Atto recitabile per fare avanti che nella compagnia si diano li panellini* and Giovanni Nardi's *Il Disperato*" *The Yale University Library Gazette* 74:3-4 (2000):126-134.

Ferraro, Bruno G. "*L'esaltazione della Croce*: rapporto tra `figura' e `figurato'" *Quaderni di teatro* 9:35 (1986): 123-34.

Inventario delle Sacre Rappresentazioni manoscritte e a stampa conservate nella Biblioteca Nazionale Centrale di Firenze, ed. Anna Maria Testaverde and Anna Maria Evangelista. Firenze: L.S. Olschki, 1988.

Kristeller, Paul. *Early Florentine Woodcuts*. London: The Holland Press, 1968.

Masi, Bartolomeo. *Ricordanze di Bartolomeo Masi, calderaio fiorentino, dal 1478 al 1526*, ed. G.O. Corazzini. Firenze: G.C. Sansoni, 1906.

Medici, Lorenzo de'. *La rappresentazione di San Giovanni e Paolo*. Firenze, [c.1498]

Molinari, Cesare. *Spettacoli fiorentini del Quattrocento*. Venezia: N. Pozza, 1961.

Newbigin, Nerida. "Art and Drama in Fifteenth-Century Florence" *The Early Drama, Art, and Music Review* 19:1 (1996): 1-26.

Newbigin, Nerida. *Feste d'Oltrarno. Plays in Churches in Fifteenth-Century Florence*. Firenze: Leo S. Olschki, 1996.

Rhodes, D.E. *Gli annali tipografici fiorentini del XV secolo*. Firenze: Leo S. Olschki, 1988.

Sacre rappresentazioni del XIV, XV, e XVI secolo, ed. Alessandro D'Ancona. Firenze: Le Monnier, 1872. 3 vols.

Serlio, Sebastiano. *Tutte l'opere d'architettura, et prospetiva*. In Venetia: Appresso Giacomo de' Franceschi, 1619.

Le temps revient / 'l tempo si rinuova: Feste e spettacoli nella Firenze di Lorenzo il Magnifico, exhibition catalogue ed. Paola Ventrone. Milano: Pizzi, 1992.

Vasari, Giorgio. *Le vite de' più eccellenti pittori*, ed. Rosanna Bettarini, comm. Paola Barocchi. Firenze: Sansoni, 1966.

Poliziano's *Orfeo*: Italian Renaissance Drama as Festival Décor

Mary Alexandra Watt

Florida University

It is perhaps a symptom of post-Enlightenment thought that modern scholars often compartmentalize, isolate and examine so many aspects of culture in discrete study units. Since it has long been common practice to treat sociology, history and literature as separate heads of inquiry, an historic social event is often studied by scholars who are completely detached from those who study the literary efforts engendered by such an event. In the case of Italian Renaissance drama the shortcomings inherent in such an approach have been particularly acute. Given the close link between public dramatic representation and socio- civic identity in Renaissance Italy, failure to consider the event which a particular work celebrated, or its intended audience, yields an analysis that negates the full experience the piece sought to embody and at the same time affixes to the piece an import and autonomy which its author or patron did not necessarily intend. Fortunately, in the past few decades, there has been movement away from this tradition and toward a broader approach,[1] one that examines not only the literary

1. As Robert Rodini suggests, "[o]f late, historians have, in fact, been giving increasingly more attention to the variety and significance of ceremony and ritual during the Renaissance" (476). Rodini further suggests that "[m]uch critical writing on the drama now seems one-dimensional and in need of revision as a result of the realization that the theatrical piece –the written text– has little to tell us unless it is viewed in the context of something much larger, the *festa*, or public festival, for which it was written and of which it was but one of several components" (477). Similarly, the work of Richard Trexler, Andrew C. Minor, Bonner Mitchell and Fabrizio Cruciani, among others, cannot emphasize enough the importance of the *festa* to any such study. Indeed it may not be imprudent to suggest that Italian Renaissance drama is merely one element of the Renaissance *festa* and ought not to be studied as an autonomous work of art.

aspects of a particular work but also its social and historical contours. While this shift by no means necessitates abandoning literary-focused critical methods, it does lead to a deeper and more fulfilling appreciation of this multi-purposed form of entertainment. Moreover, such an examination yields the fascinating conclusion that Italian Renaissance drama, more than an erudite enterprise inviting literary criticism, might be better characterized as festival décor, an audio-visual nicety coordinated thematically with all of the other elements that combined to create the great *feste* of fifteenth and sixteenth century Italy.

Since the less traditional method of analysis has not been unequivocally advocated over the last few centuries not all of the data required for such an undertaking has been preserved and catalogued in a way that might facilitate a broader-based study of some of the more prominent works of Italian Renaissance drama. This lacuna is especially evident and particularly lamentable in the case of Angelo Poliziano's fifteenth-century *Orfeo*. This pioneering work —it was one of the first secular dramas presented in the vernacular[2]— has long been the focus of scholarly attention. However, among the many studies of its humanist elements[3] and its use of *imitatio*, we find few clues as to its context other than the fact that it is often referred to as the ***Festa** di Orfeo* (emphasis mine) and that it was apparently written hurriedly and amidst great turmoil[4] at the request of one of the Gonzaga[5] cardinals. As scholars then, we are left to consider similar fact evidence if we are to have any sense of the purpose or role of the play amidst such turmoil and, moreover, if we are to have any sense of what the spectators *saw* as opposed to what the author *wrote*. That is, we must consider the cultural context, distilled from other similar occasions, and piece together a hypothesis if we are to glimpse, even remotely, the spectacle and the visual splendor of Poliziano's foray into the underworld.

---

2. According to Joseph Spencer Kennard, *Orfeo* is one of the earliest specimens of secular plays written in the vulgar tongue (89).
3. Bruno Maier points out that Poliziano considered poetry as "la civilizzatrice della barbara umanità, individuabile nel mito di Orfeo" (258). As well, while the choice of a classical subject is, in itself, a reflection of Florentine humanism, the choice of the myth of Orpheus is particularly indicative of the essential elements of such humanism. Maier goes on to suggest that "Per la sua "favola" Poliziano ha scelto il mito più caro all'Umanesimo, quello di Orfeo e di Euridice, dandoci così probabilmente il primo esempio di teatro cortegiano in volgare d'argomento profano" (268).
4. This information is taken from a letter written by Poliziano to Messer Carlo Canale in which he states that the *Orfeo* was composed at Mantua over the course of two days, "*intra continui tumulti*" (Orlando Ed. 109).
5. The Gonzaga family was the leading family of Mantua from the late Middle Ages until the seventeenth century. The last Duke in the Gonzaga line died in 1627 and Mantua was sacked in 1630.

The first step is to appreciate that, although drama would eventually emancipate itself from the dictates of the *festa* and of those who sponsored such occasions, in the context of the strict and strongly entrenched patronage systems in the city states of Renaissance Italy, playwrights, like painters, were seen as decorators whose role was to beautify and embellish the festivals that marked pivotal moments in the lives of the ruling princes and dukes. Baptisms, weddings, visits by members of other high-ranking families were marked by processions, jousts, commemorative portraits, poems and plays. Because the enduring power of a ruling family often depended, at least in part, on popular support, many of these celebrations were public occasions in which the citizens were invited to participate. At the same time, such occasions provided the ruling families with the opportunity to reinforce and entrench the civic values they themselves had propagated. As a result, there are countless examples of artisans struggling not only to meet deadlines set by demanding patrons, but also to satisfy the dictates of their patrons in terms of size, content and often even the arrangement of figures or characters.[6] Though it is difficult to imagine in this age when names of Italian Renaissance artists evoke hushed tones of reverence, at the time they were working, artists like Michelangelo and poets like Angelo Poliziano were regularly instructed by their patrons to create products ranging from love poems to honour a newly betrothed or rhymes to celebrate a ceremonial joust, to wedding portraits or frescoes to adorn bridal chambers. Yet, it would be unfair to attribute the genesis of this relationship to the patronage system alone or to the egotism of Renaissance princes. Rather, we must recognize that the notion of art for occasion has its roots, as with so much else, in the Church. In the case of drama, scholars trace a rather unswerving line from the liturgical recitation of the passion of Christ to the *sacre rappresentazioni* of the late Middle Ages. The line continues through to the Renaissance secular drama that emerges in the light of Humanism

6. Under the patronage system, the artist was to paint, write, sculpt or compose to certain deadlines, within certain parameters and in accordance with the whim of the patron. Peter Burke cites the example of Galeazzo Maria Sforza who "commanded painters to work night and day on the Castello Sforzesco" and notes that C. Corio has a story of a room painted in a single night. As well, Burke notes that Federico Gonzaga of Mantua, another important patron, wrote to Titian in 1531 asking for a picture of the Magdalen saying "and above all, let me have it quickly" (80). The fact that Titian sent it in less than a month, with a letter saying he had dropped everything in order to oblige the prince suggests that artists themselves were prepared and able to live within such confines. Burke gives other examples of Federico's impatience such as in his dealings with Giulio Romano whose assistants were not decorating the Palazzo del Te quickly enough. Similarly, Alfonso d'Este of Ferrara, says Burke " was a man of the same stamp." Apparently in 1519, Alfonso also chastised Titian for not producing a painting on time (80).

but nonetheless borrows heavily from the *sacra rappresentazione* in terms of form and language.[7] But the continuity is also one of purpose. In the Renaissance, just as much as in the Middle Ages, the subject matter and content of dramatic pieces were coordinated with the festival that the performance celebrated. For example, plays performed in the lead up to the Lenten season were customarily of a religious nature (Burkhardt 256). Similarly, the subject matter of a play was selected in accordance with its intended audience. We see, therefore, that when the play was performed by or for a confraternity, the bible story or legend performed was chosen to reflect that particular context.[8] As the Renaissance progressed, bringing with it a sense of civic pride, the celebration of the *festa* grew to encompass the civic festivals which were generally marked by spectacles ritually celebrating, reenacting or representing the civic ideals of a society.[9] It is not surprising then to find that, just as the liturgical drama was merely one component in a larger religious observance, secular drama occupied a similar complementary role in the context of the great secular festivals that marked the pivotal moments in the life of the city — (or at least of its rulers).

---

7. Such pieces often began with an introductory dialogue between Apostles, Prophets, Sibyls, Virtues and Fathers of the Church, and sometimes ended with a dance (Burckhardt 259).

8. The term *sacra* ***rappresentazione*** (emphasis mine) recognizes the iterative or repetitive quality of such drama. These performances were re-enactments of existing episodes taken from the collective consciousness of a particular group and, as part of an elaborate ritual, were constant reminders of the principles and beliefs upon which that society was based. The expansion of the dramatic presentation into the confraternity setting added another contextual determinant to the subject or content of the drama. Thus, the intended audience came also to dictate, to a certain extent, the subject matter and content of a performance piece.

9. Princely weddings, canonizations, the awarding of doctoral degrees, entrances to cities were all marked by spectacles, again ritually celebrating the civic ideals of a society (Burckhardt 261). Within this context, the content of the dramatic representation was equally important as the dramatic piece continued to serve the purpose of emphasizing the importance of the occasion. As was the case in religious drama, the intended audience was also a content determinant. The triumphs, jousts and other spectacles associated with such ideals increasingly relied upon allegorical and mythological figures to represent abstract concepts such as civic pride (as in the case of San Giovanni Battista Day in Florence) and prosperity and fertility (as in the marriage celebrations of its ruling citizens). Burckhardt notes the communal nature of such representations and the existence of "the universal familiarity of the people with the poetical basis of the show." The majority of the spectators, at least in the cities, he suggests, understood the meaning of the mythological figures, and could guess without much difficulty at the allegorical and historical, which were drawn from sources familiar to the mass of Italians (258). This communal element also served to reinforce the projected ideals. Accordingly, it was necessary that the content of dramatic pieces associated with a *festa* be universally intelligible to their intended audiences.

Bearing this in mind, let us now consider the occasion that Poliziano's work was intended to embellish. The first difficulty, however, in addressing the context of the *Orfeo* is brought to light by the substantial critical debate concerning the actual date of its composition. For some time it was believed that the *Orfeo* was first recited in Mantua in July 1471[10] under the auspices of the Marquis Ludovico Gonzaga and the Cardinal Francesco Gonzaga as a part of the festivities that welcomed Duke Galeazzo Maria Sforza and the Duchess of Milan. It is now generally accepted that the play was written in 1480 to mark the double event of the wedding of Clara (Chiara) Gonzaga and Alberto di Monpensiero and the betrothal of the teenaged Francesco Gonzaga and eight-year-old Isabella D'Este.[11] However, details concerning its performance are sparse. To get some sense of what the *Orfeo* looked like and its role in decorating Mantua, it is helpful to consider some other near contemporaneous occasions celebrated in the same social circles for which Poliziano was creating.

---

10. A number of the earlier critics suggest that Poliziano wrote the play in July of 1471. Louis Lord, for example, states that the "*Orpheus* was given at Mantua on the 18th, 20th and 22nd day of July 1471 on the occasion of the visit of Duke Galeazzo Maria Sforza. The play was written by Politian, who was then but eighteen years old, at the request of Cardinal Francesco Gonzaga of Mantua" (70). Others, however, give the date as 1480. Bruno Maier posits that Poliziano, during a stay in Mantua in 1480 as a guest at the Gonzaga court, composed in only two days, perhaps in June, the "*fabula*" of *Orfeo*. He goes on to say that it would probably have been staged on the occasion of the celebrations for the double engagements between Chiara Gonzaga and Alberto di Monpensiero and between Francesco Gonzaga and Isabella d'Este; but that it is not known whether it was actually performed (252). Giuseppe Amadei places the writing and performance of the *Orfeo* at Mantua, the 25th of February 1480 (155). Although he gives no indication as to the specific source of that date it appears to be a fusion of the year suggested by Giovanni Battista Picotti, that is, 1480 and the month in 1490 in which Isabella d'Este arrived in Mantua for her wedding occurring on 15 February 1490.

    Ida Maier offers a clarification of this issue, relying considerably on the work of Giovanni Battista Picotti, who reconstructed the events of Poliziano's life between 1479 and 1480. Maier comfortably rejects the hypotheses formulated by the earlier critics: "Depuis que G. B. Picotti a reconstitué l'histoire des événements intervenus dans la vie de Politien entre décembre 1479 et 1480, on a la certitude que l'*Orfeo* a été composé à Mantoue dans le courant 1480. Les hypothèses formulées pars les critiques des générations antérieures — Bettinelli, Del Lungo — en faveur des années 1471 ou 1472 (Politien aurait eu alors dix-sept ou dix-huit ans), étant une fois pour toutes écartées..." (387).

11. Although the actual wedding of Francesco Gonzaga to Isabella d'Este was in 1490, 1480 was a year of great festivities in Mantua which bade farewell to Chiara Gonzaga, Francesco's older sister who was about to depart for the country of her bridegroom, a cousin to the king of France. The betrothal of the teenage Francesco to the eight year old Isabella took place during this period and undoubtedly added to the festivities. The betrothal had been arranged by the Duchess of Ferrara who had arrived in June 1480 under the pretext of having been invited by the ambassador of Monpensiero to attend the nuptials of Chiara Gonzaga.

The first of these was the 1472 marriage of Ercole D'Este I, Duke of Ferrara to Leonora of Aragon, the future mother of Isabella D'Este. The celebrations lasted for months and spread over several cities. Theatre or, at least, representation abounded throughout the festivities that started in Rome where the bride, "dressed in gold brocade, flashing with jewels and gems," was fêted by Cardinal Pietro Riario, who presented a sumptuous banquet at which mythological scenes and Greek fables were set forth upon the tables in life-sized shapes of pastry. The theatrics continued after the meal with a dance performed by eight pairs of famous lovers of antiquity. During the dance eight "fierce" centaurs rushed in to carry off dancing nymphs but were routed and driven away by Hercules. Then "there was the representation of Bacchus and Ariadne, with many other most beautiful things of very great and inestimable expense" (Gardner 135-136).[12] For our purposes, it is interesting to note that a version of the Orpheus story was amongst the many pantomimes performed.

From Rome, Leonora traveled to Florence[13] where, on June 22 she was greeted with similar revelry. She then continued on to the Ferrarese frontier where she was met by the duke and his nobles on July 3. Leonora was brought into Ferrara by water. The river banks were lined with dancing and music and country people in gala attire. When Leonora finally rode into the city, she was dressed in gold cloth with her hair flowing freely. After the wedding there were eight days of public holiday and festivities including balls, tournaments and a variety of amusements and sport.

The second occasion which bears consideration is the 1486 visit to Ferrara by Francesco Gonzaga, by then the Marquis of Mantua, to visit his fiancée, Duke Ercole D'Este's daughter, Isabella. This visit is of particular interest because it involves the same parties whose engagement, it is supposed, was celebrated by Poliziano's *Orfeo*. To help celebrate the occasion Ercole sponsored a performance of Plautus's *Menaechmi* for which an entire city with houses, walls and battlements realistically portrayed was constructed in the *Cortile nuovo* of Ercole's palace. An estimated ten thousand people attended. At one point in the action, a boat with oars and sails and ten people aboard was propelled

12. See also Corio vol. 3, 267-275; Corvisieri in general; Burckhardt 263; Pastor 430-433 and Welsford 86.

13. The visit is mentioned in Poliziano's elegy *In albieram albitiam*, lines 59-68: "Annua pelliti referentem sacra Joannis/ Extulerat roseo Cynthius ore diem,/ Cum celebres linquens Sirenum nomine muros,/ Herculeumque petens regia nata torum,/ Candida syllanae vestigia protinus urbi/ Intulerat, longae fessa laborae viae./ Pro se quisque igitur pueri juvenesque senesque/ Illius adventum celebrant; atque unicus urbis/ Est vultus, festo murmure cuncta fremunt."

across the courtyard.[14] As was the vogue at the time, fireworks followed the show.[15] In this instance, as is the case with so many Renaissance performances, the evidence suggests that the audience was more enthralled by the visual effects of the play than with its content or style. Rarely do we find a critique of the acting ability of the players or the quality of the script. On the other hand, there are ample accounts of spectacular visual effects cleverly engineered to make angels and devils appear, mountains crack open and ships ply storm-tossed seas.[16] It is apparent that what a play looked like was important not only to the enjoyment of the spectators and guests but to the prestige of the patron of the celebration. The great number of missives sent by ambassadors to their respective lords describing theatrical representations, attest to the importance aristocrats placed on keeping abreast of new developments in spectacle.

By 1501, the festivities surrounding princely events had become even more lavish than many could have imagined a mere thirty years earlier. To be fair, the marriage of Lucrezia Borgia, daughter of Pope Alexander VI, to Don Alfonso D'Este, son and heir of Duke Ercole D'Este I, was somewhat unique in terms of the parties involved. But even at that, the nature of the presentation is a good indicator of the types of spectacle and the role that theatre played in the marriage festivities.

Like her father-in-law's marriage, Lucrezia's marriage (not her first!) was celebrated in a number of cities starting in Rome where balls, comedies, allegorical shows and dance pieces surrounded the proxy marriage at the Vatican on December 30. On New Year's Day triumphs

---

14. It should be noted as well that while the 1486 performance was outdoors, soon after it became more usual to present comedies indoors. The regular term for this purpose became *sala*, or salone, and where the word *teatro* or *anfiteatro* appears it refers to arrangements for seating the spectators (Anderson 7).

15. For a fuller description of the event, see Gardner 216.

16. Well known amongst these spectacular effects were those of Leonardo Da Vinci, in particular a *Paradise* devised by him in 1490 to welcome back to Milan, Gian Galeazzo, Duke of Milan, and his newly wedded wife, Isabella of Aragon in 1490. Much of our information with respect to such spectacles comes from contemporary accounts and is, therefore, at best, an interpretation of what the event might have looked like. Carlo Pedretti, for example, draws on Bernardino Bellincioni's *Rime* and the anonymous *Relazione* to conclude that Leonardo had designed a heaven in the form of a "mezzo ovo" (half egg) bordered by the signs of the zodiac, with niches for the "planets." These seven planets apparently moved like characters; walking around or crossing the scene during the course of the action (30). An anonymous description in the Estense Library in Modena confirms that the *Paradise* was comprised of one hemisphere whose interior was gilded and decorated with the signs of the zodiac and wherein numerous lamps represented the stars. In the niches there were seven divinities who conducted an animated debate then descended onto the summit of the mountain. Then Jupiter sent Apollo, escorted by the graces, the virtues and the nymphs, to the duchess, to render her homage (Jacquot 1963 89). See also Welsford 87.

of various heroes of antiquity were performed in the streets of Rome and comedies were acted in the Vatican. A *morisco*[17] was performed in the Pope's chamber upon a stage decorated with foliage and lit by torches. After a short eclogue, a jongleur dressed as a woman danced another *morisco* to the accompaniment of tambourines. Caesar (Cesare) Borgia himself took part in the performance and was recognized in spite of his disguise. Trumpets announced a second performance and a tree appeared with a Genius sitting on top of it reciting verses. At the end of his recitation, he dropped down the ends of nine silk ribbons which were taken by nine masked performers who danced about the tree. This *morisco* was well received and loudly applauded. At the end, the Pope asked his daughter to dance. Lucrezia obliged him by dancing with one of her female attendants, a native of Valencia. Soon after, all the men and women who had taken part in the performance joined in (Welsford 89). What is interesting to note is the involvement of the honourees in the spectacles. In addition to Cesare's involvement, a bullfight was staged in which Lucrezia's brother, wearing "a gold braid" took part. It would seem that, as part of a celebration, theatrical representation was intended to spur on festivity much as, in modern times, many entrepreneurs have succeeded at staging "medieval feasts" in which the performers encourage the "spectators" to participate and thereby enhance the party experience of the audience.

We also see that there were traditional or, at least, favourite pieces of theatre amidst the festivities as Plautus's *Menaechmi* was once again performed. And, as usual, the finale tended to spectacle, in this case, no doubt intended to recall the 1486 performance in Ferrara. For here in Rome, the presentation culminated in an allegorical performance in which Mercury attended Ferrara in a triumphal chariot that passed in honor across the stage (Welsford 88-89). On this occasion the importance of the performance to a patron's prestige is reiterated as the Ferrarese ambassador at Rome felt compelled to send to his master a detailed account of the *Menaechmi* and the allegorical performance (Gregorovius 218-221).

Lucrezia, like Leonora before her, then travelled on to Ferrara, greeted along the way by a variety of presentations described by David Brubaker as "audacious conceits displayed in *tableaux* that arose before her"(21). It is clear from the descriptions of these "conceits" that, in addition to their encomiastic role, they were intended to decorate the parade route with "play acting" and representations that were visually pleasing. At Foligno, for example, one "conceit" presented the Lucrezia

17. A *morisco* (plural: *morischi*) was a dance often performed during festivals and between acts of a larger dramatic presentation. According to Enid Welsford, by the sixteenth century it had developed into a sort of *ballet d'action* in which the dancers were costumed and played out a variety of roles and episodes, often taken from mythology (85).

of Ancient Rome who was declared surpassed in virtue by the living Lucrezia. In another, Paris judged again when presented with Lucrezia. And in yet another a performer dressed in the full regalia of a sultan and situated in a Turkish galley promised, for Lucrezia's sake, to restore Christian lands.

At Ferrara the real fireworks began — literally. Don Alfonso's prized artillery fire, intended to herald Lucrezia's arrival, so unnerved her horse that she was thrown and had to continue on a more docile mule for her entry into the city. As for the actual train that accompanied Lucrezia, Appendix I provides some idea of the opulence and size of her entourage. But even so, the visual prestige of the procession was not the entire focus of the event. Certainly, the populace watched as the procession was routed past triumphal arches complete with allegorical scenes, but the spectators would also have been watching the reaction of the members of the procession to the spectacle unfolding around them. Lucrezia's entrance into the main piazza, for example, was met with performing acrobats including two who hurled themselves from a tower at her feet only to be saved by an "invisible rope." Lucrezia's reaction to such a startling display would no doubt have played an important part in the creation of the festive atmosphere.

For the inevitable theatre events, Duke Ercole erected a large shallow stage, likely in the area of ten by eighty feet, in a large hall with amphitheatre staging. During the festivities, Duke Ercole arranged nightly performances of classical comedies, with *intermezzi*[18] of music and *morischi*. The *intermezzi* and *morischi* featured armed gladiators, horned shepherds, Moors with burning tapers in their mouths, satyrs dancing to the sound of a musical box inside an ass's head and peasants performing the whole round of their agricultural labour. Enid Welsford notes,

> "One *morisco* was led by a young woman riding upon a car drawn by a unicorn. On the car appeared several persons bound to the trunk of a tree, and four lute players seated under the bushes. The captives, having been freed by the young woman, descended from the car, and danced while the lute players sang beautiful canzoni" (88).

More than a hundred performers were employed and their costumes, described as "rich apparel," were displayed ahead of time so that the costumes themselves constituted a species of spectacle. This focus on the size of the production and the ostentation attached to the clothing of the performers suggests that the main purpose of theatre in this period was to delight visually, to create an event more focused in the aesthetic than in the literary or thespian aspects of theatre.

18. An *intermezzo* (plural: *intermezzi*) is a short presentation inserted between acts of a heavier dramatic presentation. *Intermezzi* often consisted of brief episodes of dancing, music or symbolic pantomimes (Welsford 85).

That Don Alfonso and his brother Don Giulio danced in at least one *intermezzo* further supports the contention that the purpose of much of this drama was to augment and enhance, not simply accompany, the festivities. That is, the performance of certain pieces of theatre comprised just one part of a highly orchestrated agenda to create a festive atmosphere or mood. The visual dazzle of costumes, the pomp of the processions, the astounding quality of the special effects, combined with the continual mood of masquerade in which the real and mundane were transformed into the fantastic and often death-defying, would create a lasting impression of an event removed from ordinary time.

It is in this context that we ought to consider Poliziano's *Orfeo*. As was mentioned above, while in the past scholars have encountered substantial difficulties in dating the script, there is at least now some consensus as to when it was written. Unfortunately, there is no such agreement as to whether or not the play was actually ever performed. However, given the timing of the event and its cultural milieu, it is not imprudent to assume that if Poliziano's *Orfeo* was presented, it was in circumstances, if not quite as spectacular as some of the occasions described above, then in very similar surroundings. We know, for example, that Poliziano had witnessed the 1472 visit of Leonora to Florence.[19] We can, therefore, conclude that Poliziano was aware of the type and extent of festivities which accompanied wedding celebrations. We know as well, that members of the leading families of Italy, including the Gonzaga, were interested in the types of presentations and spectacles offered by their peers.

The fact that the play is written in the vulgar tongue, one of the earliest secular plays to be so, also suggests that it was intended for a large and broad audience. Similarly, the inclusion of the encomium praising the Gonzaga family indicates that the play was intended not merely for the purpose of appeasing Poliziano's patron but was to be heard by the members of other families and to entrench the notion of Gonzaga virtue, especially to the Este, a more powerful and more cultured family. The general invitation to participate in the bacchanalia that is featured in the closing scenes[20] suggests that indeed the play was intended as a spur to festive behaviour and was not intended purely as a free-standing artistic endeavour.

19. See note no. 13 above.

20. "Thou art drunken, that I know. Let everyone do as I do. Let everyone drink as I drink. Let everyone follow thee, O Bacchus. Let everyone cry, O Bacchus, Bacchus and drink down the wine. Then with our din we will shatter the wine flasks. Let everyone shout evoè, evoè. Let everyone follow thee, O Bacchus. Bacchus, Bacchus, evoè, evoè" (Lord 102).

The costumes would, of course, have been fanciful and stylized in accordance with Humanist perceptions of classical dress. An allegorical figure of Iris attributed to Vasari (Appendix II), provides some sense of Renaissance costume design. However, in the absence of sketches directly attributable to the performance, there can, of course, be no certainty as to how the performers were dressed. As far as the physical performance space is concerned, Isidoro Del Lungo suggests that if indeed *Orfeo* was performed, it was likely performed in a part of the Gonzaga palace or hall set aside or designed for theatre rather than in a distinct building. Given the fact that as late as 1486 the Este were still performing their plays outside in the *cortile* or courtyard, it is just as likely that the play was performed outside.

As far as what the sets looked like, it is difficult to tell. It is unlikely that the play was performed before the "painted scenes" which started to appear in the 1480s.[21] However, we can surmise, in light of the pastoral elements of the play, that it may have been set against a rustic backdrop not unlike that used during the celebration of Lucrezia Borgia's marriage to Alfonso D'Este, that is, a stage decorated with foliage and lit by torches. The descent into the underworld is more problematic. There exists a series of sketches by Leonardo Da Vinci[22] that indicate stage plans for a mountain that would split open to allow the representation of a descent into the underworld.[23] These sketches (Appendix III), have been the subject of substantial conjecture ever since it was suggested that they were prepared specifically for Poliziano's *Orfeo*. It has now been determined that the sketches likely date from around 1506 or 1507 when Leonardo was in the service of Charles D'Amboise.[24] Accordingly, they were not likely to have been

21. I suggest this is unlikely because of a letter which speaks of the first of these appearing in Rome during an early 1480s performance sponsored by Cardinal Raffaele Riario (Anderson 3). If such a notable event had occurred in 1480, one would have expected there to be some written record of this in a time which put great store in anything novel. Moreover, the fact that we do not know whether the play was performed or not suggests, at very least, that there was nothing novel about its performance if indeed it did make it to the stage.

22. Arundel Codex 263 (224r and 231 v).

23 The sketches are of an apparatus permitting the opening and closing of a mountain whose hollow interior has the form of a semi-circular vault. Relying on a system of two counterweights housed under the floor of the scene, the machine causes two vertical axles to pivot at the same time in inverse directions; thus opening the mountain. A person can then emerge from a trapdoor situated in the centre of the cavern. The two axles that make the mountain move conceal their mechanical function within their decorative function, that is, they resemble two columns supporting the vault of an underground palace (Jacquot 1963 90).

24. Kate T. Steinitz noted that the young musician Atalante Miglioretti, friend and student of Leonardo, was likely considered as the ideal actor for the role of Orpheus in the musical drama composed by Angelo Poliziano which she accepted as having

used in preparation for the representation of the *Orfeo* in connection with the Gonzaga nuptial festivities.

The drawings, however, do give us some idea of the type of effect which would have been produced for a presentation of an Orpheus play. In Leonardo's designs there is a mountain with a small door in the centre and several small steps leading up to it. At Orpheus's invocation the mountain would have opened so as to transform the scene to represent the underworld. Carlo Pedretti suggests that at this point the countryside would have been suddenly and completely darkened with the only source of light emanating from the cavern. Upon Orpheus's return to earth the mountain would have closed up and the bacchanalia would have closed the play (30). Again, while there is no compelling proof that a Leonardo type model was the one employed in 1480, it is likely that some type of contraption or illusion would have been employed to change the scene from the pastoral to the infernal.

The lack of certainty as to whether or not the play was ever performed, while frustrating, does lend credence to the suggestion that Italian Renaissance drama was hardly the focus of the critical attention it receives today but rather was simply part of the decorative background to be remarked upon only when the costumes were particularly splendid or a guest of honour participated or some astonishing stage effect was presented. Moreover, the apparent lack of concern for preserving performance details (date, place, etc.) further supports the notion that theatre, or drama, was merely one more component of the visual decoration of a Renaissance city during festival time, an elaborate mask or living fresco, as it were. Like the other elements of festival décor, the subject matter of the play was intended to fuse with and, at the same time, highlight the type of festivity; a bacchanalia for a wedding feast, a *sacra rappresentazione* for a religious festival or, for a state visit, a revival of a classical piece, rewritten to enhance the stature of those being celebrated. In short, much of the

---

been presented for the first time at Mantua, probably in 1471. However, in light of the subsequent findings rejecting this date, her conjecture is not particularly helpful in determining the purpose of Leonardo's drawings. Carlo Pedretti notes that there appear to have been plans for the performance of the *Orfeo* at the court of Isabella D'Este between 1490 and 1500 but that these all seem to have fallen through due to the fact that Atalante —the same Atalante mentioned by Steinitz— established at Florence, did not respond to the duchess of Mantua's invitation. While Pedretti recognizes that the drawings might seem to correspond to thwarted plans for a 1491 performance, he disputes that Da Vinci prepared them at that time. Rather, Pedretti's paleographic examination of the two folios of the Arundel Codex places them around 1506 or 1507; that is to say, the period in which Leonardo was in the service of Charles d'Amboise, who was very fond of masquerades and comedies (31). One might suppose that Da Vinci may have been reprising an earlier concept. However, there is no hard evidence to support this conjecture.

drama must have had the same effect as street minstrels, buskers and performing acrobats; that is, they provided ambiance. The role of such performers and performances was likely akin to that of mechanized department store Christmas windows in the modern era or paid costumed carolers roaming around shopping centres to fuel the "holiday spirit." These kinds of representations are not now, and were not in the Renaissance, often given much attention in terms of literary merit, nor are, nor were, such performers strictly considered "actors." These spectacles are intended to create moods, alter the décor and take an audience out of the here and now — at least until the party's over.

Appendix I

Procession of Lucrezia Borgia into Ferrara to Celebrate Marriage to Don Alfonso D'Este (1501)

75 archers in red and white

80 trumpeters in gold, purple and white satin

24 pipers and trumpeters

nobles and gentlemen of Ferrara

(70 of them adorned with gold chains)

suite of the Duchess of Urbino in black velvet and satin

Don Alfonso in grey velvet covered with scales of beaten gold
Don Alfonso's brother-in-law, Messer Annibal Bentivoglio,
son of the Ruler of Bologna

8 squires in gold brocade and purple velvet

Bride's suite: including 20 Spaniards in black and gold

5 bishops

10 ambassadors

6 drummers

2 Spanish jesters

the bride's horse (now riderless)

8 grooms

The Bride (on a mule) under a canopy carried by Doctors,
escorted by 6 of the grooms' chamberlains and the French ambassador

The Duchess of Urbino

The Duke of Ferrara

3 "Noble Ladies"

Madonna Lucrezia Bentivoglio (daughter of the Duke of Ferrara)
However
70 mules (carrying Lucrezia's dower and "worldly goods"

Appendix II

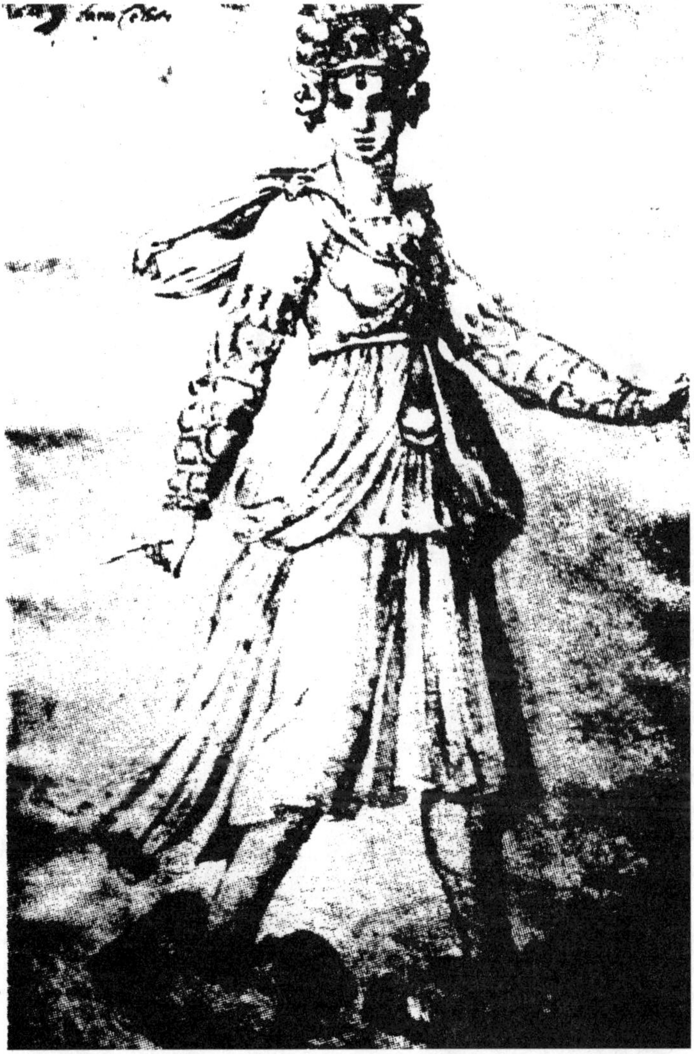

Iris

Appendix III

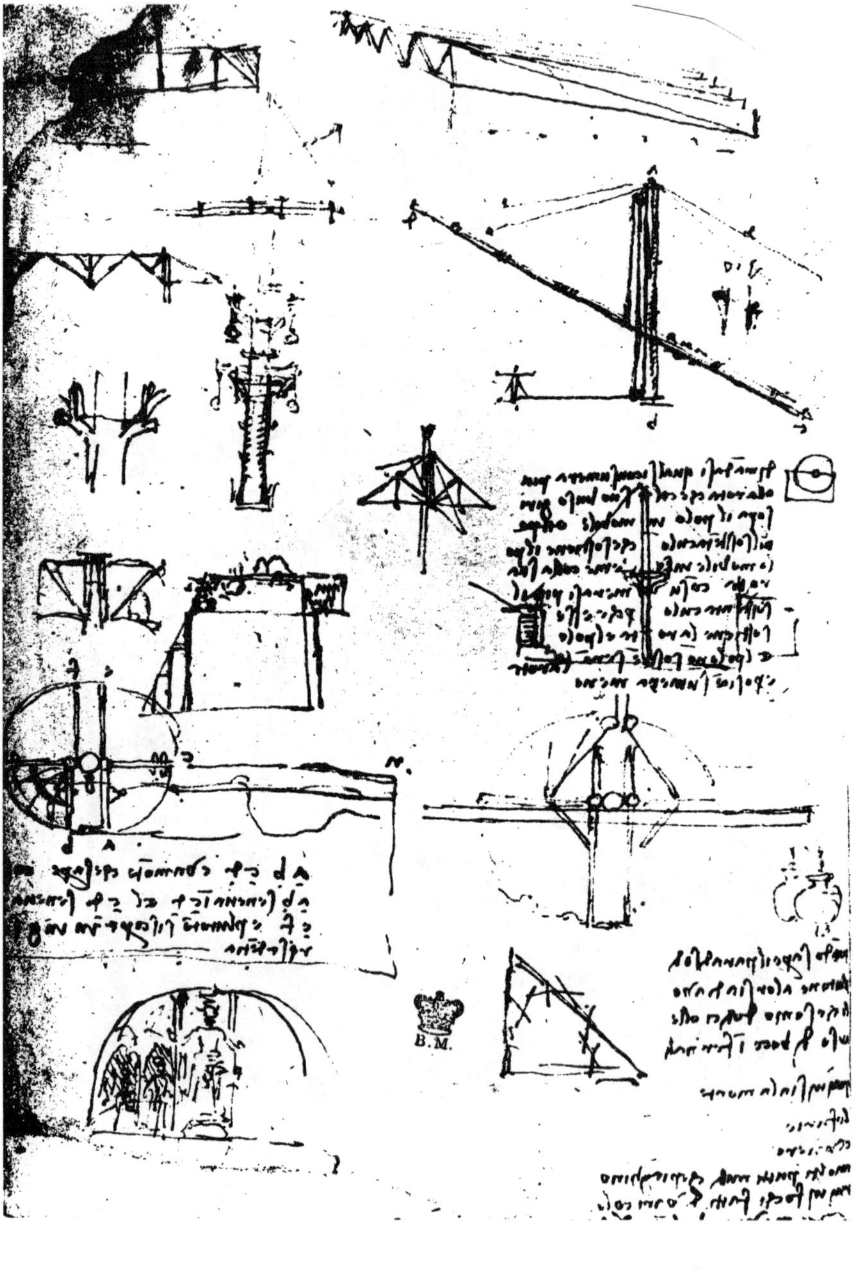

Appendix III

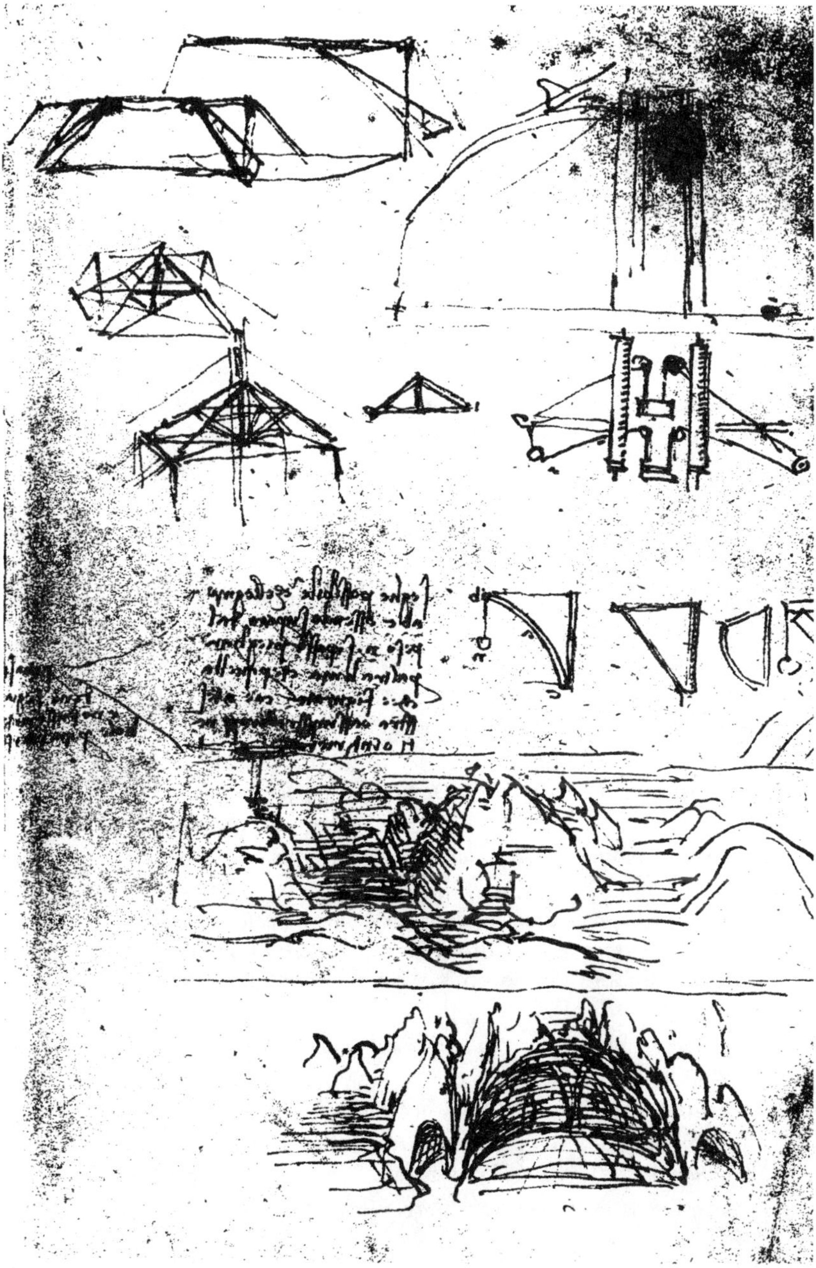

WORKS CITED AND CONSULTED

Amadei, Giuseppe. "Note sul teatro a Mantova nel Rinascimento." *Mantova e i Gonzaga nella civiltà del Rinascimento.* Mantova: Mondadori, 1977. 155-159.

Angelini, Franca. "La festa e la città." *Letteratura italiana - teatro, musica, tradizione dei classici.* Torino: Einaudi, 1986.

Apollonio, Mario. "Paesaggio dell'Orfeo." *Il Poliziano e il suo tempo.* Firenze: Sansoni, 1957. 69-83.

Attolini, Giovanni. *Teatro e spettacolo nel rinascimento.* Roma: Laterza, 1988.

Boccalaro, Mario A. *Angelo Poliziano: il poeta del bel canto.* Rocca San Casciano: Cappelli, 1951.

Brubaker, David. *Court and Commedia: Medieval and Renaissance Theatre.* New York: Richard Rosen, 1975.

Burckhardt, Jacob. *The Civilisation of the Renaissance in Italy.* Trans. S.G.C. Middlemore. London: Penguin, 1990.

Burke, Peter. *Culture and Society in Renaissance Italy 1420-1540.* London: B.T. Batsford, 1972.

Caputo, Vincenzo. *I poeti d'Italia in trenta secoli.* Milano: Gastaldi, 1962.

Clubb, Louise George. "Pastoral Elasticity on the Italian Stage and Page." *The Pastoral Landscape.* Ed. John Dixon Hunt. Hanover: University Press of New England, 1992. 111-127

Corio, B. *Storia di Milano.* Vols. 2, 3. Eds. H. Butti and C. Ferrario. Milano, 1856. Rep.1857.

Corvisieri, C. "Il Trionfo romano di Eleonora d'Aragona." *Archivio della Società di Storia Patria.* Rome, 1878. Rep. 1879.

Cruciani, Fabrizio. "Per lo studio del teatro rinascimentale: la festa." *Biblioteca Teatrale* vol 5, 1972. 1-16.

"Diario ferrarese, dall'anno 1409 fino al 1502, di autori incerti." *Rerum italicarum scriptores.* vol. 24. Muratori.

Del Lungo, Isidoro. *La patria e gli antenati d'Angelo Poliziano.* Firenze: Cellini, 1870.

____. *Florentia: uomini e cose del Quattrocento.* Firenze: Barbera, 1897.

Eisenbichler, Konrad. "Confraternities and Carnival: The Context of Lorenzo de' Medici's *Rappresentazione di SS. Giovanni e Paolo." Medieval Drama on the Continent of Europe.* Eds. Clifford Davidson & John H. Stroupe. Kalamazoo: Medieval Institute Publications Western Michigan University, 1993. 128-139

Fletcher, Jefferson Butler. *Literature of the Italian Renaissance.* Port Washington: Kennikat Press, 1934.

Gardner, Edmund G. *Dukes and Poets in Ferrara.* New York: Haskell House, 1968.

Garin, E. "Novità dell'umanesimo." *Antologia della critica letteraria.* Vol II. *Dall'Umanesimo al barocco.* Ed. Giuseppe Petronio. Bari: Laterza, 1963. 3-19

Gregorovius, I. Ferdinand. *Lucretia Borgia.* Trans. John Leslie Gardner. London, 1904.

Jacquot, Jean. "Dalla festa cittadina alla celebrazione medicea: storia di una trasformazione." *Quaderni di teatro* vol 2, no. 7 (March 1980): 9-22.

——, ed. *La vie théâtrale au temps de la Renaissance*. Paris: Institut Pédagogique National, 1963.

Kennard, Joseph Spencer. *The Italian Theatre*. Benjamin Blom: New York, 1934.

Lo Cascio, Renzo. *Poliziano*. Palermo: Palumbo, 1970.

Lord, Louis E., ed., trans. *A Translation of the Orpheus of Angelo Politian and the Aminta of Torquato Tasso*. London: Humphrey Milford, 1931.

Maier, Bruno. "Agnolo Poliziano." *Letteratura italiana: I Maggiori*. Milano: Marzorati, 1956. 245-302.

Maier, Ida. *Ange Politien: La formation d'un poète humaniste*. Geneva: Droz, 1966.

Malagoli, Luigi. *Le Stanze e l'Orfeo*. Roma: Tosi, 1941.

Mutini, Claudio. *Interpretazione del Poliziano*. Roma: IDEI, 1972.

Pastor, Ludwig. *Geschichte der Papste im Zeitalter der Renaissance*. 3rd. ed. 3 vols. Freiburg im Breisgau, 1891-1895.

Pedretti, Carlo. "Dessins d'une scène, exécutés par Léonard de Vinci pour Charles D'Amboise (1506-1507)." *Le lieu théatral à la Renaissance*. Paris: Éditions du Centre National de la Recherche Scientifique, 1964. 25-34

Pescasio, Luigi. *Rinascimento mantovano*. Mantova: Citem, 1987.

Poliziano, Angelo. *Prose indedite e poesie latine e greche edite e inedite*. Hildesheim: Verlag, 1976.

——. *Poesie italiane*. Introd. Mario Luzi. Ed. Saverio Orlando. Milano: Rizzoli, 1976.

—— *Stanze Orfeo rime*. Ed. Sergio Marconi. Milano: Feltrinelli, 1981.

Rodini, Robert J. "The *Festa* and Theater: A Decade of Research." *Forum Italicum* 14:3 (1980): 476-481.

Rospigliosi, William. *Writers in the Italian Renaissance*. London: Gordon & Cremonosi, 1978.

Sapegno, Natalino. "Il sentimento umanistico e la poesia del Poliziano." *Antologia della critica letteraria*. Vol II. *Dall'Umanesimo al barocco*. Ed. Giuseppe Petronio. Bari: Laterza, 1963. 214-232.

Simon, Kate. *A Renaissance Tapestry: The Gonzaga of Mantua*. New York: Harper & Row, 1988.

Steinitz, Kate T. "A Reconstruction of Leonardo da Vinci's Revolving Stage." *The Art Quarterly* XII 4 (1949): 325-338.

Sturm, Sara. *Lorenzo de'Medici*. New York: Twayne, 1974.

Symonds, John Addington. *Renaissance in Italy*. Part I. London: Smith Elder & Co., 1881.

Tarugi, Giovannangiola Secchi. "Cristianesimo e umanesimo in A. Poliziano." *Il Poliziano e il suo tempo*. Firenze: Sansoni, 1957. 335-337.

Tonelli, Luigi. *Il teatro italiano dalle origini ai giorni nostri*. Milano: Modernissima, 1924.

Trexler, Richard C. "Florentine Theatre, 1280-1500. A Checklist of Performances and Institutions." *Forum Italicum* 14:3 (1980): 454-475

Vaccarella, Giovanni. *Saggio sulla rinascenza e la poesia di Agnolo Poliziano*. Palermo: Pruilla, 1921.

Welsford, Enid. *The Court Masque. A Study in the Relationship between Poetry and the Revels*. New York: Russell & Russell, 1962.

Zorzi, Elvira Garbero. "La festa cerimoniale del Rinascimento. L'ingresso trionfale e il banchetto d'onore." *Scene e figure del teatro italiano*. Eds. Elvira Garbero Zorzi & Sergio Romagnoli. Reggio Emilia: Società Editrice il Mulino, 1985.

De Sommi on *Mise en Scène*

Anna Migliarisi

Acadia University

My paper concerns *mise en scène* as conceived and documented by sixteenth-century director Leone De Sommi (1527-1592)[1], also known as Leone Ebreo of Mantua, in his *Quattro dialoghi in materia di rappresentazioni sceniche* (1565).[2]

The *Quattro dialoghi* consist of four dialogues between a fictional director called Veridico ("the truth teller"),[3] and two noblemen, Santino and Massimiano, in which De Sommi deals with the following eight topics: how to choose a play, choose the actors, work with actors, costume a show, set a stage, work with lights, stage pastorals and integrate intermezzi, and unify production through the harmonization of actors, lights and other elements: "che tutta insieme sia poi un corpo bene organizzato et unito, non sensa polsi ne senza spirito" (2:31).[4] Thus

---

1. Biographical information on De Sommi may be found in D'Ancona; Marotti's introduction to *Quattro dialoghi*; Botuk.
2. References to De Sommi's *Quattro dialoghi* will appear parenthetically in the text. The introduction to *Quattro dialoghi* is dated 1556 but most De Sommi scholars, including D'Ancona and Marotti, believe the dialogues were composed, in part, about a decade later. Allardyce Nicoll in the introduction to his English translation of De Sommi's work in *The Development of the Theatre* states: "...though they were begun in that year, they were certainly not completed until at least a decade later. The surest clues are the reference to Flaminia and to Leono Aretino. Flaminia made a great stir when she came to Mantua in 1567 and Leono Aretino's work (sic) for Duke Gugliemo's wedding was carried out in 1561. One might suggest that the composition of the original manuscript was undertaken about this time; it may be that the copyist's date 1556 was put in error for 1565." (237).
3. The reader should note that I often use these names interchangeably.
4. That together the whole is a well organized and unified body lacking neither pulse nor spirit (B- R 85). Nicoll translates this passage as: "... the whole taking shape as a well planned organism, unified by a dominant spirit." (248).

De Sommi's methodology involves the interpretation of abstract impressions evoked by the initial reading of the play text and their transformation into concrete images on stage. A comparison between De Sommi's method and Jacques Copeau's definition of the directorial process in his essay, "La Mise en scène" (1935) reveals these directors have much in common: "Directing is the sum-total of artistic and technical operations which enables the play as conceived by the author to pass from the abstract, latent state, that of the written script, to concrete and actual life on the stage." (qtd. in Cole and Chinoy 214)

In Dialogues One and Two, De Sommi discusses his theoretical views of drama as they relate to the art of writing plays. De Sommi believed that writing and directing were part and parcel of a similar creative process. His ideal director is in fact also the author of the play (3:46); consequently, knowledge of the principles of good play-writing goes hand in hand with the ability to discern the scenic value of the play text. In Dialogues Three and Four De Sommi deals specifically with the scenic elements of a dramatic production: costumes, setting, and lighting. This section is distinguished by bringing to light a number of innovations in the art of directing: a performance theory, a method of working with actors, a director's workbook that organizes and documents the director's vision and method of constructing a theatrical performance, and innovations in the use of scenic light and colour for psychological effect.

In *Theatre Through the Ages*, theatre historian Cesare Molinari observes that in the fifteenth and sixteenth centuries there were no real experts in theatrical representation in a specialized modern sense, except De Sommi, who devoted himself almost exclusively to the study and practice of theatre (125). De Sommi wrote plays, designed settings and costumes, stage-managed and directed a variety of theatrical entertainments at the Gonzaga court in Mantua between 1556 and 1592. He directed productions outside of Mantua, in the duchies of Savoy, Turin, and, between 1538 and 1556, at the Este Court in Ferrara, where he played an active role, as a director, dramaturge, and choreographer in the early staging experiments of Giambatista Guarani's well-known pastoral, *Il pastor fido* (1590).

In discussing De Sommi's instructions to the director, I challenge a common assumption among theatre historians that there were no directors in the modern sense of the term until the late eighteenth and early nineteenth centuries and no formal treatments on the art of directing worthy of notice. My argument is that while working within a tradition of sixteenth-century rule-based classicism De Sommi's theory and methodology, as set down in his *Quattro dialoghi*, is situated outside the directorial practice inherited from the late Middle Ages.

Quattro dialoghi was written principally as a model of practical instruction on the art of directing for other theatre professionals rather than as abstract theory for scholars and playwrights. Theatre historians Marotti and Molinari observe that theories of performance and directing are in themselves uncommon for this period; *Quattro dialoghi* covers all aspects of drama, from theory to performance, at a time when dramatic theory, textual criticism, scenography and representation were treated as autonomous phenomena (Marotti LXIII; Molinari 125-6). De Sommi positions the director in a strategic position as the "author" of the *mise en scène,* whose primary function is the synthesis of all of the elements that are "put in the scene" as the term literally means in French. *Quattro dialoghi,* my research shows, is the first systematic account of the art of the professional director in western theatre.

COSTUMES

As a general rule, Veridico's instructions on costumes emphasize external beauty: lavish designs, sumptuous materials, and evocative colours. In his view, costumes must create visual splendour for the audience while revealing individual characterizations, and adhering to conventions of propriety and verisimilitude. The design of the costumes is circumscribed by the author's directions in the literary text. However, Veridico suggests that the imaginative director—in cases where the writer does not provide concrete directions or where the writer simply provides a generic description of the characters ("a young shepardess,") may play with the boundaries of the secondary directions (3:53).[5]

Veridico instructs the director to dismiss Greek lexicographer Iulius Pollux's rules of dress[6] on the grounds that they are too restrictive and little known or appreciated by the modern spectator. The director must strive always to dress the actors in elegant costumes because they greatly increase the reputation and charm of both comedy and tragedy (3:47-8). Veridico's servants are dressed as elegantly as their masters and class distinction is revealed by the degree of lavishness in the design of the individual costume. If a servant is dressed in velvet or coloured satin, for example, then the director must enhance the "master's" costume with embroidery or fancy ornaments such as buttons, jewellery, or beading to ensure that class distinction is obvious

5. By secondary directions I mean directions which are integrated directly into the dialogue. De Sommi was an accomplished costume designer in his own right; his call for expertise in this area of production and his scattered comments on the exceptional talent of master-director Veridico represents a self-conscious affirmation of De Sommi's status in the theatre culture of his day.

6. In the *Onamastikon*, Pollux describes various aspects of Greek theatre practice, including the treatment of tragic and comic masks: old men wore white robes; young men wore purple robes; slaves wore ragged garments; matrons wore yellow robes, and so on. See Nagler *Source Book* (7-15). Theorist Franciscus Robortello makes mention of Pollux in his 1545 commentary *On Comedy* in Herrick, *Comic Theory* (227-239).

to the audience. Veridico frowns upon dressing characters in wretched, threadbare skirts, and doublets that are torn or ragged, even in the case of costumes for characters such as servants, misers, or parasites, on the grounds that *quei cenci* (these rags) would compromise the visual splendour of the *mise en scène* (3:49).

According to Veridico, the director must make every effort to dress the actors as differently from one another as possible, since variation assists the actor in particularizing the character being portrayed and, at the same time, serves as a visible cue for the spectator attempting to follow the plot of the play. Such distinction is particularly important in the representation of comedies and pastorals with double plots and large casts of characters. Differentiation between characters in a complex comedy, for example, might be achieved through attention to detail in the cut and colour of the costumes and in the use of accessories.[7] Four servants might be distinguished by the colour and style of their livery: one in white with a hat, one in red with a little cap on his head, the other in a uniform of all different colours, and the last in a velvet cap and a pair of knitted gloves. Two lovers might be dressed in similar colours or textures yet be differentiated by the length and style of their clothing: one with a cloak, the other with an overcoat; one with feathers in his cap, and the other with gold and without feathers; and so on (3:49).

With respect to the colours and textures of the fabrics employed, De Sommi believes colour creates and effects the mood of the actor as well as that of the spectator viewing the play. For this reason, he favours a variety of primary, bold and bright colours, and he cautions against the use of black or very dark colours, particularly in the staging of comedy, since he believes they evoke a sombre mood (3:49-50). The colours employed, therefore, must always compliment both the thematic concerns of the play and those of the actor's interpretation. A joyful comedy, for example, would be best served with bright colours and crisp fabrics; the actor would compliment this visual vivacity with an energetic delivery of the text and an expressive use of movement and gestures (3:49-50).[8]

---

7. Veridico is particularly fond of the use of hats with variously cut and coloured feathers to particularize and distinguish individual characters.

8. Here we see De Sommi's concern with the whole aesthetic and emotional experience of the play. Further evidence of this may be found in Veridico's reference to staging the pastoral: "dico che, sí come nella lor testura le si ricerca il verso, così bisogna che chi li veste o essercita, facci accompagnare le presenza et i movimenti di chi vi recita alla gravità che con li versi li avrà dato il poeta" (3:54). I shall say that, just as verse is required in their compositions, thus is it necessary for whomever costumes or directs to have the presence and the movements of the players be in keeping with the gravity which the poet will given them [the poems] with his verses (B-R 147).

Exotic costumes, far removed from custom, may be introduced in the representation of comedy. They add charm and novelty to the *mise en scène* which pleases the modern spectator, who delights in viewing things strange and out of the ordinary (3:50). Exotica also enhances verisimilitude, on the grounds that theatrical situations involving foreign or unrecognizable persons are, invariably, more probable than the formulaic dramatic situations of popular comedy. The comedy Veridico is directing in *Quattro dialoghi* is, in fact, a classic comedy; it will be set in Constantinople, in order to introduce "uncommon" clothes, which Veridico believes will add a little charm to the show (3:50).

In the representation of tragedy, Veridico encourages the director to dress the actors in the elegant clothing seen in antique sculptures and paintings rather than in the modern style. In addition, since tragedy deals with exalted figures such as kings and noblemen, the fabrics and colours employed must be visually striking. Veridico states his preference for tragedies that feature large casts of characters with gladiators, soldiers, and squads of armed men since these plays permit the director to introduce a variety of splendid accessories and weapons, which, he maintains, are always a most beautiful sight (3:50).

Veridico's guidelines for costume design for comedy and tragedy apply to the pastoral. The designs must be subordinate to the secondary directions provided by the writer, the characters must be dressed as differently from one another as possible in order to provide scenic contrast, and the final choices in the design of the costumes are approved by the director and determinable only through actual experimentation in rehearsals under working lights and against scenic perspectives. Veridico creates a standard design for both shepherds and wood nymphs which he then particularizes for each character through the use of colour, cut, and accessories.

Actors portraying shepherds are uniformly dressed in sleeveless tunics covered with leopard or other animal skins. The legs and arms completely covered with flesh-coloured cloth, except in the case of actors that are young and handsome, who may leave their limbs bare. They wear either socks or *cothurni* (buskins), and are never allowed to appear on stage with bare feet. Differentiation in a chorus of shepherds might be revealed by the colour of the tunic, the type of skins, or the way that the skins are placed on or off the shoulder, secured at the waist, and so forth. Shepherds generally carry a small flask, or wooden bowl attached at the waist, and others have a water pouch slung over the shoulder. Each shepherd carries a walking stick, and each stick is particularized—some are evenly cut and sanded, and others are ornamented with leaves or flowers. Differentiation between shepherds is also achieved with contrasting hair styles and wigs, make-up, and by the individual actor's carriage and gestural behaviour (3:51-2).

Nymphs are dressed in sleeved blouses that are variously decorated with ribbons of coloured silk, buttons, or pieces of jewellery. Veridico advises having the blouses well starched before the sewing on of these colourful details so that the buttons and jewels will stand out and glitter evocatively in the lights. Skirts that vary in colour and fabric are worn to ankle length, feet are clad in elegant gold slippers in the antique style (sandals), or, in boots of coloured leather, and a cloak is draped over one shoulder. Nymphs are fair-haired, in the Petrarchan tradition, with long thick tresses that flow freely and naturally over the shoulders; Veridico provides specially designed wigs for the actors to create this effect. Differentiation between nymphs on stage is achieved by the use and placement of coloured garlands and ribbons in the hair, flowing veils, and stage properties such as hunting spears, and bows and arrows (3:52-3).

If animals are used on stage, and Veridico favours the use of real dogs and other small creatures in his *mise en scène*, then they too must be suitably dressed, preferably in elegant collars and pretty coverlets that coordinate, presumably, with the colours of the costume of the particular actor assigned to lead the animal on and off the stage (3:53-4).

Veridico distinguishes between street clothing and stage costumes on the grounds that they are conditioned by different criteria. While costumes may appear to be as fashionable as street clothing, they are purposely designed and constructed to reveal and express character and dramatic situation on stage. The costume should help "transform" the performer; the character must always "mask" the identity of the actor (3:50), a direction that provides us with further evidence of the director's (De Sommi's) dominant position in the selection and shaping of the various scenic elements.[9]

LIGHTING

De Sommi's instructions on lighting, based on the established Serlian principles that light simultaneously illuminates and decorates (Bergman 44),[10] are distinguished by a series of innovations that reveal De Sommi's sophisticated knowledge of the art of staging: strategic placement of lighting fixtures to illuminate both actors and scenery,

9. De Sommi's authority as a director at the court of Mantua was striking. He organized and conducted both acting and technical rehearsals and he had final say all virtually all matters pertaining to production. Yet most theatre historians claim the actor was the dominant artist of the theatre until the appearance of the Duke of Saxe-Meiningen (1826-1914) in Germany, who is generally considered the first director of the modern theatre (Brockett 429).

10. Of course the most basic decorative lighting in the theatre would elicit striking effects on a sixteenth-century audience accustomed to fairly dim everyday lighting conditions, both in and out of doors (Bergman 44).

shades to conceal visible sources of decorative light, reduced lighting in the auditorium in order to intensify the light on the stage, practical suggestions to minimize the amount of toxic smoke circulating in the theatre, and psychological considerations in the use and placement of lights in the scene.

Veridico illuminates the stage picture from above the stage, using the principal sources of lighting available to the theatre practitioner in the sixteenth century: torches, tallow candles, oil lamps, and (standing and fixed) candelabra. Veridico favours the placement of lights (torches) on the roofs of the houses on the stage. This practice is associated with the well-documented festival culture of the Italian Renaissance during which fireworks and lighting were often the central attraction of the festivities, and bonfires and torches were secured on top of towers and rooftops to create a sense of anticipation for the first appearance of the unveiled scene (4:63). It also reflects De Sommi's belief that this placement created a sense of "gladness and joy" in the theatre, reinforcing the traditional end of comedy: to impart delight and relieve the spectator of troublesome thoughts.

Transparent and coloured glass frames (Serlian *bozze*) are used to cover all visible sources of decorative lighting. This technique both minimizes the brilliant light striking directly upon the eye of the spectator and produces evocative visual effects, softening and diffusing the light that it filters in the scene (4:64). Veridico makes use of invisible and concealed lighting sources with strategically placed reflectors or small mirrors. The mirrors reflect the concealed lights placed behind the columns and between the decor frames of the setting. This technique helps impart texture and subtle depth to the decor, enhances the visual beauty of the *mise en scène*, and creates an atmosphere on stage which corresponds to the spirit of the play being represented (4:64).

In lighting the auditorium, Veridico reduces the number of standing lamps (candelabra) from the standard 250 or so to twelve in order to intensify the light on the stage (4:65). He positions the lamps behind the spectator rather than at the front of the stage (the latter customary during this period) (4:65).[11] This placement behind the seats renders the lighting source invisible to the audience. It has the added advantage of reducing smoke in the theatre, which at times could literally "cloud" the spectator's vision. Innovative use and arrangement of lights reveals De Sommi's advanced knowledge of the science of optics. A person standing in shadow will see a distant illuminated object more clearly than if he stands in light himself: "… perchè la vista va piú unita all'obietto, senza vagare, o, secondo il parere d'i peripatetici, l'obietto si viene piú unitamente ad appresentare a

11. Positioning the lamps at the front of the stage was customary during this period.

l'occhio" (4:65-6). By placing only a few lamps in the auditorium, and rendering the stage as bright as possible, Veridico differentiates between the acting and viewing areas, and effectively introduces the darkened auditorium of modern theatre practice.[12]

Veridico emphasizes psychological realism in his use and placement of the lights on the stage. He argues that colour and intensity can influence the mood of both the actor and the spectator. He favours treating comedies with a brightly lit ("joyous") stage that gradually transforms into a melancholy semi darkness, since all plays of this genre begin in a state of harmony, or light, and move towards darkness: "non sarà mai isconvenevole il destar l'animo alla letizia più che sia possibile, benché segua poi nelle tragedie alcune rovine o morti" (4:63).[13] Veridico instructs the director to underscore the structural movement of tragedy with a corresponding visual play of light in order to induce specific emotional effects in the spectator. Veridico describes a production of a tragedy he directed to illustrate this technique. He had the stage brightly lit during the opening episode of the tragedy, in order to awaken the soul of the spectator to "gladness," a mood sustained until the first unhappy incident of the drama: the unexpected death of a queen. The chorus reveals this tragic turn of events and laments that the sun itself could not bear to see such ill and so it too "darkened." Veridico directed the scene to have most of the stage lights, which were not used to light the perspectives, extinguished at this precise line in the text, a mood-inducing technique which, he claims, proved effective in creating a profound impression of horror (catharsis) among the spectators, and won universal praise for Veridico's direction (4:63-4).

Finally, Veridico provides a cautionary note regarding the principal hazard associated with sixteenth-century lighting equipment: the smoke produced from the oil lamps and candles, both on and off the stage and in the auditorium. While Veridico believes these lighting instruments are effective in creating an atmosphere of soft, perpetually moving light flickering on the back cloths, they also produce an overabundance of smoke which forces the actors to move downstage, far from the painted perspectives, shattering the harmony of the stage impression.[14] Veridico proposes circulating the air out of the theatre

12. Stage director Angelo Ingegneri advocated this principle twenty years later in *Della poesia rappresentativa e del modo di rappresentare le favole sceniche* (1598). The fully darkened auditorium appeared in Italian opera houses towards the end of the seventeenth century; elsewhere in Europe lamps and candles were employed until the coming of gas in the nineteenth century (Bergman 65).

13. It would never be out of order to awaken the soul as much as possible to gladness, even though in tragedies some ruin or death may follow (B-R 174).

14. The toxicity of the smoke would vary with the quality of the wax and wick employed. Beeswax candles, although expensive, produced the most constant light. Tallow

through a number of vents in the ceiling behind the proscenium and on the floor of the stage. Veridico observes, with some severity, that this is a technical matter of some importance in the successful presentation of a play, one which, as far as he is concerned, few of his contemporaries pay sufficient attention. He cautions the director to take adequate pains to ventilate the stage before the actual performance begins. Ventilation will prevent the appearance of a screen of smoke suspended in midair, which he claims "blinds" the spectators and makes actors appear like "ghosts" rather than men (4:65).

STAGE SETTINGS

Veridico's discussion of stage settings in Dialogue Four takes place in his theatre, where we find our master director seated in the auditorium ordering his technical crew to light lamps and reliefs in preparation for a technical rehearsal, while courtiers Santino and Massimiano wait to view the full effect of the perspective scenery. Throughout this section Veridico emphasizes the visual appeal of modern perspective scenery and the problems associated with re-creating the scenic splendour of classical antiquity in contemporary performance.

Theatre historian Ronald W. Vince observes that "Renaissance knowledge of Greek and Roman theatres was derived principally from [the Roman architect] Vitruvius, whose *De Re Architectura*" contained descriptions for comic, tragic, and pastoral scenes codified by Sebastiano Serlio (1475-1554) in his *Architettura* written in 1545 (7, 11-2, 103).[15] In Dialogue Four, Veridico is referring to Serlian three-dimensional perspective scenery: "gl'aparati devono esser sempre nei modi piú belli che sia possibile; le quale cose inparticolare lassando al giudicio de i lor professori" (4:61).[16] Here Veridico defers to the judgment of artists and architects for "particulars," that is to say, the painting and the construction of the scenery, which is not unusual since scene design, until the mid-seventeenth century, was the primary responsibility of painters and architects; however, as observed in other areas of production, director Veridico has enormous creative influence over the final impression brought to the stage. "His" director, whose primary function is the synthesis of all of the elements, is the creator of the *mise en scène*.

candles made from vegetable or animal fat were less costly but produced more smoke (Bergman 53-54).

15. Descriptions and illustrations of Serlio's three perspective scenes may be found in Nagler *Source Book* (73-8).

16. The sets must always be done in the most beautiful styles possible; and, leaving these things, in particular, to the judgement of their professors (B-R170).

Underlying Veridico's instructions in this area of production is a fundamental concern with harmonizing the "ideal" with modern taste and conventions. His pastoral setting, for example, is an elaboration on Serlio's rustic scene.[17] Veridico insists that the manner and styles of settings must always coincide with the demands of the text and be treated in the context of performance. Moreover, as he states in "Dialogue Three," the actors' costumes, movements, and gestures, must be reconciled with, rather than serve as competition for, the scenic background. Most theatre historians acknowledge the Duke of Saxe-Meiningen (1826-1914) as the "first" modern director because he harmonized acting with the demands of the pictorial stage (Cole and Chinoy 22). In principal, De Sommi's approach appears three hundred years earlier.

As Veridico's scenery gradually appears, Massimiano comments on the mesmerizing effects of the new art of scenic painting: "veramente gran forza ha quest'arte della pittura, quand'ella è bene intesa; ché, a star qui, tanto mi inganno, che, bench'io sappia quella non esser altro che una tela piana, par una strada che corra mezzo miglio" (4:59).[18] In response, Veridico makes a comparison between the arts of the actor and the scenic painter: both the painter and the actor tell a story in space, the painter through the use of colour and canvas, the actor through his body and spirit, or, "vivacity." Both have a power at their

---

17. In *Quattro dialoghi,* De Sommi codified a design and directorial approach that became standard practice in the representation of pastoral drama. His setting was a dense "joyful" landscape of actual foliage, flowers, trees bearing fruit, and live birds perched in tree branches that sang songs intended to arouse feelings of joy in the spectators. The fore-stage, adorned to represent a flowery field, was the principal acting area for the actors. In the distance, mountains, valleys, cottages and caves are painted in conformity with the laws of perspective (4:66-7). Veridico states his preference for the use of real animals on stage, such as rabbits and other small creatures, that wander in and out of the setting from time to time. He does not indicate how this appearance of the animals on stage is executed in performance, but it is likely that crew-members would be assigned to direct the animals into position. Singing birds, for example, were probably placed in the setting by De Sommi-Veridico or his scenic artists prior to the lowering of the curtain. The challenge associated with the use of real animals in the *mise en scène* would be felt, no doubt, when moving the creatures off the stage at strategic moments of the drama. As we know from Veridico's instructions on costumes, shepherds and nymphs were often assigned dogs and other small animals as stage companions. We may assume that each actor was responsible for leading his or her animal off stage when necessary. In the case of hares or birds it is likely that these creatures would, respectively, scurry off stage or fly out of the *mise en scène* at their own will—unexpected occurrences which presuppose a number of challenges for the director in the successful realization of this genre.

18. This art of scene painting [in perspective] really has a great effect, when it is well done; because while I stand here I am deceiving myself so much, that, even though I know that is only a flat canvas, it seems to me to be a street that runs on for half a mile (B-R 169).

command to make fiction seem real: "Questa forza istessa avrà il perfetto comico che quantunque sappiamo che egli ci recita una favola, se sarà diligente nel rappresentarla, ci parrà un sucesso veracissimo" (4:59).[19]

When courtier Santino comments on the beauty of Veridico's setting, Veridico responds by saying that the modern director has a variety of models and styles from which to draw upon; however, the choices made by the *buon corago* must always coincide with the requirements of the text and be treated in the context of performance (4:59-60). Central to this discussion is Veridico's recognition that the new art of perspective scenery must serve the aesthetic requirements of the production as a whole, rather than be an end in itself. Botuk makes this observation in her study of De Sommi: good perspective painting, which De Sommi insists upon, "cheats the eye of the spectator" while drawing the audience into the dramatic illusion on the stage (175).

CONCLUSION

In his discussion of dramaturgy, Veridico conceives the perfect play-text as a literal and figurative "whole" body, which he describes as a well-planned organism unified by a dominant spirit. Just as in the human body there is no part made in vain, a play is perfect when the omitting of the smallest part renders it imperfect. The main theme is the play's heart and soul, which gives life to all its various parts: "sí come il cuore destribuisce lo spirito a tutte le membra, cosí il soggetto dispensarà le sue sustanze a tutte le parti di questo poema, talché non paia esservi cosa soverchia né oziosa, sí come nel corpo nostro non è membro alcuno fabricato invano" (2:32).[20]

Veridico believes it is the function of the director to grasp, distil and physically express this meaning in an appropriate form on stage. The poet provides "flesh," the actor "spirit," and the director transforms flesh and spirit into a unified, organic whole, integrating all the theatrical arts at his disposal (settings, costumes, lights, colour, figure expression and movement) into "soul." This highly complex transformational process from page to stage, which differentiates performance from literary text, presupposes the necessary presence of a controlling eye, the *buon corago*, to assess, refine and synthesize the various scenic elements.

19. This same effect must the perfect comic actor have, in that even though we know he is reciting fiction to us, if he is diligent in his performance, it will seem a very real event to us (B-R 169).

20. Even as the heart distributes its spirit to all its members, so the theme of the play should send its spirit into all the parts of the work, giving the impression that nothing is extraneous or without purpose any more than the body has been created in vain (My translation).

De Sommi's understanding that each play embodies an inner meaning or soul, which the director must access and express in a suitable form on the stage, could be compared to the aesthetic principles of counterparts in the modern theatre. Otto Brahm (1856-1912) believed "the director is a man who must be 'sensitive to the inner spirit of a work... without getting bogged down in hollow conventions.' One of [his] major tasks in the Freie Bruhne was to find actors to accomplish this goal." Constantin Stanislavski (1863-1938) "was intrigued by the perfection of external realism. [His work on Gorky's *The Lower Depths*] made him 'aware of the inner meaning of the play' [and led to a] growing dissatisfaction with the limitations of external realism... and a new appreciation of the playwright." (Cole and Chinoy 30, 33, 35, 107).

In principle, De Sommi's methodology is not significantly different. His concern in *Quattro dialoghi* is to codify an external form of representation. De Sommi's "plan" embodies sixteenth-century pictorial illusionism; however, his instructions, in the areas of acting and stage lighting, for example, are distinguished by a preoccupation with realism (Cole and Chinoy 16). De Sommi's literal and figurative body, the play, has a heart that provides spirit to all of its members. Similarly, Stanislavski's notion of the soul of the play, or superobjective, is a heart that is life-giving, a main artery that provides nourishment and life to all the parts (256). Structurally, De Sommi's perfect play needs all of its parts but no more than those parts. According to Stanislavski, the most insignificant detail, if it is not related to the superobjective, will stand out as superfluous or wrong. A play with "a deformed, broken back bone cannot live" (260-1). In Stanislavski's view, the soul of the drama is the principal creative impetus for actors to begin building a character; the primary mission of the actor is to create the life of the human spirit. De Sommi's work with the actor, as revealed in Dialogue Three, begins with a reading of the whole play so that each actor may be instructed in its theme or subject matter; from there, the actor's duty is to fully comprehend the nature or spirit of the characters and reveal it in suitable vocal and gestural behaviour (3:39).

Although other significant comparisons could be made between De Sommi and modern directors, we must bear in mind that De Sommi's *mise en scène* was quite distant from the stage of twentieth-century naturalism. The explicit similarities in the principles of De Sommi and his modern counterparts are less significant than the overall comparisons to be made between De Sommi's methodology and modern directorial practice.

In conclusion, the *Quattro dialoghi* represent De Sommi's conscious attempt to codify theatrical representation from the point of view of the director. In "Dialogue One," De Sommi states: "mi par assai degna questa facoltà scenica di essere trattata molto piú curiosamente, et con discorso piú particolare di quello che sin ora sia fatta da' scrittori antichi o moderni" (1:7).[21] Since no rules on directing a play were inherited from the Middle Ages, De Sommi filled this void by providing a point of reference for new advances in acting, directing and stage craft: "ho giudicato non essere vana fatica il raccogliere questo ragionamente ... non però con pensiero di satisfare intieramente, ma piú tosto con animo di incitar altri a supplire ov'io sarò manchevole" (A' lettori: 7).[22]

WORKS CITED

Bergman, Gosta M. *Lighting in the Theatre.* Stockholm, Sweden: Almquist and Wiksell, 1977.

Blanchard-Rothmuller, C. A. "Four Dialogues on Stage Representation: A Translation with Introduction and Notes," Diss., Indiana U, 1973.

Botuk, Wendy Sue. "Leone De Sommi: Jewish Participation in Italian Renaissance Theatre," Diss., New York U, 1991.

Brockett, Oscar. *History of the Theatre.* 7th ed. Boston: Allyn and Bacon, 1995.

Cole, Toby, and Helen Krich Chinoy. Eds. *Directors on Directing: A Source Book of the Modern Theatre.* Rev. ed. Indianapolis: Bobbs-Merrill, 1963.

D'Ancona, Allesandro. *Le origini del teatro italiano.* 2 vol. Torino:Ermanno Loescher, 1891.

De Sommi, Leone. *Quattro dialoghi in materia rappresentazioni sceniche,* ed. Feruccio Marotti. Milan: Il Polifilo, 1968.

Herrick, Marvin T. *Comic Theory in the Sixteenth Century.* Urbana: U Illinois P, 1964.

Ingegneri, Angelo. *Della poesia rappresentativa e del modo di rappresentare le favole sceniche.* ed. Maria Luisa Doglio. Modena: Edizioni Panini, 1989.

Marotti, Ferrucio. "Introduzione." De Sommi xv-xxxv.

Molinari, Cesare. *Theatre Through the Ages.* Trans. Colin Hammer. London: Cassell, 1975.

Nagler, A. M. *A Source Book in Theatrical History.* New York: Dover, 1952.

Nicoll, Allardyce. *The Development of Theatre.* 3rd ed. London: George Harrap, 1927.

---

21. [The art of directing] is worthy of being treated more diligently and with more detailed attention, than anything written up to now by ancient or modern writers (B-R 4-5).

22. [I] have deemed it not a vain undertaking to gather together these discourses ... not, however, with the thought of satisfying completely, but rather with the desire to urge others to supplement that in which I shall be insufficient (B-R 5).

The Oxford Illustrated History of Theatre. ed. John Russel Brown. Oxford, New York: Oxford UP, 1995.

Serlio, Sebastiano. "Architettura." Nagler 73-8.

Stanislavski, Constantin. *An Actor Prepares*, trans. E. Reynolds Hapgood with an Introduction by John Gielgud. New York: Theatre Arts Books, 1936.

Vince, Ronald W. *Renaissance Theatre: A Historiographical Handbook*. London, England and Westport, Connecticut: Greewood 1984.

Vitruvius Pollio, Marcus. *Ten Books on Architecture*. Trans. Morris H. Morgan. Cambridge, Mass.: Harvard UP, 1914.

Descrizioni liriche di temi teatrali nel poema epico del Marino

Francesco Guardiani

UNIVERSITY OF TORONTO

Ici la Comédie apparaît un example
Où chacun de son fait les action contemple:
Le monde est un théâtre, et les hommes acteurs.
RONSARD[1]

SEBBENE DA ANNI ORMAI, grazie al lavoro fondativo di Padre Pozzi e a quello di tanti altri studiosi che hanno ripercorso sulla sua traccia lo sterminato *corpus* del Marino[2], si dia per scontata la gloriosa ammissione del poeta nella schiera dei classici della letteratura italiana[3],

1. Il passo, forse non ignoto al Marino, è tratto dall'epilogo di una commedia recitata a Fontainbleau nel 1564. Lo colgo in Curtius, citato anche più sotto per una carrellata storico-linguistica sull'uso delle metafore teatrali (*European Literature* 138).

2. Si ricordano di Giovanni Pozzi, oltre alla storica edizione dell'Adone del 1976, l'edizione delle *Dicerie sacre* unita a quella della *Strage de gl'innocenti*, del 1960, e i due importantissimi articoli, "Metamorfosi di Adone" e "Ludicra mariniana", rispettivamente del '71 e del '73. Delle altre opere mariniane vanno ricordate le edizioni delle varie parti della *Lira* finora pubblicate (*Rime amorose, Rime Marittime, Rime Boscherecce, Rime Lugubri*), l'edizione della *Sampogna* di Vania de Maldé e quella doppia di Gian Piero Maragoni (*La Sferza e il Tempio*). Per quel che riguarda gli studi critici, mi limito a segnalare, con i miei lavori (*La meravigliosa retorica dell'Adone*, la *Lectura Marini, The Sense of Marino* e *Going for Baroque*), la densissima rassegna del compianto Giorgio Fulco.

3. Si è parlato (dopo Croce) dell'ingresso di Marino in Parnaso già dai tempi di Carlo Calcaterra e del suo, appunto, *Parnaso in rivolta* (1940); si è discusso, poi, a vari livelli di ironia, sulla classicità dell'*Adone* che, nell'edizione Pozzi, è uscito nella collana dei Classici Mondadori. Ironia della sorte: Marino entra fra i "classici", (i.e. fra i poeti "letti in classe") proprio quando si decentralizza la situazione, per così dire, quando tutto è classico o niente lo è più, per un rimescolamento di giudizi critici e storici che tendono all'appiattimento di valori ed esperienze del passato letterario entro il proprio più ampio contesto culturale, più che alla celebrazione del genio del singolo autore.

non si può certo dire che le opere del Napoletano siano di larga diffusione: il vasto pubblico continua ad ignorarle del tutto, mentre gli accademici, benché siano perfettamente consci del giusto, nuovo rilievo assegnato al poeta, stentano, esitano e tardano a valorizzarlo in campi che non siano di puro specialismo monografico. Marino, insomma, è studiato soprattutto da chi si occupa di nuove edizioni delle sue opere, mentre mancano saggi critici volti a integrarlo nella cultura del suo tempo e a dare alla sua figura la giusta dimensione accanto ai suoi grandi contemporanei, da Campanella a Galileo, da Caravaggio a Monteverdi (per restare in ambito italiano, ché il discorso si potrebbe agevolmente ampliare con pertinenti riscontri e accostamenti a Lope de Vega e a Góngora, e perfino a Shakespeare).

Fra le varie cause della 'mancanza di popolarità', chiamiamola così, del poeta dell'*Adone*, va senz'altro considerata l'indubbia mancanza di chiarezza ideologica, malamente interpretata per secoli come "carenza d'ingegno filosofico" (secondo la citatissima sentenza dello Sforza Pallavicino nelle sue *Vindicationes*) mentre si trattava di sovrabbondanza di ingegno poetico nel bel mezzo della peggiore controriforma, quella degli ipocriti, in cui il tiratissimo gioco del *non dire dicendo* o del *dire non dicendo* poteva farsi, nel pericolo, altamente raffinato[4]. E va poi considerata l'ampiezza enorme dei testi, dell'*Adone* in particolare che è stato detto, a ragione o a torto, "l'opera più lunga della letteratura italiana": una lunghezza sicuramente estesa, nella mente di chi per primo ha enunciato la frase, dal fatto che l'intera *fabula* del poema si poteva agevolmente racchiudere in una manciata di ottave, mentre al Marino ne sono servite più di cinquemila. Evidentemente il poeta non considerava la narrazione, che costituisce tradizionalmente l'ossatura dell'epica, una priorità: *L'Adone* è anzi, sostanzialmente, opera descrittiva e non narrativa, il che ha creato in passato e crea ancora oggi non pochi ostacoli di lettura e di interpretazione.

Per tutte queste difficoltà non dovrebbe dispiacere se, dopo aver dichiarato l'obiettivo di questo studio, mi permetto di indugiare un po' sui luoghi dell'*Adone* in cui esso è nato. Nel titolo ho parlato di descrizioni *liriche* di temi *teatrali* nell'*epica* del Marino per avviare il discorso col *significare* la fusione dei tre generi letterari aristotelici voluta e applicata dal poeta nell'*Adone*. È una fusione problematica

4. È difficilisimo capire la posizione ideologica del Marino che fa del tutto, infatti, per confondere e depistare il lettore. Il Marino, bisognerà sempre ricordare quanto risultò a Pozzi nelle prime indagini sul poema maggiore, "è un poeta fondamentalmente antifrastico" ("Ludicra mariniana" 143). E su questa traccia penso non sarebbe azzardato definire *L'Adone* un'opera a chiave, con il catenaccio ben in vista lì nel prologo del poema: "Ombreggia il ver Parnaso e non rivela / gli alti misteri agli umili profani, / ma con scorza mentita asconde e cela, / quasi rozo Silen, celesti arcani" (1.10).

perché non avviene soltanto a livello retorico, ma anche e soprattutto a livello ideologico, come spero apparirà chiaramente verso la conclusione. Va detto, innanzi tutto, che questa fusione è contraria alla tendenza generale del periodo. Nell'autunno del Rinascimento, che è anche preludio della modernità, si tende infatti alla distinzione e alla specializzazione delle forme, alla loro classificazione capillare e all'incasellamento dei temi nelle forme e nei generi pertinenti: si tende, insomma, a un vero e proprio sapere parcellare: non solo sapere letterario (per cui si pensi alla citatissima *Poetica d'Aristotele vulgarizzata et sposta per Ludovico Castelvetro*, del 1570), ma sapere *tout-court* (per cui si pensi alle consultatissime enciclopedie di Tommaso Garzoni, dal *Teatro dei vari e diversi cervelli mondani*, del 1683, alla *Piazza universale di tutte le professioni del mondo*, del 1685, al *Serraglio degli stupori del mondo*, del 1613, che è l'opera ultima del Garzoni, portata a compimento dopo la sua morte dal fratello Bartolomeo).

Ebbene, il Marino non fa questo: non rispetta, per così dire, l'umor del secolo sul fronte mediale, ovvero degli strumenti intellettuali di percezione della realtà. Egli fa, anzi, il contrario: dove gli altri separano egli unisce; dove gli altri analizzano, egli mira alla sintesi.

E per sintetizzare, *in fine*, il nostro proposito, possiamo dire che a noi ora importa verificare come il Marino alla metafora dell' 'universo come libro', che con logica moderna e, anzi, addirittura 'tipografica', piacque a Galilei[5], preferisca quella del 'mondo come teatro'[6], ovvero del magmatico 'gran teatro del mondo' di cui egli ci dà un'amplissima e conclusiva, straordinariamente pregnante descrizione nell'ultimo canto dell'*Adone*, non a caso intitolato "Gli spettacoli".

Un altro tradimento fondamentale della poetica del tempo, da mettere in relazione alla inclusività del gran teatro del mondo, è quello relativo alla allora corrente gerarchia dei sensi, da Marino platealmente rifiutata nei canti 6, 7, 8. L'idea corrente era quella aristotelica secondo cui il senso più alto è da ritenere quello degli occhi, ovvero la vista; mentre quello più basso è il senso diffuso in tutta la superficie del corpo

---

5. Ecco il famoso passo del *Saggiatore*: "La filosofia è scritta in questo grandissimo libro che continuamente ci sta aperto innanzi (io dico l'universo), ma non si può intendere se prima non s'impara a intender la lingua, e conoscere i caratteri ne' quali è scritto. Egli è scritto in lingua matematica, e i caratteri son triangoli, cerchi, ed altre figure geometriche, senza i quali mezzi è impossibile a intenderne umanamente parola; senza questi è un aggirarsi vanamente per un oscuro laberinto".

6. Entrambe le metafore sono molto antiche; vedi a proposito Curtius ("Theatrical Metaphors" 138-144, e "The Book as Symbol" 302-347, entrambi in *European Literature*) e Mario Costanzo ("Il gran teatro del mondo" 239-278). Entrambe hanno una certa diffusione nel primo Seicento, ma chiaramente indicano diverse percezioni della realtà. E il barocco, *in nuce*, è proprio questo: tensione risultante dallo scontro di opposte visioni del mondo. La scelta metaforica di Marino ha forse la sua origine filologica, come si accennava sopra, nel Ronsard dell'esergo.

e concentrato nei genitali, ovvero il tatto. La formalizzazione forse più autorevole della suprema eccellenza della vista è nel *Paragone delle arti* di Leonardo Da Vinci, che un'edizione recente di Claudio Scarpati ci permette ora di apprezzare appieno. Per tutto il Cinquecento si procede con questo principio fino a Marino, che lo rovescia.

Tanto ci occorre sapere per capire, nell'*Adone,* l'ubicazione e la struttura del teatro al centro del palazzo di Amore, al centro dell'isola di Cipro, che è il centro del mondo. Come è noto, il palazzo ha quattro torri quadrate ai lati e una circolare al centro. Le torri laterali rappresentano i sensi 'minori', mentre quella circolare–un ovvio simbolo fallico–è riservata al tatto. Ora io propongo che si intenda l'ubicazione del teatro *in cima* alla torre del tatto con tutte le implicazioni che tale collocazione può comportare. Marino è quanto mai incongruo nella descrizione dei dettagli delle sue creazioni architettoniche, nonostante la famosa dichiarazione massonica del canto sesto: "trovano in sì perfetta architettura / il compasso e lo squadro ogni figura" (6.10). Non entro qui in discussione su chiose di Pozzi, di Giambonini o anche di Maragoni intorno all'*ars edificatoria* del Marino[7]. Voglio dire però che quanto più improbabile o inverosimili appaiono le descrizioni nell'*Adone* tanto più chiaramente esse assumono un significato simbolico; come, per esempio, nella zona finale del poema, nel luogo in cui il narratore dichiara che Cipro non è un'isola ma è legata al continente[8]. Il teatro, comunque, in cima alla torre circolare (inscritta vitruvianamente nel quadrilatero degli altri sensi), non è tanto un argomento interpretativo quanto una semplice verifica, perché è lì che, a ben vedere, lo ha messo il Marino stesso:

> Qui tace [Venere] e poi di quella torta scala
> che di mezzo al cortil gli archi distende,
> gli eburnei gradi, onde si monta e cala,
> preme e col bell'Adon in alto ascende. (5.112)

Il teatro è di forma quadrata ed è iscritto nel perimetro circolare della torre del tatto (a sua volta iscritto nel quadrilatero degli altri quattro sensi). Ogni lato è dedicato a uno dei quattro elementi del

---

7. Cfr. Pozzi nel commento al canto sesto dell'*Adone* (324-326). Si veda, inoltre, Giambonini, "Il compasso e lo squadro nelle architetture del Marino" e Maragoni, "Marino letto e misurato".

8. Ad un certo punto del poema, dopo che Adone è stato eletto re, l'isola di Cipro, ovvero il suo reame, non è più un'isola: "Cipro, bench'or dal'isola diviso / sia 'l continente, era già unita a quello" (*L'Adone* 16.256). Pozzi, portando in campo la *Naturalis historia* di Plinio, non si dà conto di questa uscita del Marino. A me sembra che il poeta tradisca deliberatamente la realtà per mettere in evidenza il significato simbolico. La spiegazione dell'enigma potrebbe essere che non solo a Cipro, ma a tutto il mondo si espande il regno spirituale di Adone.

creato, con descrizioni opportune, perché questo teatro è, prima di ogni altra cosa, rappresentazione del mondo. La logica del Marino è perfettamente descritta da Giovanni Pozzi: "Se il mondo è un teatro, il teatro è costruito come il mondo" (*L'Adone*, Tomo 2, 320).

> Nele facciate [...]
> l'ordin degli elementi è compartito
> ed ha ciascun nella sua propria sfera
> ogni pesce, ogni augello e ogni fera.
>
> In ogni spazio v'ha quel dio ritratto
> che di quell'elemento ha sommo impero,
> e ciascuno elemento è sculto e fatto
> d'una materia somigliante al vero.
> Vermiglio il foco è d'un rubino intatto
> ceruleo l'aere è d'un zaffir sincero,
> di smeraldo ridente e verdeggiante
> fatta è la terra e l'acqua è di diamante. (5.113-114)

Le descrizioni del Marino sono sempre tridimensionali per cui abbiamo anche la volta celeste sul soffitto e il "tartaro profondo" rappresentato sul pavimento, in cui "vedesi il re del tenebroso mondo" che ha "seco l'orride dee di Flegetonte / cui fa pompa di serpi ombra ala fronte" (5.115).

Si appresta la rappresentazione. Il capocomico è Mercurio:

> Mercurio è quei che i personaggi appresta
> Ed essercita e prova ogn'istrione
> E ciascuno d'essi in lieta parte o mesta
> Secondo l'attitudine dispone
> Né seco già di recitar consente
> Turba vulgar di mercenaria gente. (5.122)

Nell'ottava seguente, più che polemica come questa (pare, nell'ultimo verso, scritta contro gli attori della commedia dell'arte), parodica, Marino fornisce un'affollata serie di personificazioni che secondo la sua poetica occorrono per fare una buona tragedia: Invenzione, Favola, Poema, Ordine, Decoro, Armonia, Facezia, Arguzia, Energia, Eloquenza e Poesia, per finire con numero, metro, misura e musica. Egli fa, insomma, con tante ridondanze di cui si è ben accorto lo Scrivano, i versacci al Castelvetro che nella *Galeria* era stato fatto a pezzi, frantumato, dal più 'liberale' Annibal Caro, come un "Castel di vetro".[9] L'ottava manda in bestia lo Stigliani o, anzi, lo fa felice perché

---

9. Ecco il madrigale della *Galeria*, intestato ad Annibal Caro.

> Son io novo Anniballe: l'altro pugnò con l'armi,
> Io guerreggio co' carmi.
> Quei Sagunto domò con la man forte,

dimostra (dimostrerebbe) la totale ignoranza di Marino in fatto di poetica. Ecco il materano nell'*Occhiale*:

> Qui l'autore veramente per li multissimi errori che piglia, mostra di non sapere che cosa sia arte poetica, ma di parlare a caso, ed a caso anche comporre. I quali errori io registrerò tutti ad uno ad uno col replicare il testo a pezzo a pezzo. (*L'Occhiale* 186 [ma 190])

Il fatto è che Marino conosce la poetica almeno quanto Stigliani, ed è anzi proprio perché ha ben a mente il trattato del Castelvetro che si lancia all'attacco, per così dire, esautorando le forme retoriche più solide con l'invenzione più libera, come avremo modo di verificare più sotto. Basti intanto, a questo punto, ricordare che il titolo del canto, "La Tragedia", che ovviamente fa riferimento alla messa in scena del mito di Atteone (e quindi sia alla *fabula* che al genere letterario, ovvero alla tragedia) è svilito del tutto sia per quel che riguarda la storia stessa (che non fa impressione a nessuno e non crea, quindi, alcuna tensione narrativa) e sia soprattutto per quel che riguarda il genere letterario. La tragedia cinquecentesca, ricca di trame sconvolgenti, di inganni, di immagini cruente, di riconoscimenti fatali e di sangue, è il vero obiettivo polemico del Marino che include nella placidissima rappresentazione anche un balletto e un concerto.

Fabula della tragedia è il mito di Atteone, il giovane cacciatore disperso nel bosco, che per aver osato vedere Venere nuda al bagno con le sue ninfe viene trasformato in cervo e sbranato dai suoi stessi cani.

La prima scena è luminosissima. In apertura "selve, statue, palagi agli occhi offerse / la cortina real quando s'aperse" (5.121). Mercurio, regista e autore oltre che capocomico, fa il prologo ed annuncia che il soggetto "è d'Atteone il miserabil caso" (5.124). Entra in scena Atteone, "che vien con archi e dardi e cani e corni / e da molti scudier cinto si vede" (5.125), ed ecco che spuntano "damme e camozze e cavriuoli e lepri" (5.125) che si mescolano nel pubblico, vanno a lambire la veste di Venere e si rifugiano, infine, in grembo ad Adone (5.126), in ossequio alla mitezza tutta femminile del suo carattere, che persino le bestie capiscono, le stesse bestie di cui egli è cacciatore. (Tale è la sua 'qualifica,' ovvero il suo ruolo narrativo che, benché egli resti a carniere vuoto per tutto il poema, lo porterà alla morte in una battuta di caccia).

---

ed io vinto ho l'Oblio, vinta la Morte.
Ei s'aperse in Italia a forza il calle,
anch'io le vie piu chiuse
de l'italiche Muse
con l'ingegno trapasso, e spiano, e spetro:
e l'Alpi mie son un CASTEL DI VETRO.

Nella seconda scena appare la *machina* barocca, ovvero, con una similitudine, il palcoscenico mobile, l'ordigno girevole che permette una rapida e completa mutazione di scena:

> Come congiunti in un sol globo il mondo
> duo diversi emisferi insieme lega,
> per l'orizzonte che dal sommo al fondo
> la rota universal per mezzo sega,
> così l'ordigno che si gira in tondo
> vari teatri in un teatro spiega,
> senon che dove quel n'abbraccia duo,
> questo più ne contien nel cerchio suo. (5.128)

La macchina dell'asse rotante è ciò che fa speciale questo teatro, ovvero l'elemento che rende contemporaneo, d'avanguardia, e quindi barocco, il teatro del Marino, altrimenti costruito, nella sua pianta generale, quadrata, su un modello ideale di chiaro stampo rinascimentale. Più precisamente, potremmo parlare qui di scena mobile barocca in un teatro rinascimentale[10].

Con la nuova scena si introduce il balletto, ovvero: il palcoscenico ruota e ci si trova di fronte a "spelonche opache... foreste amene / piagge fresche, ombre fosche e chiari fonti" (5.132). Il Marino non dimentica, immerso nel suo teatro, inserito nel poema epico, il linguaggio evocativo della lirica, le allitterazioni, le paronomasie. Ed in questo luogo idillico, attorniato da uno stuolo di ninfe, "discende Apollo da que' verdi monti, / imitando quaggiù, vaghe e leggiere, / le danze che lassù fanno le sfere" (5.133).

Finisce il balletto e si passa alla caccia, presentata come una battaglia (5.135), mentre alla *audience* reale, a Venere e ad Adone, vengono serviti dei rinfreschi (5.137). Fa seguito, alla presentazione di Atteone stanco in cerca di un rifugio per riposarsi, una terribile tempesta, anche in questo caso con grande dispiego di mezzi scenici (5.139- 141). La varietà vuole che alle scene concitate succedano quelle placide. Ed ecco che cosa troviamo alla fine della tempesta:

> Ciò fatto, il bel teatro ancor si chiude
> poi si vede sgorgar vaga fontana,
> dove tra molte sue seguaci ignude
> stassi Atteone a vagheggiar Diana. (5.143)

Atteone viene trasformato in cervo (5.143); si fa notte in teatro e appare per mezzo di un'altra macchina, dal basso, una "prospettiva

10. È quanto risulta, giustamente, alla Peters: "It is evident that while Marino's theatre recalls the classical structures of the earlier Renaissance, his stage has nothing of the static presentation of the classical *scaena*, but rather is completely typical of the "scena mobile" of the late-*Cinquecento* and early Baroque" ("The Theatre and the Stage" 97).

superba... / con ricca mensa e sontuosa e grande / e v'ha de' sommi dei tutto il consesso / con tal pompa d'arnesi e di vivande, / tanto tesor, tanto splendor... / che sembra apunto il ciel calato in terra" (5.145). Per questa *audience* divina che sta sul palco e per quella umana e divina che assiste dall'altra parte, si ha ora un concerto, molto 'inclusivo', descritto in questa notevolissima ottava:

> Concerto allor di musici concenti
> da basso incominciò, d'alto e da lato
> e concordi s'udir vari istrumenti,
> qual da man, qual da gamba e qual da fiato,
> ed acuti e veloci e gravi e lenti
> alternar versi al pasteggiar beato,
> e rispondersi insieme in molti cori
> mute di ninfe e sinfonie d'amori. (5.146)

Finito il concerto si ha la scena conclusiva della tragedia di Atteone, ovvero del giovane cacciatore sbranato dai suoi stessi cani. Adone non vi assiste perché si è addormentato in grembo a Venere. Marino lo descrive con una similitudine che è, ancora una volta, un tradimento di genere letterario, sia dell'epica che della tragedia: Adone addormentato ci appare "in quella guisa che, dal primo sole / tocco talor, papavero vermiglio / piegar la testa sonnacchiosa suole" (5.148). Il papavero è archetipo principale e antichissimo dell'idillio, ed è figura, come in *Remembrance Day*, di giovinetto perito o che perirà di morte violenta. La conclusione della storia ad Adone sarà raccontata da Venere, ma evidentemente non fa l'effetto sperato sul giovane amante. Aveva infatti ammonito Venere: "molto move l'esempio e per la vista / maggior che per l'udir fede s'acquista" (5.111). L'esempio doveva servire a far sì che Adone abbandonasse la sua passione sportiva perché era stata profetizzata la sua morte proprio nel corso di una battuta di caccia.

Possiamo già da qui cominciare a tirare alcune conclusioni, ovvero ad allargare il contesto che ce le mostrerà da solo in tutta evidenza. Rimandiamo l'interpretazione, ritrovandoci prima, sul fronte della poetica mariniana, insieme a Pozzi:

> Due sono gli elementi che contano a livello di pensiero poetico. Primo, la svalutazione della tragedia, superata dall'interesse per il balletto. È una presa di posizione polemica contro la situazione letteraria cinquecentesca, pari all'impegno che il poeta mette in atto nel corrodere gli istituti del poema eroico: ora, tragedia e poema eroico costituivano i generi letterari su cui il cinquecento fondava il suo prestigio poetico. Secondo, la macchina teatrale: essa non è solo un modo di rappresentare in termini modernissimi i problemi dello spettacolo, ma è quasi un'immagine e un riassunto di quello che è *L'Adone*, poema per macchine (ciò è possibile in quanto per un uomo

come il Marino, la metafora è una macchina ed il poema è una metafora). (*L'Adone*, t. 2, 322)

Così come a niente servirà la premonizione della morte violenta illustrata dalla tragedia di Atteone, inutili saranno i mesaggi ricavabili dagli *exempla* contenuti nello stesso canto, cioè dalle storie di Narciso ed Eco, Ganimede e Giove, Ciparisso e Apollo, Ila ed Ercole, Attide e Cibele: sei *fabulae* in tutto se si conta anche quella, la più esemplare, di Atteone e Diana. Queste storie, però, diventano estremamente funzionali quando vengono rapportate ad altre storie collocate nella zona finale del poema, dove cioè, come credo di aver dimostrato nei miei lavori precedenti, tutti i simboli vengono finalmente scoperti quando non apertamente dichiarati. Anche le storie del canto 19 sono sei: Giacinto e Apollo, Pampino e Bacco, Aci e Galatea (e Polifemo), Calamo e Carpo, Leandro ed Ero, Achille e Chirone (e Deianira).

Nel primo gruppo di racconti, per Pozzi, si riconosce "un principio etico, cinico insieme e pessimistico, . . . poiché tutti quanti essi iniziano allo stesso modo, con un incontro di un mortale con una divinità e tutti finiscono in modo differente" (*L'Adone,* Tomo 2, 301). Negli altri racconti, invece, quelli al canto 19, narrati per consolazione di Venere dopo la morte di Adone, abbiamo che l'incontro di un mortale con la divinità porta sempre allo stesso risultato, ovvero al conferimento dell'immortalità. Nel caso di Galatea, Aci e Polifemo, che per estensione testuale corrisponde all'Atteone del canto 5, abbiamo che l'immortalità viene data anche allo stesso mostruoso e crudele gigante. Abbiamo quindi una opposizione apparentemente perversa di destini: un giovinetto innocente è ucciso, mentre un arrogante energumeno, omicida per giunta, è premiato con il dono dell'immortalità. Vedremo fra poco la logica di questa opposizione.

Intanto osserviamo che, come dopo gli *exempla* del canto quinto si passava al teatro per la recita di Atteone, dopo gli *exempla* del canto 19 si entra nel mondo magico degli spettacoli, ovvero del teatro del mondo nuovo, descritto nelle ultime 515 entusiasmanti ottave del poema che ho avuto la ventura di definire, esattamente 10 anni fa nella *Lectura Marini,* "il gran teatro del mondo ovvero il mondo a teatro"[11]. So bene che è odioso autocitarsi ma qui mi tocca proprio, seppure con la speranza di poter presto citare da altri, amici svizzeri in particolare, che

11. Pozzi, come è noto, ha seguito un'altra strada nell'interpretazione del canto 20, presentandolo come "dopo poema", o poema aggiuntivo, data la sua vasta dimensione (515 ottave) e dato che la storia del giovinetto ucciso dal cinghiale a questo punto si è ormai definitivamente conclusa (cfr. *L'Adone*, t. 2, 695-697). È curioso, comunque, verificare come la Peters, che con grande acume ha notato le affinità fra il teatro del canto 5 e il Palazzo delle Arti del canto 10, "palagio ch'al modello, a la figura / quasi d'anfiteatro avea sembianza" (10.117), (cfr. "The Anatomical Machine 104), non abbia anche visto le metafore teatrali del canto 20.

continuano a occuparsi non solo di Marino, e non solo dell'*Adone*, ma specificamente del canto 20. Ecco come aprivo, nel 1989, "Il gran teatro del mondo, ovvero il mondo a teatro":

> L'intero universo ha risposto all'appello di Venere: nella gran "piazza ovata" (ott. 18) antistante il meraviglioso "palagio d'Amore" accorrono le potenze del cielo e dell'inferno unendosi a "vulgo e baronaggio" (ott. 20), provenienti da ogni luogo della Terra. In perfetta armonia ("l'ordin non si confonde...", ott. 14, 20) e con la cooperazione delle forze della natura ("sereno il ciel... tranquillo il mar... verdeggiante la terra", ott. 8-10) si riempiono gli stalli del "circo" o "teatro" (ott. 18) che fanno da corona all'"alto tribunal" (ott. 20) di Venere, ed hanno così inizio i giochi, o meglio gli "spettacoli" adonii per immortalare il ricordo del tenero giovinetto quindicenne ucciso dalla bruta violenza del cinghiale.
>
> (*Lectura Marini* 325)

E continuavo:

> Il nuovo mondo mariniano, annunciato con tanti *exempla* nel penultimo canto, si spalanca con gli "Spettacoli". Altre figure del cinghiale e di Adone riappaiono qui, altri accostamenti di simboli opposti, ma ora le antitesi si risolvono in maniera chiara e definitiva e così, finita l'elegia, il canto prende una dimensione trionfale [...] Il nesso principale che lega gli opposti non è più suggerito da allusioni e rimandi, ma dichiarato dalla nuova identità di Venere: dimesso l'abito dell'amante privata, ora veste i paramenti solenni che la fanno figura di una *charitas* entro cui tutto si raccoglie. Si può notare come la dea ora eserciti il suo nuovo ruolo soprattutto alla fine di ogni gara, quando premia vincitori e vinti, addolcisce le ire dei contendenti e spegne in essi ogni desiderio di rivalsa. E, del resto, per mezzo della pubblicazione del cartello, all'alba della prima giornata, ella chiarisce subito la natura dei giochi adonii: "...non saranno invan sparsi i sudosi / né poveri di palme trionfali / invidia avranno i vinti ai vincitori" (ott. 24).
>
> (*Lectura Marini* 330)

C'è proprio da interrogarsi qui sull'evento su cui si imperniano tali rivolgimenti. Che cosa è successo per giustificare un ribaltamento così 'plateale' della storia e dei personaggi? Che cosa è successo, per restare nel mito, fra le storie che anticipano la tragedia di Atteone e quelle che seguono la tragedia di Adone? Che cosa è successo che ha cambiato il destino del bell'Atteone, sbranato dai cani, in quello del mostruoso Polifemo, "premiato" con l'immortalità? Che cosa è successo che ha cambiato il teatro da parodia aristotelica a 'gran teatro del mondo'? La risposta è semplice e complessa insieme: fra i due teatri c'è la morte di Adone, conscia e anzi volontaria, ed anzi cristologica: vittima sacrificale, votata alla redenzione dell'intera umanità, come ormai, credo di aver dimostrato a sufficienza[12], non si può più evitare di riconoscere. Ed è così che con la trasformazione / resurrezione di Adone la tragedia diventa commedia e il poema epico diventa, secondo il famoso ossimoro dello Chaplain, "poëme de paix" (cfr. *L'Adone* 33).

Qui con i dovuti rimandi potrei fermarmi; ma in appendice vorrei aggiungere due parole almeno su questa incredible dimensione del teatro in Marino, diametralmente opposta alla metafora del 'mondo come libro'. Nel Seicento, e per Marino più che per ogni altro autore, non si è ciò che si è, ma ciò che si vuole essere: in una continua, cosciente e costante proiezione di sé, come appunto in un gran teatro in cui tutti fanno la loro parte, esplicando così, individualmente, la comune attività creativa dell'uomo, ovvero ciò che lo rende "artificioso" e "divino" insieme; non per niente questi sono i termini fra i più ambiti dai poeti del tempo. E se, *in fine*, la 'divinità poetica' del Marino su cui, Achillini *in primis*, giuravano i contemporanei, non fosse semplicemente da noi scartata come iperbole barocca, roboante e vuota, forse potremmo acquisire una migliore, più giusta e utile intelligenza della spiritualità del *poema grande* e di quella del suo tempo.

OPERE CITATE

AA.VV. *Going for Baroque: Cultural Transformations 1550-1650*. A cura di Francesco Guardiani. Ottawa: Legas, 1999.

AA.VV. *Lectura Marini*. A cura di Francesco Guardiani. Ottawa: Dovehouse, 1989.

AA.VV. *The Sense of Marino: Literature, Fine Arts and Music of the Italian Baroque*. A cura di Francesco Guardiani. Ottawa: Legas, 1994.

Calcaterra, Carlo. *Il Parnaso in rivolta*. Milano: Mondadori, 1940.

Costanzo, Mario. "Il gran teatro del mondo", *Dallo Scaligero al Quadrio*. Milano: All'insegna del pesce d'oro, pp. 239-78.

Curtius, Ernst Robert. *European Literature and the Latin Middle Ages*. Trans. from German, Willard R. Track. Princeton: Princeton UP, 1973.

Fulco, Giorgio. "Giovan Battista Marino", *Storia della letteratura italiana*. Vol. 5: *La fine del Cinquecento e il Seicento*. Roma: Salerno editrice, 1997, pp. 597-652.

12. Sia con le pagine interpretative di "*Inventio*: Dal madrigale al *poema grande*", che con i due saggi, "Canto XVIII: LA MORTE. I trastulli del cinghiale" e "Canto XX: GLI SPETTACOLI. Il gran teatro del mondo, ovvero il mondo a teatro" della *Lectura Marini*. Un breve *addendum* sulla identificazione di Adone con Cristo si trova anche in "*Gli alti misteri ai semplici profani*: A Didactic Approach for *L'Adone*" contenuto in *The Sense of Marino*.

Galilei, Galileo. *Il Saggiatore*. In Luigi Russo, *I classici italiani dal Cinquecento al Settecento*. Firenze: Sansoni, 1975.

Giambonini, Francesco. "Il compasso e lo squadro nelle architetture del Marino", *Strumenti critici*, 8 (1974): 323-43.

Guardiani, Francesco. *La meravigliosa retorica dell'*Adone *di G. B. Marino*. Firenze: Olschki, 1989.

Maragoni, Gian Piero. "Marino letto e misurato", *Dismisura*, 11 (1982): 57-60.

Marino, Giovan Battista. *Dicerie sacre e la strage de gl'innocenti*. A cura di Giovanni Pozzi. Torino: Einaudi, 1960.

____. *L'Adone*. A cura di Giovanni Pozzi. 2 tomi. Milano: Mondadori, 1976.

____. *La sampogna*. A cura di Vania De Maldé. Parma: Fondazione Bembo/Guanda, 1993.

____. *La Sferza e il Tempio*. A cura di Gian Piero Maragoni. Roma: Vignola, 1995.

____. *Rime amorose*. A cura di Ottavio Besomi e Alessandro Martini. Modena: Panini, 1987.

____. *Rime boscherecce*. A cura di Janina Hauser-Jacubowicz. Modena: Panini, 1991.

____. *Rime lugubri*. A cura di Vincenzo Guercio. Modena: Panini, 1999.

____. *Rime marittime*. A cura di Ottavio Besomi, Costanzo Marchi e Alessandro Martini. Modena: Panini, 1988.

Peters Coy, Susanna. "The Theatre and the Stage of Marino's *Adone*: Canto V", *Modern Language Notes*, 98 (1983): 87-110.

Peters, Susanna. "The Anatomical Machine: A Representation of the Microcosm in the *Adone* of G. B. Marino." *Modern Language Notes* 88 (1973): 95-110.

Pozzi, Giovanni. "Ludicra mariniana." *Studi e problemi di critica testuale* 6 (1973): 131- 162.

____. "Metamorfosi di Adone." *Strumenti critici* 5 (1971): 334-356.

Scrivano, Riccardo. "Canto V: La Tragedia – Amplificazione per ripetizione." *Lectura Marini*. A cura di Francesco Guardiani. Ottawa: Dovehouse, 1989.

Dalla botola sciasciana alle scene plastiche: elementi per una storia della messinscena del *Riscatto d'Adamo*

Salvatore Bancheri

UNIVERSITY OF TORONTO

1. NOTIZIE BIO-BIBLIOGRAFICHE SU FILIPPO ORIOLES

Su Filippo Orioles[1], autore del *Riscatto d'Adamo nella morte di Gesù Cristo,* si hanno scarse e incerte notizie, essendo, come lo definisce il marchese di Villabianca nel suo *Diario Palermitano,* una "persona minuta". Nacque a Palermo nel 1687 e morì all'età di ben 106 anni, nell'agosto del 1793. Ed è per la sua veneranda età che è ricordato dal diarista palermitano:

> Agosto 1793. Per due ragioni mi prendo l'eccezione di far nota in queste memorie della morte di una persona minuta qual fu Filippo Orioles. La prima perché egli fu un buon poeta e improvvisatore di versi latini, avendo lasciato il suo nome nei pubblici torchi colle sue opere di drammi, e posto in scena il mortorio di Cristo e vite di santi. La seconda è che portava l'età di centosei anni, che rade volte si vive dagli uomini. (VIII, 191)

Di lui, Ugo Antonio Amico scrive:

> Lo dicono valente improvvisatore in lingua latina; d'una memoria felicissima tanto da ritenere a mente parecchie prediche degli oratori nella quaresima, e così per l'appunto da esser messe a stampa, senza che una sillaba vi fosse sbagliata. (8)

Anche della produzione letteraria dell'Orioles poche sono le documentazioni e spesso si hanno solo dei titoli; si conoscono solo 10 opere drammatiche:

---

1. Per maggiori informazioni su Filippo Orioles, sulle sue opere e sulle messinscene del *Riscatto,* si vedano: S. Bancheri, "Nota critica"; S. Bancheri; "Una sacra rappresentazione settecentesca a Toronto".

1) *L'amor trionfante*[2].
2) *La notte in giorno nella nascita di Gesù Cristo*, opera sacroscenica, dedicata al Signore Gius.pe Emmanuello Massa, Caccamo, e Branciforte. Palermo: Valenza, 1745.
3) *L'alchimia in contesa*, commedia. Palermo: [senza editore], 1746.
4) *Il riscatto d 'Adamo nella morte di Gesù Cristo*, tragedia, dedicato al merito distinto del sig. Giuseppe Baldi e Platamone. Palermo: Eredi D'Aiccardo, 1750.
5) *La servitù disciolta nella morte di Gesù Cristo*, tragedia dedicata al signor Tommaso Celestri, e Grimaldi de' marchesi di S. Croce. Palermo, Eredi D'Aiccardo, 1751.
6) *II S. Elia*, opera tragicomica, dedicata al sig. Francesco Costanzo. Palermo: Angelo Felicella, 1753.
7) *L'eroina d'Oreto overo la S. Rosalia*, opera sacro-scenica. Palermo: Francesco Ferrer, [senza data][3].
8) *L'anticristo*[4].
9) *La conquista di Gerosolima*, opera scenica, dedicata al gran merito del Sig. marchese Stefano Airoldi. Palermo: D. Gaetano M. Bentivenga, 1785.
10) *Il San Basilio Magno*, opera sacro-scenica[5].

---

2. Di quest'opera, a cui si fa riferimento nella lettera dedicatoria alla *Notte in giorno*, non siamo riusciti a trovare copia. Si tratta molto probabilmente del *Riscatto d'Adamo*, presentato sotto altro titolo: si veda S. Bancheri, "Nota critica", pp. XXXII, XCIII e CLII-CLIII.

3. L'anno di pubblicazione della S. *Rosalia* è da collocarsi tra il 1750 e il 1779, come si può dedurre dai seguenti elementi: 1) In una nota a mano nella copia della Biblioteca del Museo Teatrale alla Scala di Milano si legge che l'opera "Si rappresentò nella città di Vizini Festa di S. Gaetano Tiene Fiera 5 e 7 agosto 177_". L'ultima cifra della data è resa di difficile lettura da una rilegatura poco accurata. Le possibilità sembrano essere 1771/1778/1779. 2) L'editore Francesco Ferrer svolse la sua attività nel periodo 1750-1797. Per maggiori ragguagli, si veda: S. Bancheri, "Nota critica", XXXIII- XXXIV.

4. Quest'opera, di cui alla pubblicazione della mia edizione critica del mio *Riscatto d'Adamo* si conosceva solo il titolo, è ora così catalogata presso la Biblioteca centrale della Regione siciliana di Palermo: *L'anticristo*. Opera traggica [sic] composta da Filippo Orioles palermitano. In Palermo per Gio. Battista Gagliani, si vendono dal medesimo stamp. alla calata di S. Franc., 1781. Collocazione Antiqua Y.7.11.28. Purtroppo, durante la mia recentissima e breve visita (luglio 1999) alla biblioteca palermitana, non mi è stato possibile prendere in visione l'opera in quanto gli addetti ai lavori, dopo vari tentativi, non sono riusciti a trovarla sugli scaffali. Giorni prima della consegna alla stampa del presente studio, mi è arrivata conferma che è stata approvata la mia richiesta per un microfilm dell'opera.

5. Del *San Basilio Magno*, di cui sto preparando un'edizione critica, sono riuscito a trovare solo un manoscritto del 1786 presso la Biblioteca centrale della Regione siciliana, ai segni VII.B.6. Per ulteriori informazioni, si veda: S. Bancheri, "Nota critica", XXXII-XXXIII e XL-XLIII.

2. Fortuna del *Riscatto*

L'edizione del 1750 segnò una svolta definitiva nel successo del *Riscatto.* Infatti, l'opera – per dirla con il Pitré — "acquistossi celebrità in tutta l'isola" (15) e parve la migliore fra tutte le varie passioni di Gesù Cristo. La popolarità determinò un successo di edizioni e di rappresentazioni. I lavori a stampa, oltre che con il titolo di *Riscatto,* uscivano anche con il titolo popolare di *Martorio* o *Passione di Gesú Cristo,* spesso senza l'indicazione del nome dell'autore. Il *Riscatto,* inoltre, fu divulgato tramite copioni manoscritti che presto invasero molti paesi della Sicilia e furono e sono tuttora conservati gelosamente come copie originali e uniche.

I vari studiosi dell'Orioles sono consci dell'immensa fortuna del capolavoro del drammaturgo palermitano e ne parlano sempre in modo lusinghiero. Il Mira osserva che "la produzione fu bene accolta e tanto famosa si rese di essersi data in moltissimi teatri, ed in taluni anche sinoggi [...]"; asserisce, inoltre, che la tragedia — di cui si conoscono moltissime edizioni, le quali "non torna tutte numerare" — continua ad essere ristampata in edizioni "pessime e deturpate che conviene meglio tacerle e lasciarle alla dimenticanza". (154)

Sempre in modo alquanto vago l'Amico scrive al Ferrazzi che l'Orioles " è pur l'autore del *Martorio di Cristo,* ripubblicato cento volte, e rappresentato anco oggidì nella settimana santa". (Ferrazzi 306)

Il Pitré sostiene che in Sicilia il *Riscatto* trovò tanto favore che "maggiore non n'ebbe forse mai nessuna tragedia di autor siciliano" e aggiunge che esso, "moltiplicato per ricopie e ristampe" e "pubblicazione quasi ordinaria delle tipografie palermitane di Francesco Ferrer e di L. D'Asaro", "venne recitato nei teatri e nelle chiese, nelle piazze pubbliche e nelle case private, qua ridotto, colà ampliato, altrove preso a fonte delle *Cene parlanti* e delle *Deposizioni dalla croce*". (17)

A dimostrazione della sua popolarità ai nostri giorni, il *Riscatto* ha trovato una degna collocazione anche nella narrativa di Leonardo Sciascia e precisamente nelle pagine conclusive di *A ciascuno il suo:*

> [...] e di quel povero professore Laurana — continuò il commendatore — che è scomparso come Antonio Patò nel *Mortorio.*
>
> Cinquant'anni prima, durante le recite del *Mortorio,* cioè la Passione di Cristo secondo il cavalier D'Orioles, Antonio Patò, che faceva Giuda, era scomparso, per come la parte voleva, nella botola che puntualmente, come già un centinaio di volte tra prove e rappresentazioni, si aprì: solo che (e questo non era nella parte) da quel momento nessuno ne aveva saputo più niente; e il fatto era rimasto in proverbio, a indicare misteriose scomparizioni di persone e di oggetti. (134)

Su questa citazione scasciana, Andrea Cammilleri ha costruito addirittura uno dei suoi più recenti romanzi, *La scomparsa di Patò*, soffermandosi, in particolare nei primi capitoli, suol Riscatto e sulla sua messinscena.

3. Datazione

Il notevole successo tipografico dell'edizione del 1750, determinato dal fatto che i primi editori basarono su di essa le loro ristampe, riconoscendola cosí tacitamente quale testo ufficiale, ha portato i critici, anche se a volte con dovute riserve, a vedere in essa l'*editio princeps*. Noi, pur senza disconoscerne l'importanza, non crediamo che essa sia stata la prima: infatti, che l'opera fosse stata stampata anteriormente lo si sospetta dalla dedica, nella quale si legge:

> Questa sacra rappresentanza della Passione di N.S.G.C. rinasce dai torchi con diversa idea e con altro aspetto dalla prima[6].

E ancora:

> Avendo dunque io sempre presente quella pronta soddisfazione, colla quale voi interveniste alle recite di quella prima mia Rappresentazione, fatta in questa Città, spero che da voi debbasi gradire lo stesso componimento, che vi presento da me rinnovato. (Amico 8)

Eventuali dubbi sull'esistenza di una o più edizioni anteriori a quella del 1750 vengono fugati dalla considerazione della fortuna delle rappresentazioni del *Riscatto* prima del 1750. Il Pitré afferma che "prima della metà del sec. XVIII il *Riscatto di Adamo* era stato recitato più e più volte in Palermo". (16) L'Orioles stesso nella sopracitata dedica parla di "recite di quella mia prima Rappresentazione". Nelle *Siculae sanctiones*, in una lettera del Viceré La Viefuille al capitano della città di Palermo, datata 20 marzo 1750, si legge:

> *Vel sacras Comicorum recitationes in Ecclesis habendas 'Capitanei' jurisdictioni subjectas esse decernitur.*
>
> Ha fatto a me ricorso una compagnia di dilettanti Comici per voler accordata la licenza di rappresentare il mortorio di N. S. nella Chiesa di S. Pietro Martire, ove han situato il teatro, ed avendo io accordato loro il permesso, che mi fu richiesto, prevengo V. S., a cui appartiene la giurisdizione d'invigilare, e curare, che non succedessero inconvenienti ne' pubblici teatri, acciò faccia ella assistere quegli ufficiali di sua Corte in detto luogo di S. Pietro Martire, nella stessa guisa, che assistono ne' teatri di questa capitale, e prevenire tutti quegl'inconvenienti, che potessero accadere in detto luogo, ove si

---

6. La dedica è riportata parzialmente dal Pitré (16). Anche U. A. Amico (7-8) riporta la frase con leggere varianti.

rappresenta il riferito mortorio; e nostro Signore la feliciti. Palermo a' 20 di Marzo 1750. (Gervasium II, 430)

Recite del *Riscatto* non furono effettuate soltanto a Palermo, ma persino a Napoli. Il Croce, nei *Teatri di Napoli, si* riferisce a rappresentazioni della tragedia dell'Orioles che risalgono addirittura al 1731, cioè a quasi vent'anni prima della edizione del 1750:

> Nel 1738 e nel '39 fu impedita la recita ai Fiorentini e al Nuovo, nei giorni di Pasqua, dell'*Opera della passione di Gesú Cristo* (di Filippo Orioles, palermitano), la quale pel passato era stata solita a farsi o in case di privati gentiluomini o in oratori "con somma decenza e compungimento"; ed "io stesso (scriveva l'uditore dell'esercito nel marzo '39) otto anni sono ne fui una volta spettatore in una casa vuota di San Carlo delle Mortelle, recitata dal marchese de Simone e da altre persone distinte con tanta proprietà e devozione, che quasi continuamente si pianse"; senonché, offerta in pubblico e con fini di lucro, dava luogo a chiassate e scandali. Qualche anno dopo, nel '51, giunse a notizia dell'uditore che nella via che dai Fiorentini va a largo del Castello, in una stanza a pianterreno, si recitava appunto l'opera della Passione, vendendosi i biglietti senza riscuotere il prezzo all'entrata per poter asserire con frode che non era fatta per lucro; e tosto venne di nuovo proibita. (*I teatri di Napoli dal Rinascimento alla fine del secolo decimottavo,* 188-189)

Le notizie forniteci dal Croce non lasciano adito a dubbi sul fatto che il *Riscatto* esistesse già nel 1731 e, quasi certamente, anche prima.

4. Le rappresentazioni

Voler seguire la fortuna scenica del *Riscatto* risulta impresa ardua, in quanto l'opera è stata — e viene tuttora — rappresentata quasi annualmente durante il periodo pasquale. Già il Pitré aveva dedicato a questo argomento diverse pagine dei suoi *Spettacoli e feste popolari.* La vastità dell'argomento non ci consente, in questa sede, né di ripetere le informazioni forniteci dal Pitré né tantomemo di presentare le illustri rappresentazioni ottocentesche di Acireale e di Caltanissetta[7]. Ci proponiamo solo di aggiornare lo studio del Pitré, segnalando alcune rappresentazioni del *Riscatto* di cui siamo a conoscenza, e di soffermarci sulla rappresentazione del *Riscatto* a Delia (CL), con particolare riferimento alla scenografia.

La prima indicazione concerne alcune mancate rappresentazioni del *Riscatto* a Cava (Salerno). A fornirci le notizie è il Croce:

> Nel [giugno] 1783 fu negato il permesso a un D. Francesco M. Apuzzo e compagni che volevano rappresentare "l'opera tragica, che porta il titolo della passione del nostro Signore Gesú Cristo, composta da

7. Si veda S. Bancheri, "Nota critica", CLV.

Filippo Orioles di Palermo" [...] Nel [28 maggio] 1790 i Cavaiuoli tornarono alla carica per rappresentare l'opera *Il Riscatto d'Adamo,* e la Deputazione dei teatri dubitò giustamente che non fosse altro se non *l'Opera della passione,* per la quale s'era già negato più volte il permesso. (*I teatri di Napoli dal Rinascimento, secolo XVI-XVIII,* 713- 714)

Una corrispondenza non firmata de *Il Giorno* di Napoli ci informa che il giovedì e il venerdì santo del 1926 nella frazione Cellia del comune di Polia (Catanzaro) fu rappresentata con enorme successo e con "mirabile esecuzione" l'opera del drammaturgo palermitano. Durante la scena della impiccagione di Giuda la folla fu "pervasa di terrore", e vivamente commossa durante quella della Crocifissione, "tanto che furono pochi coloro che non si lasciarono vincere dal pianto". (3)

A Montemaggiore Belsito, in provincia di Palermo, le recite del *Riscatto* risalgono agli inizi del secolo: l'opera del drammaturgo palermitano viene rappresentata, con le solite modifiche, all'incirca ogni cinque anni. Nel 1930-1935 la filodrammatica di questo paese rappresentò la tragedia dell'Orioles presso il Teatro Biondo di Palermo.

Ad Albi, in provincia di Catanzaro, le rappresentazioni del *Martorio*, chiamato semplicemente *L'Opera,* risalgono almeno alla seconda metà degli anni Venti. Si sono avuti allestimenti scenici certamente negli anni 1946, 1948, 1952 e 1988. Quest'ultima rappresentazione — ci informa il prof. Rocco Mario Morano[8] — ha avuto luogo, "dopo 36 anni di interruzione, il 27-3-1988 nel Piazzale Oliveto dinanzi a circa 1500 spettatori ed è durata dalle 11 alle 19". La discontinuità cronologica della rappresentazione dell'Opera ad Albi è dovuta a motivi economici: infatti — ci spiega ancora il Morano — "essa avveniva quando le annate relative alla raccolta delle olive erano buone. La vendita dell'olio permetteva alla popolazione di affrontare le spese occorrenti". Il *Martorio* ad Albi è stato importato dal vicino paese di Tiriolo (Catanzaro), "dove esiste, a quanto sembra, dal secolo scorso la consuetudine di rappresentare annualmente (o quasi) il "martorio". Mi dicono che il "martorio" è stato rappresentato a Tiriolo due anni or sono".

Rappresentazioni del *Martorio* si sono avute anche a Joppolo Giancaxio (Agrigento), come segnala Alfonso Zaccaria in un suo articolo. Lo studioso tuttavia non rende giustizia al *Riscatto* dell'Orioles, definito "letterariamente orribile e popolarescamente (perché schematico, approssimativo, candido) suggestivo." (481) L'Orioles di Joppolo — aggiunge il critico — è quello universalmente noto, ovvero

> tenacemente avvinghiato alle sacre scritture per snodare la sua risaputa trama di sudore e di sangue, alquanto truculenta perché non addolcita e diluita dalle parabole e perifrasi poetiche simbologie e

8. R.M. Morano, in una lettera datata 3 maggio 1988 a me indirizzata, tiene a precisare di aver attinto le notizie di cui sopra dall'amico A.F. Corea.

> piacevolezze narrative dei testi evangelici, ma fosca anche intenzionalmente, credo per far presa sulla platea, che l'autor doveva ben sapere incline (specie a quei tempi) alla gagliarde coloriture, al *décor* tinteggiante il più possibile. (483)

Lo Zaccaria cerca anche di spiegare i motivi del successo secolare della tragedia dell'Orioles:

> Ed è un fatto che il "Mortorio" non è mai venuto a noia alle masse siciliane, che fin qui, da due secoli e passa, hanno conosciuto la Passione [...] più per il tramite del verseggiare enfatico, aulico-pretenzioso, stampellato e a volte anche francamente ridicolo, senza barlume di interiore verità, del cavalier Orioles panormita, che per pratica di testi canonici e frequenza di visitazioni chiesastiche. (483)

Le accuse dello Zaccaria sono senza dubbio infondate e la sua definizione del *Riscatto* come opera "letterariamente orribile" ci lascia il dubbio che la tragedia consultata dal critico non sia quella dell'Orioles, ma uno dei tanti rimaneggiamenti, con fraintendimenti e contaminazioni di stili propri della tradizione popolare.

Nella prefazione e nell'appendice all'edizione del 1967 del *Riscatto,* Damiano Barcellona ci dà alcune interessanti notizie sulle recite del *Martorio* ad Alia (Palermo), dove le rappresentazioni risalgono alla metà del 1800: si sono avute recite nel 1854, nel 1882, 1892, 1898, 1905, 1914, 1920/21, 1928, 1935, 1949, 1950, 1965, 1969, 1973 e 1977. Le rappresentazioni avevano luogo in conformità con lo spirito liturgico della passione:

> Il Venerdì Santo, ad Alia, si andava al Martorio come ad un prolungamento dei Sacri Riti che si erano celebrati in Chiesa qualche ora prima. Tutto il popolo si recava in piazza, dinanzi al grande palco costruito accanto alla Chiesa di S. Anna o di Santa Rosalia, e là, con l'animo ancora compenetrato dalla commossa rievocazione del mistero della Redenzione contemplato nelle funzioni liturgiche, assisteva alla Sacra Rappresentazione, che, nelle sei o sette ore di spettacolo vario e drammatico, riproduceva plasticamente, con artistiche e sempre aderenti interpretazioni, il racconto della Passione di Gesù [...]. (Barcellona 5)

La preparazione del *Martorio* era molto faticosa e accurata; le spese erano ingenti:

> Le *prove* della *recita* si facevano accuratamente, alcuni mesi avanti, nelle lunghe serate d'inverno, dagli *attori,* che venivano scelti con il criterio non solo della loro idoneità artistica ma anche della loro capacità di religiosa immedesimazione.
>
> Alle spese per la rappresentazione si faceva fronte con la contribuzione di tutto il paese. (Barcellona 5-6)

Gli stessi fenomeni si verificano anche a Delia (Caltanissetta), dove la tradizione risale, secondo il La Verde, alla seconda metà del secolo XVIII. (80) La tradizione è bipartita in "Martorio" e "Scinnenza". Il "Martorio", il quale non è altro che il *Riscatto* modificato ed ampliato, si rappresentava ogni quattro o cinque anni durante il periodo della Quaresima. La "Scinnenza" (che significa "Deposizione") ripropone le ultime scene del *Riscatto,* modificate ed ampliate (La Verde 82). Le rappresentazioni sono allestite annualmente durante la Settimana Santa e si svolgono all'aperto. A queste scene se ne sono man mano aggiunte altre, tanto che il *Riscatto* è ormai rappresentato quasi per intero. Ed è probabilmente per questi motivi che ultimamente il "Martorio" non è stato più rappresentato.[9] I deliani — scrive il La Verde — hanno un culto per il *Martorio:*

> Non c'è professionista, artigiano o contadino che non ne sappia a memoria alcune parti. I versi più famosi sono entrati nel linguaggio popolare ed hanno trovato il loro posto accanto ai proverbi più comuni. Non è raro sentire citare, non solo dagli uomini, ma anche dalle donne, versi del "Mortorio" che conferiscono particolare efficacia ai loro discorsi. (90)

Le rappresentazioni sono allestite annualmente durante la Settimana Santa e si svolgono all'aperto. Le scene nelle rappresentazioni a Delia hanno subito, in particolare negli ultimi venticinque anni, dei miglioramenti notevoli, dovuti anche ad una maggiore indipendenza e stabilità economica da parte dell'associazione che cura le manifestazioni pasquali. Tra il 1960 e il 1967 circa, il comitato organizzatore delle feste pasquali aveva a disposizione 3-4 scene, dipinte da artisti locali (si fa il nome di Calogero Talluto) su sacchi di cemento uniti e incollati insieme; dal 1967 al 1976 si utilizzaronno invece delle scene dipinte su tela da Calogero Talluto e Paolo Marchiolo (per esempi di scene usate dal 1960 al 1976 si vedano foto 1-4). Dal 1976 ad oggi si utilizzano delle scene su masonite, costruite, su progetto di Francesco Paolo Marchiolo, dal falegname Angelo Lo Porto e tinteggiate dal decoratore Angelo Fazio: si tratta di sei parallelepipedi di 2,20 di altezza e di 1.10 di larghezza, contrassegnati da lettere e numeri (facciate), che nella giusta combinazione formano le circa sette scene essenziali delle rappresentazioni a palco (per un esempio, si veda foto 5). La composizione delle scene non presenta difficoltà: è come ricostruire un puzzle tridimensionale di pochi tasselli, addirittura numerati e con una chiave di composizione (foto e disegni). Le scene ricomposte rappresentano le mura di Gerusalemme (foto 6), il sinedrio,

9. Per le rappresentazioni del *Martorio* a Delia, si veda Bancheri, "Nota filologica", nota 23.

un esterno per l'ultima cena (foto 7), l'orto del Getsemani, il pretorio di Pilato (foto 8), la regia di Erode, il cortile romano per la flagellazione (foto 9). Comunque, le possibilità per la creazione di altre scene usando diverse combinazioni sono parecchie (come si potrà vedere anche dalle immagini dei quadri plastici, foto 10-11).

La versatilità di questo sistema scenografico ha portato, a partire dal 1980 circa, ad una introduzione graduale dei cosiddetti quadri plastici nelle manifestazioni pasquali di Delia.[10] Si tratta di messinscene — curate da Orazio Strazzeri e ispirate al *Gesù di Nazareth* di Zeffirelli — di episodi essenziali della vita pubblica di Cristo, dalla durata di circa 10 minuti, con la partecipazione di circa 30-50 personaggi, tutti in costume dell'epoca: alcuni quadri hanno un sottofondo musicale, altri sono commentati, altri ancora mimati. Si sono avuti quadri plastici per il discorso della montagna (foto 12), la flagellazione (foto 9), la resurrezione (foto 13), i miracoli, la resurrezione di Lazzaro (foto 14), la moltiplicazione dei pani, il miracolo del sordomuto e quello dello zoppo. Si rappresentano circa 4-5 quadri plastici all'anno, in base alle necessità dell'intera manifestazione pasquale e per garantire ad essa una qual certa varietà tra un anno e l'altro. Usando il sopraddetto sistema scenografico a combinazione, si sono create nuove scene per ognuno di questi quadri: per esempio, per le tentazioni del diavolo si usa il bosco con mura di Gerusalemme; per il discorso della montagna si hanno degli alberi con veduta delle mura di Gerusalemme (foto 12); per la resurrezione ancora degli alberi (foto 13). Il successo dei quadri plastici ha indirettamente portato anche ad un leggero allontanamento dalla tragedia dell'Orioles. Infatti, alcuni dei quadri plastici sopra menzionati hanno anche delle scene corrispondenti nel *Riscatto* dell'Orioles, e pertanto, per evitare duplicazioni, non si rappresenta mai nello stesso anno il quadro plastico e la scena dell'Orioles.

Come miglioramento della scenografia sono anche da vedere gli investimenti, negli anni novanta, in alcune trombe egiziane e in una biga romana per l'ingresso di Pilato prima della condanna di Cristo. Quest'ultimo elemento ha anche determinato un ulteriore allontanamento dal testo dell'Orioles, con la ristrutturazione delle entrate del pretore romano.

Anche i costumi hanno subito, con il passare degli anni, dei cambiamenti notevoli: si è passato infatti da costumi scarni, poco accurati da un punto di vista storico e addirittura appartenenti ad epoche moderne, a costumi dai colori più vivaci e storicamente più veri: per esempio, le guardie del sinedrio vestivano una volta come soldati romani, mentre una Veronica degli anni '50 (foto 15) porta l'abito di

10. Il primo quadro plastico fu introdotto nel 1969, in occasione dell'ultimo *Martorio* rappresentato a Delia.

suora. Oggigiorno invece i dettagli sia nella scenografia, che nei costumi, nel trucco, nelle sfumature dell'illuminazione, sono estremamente ben curati da un gruppo di esperti locali.

Le manifestazioni pasquali a Delia, che il Buttitta qualifica come "imponenti" (30), devono il loro successo non solo alla rappresentazione del *Riscatto*, ma a tutto un complesso di manifestazioni, che dura tutto l'arco della settimana santa, e ad una attiva partecipazione dell'intera popolazione della cittadina dell'entroterra siciliano. L'intera Delia diventa letteralmente il palcoscenico per la tragedia dell'Orioles: la Via Crucis si svolge tra le strade cittadine, mentre la crocifissione e la deposizione hanno luogo davanti alla pittoresca Chiesa del Calvario (foto 16-19); al testo dell'Orioles sono anche associati anche altre attività pasquali, come quelle delle lamentazioni per la morte del Cristo, la processione dell'Urna e dell'Addolorata, l'incontro tra Cristo risorto e la Madonna[11] (foto 20). Singolare quest'ultima manifestazione perché l'incontro tra le due statue, che avviene in una strada a ripida discesa della cittadina, si svolge al ritmo di una marcia tradizionale e con la partecipazione attiva del pubblico. Il La Verde così descrive questa manifestazione:

> La Madonna, appena scorge il Figlio, ha un momento di esitazione, ma il Salvatore Le va decisamente incontro. La Madre Lo riconosce, il velo nero cade giù e i due si affrettano ad avvicinarsi come spinti da un forte desiderio di abbracciarsi e di baciarsi. Le sacre immagini della Madre e del Figlio, sollevate sulle bare ed inclinate, stanno per qualche secondo l'una di fronte all'altra come per parlarsi e scambiarsi parole d'affetto, mentre tutte le campane suonano a stormo e la musica esegue un'allegra e rumorosa marcia tradizionale. (96)

Quando le due statue si distaccano, il Cristo riparte velocemente ed in salita, seguendo il ritmo dell'allegra marcia. Lungo il percorso delle due statue, fanno fila gli sbandieratori, come se facessero arco per il passaggio di Cristo e della Madonna; il pubblico batte le mani a suon di musica. (foto 20)

Durante la settimana santa, Delia, cittadina di circa 4500 anime, ospita per le manifestazioni pasquali circa 30.000 persone. Alcuni fattori essenziali che hanno contribuito, secondo noi, al successo ormai secolare delle manifestazioni sono: 1) l'aver saputo saggiamente amministrare queste manifestazioni religiose; 2) l'aver saputo rinnovare i costumi, la scenografia e la musica, imbandendo anche concorsi a premi; 3) l'aver alimentato non solo la messinscena del testo dell'Orioles, ma anche un vasto complesso di tradizioni pasquali; 4) l'aver creato un vivaio di attori per queste rappresentazioni; 5) l'aver

---

11. Per ulteriori dettagli su queste manifestazioni, si vedano La Verde 74-113 e Caramanna.

saputo rendersi indipendenti anche per ciò che concerne i costumi, allestiti ormai localmente; 6) l'aver creato una specie di scuola per sbandieratori, ormai molto richiesti in altri paesi della Sicilia; 7) l'aver soprattutto ispirato i cittadini a preservare e vivere a pieno queste tradizioni. Grazie a questo attaccamento alle proprie tradizioni pasquali, dal 1977, il *Riscatto* dell'Orioles è riproposto regolarmente a Toronto (Canada) con il patrocinio del Delia Social and Cultural Centre.[12] (foto 21-22)

OPERE CITATE

Amico, Ugo Antonio. *Prefazione* a Orioles, Filippo. *La conquista di Gerosolima.* Palermo: Giannone e Lamantia, 1887.

Bancheri, Salvatore. "Una sacra rappresentazione settecentesca a Toronto". *Italian Canadiana* 7 (1991), 121-134.

Bancheri, Salvatore. "Nota critica" e "Nota filologica" a Orioles, Filippo. *Il riscatto d'Adamo nella morte di Gesù Cristo.* Edizione critica a cura di Salvatore Bancheri. Rovito (Cosenza): Marra Editore, 1995.

Barcellona, Damiano. "Prefazione" a F. Orioles. *Il Riscatto d'Adamo nella morte di Gesù Cristo.* Palermo: Scuola Arti Grafiche "D. Orione", 1967.

Buttitta, Ignazio. *Pasqua in Sicilia.* Palermo: Grafindustria editoriale, 1978.

Cammilleri, Andrea. *La scomparsa di Patò.* Milano: Mondari, 2000.

Caramanna, Pasquale. *La settimana santa a Delia.* Caltanissetta: Tipografia Lussografica, 1990.

Croce, Benedetto. *I teatri di Napoli dal Rinascimento, secolo XVI-XVIII.* Napoli: Pierro, 1891.

Croce, Benedetto. *I teatri di Napoli dal Rinascimento alla fine del secolo decimottavo.* 5ª ed. Bari: Laterza, 1966.

Ferrazzi, G.J. *Torquato Tasso. Studi biografici critici bibliografici.* Bassano: Pozzato, 1880.

Gervasium, Nicolaum. *Siculae sanctiones.* Palermo: Pietro Bentivegna, 1750-1752. 3 vols.

Il Giorno di Napoli. 7-8 aprile 1926, p. 3.

La Verde, Luigi. *Folklore di Delia.* Caltanissetta: Tipografia Lussografica, 1990.

Mira, Giuseppe Maria. *Bibliografia siciliana ovvero gran dizionario bibliografico delle opere edite e inedite, antiche e moderne di autori siciliani o di argomento siciliano stampate in Sicilia e fuori.* Vol. II. Palermo: 1875; rist. New York: Burt Franklin, 1960.

12. Si veda Bancheri, "Una sacra rappresentazione settecentesca."

Pitré, Giuseppe. *Spettacoli e feste popolari siciliane.* Vol. XII di *Biblioteca delle tradizioni popolari siciliane.* Palermo: Pedone Lauriel, 1881.

Sciascia, Leonardo. *A ciascuno il suo.* 5ª ed. Toronto: Einaudi, 1975.

Villabianca (marchese di), Francesco Maria Emanuele e Gioeni. *Diario Palermitano,* "Agosto 1793", t. VIII, p. 191. Manoscritto inedito, Biblioteca Comunale di Palermo, segnatura Qq D 100.

Zaccaria, Alfonso. "Venerdì Santo in Sicilia con "Mortorio"," *Cronache parlamentari siciliane* 17, No. 9-10 (1977), 481-486.

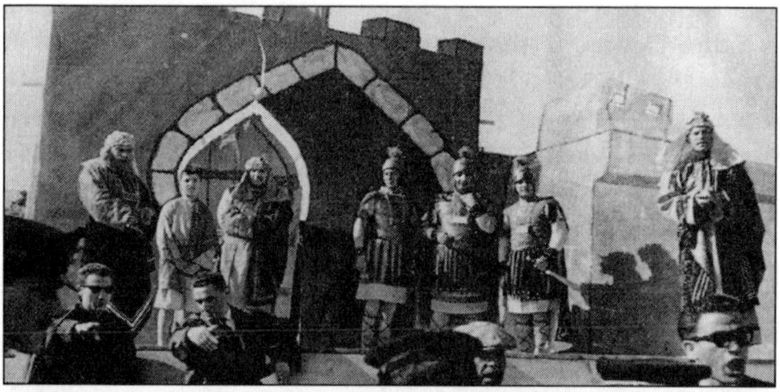

Foto 1

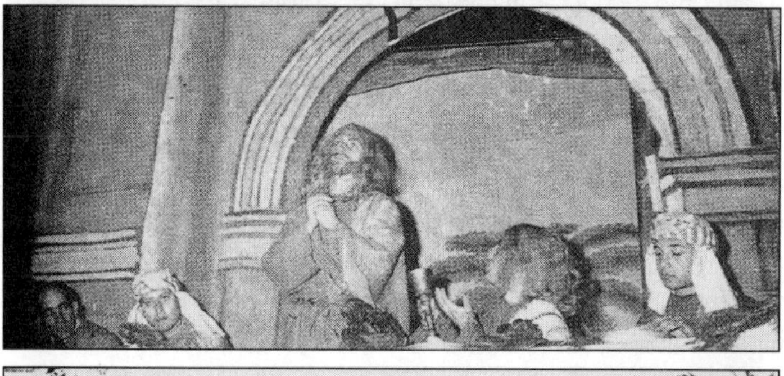

Foto 2

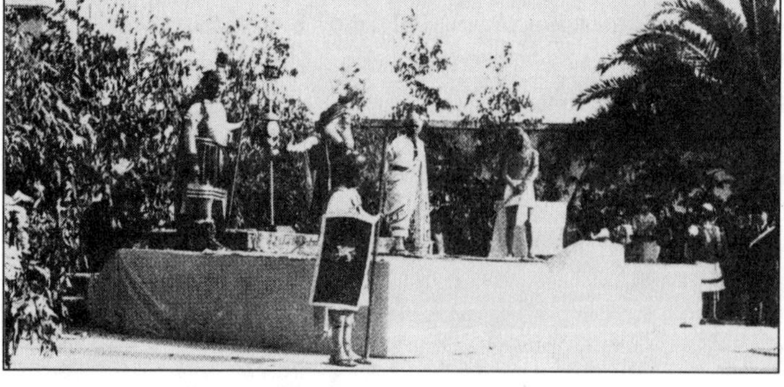

Foto 3

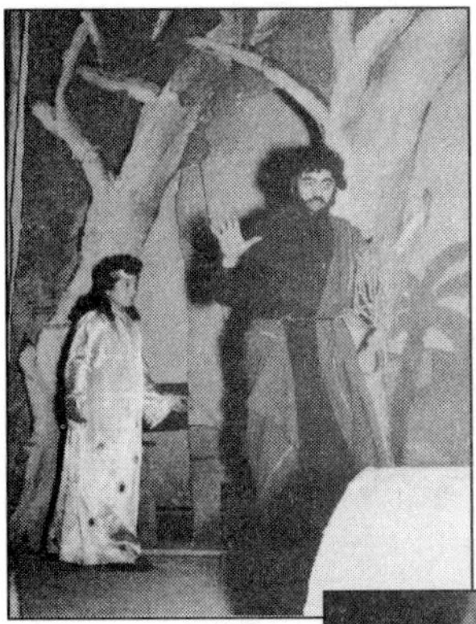

Foto 4

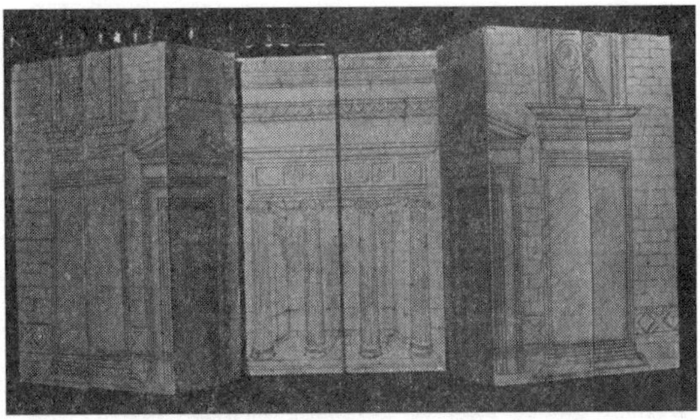

Foto 5

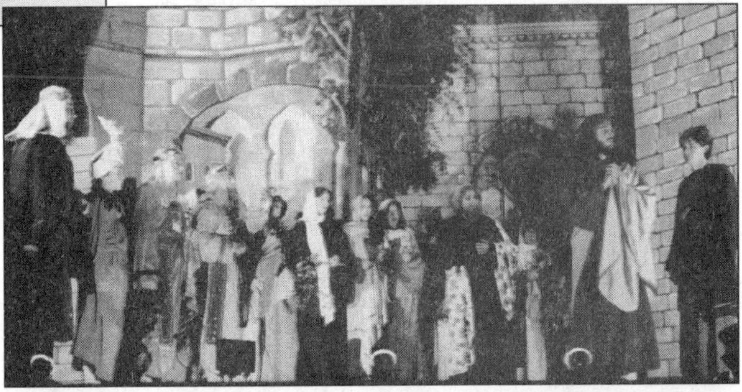

Foto 6

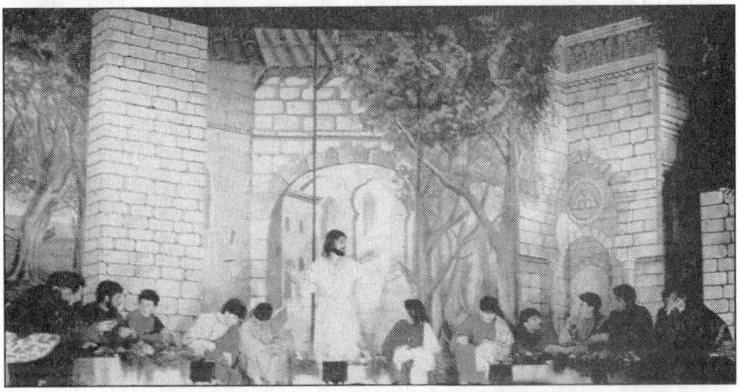

Foto 7

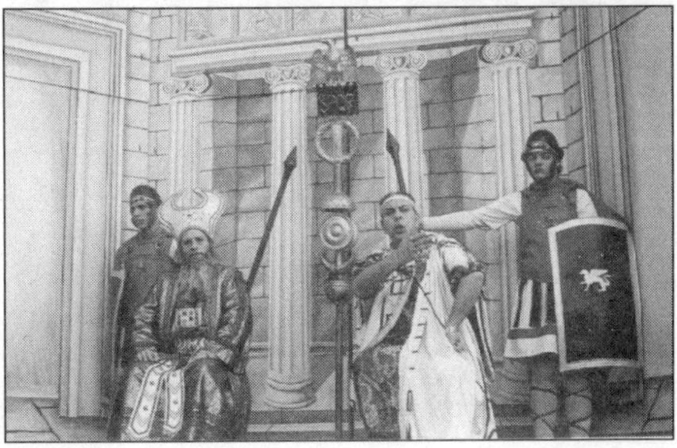

Foto 8

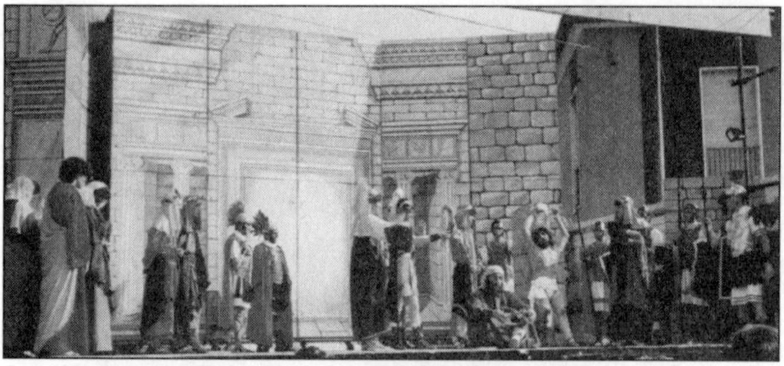

Foto 9

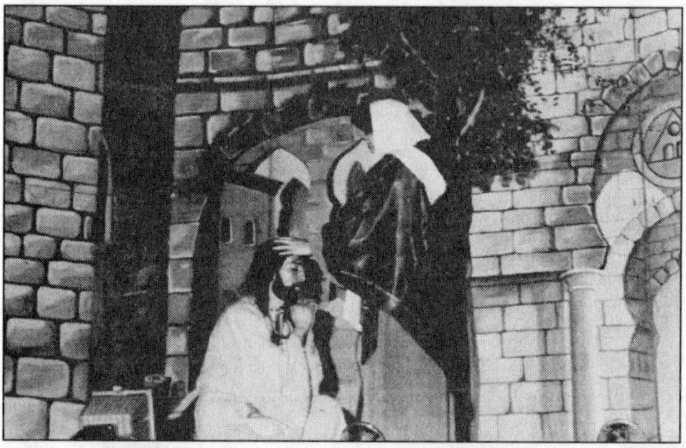

Foto 10

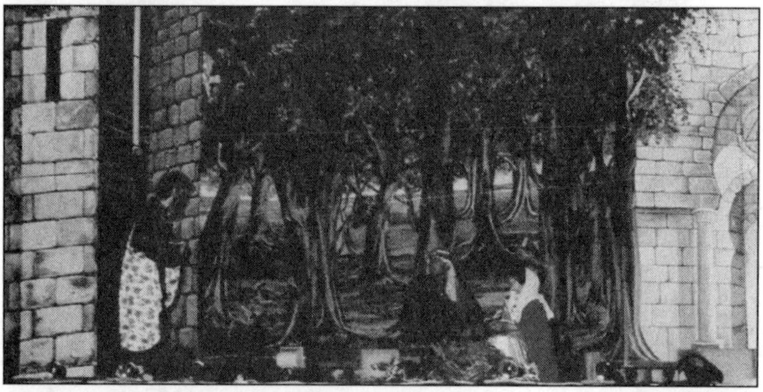

Foto 11

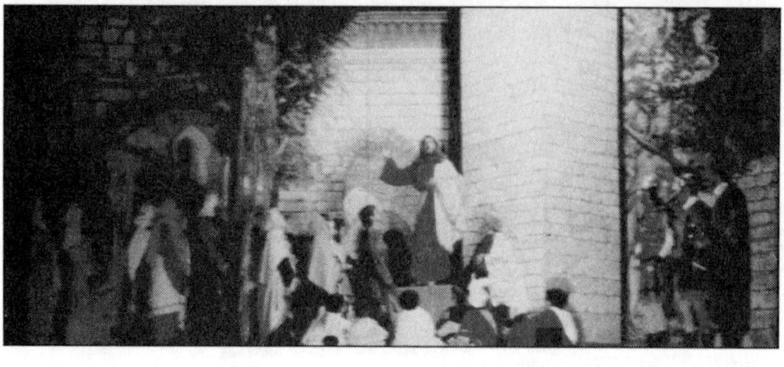

Foto 12

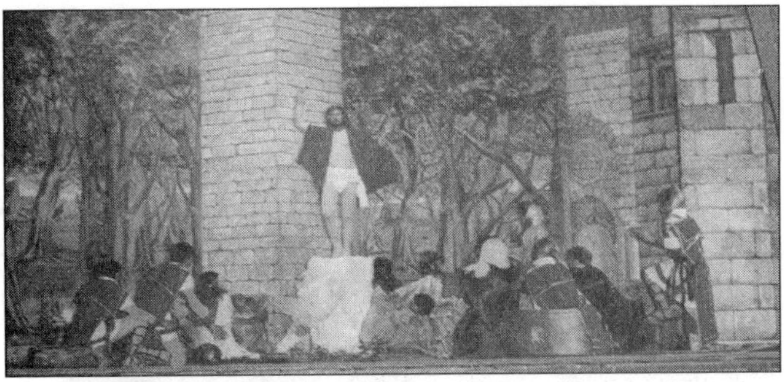

Foto 13

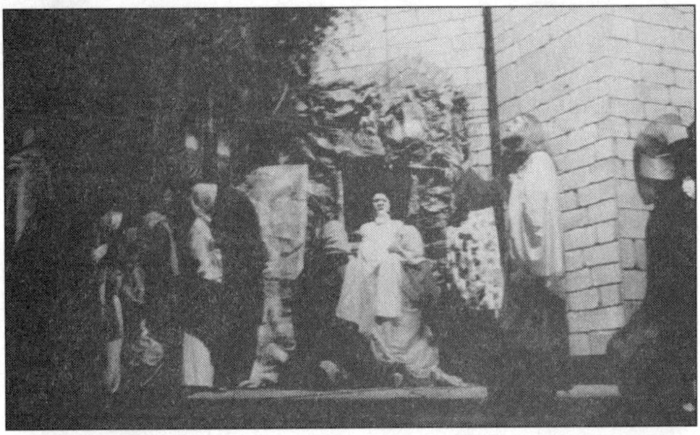

Foto 14

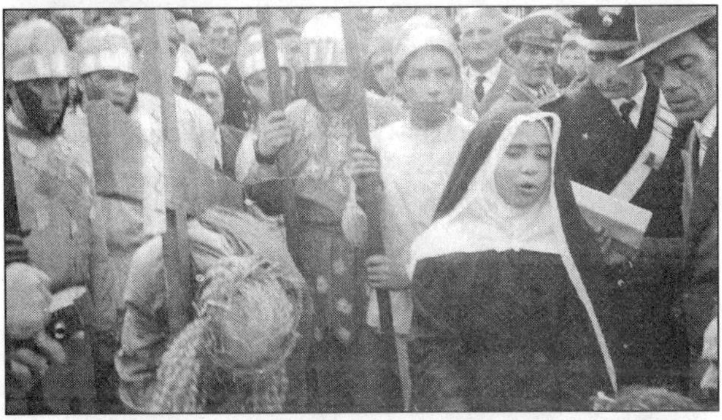

Foto 15

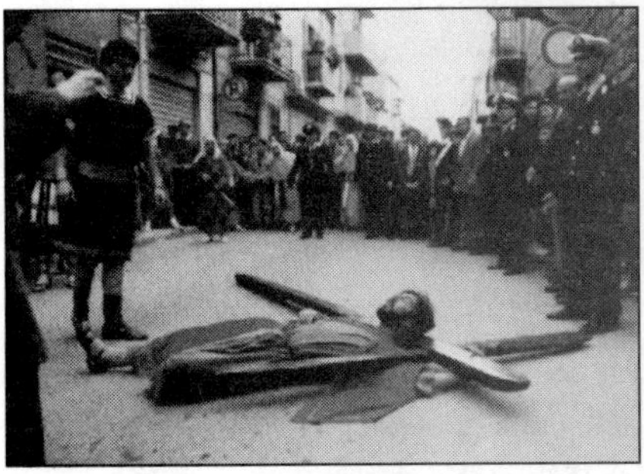

Foto 16

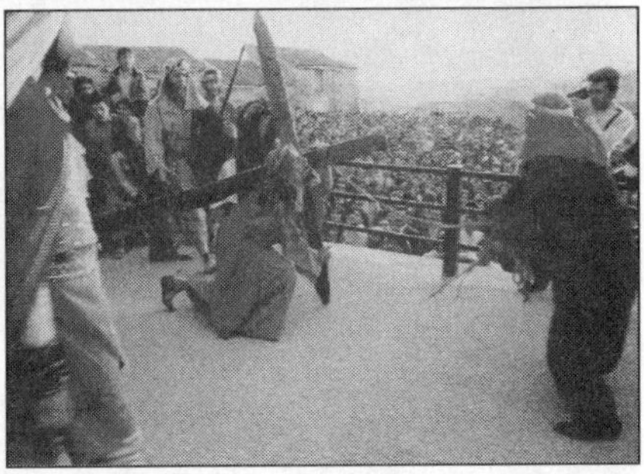

Foto 17

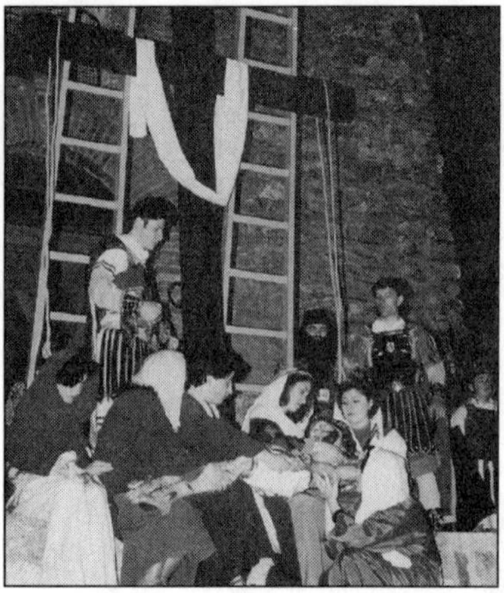

Foto 18

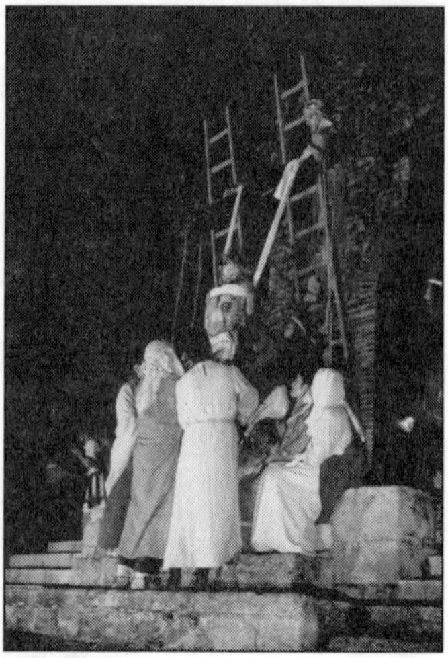

Foto 19

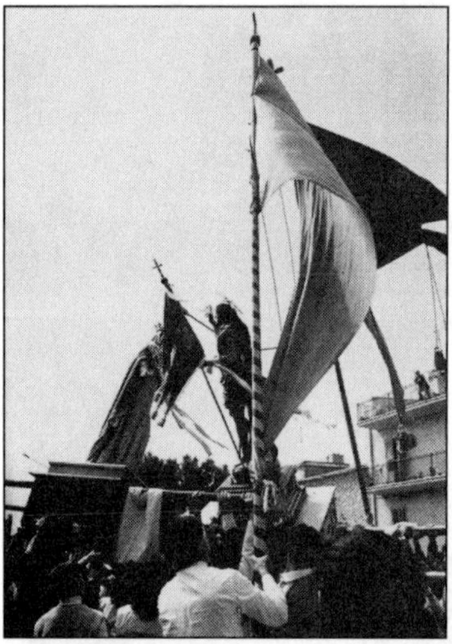

Foto 20

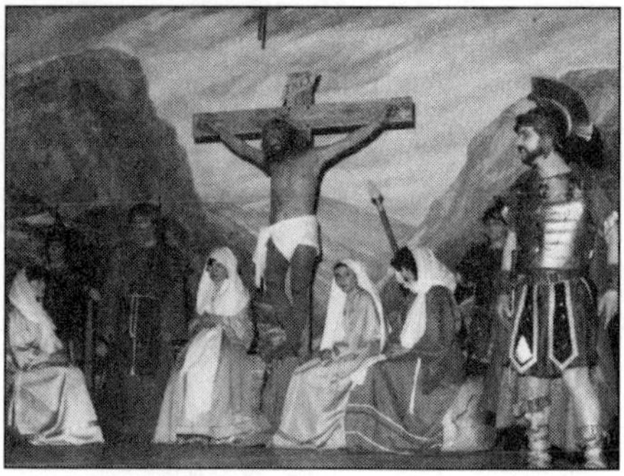

Foto 21

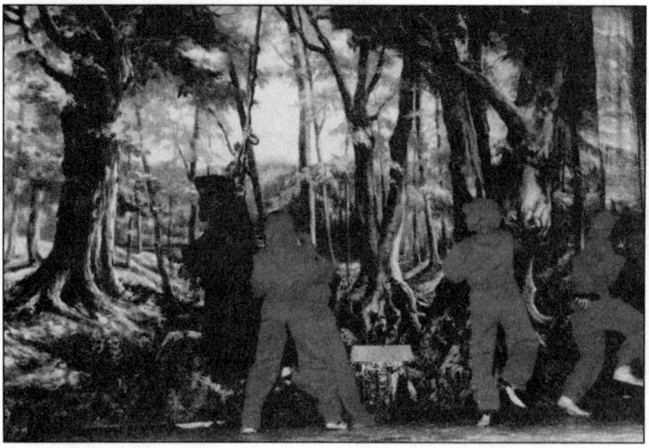

Foto 22

Visualizing the Restoration: "Neo-baroque" Costuming at the Stratford Festival

Nancy Copeland

University of Toronto at Mississauga

Although the Stratford Festival at Stratford, Ontario was founded in 1953 to stage Shakespeare's plays,[1] comedies of the "long Restoration"—the period of English drama between 1660 and about 1715— have formed part of its repertoire since 1964, when Michael Langham directed Wycherley's 1675 comedy, *The Country Wife*. Since then, as part of Stratford's inclusion of "an independent classical tradition, separate from the Shakespearean mandate" (Hayes 6), *The Country Wife* has been staged twice more; while *The Way of the World* and *Love for Love*, both by Congreve, *The Relapse* by Vanbrugh, and *The Beaux Stratagem* by Farquhar have been staged once each.[2] Although the *Stratford Festival 1999 Visitors' Guide* emphasizes the Festival's "matchless variety of theatrical entertainment" from "classic comedies" to "thrilling musicals"(3), the Festival remains the site of the most frequent, as well as the best documented, Canadian revivals of the English comedies of this period. Since, as with all revivals, productions of these plays involve the translation of an alien culture into a theatrical idiom that is accessible to its target audience, they are at least as much about current concepts of the "Restoration" as they are about the individual plays. This paper will focus on one aspect of this process—

1. The Festival was originally named the Stratford Shakespearean Festival, but in 1960, "Shakespeare" was removed from the title "in order to indicate its expanded mandate" (Hayes 6-7).

2. See Somerset for information on productions up to 1990. For an up-to-date list of productions see the Festival Archive webpage, accessible through the Festival's website (www.stratford-festival.on.ca). I have attended performances of all the Festival's productions of Restoration comedy except the 1964 *Country Wife*; the programs, etc. to which I refer are in my personal collection.

costume design. As the theatre scholar Jessica Munns has noted, in arguing for historically accurate design: "costume *is* a serious matter," a "language" "encoding ways of perceiving, thinking, seeing and being" (23-24). Equally, changing ideas about the late-Stuart period can be traced through twentieth-century costume design.

The Stratford Festival's Restoration programming participates in the established practices common to Great Britain and North America in being drawn from among the work of the "big five" canonical authors, of whom only Etherege has been overlooked at Stratford (Wertheim xvi). Its costuming practices equally take their place within the succession of stylistic paradigms through which the period has been conceptualized in the mainstream theatre. The first influential twentieth-century revivals of Restoration and eighteenth-century comedy, Nigel Playfair's in the 1920s, established a style that dominated mainstream productions of Restoration comedy until the 1960s (Nyberg 3-4). This style conveyed a concept of the period recalling Charles Lamb's famous characterization in his 1822 essay, "On the Artificial Comedy of the Last Century." In this essay, Lamb sought to defend these plays from their reputation for obscenity by arguing that they are "a world of themselves almost as much as fairy-land," without any applicability to social life (568). The twentieth century production style that realized this concept portrayed a play-world that was self-consciously artificial, exaggerated, and fantastic. For Playfair's 1924 production of Congreve's *The Way of the World* (1700), the costumes designed by Doris Zinkeisen "were 'as gorgeously polychromatic as possible.'. . ."[3] Simplified period silhouettes are rendered in Zinkeisen's designs in bright, contrasting solid colours: a bright orange coat and green waistcoat for the fashionable Mirabell; a green coat and raspberry stockings for the pretender to fashion, Witwoud; a raspberry gown over a powder blue petticoat for the genteel Mrs. Fainall; and a lime green coat with yellow trim, worn with raspberry gloves, for the villainous Mrs. Marwood. The heroine Millamant's pale blue satin gown over a three-tiered white petticoat, worn with a white headdress and a blonde wig, creates the effect of a wedding-cake ornament.[4] "Fantasticated," the epithet applied by the *Times* reviewer to this production, is used by J. L. Styan to characterize this influential concept of the "Restoration" as a whole (40).

A later example of "fantasticated" costuming is provided by Oliver Messel's designs for Tyrone Guthrie's 1936 Old Vic production of Wycherley's *The Country Wife*. Messel was part of the anti-modernist,

3. A. B. Walkley *Times* rev. qtd. Styan 39.

4. For Zinkeisen's designs see Playfair *Story of the Lyric Theatre*, facing 165, 180, 184; for the realized costumes see Playfair *Hammersmith* 256 and Styan 97.

painterly school of post W.W.I English theatre designers, whose work was characterized by "formalised or highly decorative elements."[5] The catalogue to the posthumous exhibition of his work in 1983 described him as "essentially a pastiche-maker from historical styles" and the design historian Sybil Rosenfeld identified his "poetic imagination and a sense of period fantasy" as distinguishing traits (Pinkham 22, 34). His designs for *The Country Wife* epitomize these qualities. The costumes were aestheticized fantasies based on period styles that combined bold stripes, oversized, stylized brocade patterns, strong contrasts, and exaggerated shapes to produce a decorative, almost cartoon-like effect.[6]

In the 1960s the "fairy-land" conception of the period's drama was briefly displaced by one that stressed the social reality of the plays, with a corresponding change from decorative to functional design. The frivolous irrelevance of the earlier style was opposed by an attempt to treat the plays as examples of gritty social realism (Trussler 9). The watershed production for this stylistic shift was the version of Farquhar's *The Recruiting Officer* (1706) directed by William Gaskill for the National Theatre in 1963. Gaskill was "partly influenced" by the Berliner Ensemble production of Brecht's *Trumpets and Drums*, an adaptation of Farqhuar's play, which had toured to London in 1956 (Gaskill 56). In rehearsal, Gaskill distinguished a "small town realism" suitable for *The Recruiting Officer*, with its Shrewsbury setting, from the "urban airs and graces" appropriate to staging Congreve (Farquhar 14). The design was by René Allio, who had designed Brecht-inspired productions for Roger Planchon at the Théâtre de la Cité in Villeurbanne (Daoust 16). His costumes for *The Recruiting Officer* were simple and realistic —in the sense of looking like clothes, rather than costumes— but they were not precisely historically accurate. For example, Gaskill remarked that "the men looked better in the shorter tie-back hair" of a later period, so the attractive men, Plume and Worthy, did not wear the long wig fashionable in 1706, when the play was first performed (Gaskill 56). Similarly the women's hair-styles were more twentieth- than eighteenth-century and their costumes evoked the period in their silhouette but not in their details. But overall the costumes offered a striking contrast to the fantastic creations of the earlier style, thus creating an impression of realism.[7] This approach to the period had a vogue in Britain in the sixties and the early seventies, when it was applied to a range of playwrights, including Congreve

5. Sybil Rosenfeld in Pinkham 34.
6. Black and white photographs of these costumes are reproduced in Styan 85, 142, 249, in Castle 105, and in Pinkham, figs. 42 and 43.
7. Tynan's edition of the play, which is a record of Gaskill's production, is copiously illustrated with black and white production photographs.

(Nyberg 7).[8] At Stratford, the influence of this kind of realism could be seen in Daphne Dare's elegant, subdued period costumes for *The Way of the World* in 1976, which complimented the "simplicity and straightforwardness" of Robin Phillips's approach to the play (Fraser 15).[9] Productions are still designed in this style,[10] but its legacy can be seen mainly in the "natural" or realistic costume that has formed part of the eclectic "Restoration" design vocabulary since the 1970s.

The dominant style since the 1970s has been characterized by Lennart Nyberg as "the stylized and theatrical mode" (11-13). In costuming this mode has resulted in a return of artificiality and exaggeration, often transmuted into the grotesque. An early example, a production of Vanbrugh's *The Relapse* (1696) directed by Trevor Nunn for the Royal Shakespeare Company in 1967, featured a "gorgeous" design by Christopher Morley, which included costumes that were "predominantly silver, with contrasting pinks" (Marcus 38). The centrepiece of the production was Lord Foppington, a "coxcomb" who imagines himself to be the pinnacle of fashion. Donald Sinden's extravagant appearance in the role, "a rouged puppet" in an enormous "rose-pink" wig and a knee-length waistcoat with a wired hem, was partly indebted to the female impersonator Danny LaRue.[11]

Nunn's juxtaposition of such "grotesque theatrical exuberance" with "scenes of low-key naturalism" was criticized by some reviewers as "a sign of stylistic inconsistency" according to Nyberg (10), but stylistic inconsistency has become the norm for late-twentieth-century productions. The eclecticism of these productions often juxtaposes "natural," or (quasi-) "realistic" design with artificiality, within overall concepts that may freely mix period styles and degrees of fantasy and exaggeration. This is essentially a postmodern approach to the plays that picks up on their potentially "neo-baroque" elements: theatricality; startling juxtapositions and other manifestations of the grotesque; hybridity; a delight in surfaces and in the pleasure of spectacle, and "a strong sense of contrivance … and artifice" (Turner 28) — aspects of the baroque that have an affinity with postmodernism.[12]

8. Peter Wood's 1965 production of Congreve's *Love for Love* for the National Theatre, with costumes by Lila de Nobili, was a particularly notable and successful example of this style (see also Trussler 9).

9. The program for the production included five black and white photographs.

10. For example, Peter Hartwell's designs for Max Stafford Clark's 1988 production of *The Recruiting Officer* for the Royal Court.

11. Marcus 39; Irving Wardle *The Times* (18 August 1967), qtd. Nyberg 10; Sinden 168-169. Styan reproduces a photograph of Sinden's Foppington (53).

12. See also Moyes. I have taken the term "neo-baroque" from Calabrese, although the analogies between the baroque and neo-baroque which are relevant to my argument differ from his.

This "neo-baroque" style has become the norm for Restoration comedy at the Stratford Festival. Although the designs for these productions are based on historical research and contribute to "period" productions, they embody a "neo-baroque" aesthetic. Within many productions, a particular kind of eclecticism prevails: within an overall design concept, central and normative characters are costumed "naturally" or "realistically," while fops and other eccentric or satirized characters are costumed extravagantly, or grotesquely. An early example is provided by Desmond Heeley's designs for *The Country Wife*, directed by Richard Cottrell in 1983, which subtly mixed period styles. For example, the naïve Margery Pinchwife, when at home, wore a "natural" costume: a pretty, simply-constructed full-skirted dress in a pastel floral pattern, accessorized with a lacy scarf, apron, and mob cap. This design was apparently inspired by the simpler styles of the early Georgian period (1714-1727) rather than by the more rigid and formal styles of the 1670s when the play was written, or by the loose, informal "undress" of the same period. On the other hand, the cuckold Sir Jasper Fidget wore the extravagant full breeches, long brocaded coat, and broad brimmed hat —lavishly decorated with ruffles, lace, and feathers — that would have been fashionable in 1675, when the play was first performed. His worldly, adulterous wife, Lady Fidget, was dressed in the style of the 1690s, with an elaborate, towering hair style and head piece. In both cases, the effect was one of grotesque (and in Sir Jasper's case, ludicrous) artificiality.[13]

Ann Curtis's lavish costumes for David William's 1990 production of Congreve's *Love for Love* and for Douglas Campbell's 1995 production of *The Country Wife*, present variations on this underlying concept. In *Love for Love*, the lovers, Angelica and Valentine, were dressed in sumptuous but comparatively "realistic" period style. In the production's signature image, reproduced on a publicity postcard as well as in the program, Valentine wears a conspicuously natural-looking wig and Angelica wears a white brocade jacket, typical of her costumes throughout the production. Within the overall design plot her colour scheme suggested her moral superiority to the other characters, while also being in better taste than the costumes of the other women in the play. These normative characters were surrounded by emblematically costumed grotesques who, along with the Jacobean architecture of the set, brought out the play's debt to humours comedy. Sir Sampson Legend, Valentine's father, was gaudily dressed in red and gold that corresponded to his combustible temperament. Scandal, Valentine's "free speaking" friend, known for murdering reputations, was a

13. For designs and photographs of the costumes, see the 1983 souvenir program, the production program, and Prosser.

funereal presence dressed completely in black, with a black wig and unnaturally white face, suggesting that he suffered from an excess of black bile. Mrs. Frail, a "woman of the town" with "no great stock of … reputation," was costumed in bright orange, with hair to match.[14]

The 1995 *Country Wife* introduced Horner, the sexual predator, in a dressing gown that exposed his pox-scabs, but sought to convey the "foulness" of the fop Sparkish through a frothy fantasy of cream brocade and lace accessorized with lavender-tinted spectacles, using "the colours you find in bad cheese" to represent this character's (and others') "putrefaction."[15] Curtis's Margery Pinchwife, like Heeley's, wore a simpler gown than the other women, but its gold brocade was, significantly, decorated with small lavender bows — suggesting, in the light of Curtis's comments, her propensity for immorality. The virtuous Alithea stood out by appearing in an understated, natural costume, which included a "handkerchief" covering her bosom.[16]

Susan Benson's costumes for Richard Monette's 1989 production of *The Relapse* clearly convey the similarity between the post-seventies "theatricalized" style and the "aestheticized" style of the first part of the twentieth century. Predictably, the most extreme designs were worn by Lord Foppington, whose costumes were "fantasias of gaudy colours and synthetic glitter" (Copeland 266), that one reviewer compared successively to "a Baroque church" and "Hindu temples," as the colour scheme moved from purple to gold (Conlogue C7; Sidnell 159). Benson's designs did not make a clear distinction between "realistic" and grotesque characters, or between the "natural" and the artificially social. Instead, they created an overall impression of complete artificiality and contributed substantially to the production's effect of over-the-top fantasy. The central couple, Loveless and his wife, Amanda, were colour-coordinated in purple costumes and red wigs; while their tempters to adultery, Berinthia and Worthy, were dressed in white and black respectively — colour schemes that also included their wigs, which in Berinthia's case was an enormous, tousled platinum creation. The rustic characters were costumed in keeping with a dominant pumpkin motif: orange and brown dominated, and the Nurse was padded to "resemble the vegetable in shape, as well as in color…" (Copeland 266).

The "neo-baroque" aesthetic in Restoration costuming is well-suited to the house style of the Festival, which, as Richard Knowles has pointed out in writing about its Shakespeare productions, is characterized by a consistent "'to-be-looked-at-ness'" that is the product of "[t]he sheer quality of the work done by Stratford's staff—

14. Congreve, dramatis personae and 2.1.441; Copeland 1, 2.

15. Ann Curtis, note on the costumes in the 1995 *Souvenir Programme* 22.

16. See the production photographs in the 1995 *Souvenir Programme* 20, 21. 23.

and the expectation of excellence-on-parade that this has produced over the years . . ." ("Shakespeare" 216).[17] As a result, the productions become at least as much about "Stratford" —specifically the tradition of lavish, beautiful costuming— as they are about the specific play being staged. At best, the two elements may coincide: Kate Taylor's review of Campbell's *Country Wife* observed that the design "builds up a suffocating mass of material wealth" putting "the overwrought design that is typical of Stratford these days . . . to good thematic purpose" (C1). In contrast, Michael Sidnell commented of Monette's *Relapse* that it "emphatically played Restoration theatre," rather than the "social truth" of the libertine relapse that gives the play its title (159).

Indeed, whatever the intentions of the production team and the qualities of the individual plays, these productions stage a common concept of the Restoration. The "neo-baroque" style that has dominated the post-seventies designs at Stratford combines with the Festival's lavish house style to produce a "Restoration" that is a postmodern "fairy-land:" it includes the grotesque, and sometimes —especially in Ann Curtis's designs— conveys some of the plays' social satire, but it nonetheless recalls the aestheticized escapism of the productions from the first part of the century through its overwhelming artificiality and extravagant "otherness." Despite concepts as different as Curtis's and Benson's, the effect of the common extravagance and conspicuous consumption of the designs predominates. They consequently help to perpetuate the common twentieth century conception of Restoration drama identified by Simon Shepherd: "parochial" rather than "universal," frivolous, "neither humanly relevant nor theatrically profound" (Shepherd and Womack 178).

This is the view of the period that the social realist productions of the sixties and seventies were intended to combat. Another alternative is presented by a kind of "neo-baroque" design that has yet to be applied to plays of this period at the Stratford Festival: postmodern metaphoric productions of the sort that are commonplaces of Shakespeare production. They too are characterized by eclecticism, theatricality, and artifice, but in such productions the metaphor is specific to the play, not the period. They provide a specificity that is missing from the Stratford designs and assert the meaningfulness of the plays to their late-twentieth century audience. An excellent example is provided by Anthony Ward's designs for Phyllida Lloyd's Royal National Theatre production of *The Way of the World* in 1995. The costumes were conflations of period and contemporary styles that

---

17. "To-be-looked-at-ness" is Laura Mulvey's term for the connotation of women in their "traditional exhibitionist role," in which "their appearance [is] coded for strong visual and erotic impact" (33).

repeatedly led critics to invoke Vivienne Westwood's designs, themselves examples of postmodern pastiche, often inspired by baroque costume (McRobbie 110). The fop Witwoud was described by one reviewer as "a dead ringer for Malcolm McClaren," Westwood's erstwhile partner in punk, "in flyaway ginger hair and loud checked suit." The underlying concept was interpreted by John Peters in the *Sunday Times*: "Anthony Ward's designs, modern but with a baroque flamboyance, are a silent comment on the fact that our society, like Congreve's, is intensely fashion-conscious and almost bigotedly unrestrained...."[18] A contrasting example is provided by Catherine Armstrong's costumes for the 1994 production of Aphra Behn's *The Rover* (1677) directed by Jules Wright for the Women's Playhouse Trust. The central directorial concept, which conveyed the national divisions in Behn's play through multi-racial casting intended to evoke"gender and power relations in contemporary London," was extended by the costuming (Goodman 178).[19] The expatriate Englishmen were costumed in white linen suits, the local characters wore pajama-like tunics and loose pants, and the courtesan outsider was costumed in traditional South Asian dress. This kind of metaphoric design, like Ward's, suggests that, in the words of postmodernist director Peter Sellers, "[a] classic is a house we're still living in...."[20]

The "neo-baroque" Restoration produced by the Festival designers, on the other hand, is remote both from the historical difference inscribed in the plays and from the immediate circumstances of their reproduction. It is, instead, a standardized product suited to an industrial model of theatrical production usually associated with corporations such as Livent, for which, as Alex Fallis writes in an article about the international tour of *The Phantom of the Opera*, "[t]he product is the same the world over" (42-43). Knowles has argued convincingly that the Stratford Festival of the last two decades is also "a *multi*national theatrical corporation" that produces a "corporate bard, appropriated in the service of globalization" ("Nationalist" 41). The "neo-baroque" Restoration that has prevailed at Stratford during the same decades is the corporate form of this "not Renaissance" component of the repertoire (Shepherd and Womack 178), which elides the historical specificity, social content, and individual qualities of the plays within a generalized period style that is more powerful than any individual production concept. Despite attempts at specificity and relevance such

18. Michael Coveney *Observer* 22.10.95; John Peters *Sunday Times* 29.10.95. These and other reviews of the production are collected in *Theatre Record* 15 (8-21 October 1995).

19. Goodman's essay includes numerous black and white production photographs.

20. Qtd. in John Lahr, "Inventing the Enemy," *New Yorker* (18 October 1993): 103, qtd. Green 173.

as Horner's pox scabs, this monolithic style contributes to an unfortunate perception of the era and its plays as frivolous and decadent, but not particularly significant.

WORKS CITED

Calabrese, Omar. *Neo-Baroque: A Sign of the Times*. Trans. Charles Lambert. Princeton: Princeton UP, 1992.

Castle, Charles. *Oliver Messel*. London: Thames and Hudson, 1986.

Congreve, William. *Love for Love*. Ed. Emmet L. Avery. Lincoln: University of Nebraska Press, 1966.

Conlogue, Ray. "Lavish production dulls comedy's cynical edge." *The Globe and Mail* (31 July 1989): C7.

Copeland, Nancy. Review of *The Relapse*, by Sir John Vanbrugh. Stratford Festival, Stratford, Ontario. 22 August 1989. *Theatre Journal* 42.2 (1990): 266-267.

Copeland, Nancy. Unpublished review of *Love for Love*, by William Congreve. Stratford Festival. 24 July 1990.

Daoust, Yvette. *Roger Planchon: Director and Playwright*. Cambridge: Cambridge UP, 1981.

Fallis, Alex. "Singapore: Notes from a *Phantom* Tour." *CTR: Canadian Theatre Review* 85 (Winter 1995): 42-44.

Farquhar, George. *The Recruiting Officer*. Ed. Kenneth Tynan. London: Rupert Hart Davis, 1965.

Fraser, John. "Way of the World a triumph of wit and elegance." *The Globe and Mail* (8 June 1976): 15.

Gaskill, William. *A Sense of Direction: Life at the Royal Court*. London and Boston: Faber and Faber, 1988.

Goodman, Lizbeth. "*The Rover* in performance." *Shakespeare, Aphra Behn and the Canon*. Ed. W. R. Owens and Lizbeth Goodman. London and New York: Routledge, 1996. 175-190.

Green, Amy S. *The Revisionist Stage: American Directors Reinvent the Classics*. Cambridge: Cambridge UP, 1994.

Hayes, Elliott. "Stratford: A Classical Tradition." Stratford Festival Souvenir Magazine. Toronto: Canadian Controlled Media Communications, 1989. 6-10.

Knowles, Richard Paul."From Nationalist to Mulitnational: The Stratford Festival, Free Trade, and the Discourses of Intercultural Tourism." *Theatre Journal* 47.1 (1995): 19-41.

Knowles, Richard Paul. "Shakespeare, 1993, and the Discourses of the Stratford Festival, Ontario." *Shakespeare Quarterly* 45 (1994): 211-225.

Lamb, Charles. "On the Artificial Comedy of the Last Century." *Restoration and Eighteenth Century Comedy*. Ed. Scott McMillin. 2nd ed. New York: W. W. Norton, 1997. 567-572.

Marcus, Frank. "Behind the Masks." *Plays and Players* (October 1967): 37-39.

McRobbie, Angela. *British Fashion Design: Rag Trade or Image Industry?* London and New York: Routledge, 1998.

Moyes, Lianne. Introduction. "Contemporary Feminist Baroque." *Tessera* 24 (Summer 1998): 8- 23.

Mulvey, Laura. "Visual Pleasure and Narrative Cinema." *Issues in Feminist Film Criticism*. Ed. Patricia Erens. Bloomington and Indianapolis: Indiana University Press, 1990. 28-40.

Munns, Jessica. "*The Wives' Excuse Or Cuckolds Make Themselves* at the Swan Theatre Stratford-on-Avon, Summer 1994." *Restoration and Eighteenth Century Theatre Research*, 2nd series, 10.2 (1995): 17-31.

Nyberg, Lennart. "Restoration Comedy in the Modern British Theatre." *Restoration and Eighteenth Century Theatre Research*, 2nd series, 10. 2 (1995): 1-16.

Pinkham, Roger, ed. *Oliver Messel. An Exhibition at the Theatre Museum. Victoria and Albert Museum. 22 June-30 October 1983*. London: Victoria and Albert Museum, 1983.

Playfair, Nigel. *Hammersmith Hoy: A Book of Minor Revelations*. London: Faber and Faber, 1930.

Playfair, Nigel. *The Story of the Lyric Theatre Hammersmith*. London: Chatto and Windus, 1925.

[Prosser, David, ed.] *Dross Into Gold: The Theatre Alchemy of Desmond Heeley*. Stratford: The Gallery/Stratford, 1997.

Shepherd, Simon and Peter Womack. *English Drama: A Cultural History*. Oxford: Blackwell, 1996.

Sidnell, Michael J. "Representing Theatre: Stratford's 1989 Season." *Journal of Canadian Studies* 24 .4 (Winter 1989-90): 149-160.

Sinden, Donald. *Laughter in the Second Act*. London: Hoddert and Stoughton, 1985.

Somerset, J. Allan B. *The Stratford Festival Story: A Catalogue-Index to the Stratford, Ontario Festival 1953-1990*. New York, Westport, London: Greenwood Press, 1991.

Souvenir Programme 1995. Stratford Shakespearean Festival Foundation of Canada, 1995.

Styan, J. L. *Restoration Comedy in Performance*. Cambridge: Cambridge UP, 1986.

Taylor, Kate. "Country Wife Redeems Stratford." *The Globe and Mail* (5 June 1995): C1.

Theatre Record 15 (8-21 October 1995): 1448-1453.

Trussler, Simon."Rich and Filthy." *Plays and Players* (July 1998): 8-10.

Turner, Bryan S. "Recent Developments in the Theory of the Body." *The Body: Social Process and Cultural Theory*. Ed. Mike Featherstone, Mike Hepworth, and Bryan Turner. London: Sage, 1991. 1-35.

Wertheim, Albert. "Restoration Drama: The Second Flowering of the English Theatre." *Kiss and Tell: Restoration Monologues, Scenes, and Historical Context*. Ed. Michael Dixon and Michele Volansky. Newbury, VT: Smith and Kraus, 1993. x-xxiv.

"Your Guide to the Stratford Experience." *Stratford Festival 1999 Visitors' Guide*. Stratford: Stratford Festival, 1999. 3.

La figlia di Iorio di Gabriele d'Annunzio: un secolo di messe in scena

Enzo Zappulla

Istituto di Storia dello Spettacolo Siciliano, Catania

D'accordo con Eleonora Duse, alla cui interpretazione inizialmente la tragedia pastorale *La figlia di Iorio* è destinata, già nel settembre 1903, appena terminatane la stesura, Gabriele d'Annunzio, per il tramite di Adolfo Orvieto, ha cercato un contatto con Virgilio Talli, capocomico della più rinomata Compagnia nazionale dell'epoca.

In un colloquio alla Capponcina, ove Talli si è recato a trovare il poeta conosciuto negli anni giovanili trascorsi al collegio Cicognini di Prato, si convenne che d'Annunzio avrebbe affidato alla «Compagnia Talli-Gramatica-Calabresi» la messa in scena de *La figlia di Iorio* purché il capocomico «avesse reso possibile l'altissima collaborazione di Eleonora Duse alle prime recite della tragedia che si sarebbero fissate, in un successivo incontro, per Milano, Firenze e Roma»[1]. Accanto alla Duse d'Annunzio pensò, come protagonista della tragedia, a Gualtiero Tumiati che, precipitatosi alla Capponcina, provò «la gioia folle di ascoltare (forse il primo!) la *Figlia di Iorio* dalla sua viva voce», ma il progetto non ebbe seguito probabilmente perché se Talli poteva essere disponibile a sacrificare la Gramatica per la Duse non altrettanto intendeva fare nei confronti di Ruggero Ruggeri per Tumiati.

I preliminari per la messa in scena della tragedia proseguono con difficoltà: d'Annunzio insiste con Talli (è del 26 dicembre una lunga lettera in tal senso del poeta al capocomico) sull'opportunità che alla Duse siano riservate alcune rappresentazioni a Milano, Firenze e Roma; Talli, pur volendo soddisfare le richieste del poeta, ha di fronte una serie di problemi organizzativi anche in relazione agli impegni degli impresari del teatro «Niccolini» di Firenze e «Costanzi» di Roma circa

1. Virgilio Talli, *La mia vita di teatro, I, Memorie*, Milano, Treves, 1927, p. 165.

la possibilità di consentire la prosecuzione della *tournée* dopo le recite milanesi; Eleonora Duse e la sua compagnia, dal canto loro, sono vincolati con contratti inderogabili con teatri di Berlino e Vienna. L'attrice è libera soltanto per il mese di marzo e si è già ai primi di gennaio. Intanto sulla stampa appaiono con sempre maggiore frequenza notizie di una malattia seria della Duse che rischia di pregiudicarne la partecipazione al grande, atteso avvenimento artistico.

Il 14 gennaio 1904, a Milano, d'Annunzio firma il contratto con la «Compagnia Talli-Gramatica-Calabresi» e lo stesso giorno ne dà notizia all'amico Michetti chiedendogli di occuparsi delle scene e dei costumi.

Intanto le voci sulla malattia della Duse diventano sempre più preoccupanti e si teme non possa prendere parte alla rappresentazione milanese. E provvidenziale dovette apparire a d'Annunzio (già preso da una nuova fiamma, la duchessa Alessandra Starrabba di Rudinì, giovanissima vedova Carlotti) la malattia dell'attrice, troppo diafana, spirituale forse, per dar vita al personaggio passionale e selvaggio di Mila di Codra che meglio si attagliava alla personalità nervosa e sensuale della Gramatica. «Ho pensato a lungo a questa circostanza del mancato concorso della Duse — scrive il 20 gennaio 1904 Marco Praga a Virgilio Talli — e ne ho concluso che in ciò può essere del cattivo e del buono. Certo è che mancherà una grande attrattiva alle recite di Milano»[2]. Da quel momento il nome della Duse non è più pronunciato nelle conversazioni intorno alla messa in scena e d'Annunzio, nel corso del colloquio avuto col Talli a Verona il 30 gennaio, lo prega «di invitare Irma Gramatica ad assistere alla lettura della tragedia che egli avrebbe fatta alle tre del pomeriggio in quello stesso salone del "Londres" dove stavamo parlando»[3].

Alla lettura, durata quattr'ore, «nitida, lineare, senza musicalità distraenti», furono presenti Irma Gramatica, Teresa Franchini, Ruggero Ruggeri, Oreste Calabresi e Virgilio Talli, «tutti seduti in cerchio attorno a d'Annunzio». Ricorda Virgilio Talli:

> d'Annunzio *disse* i tre atti con cadenze ritmiche. E di scena in scena, d'atto in atto, quelle cadenze rifuggenti da ogni speciale armonia si foggiavano invece in un crescendo di armonie, fino a diventare musica, musica liturgica, canto fermo. Nessun commento durante i silenzi degli intermezzi. Ognuno avrebbe voluto liberarsi della propria emozione, ma nessuno lo osò per rispetto a quelle ore di raccoglimento che assunsero importanza di cerimonia [4].

Così Irma Gramatica molti anni dopo:

2. *Ibidem.*
3. *Ibidem.*
4. *Ibidem.*

La lettura a viva voce dell'opera era certo il contributo più diretto che d'Annunzio desse all'allestimento d'un suo lavoro. Egli era un dicitore inimitabile. Risento ancora il modo con cui, mentre il poeta scandiva o mirabilmente cantilenava gli avvenimenti della sua saga abruzzese, quelle cadenze letteralmente si imprimevano nella mia memoria. Il mio lavoro d'interprete ne fu facilitato, semplificato. Posso dire, con modestia e orgoglio insieme, che la mia creazione fu opera sua: io fonografai sulla scena i suoi ritmi. La mia *Mila* era sua; e per questo forse egli da allora mi chiamò sempre, non col mio nome, ma la sua *Mila*, la sua «Mila Selvaggia»[5].

E Ruggero Ruggeri rievocando la profonda impressione di quella lettura: «Particolarmente intensa fu la mia silenziosa commozione. Trovavo finalmente l'interpretazione che da tanto tempo il mio amore per la poesia si augurava»[6].

La decisione di mettere in scena la tragedia senza la Duse rappresentò per l'attrice un grave colpo. Da Cannes, dove s'era recata per riposare, il 9 dicembre 1903 manifesta la sua disperazione per la forzata rinunzia:

> Allora — è deciso! — Gabri — dolcezza forza — speranza — sola cosa forte e dolorosa di vita mia! — È deciso! — Io pure dico «Amen» — e così sia!
>
> Avrò con questo tutto donato per la tua bella sorte — e se il core mi si rompe — ora quest'ultima volta... e così sia!
>
> Ho sperato, mi sono illusa — ho sperato che una buona Luce avrebbe illuminato di pazienza — e che avremmo potuto attendere prima di tutto donare. — Non si può!
>
> Hai donato la Figlia di I. — L'ho donata io pure, per te, per la tua bella sorte, — e che il core se ne vada a pezzetti, non conta — non conta! Ricordati un giorno — che profondo amore — è quello che lo dona altrui[7]!

Vent'anni dopo, nel 1924, sull' «Illustrazione Italiana», Matilde Serao narra di aver assistito, affascinata e sgomenta, al capezzale della Duse, seriamente inferma nel corpo e nell'anima, per il dolore di non essere lei la protagonista della tragedia, ad un'esclusiva e straordinaria interpretazione de *La figlia di Iorio*:

> E il grido, sì, il grido prorompente: — Era mia, era mia e me l'hanno presa! — Ed ecco l'ammalata tira fuori, da sotto l'origliere, il copione

5. *Nascita di Mila di Codra*, «Scenario», numero speciale su *D'Annunzio e il Teatro*, aprile 1938, p. 185.

6. Ivi, p. 192.

7. Renzo Martinelli, *Come Mila di Codra non fu Eleonora ma Irma*, «La Nazione», Firenze, 6-7 marzo 1938.

> intiero del dramma pastorale; e, sollevata sui cuscini, comincia a leggere, qua e là, dei brani, sovra tutto quelli di *Mila di Codra*. La sua voce si rinforza: il suo viso si muta, si trapunta, si colora, si trascolora: ella recita, recita come se fosse sul palcoscenico, come se fosse innanzi a mille spettatori. Invano io mi oppongo a quello che essa fa, essa, malata, febbricitante, emottoica, invano, io tento d'impedirglielo; invano io la supplico; sono sola, il medico è andato via...; sono sola e nulla posso dire e fare. — Lasciami, lasciami — ella esclama — mi fa bene, mi consola, mi guarisce! — E riprende il folto manoscritto e ricomincia, da capo, mezzo sollevata, sollevata per tre quarti, sul suo letto, a leggere, non solo la parte di *Mila di Codra*, ma tutte le parti, recitandole, colorandole, declamandole, mormorandole, come le ha create il Poeta, dando ad ogni figura il suo carattere, ad ogni verso la sua espressione, e a me, allucinata, par di udire non una sola voce, ma tutte le voci del dramma pastorale, a me, allucinatissima, par di vedere tutta la scena e nella casa di *Lazaro di Roio* e nell'addiaccio sulla montagna e sotto il grande albero ove piangono le prèfiche di Abruzzo e tutte le figure mi par di vedere apparire, da *Candia della Leonessa* alla bionda *Vienda*, capino d'oro, dal *Santo dei Monti* a *Ornella*, tutte quante create, interpretate, rappresentate dalla sola voce e dalla sola persona di Eleonora, in una stanza chiusa di un albergo genovese, sul suo letto d'inferma, con me sola, come spettatore.[...] Fu così che io ho udita e vista la prima rappresentazione della *Figlia di Iorio*, recitata dalla sola Duse a me sola. L'altra prima rappresentazione si dette a Milano con Irma Gramatica, una settimana dopo.

Mentre Eleonora Duse consuma il suo malessere fisico e morale fervono le prove e i preparativi per il grande debutto e per l'organizzazione della *tournée*. La cura maggiore d'Annunzio e Michetti, coadiuvati dal giovane Arnaldo Ferraguti, la dedicarono alla ricerca degli oggetti, per cui i due pittori decisero di fare un viaggio all'interno dell'Abruzzo, e ai disegni di scene e costumi.

Il materiale accumulato da Michetti per realizzare i suoi dipinti fu prezioso per l'allestimento della tragedia, «dalle ampie casse aperte — riferisce Ferraguti in un articolo riccamente illustrato[8] — usciva tutta la storia del lavoro di Michetti, qui il corpetto servito per il *Corpus Domini*, là la gonna a righe azzurre e nere della *Prima e seconda nidiata*, lo scialletto di lana a palline che copriva una delle figure di *Mattinata*. *Il Voto*, i deliziosi quadretti esposti nel '95 a Venezia, tutta la serie, poco conosciuta, di tempere e pastelli, dipinti sino alla *Figlia di Iorio*, l'opera sua intera ed integra era rievocata da quelle vestigia».

I bozzetti per la scena dei tre atti — l'interno di una casa abruzzese, l'antro della grotta e un'aia assolata — furono schizzati da Michetti quasi di getto in un sol giorno; nei due giorni successivi, con l'aiuto di

8. Arnaldo Ferraguti, *L'odissea di un allestimento scenico*, «Il Secolo XX», Genova, maggio 1904.

Ferraguti, vennero trasformati in grandi bozzetti dipinti a tempera e spediti «a grandissima velocità» a Milano ove lo scenografo Rovescalli provvide a tradurli immediatamente in scene. Si era già agli ultimi giorni di gennaio e bisognava ancora pensare ai costumi per i singoli personaggi. Michetti ne calcolò complessivamente ben settantasei (per molti personaggi, infatti, i costumi cambiavano ad ogni atto). Data la ristrettezza di tempo che non avrebbe consentito di disegnare tanti *figurini*, Michetti decise di 'vestire' direttamente i personaggi comprando la stoffa, portando personalmente gli attori dal sarto per spiegare le esigenze di ogni singolo personaggio e procedere alla confezione dei vari costumi.

Il recupero degli oggetti originali fu oltremodo laborioso perché «il mal vento della speculazione aveva spazzato via ogni cosa»; fu necessario scrivere e telegrafare in ogni angolo dell'Abruzzo a parenti, amici e semplici conoscenti. Fu mobilitato l'etnologo De Niro a Sulmona perché procurasse il colascione, l'on. Masciantonio fornì antichi ori di famiglia, Pascal si incaricò di recuperare gli otri, le arche, l'arcolaio, la signora Michetti ricamava la camicia che avrebbe indossato Aligi, le donne di Orsogna recavano piatti, pignatte e boccali.

È ancora Arnaldo Ferraguti a raccontare «l'odissea» di quelle ricerche: a Chieti «in un negozio ove si aveva speranza di rintracciare qualche lembo di stoffa dei bei tempi, il proprietario ci consigliò di andare a far ricerca a Milano. Il concetto di dover andare a cercar l'Abruzzo per le vie di Milano, non ci parve più così paradossale. Nulla di singolare, infatti, disse il Mastro con convinzione. Sarebbe inesatto credere che laggiù si fabbrichi solo del panettone. Milano è l'emporio italiano». Dal canto suo d'Annunzio aveva trovato la zampogna, e a Milano l'intagliatore Rossi lavorava, su disegno di Michetti, all'Angelo e alla Madonna. La Compagnia intanto provava in una sala del «Teatro Drammatico», a Verona, ove si recarono Michetti, febbricitante, e Ferraguti per provvedere ai costumi.

Le prove, riferiscono Talli e Ruggeri, «furono lunghe, pazienti, ardentissime, sovente ma non sempre guidate dalla vigile cura di Gabriele d'Annunzio» il quale, testimonia Oreste Calabresi, vi assisteva «sorridente e tranquillo». L'interesse e l'attesa per l'avvenimento erano grandissimi. I giornali vi dedicavano molto spazio e anticipavano il testo di intere scene della tragedia. Alla prova generale fu ammesso un ristretto pubblico di giornalisti e critici. Irma Gramatica, assai affaticata dalle prove precedenti,

> più che recitare assisteva alla recitazione altrui: solo di tanto in tanto accennava all'ardua parte che ha assunta, con un filo di voce tenuissima, insinuante tuttavia, sovrattutto a chi l'ha familiare e cara[9].

9. Domenico Oliva, *Note di uno spettatore*, Bologna, Zanichelli, 1911, p. 393.

La prova terminò alle due del mattino, ma, nella fredda notte milanese, discussioni lunghe e vivaci si protrassero nei caffè della Galleria. «Sui nervi di Milano», scrisse alcuni anni dopo Domenico Oliva, l'attesa per *La figlia di Iorio* «esercitava tutto il suo fascino femminile»[10].

La sera del 2 marzo 1904 ebbe luogo il debutto sul palcoscenico del «Teatro Lirico», «colmo in modo fenomenale» in ogni ordine di posti, a dispetto dell'alto costo dei biglietti[11]. *Mila* portava gli orecchini ritratti da Michetti nel suo celebre quadro esposto a Venezia nel 1895, *Vienda* era adorna degli ori autentici che Masciantonio aveva portato da Casoli, i *pastori* erano vestiti con i velli «mondati col solfo» che d'Annunzio aveva acquistato nella campagna romana. Il pubblico milanese, «il pubblico della ricchezza, e del lusso, dei salotti e dei teatri» secondo la definizione di d'Annunzio[12], dapprima rimase incantato dalle scene che creavano, come aveva rilevato Domenico Oliva, «un effetto totale di verità», in grado di appagare l'occhio dello spettatore, ma «pareva tutto in sé raccolto, misterioso e ostile forse». In effetti fino ad allora il pubblico italiano non aveva mai mostrato particolare entusiasmo per il teatro dannunziano. Alla fine del primo atto, calato il sipario, seguì, narra Oreste Calabresi, «un silenzio sepolcrale sì che io dissi forte come a me stesso: è finita! buona notte. Ma improvviso, di lontano come una grande onda di mare che giunge e s'abbatte sulla spiaggia, risuonò come tuono un immenso applauso, al quale si univano grida di entusiasmo». Anche d'Annunzio, giunto in teatro sul finire del primo atto, ricorderà nell'intervista rilasciata a Filippo Surico quell'attimo di profondo silenzio che gli aveva fatto temere burrasca.

Unanime la stampa registra il successo della tragedia. «Fu una grande vittoria, un trionfo», scrive Giovanni Pozza sul «Corriere della Sera» del 3 marzo; e Domenico Oliva su «Il Giornale d'Italia» del 3 marzo: «il pubblico si abbandonò a una fragorosa manifestazione di gioia».

Riserve vennero tuttavia espresse per l'interpretazione della Gramatica sulle cui spalle gravava l'ombra della Duse:

> Irma Gramatica non diede al suo personaggio quel rilievo che sarebbe stato necessario: pareva quasi non osasse compiere la figura ideata dal poeta e il suo non fu che un abbozzo di interpretazione[13].

---

10. Ivi, p. 406.
11. I prezzi della prima furono: 2 lire per il «loggione», 35 lire per le «poltrone», 120 lire per i «palchi» di prima e seconda fila; 5 lire per il solo ingresso.
12. Filippo Surico, *Ora luminosa. Le mie conversazioni letterarie con Gabriele d'Annunzio*, Roma, Urbs, 1939.
13. Domenico Oliva, *La prima de «La figlia di Iorio»*, «Il Giornale d'Italia», Roma, 3 marzo 1904.

> Irma Gramatica non ha ancora trovata la giusta espressione del personaggio di *Mila*. Ella recitò ieri con grande uniformità di cadenze e di voce, togliendo così alla parte ogni finezza di sfumature[14].

> Solo la Gramatica non riuscì a dare alla sua parte il rilievo necessario. Nocque alla sua recitazione lo studio e l'urlare di cui ella fa abuso[15].

Qualche settimana dopo, a Roma, Irma Gramatica cedeva, anche per motivi di salute, la parte di *Mila* a Teresa Franchini. La nuova Mila piacque alla critica e al pubblico anche se, in qualche momento della tragedia, le faceva difetto la necessaria grandiosità venerabile e tragica.

Ma le lodi maggiori la critica le riservò a Ruggero Ruggeri che

> recitò la parte di *Aligi* con un'arte e una intelligenza interpretativa degna di un grande attore[16].

> Ruggero Ruggeri non ha smentito i suoi ammiratori, che riconoscono in lui una delle forze giovani della nostra scena. È entrato, meravigliosamente, nello spirito del mistico personaggio di *Aligi*, e lo ha fatto vivere, circonfuso da tutta l'aureola di poesia e di fede di cui l'ha avvolto l'autore[17].

* * *

Tra la prima messa in scena il 2 marzo 1904, al «Teatro Lirico» di Milano e quella della «Compagnia Drammatica Siciliana» corrono soltanto sei mesi, ma la rappresentazione in dialetto avrebbe dovuto precedere quella in lingua, tanto era il desiderio di cavalcare il successo — di pubblico e di cassa — di Grasso, se la fuga d'amore della prima attrice Marinella Bragaglia con l'amministratore Vittorio Marazzi Diligenti non ne avesse causato lo scioglimento. Nella nuova formazione la Bragaglia, passata alle scene italiane, è sostituita dalla palermitana Mimì Aguglia, anche lei giovanissima figlia d'arte (è appena ventenne), prelevata da Martoglio dal «Teatro Jovinelli», *Café chantant* di piazza Guglielmo Pepe a Roma.

Ricostituitasi la Compagnia ad opera di Nino Martoglio, dopo quattro mesi di prove — alle quali assiste anche il poeta che si dichiara entusiasta della recitazione di tutti gli attori della *Siciliana*, definita

---

14. G.P. [Giovanni Pozza], *«La figlia di Iorio», tragedia pastorale in tre atti di Gabriele d'Annunzio*, «Corriere della Sera», Milano, 3 marzo 1904.

15. Aldo Sorani, *La rappresentazione della «Figlia di Iorio» a Firenze*, «Il Giornale d'Italia», Roma, 24 marzo 1904.

16. G.P. [Giovanni Pozza], *«La figlia di Iorio», tragedia pastorale in tre atti di Gabriele d'Annunzio*, cit.

17. Leporello, *«La figlia di Iorio», tragedia pastorale di Gabriele d'Annunzio*, «L'Illustrazione Italiana», Milano, 6 marzo 1904.

«umana, naturalissima, efficace e potente»[18] —, la prima ha luogo al «Teatro Costanzi» di Roma, il 17 settembre 1904.

Ne *'A figghia di Joriu* l'accorto Martoglio introduce, d'accordo con d'Annunzio, motivi musicali siciliani, opera del maestro Alberto Favara, professore di composizione al Conservatorio di musica di Palermo, anticipando in tal modo la raffinata operazione culturale della sfortunata «Compagnia Drammatica del Teatro Mediterraneo» (1918-'19) che abilmente coniugherà, com'era stata tradizione del teatro greco, dialetto e musica.

Le scene e i costumi, ideati da Adolfo de Carolis, sono realizzati dal pittore Pietro Sassi. I ruoli principali sono così distribuiti: Giovanni Grasso: *Aliggi;* Mimì Aguglia: *Mila di Codra;* Totò Majorana: *Lazzaru di Roju;* Marianna Catalisano Balistrieri: *Cannia di la Liunissa;* Carolina Balistrieri: *Ornella.*

Il successo è «trionfale». Per tutti riportiamo l'impressione che l'autore di *Persuasione,* il filosofo e poeta Carlo Michelstaedter, goriziano di nazionalità austriaca, di formazione mitteleuropea e di estrazione ebraica, comunica ai familiari nella «notte tra il 6-7 novembre 1906» dopo avere assistito alla messa in scena de *'A figghia di Joriu* da parte della «Compagnia Drammatica Siciliana», al «Teatro Niccolini» di Firenze:

> Ritorno ora, e sono schiacciato ammalato per le impressioni provate; è una scossa continua, un affanno che sale e fa soffrire veramente, chiudendo la gola. (...) Grasso è poderoso in ogni suo gesto e in ogni accento. Ha quella voce calda intensa che dà le vertigini. Specialmente il racconto che fa al santo nel 2° atto dove non c'è niente di lirico, dove tutta la bellezza poetica è tolta dalla versione in Siciliano, è un capolavoro. Pareva di rivivere le scene precedenti in tutta la loro intensità. Una impressione simile l'avevo provata sentendo Tumiati ma molto meno forte, Grasso è spontaneo e più completo. L'Aguglia non si mantiene sempre alla stessa altezza; l'ultimo grido: "tu non puoi, tu non devi" e "la vampa è bella" non mi piacque. Ma del resto lei e tutta la compagnia sono meravigliosi e superiori certo nell'insieme a qualunque compagnia non dialettale. Fa l'impressione che la tragedia così in siciliano sia l'originale, l'italiana la traduzione, e certo d'Annunzio l'ha concepita così come noi la sentiamo da Grasso[19].

'A figghia di Joriu non può non avvalersi, oltre che dei numerosi modelli femminili della classicità, dell'esperienza teatrica siciliana, percorrendo la pastorale, fra gli innumerevoli altri, itinerari omologhi e sovrapponibili a quelli di Verga e di Capuana.

18. ——, *«La figlia di Iorio» in siciliano,* «La Tribuna», Roma, 11 settembre 1904.
19. Carlo Michelstaedter, *Epistolario,* a cura di Sergio Campailla, Milano, Adelphi, 1983, p. 139.

Sottili e tenaci precorrimenti della tragedia si colgono ne *La Lupa*, creatura primordiale e ferina, esemplare sinossi dell'eros che diviene consapevole volizione, drammatica rinuncia, totale annientamento[20]. Approdata ad una dimensione archetipa, fuori da qualsiasi tempo storico, cristallizzata nella forma di un demoniaco maleficio da esorcizzare, la *Lupa* supera nella fame di sacrificio lo scarto impietoso tra istinto e ragione, tra passione e pentimento. Pubblica meretrice, profanatrice della fedeltà coniugale, emarginata da una comunità irrigidita nella superstizione, secondo costumi antropologici e morali che condannano la pulsione erotica al femminile sacrificandola. Il lavacro di sangue accomuna la *Lupa* verghiana e la *Mila* dannunziana, entrambe incarnazione della *mavaria* ed elemento di deflagrazione dell'istituto familiare. È attraverso il loro annichilimento che la tribale società arcaica difende la propria integrità. Ma se per la *gnà Pina*, trasgressiva fino in fondo, con la carne bruciante e l'anima piagata, l'amore è essenzialmente passione erotica, per *Mila* diviene riscatto mediante la rinuncia e l'abnegazione eroica. Con la castità e la morte *'A figghia di Joriu* monderà l'infamante passato, offrendo una nuova immagine di sé giacché la verità potrà essere testimoniata da *Ornella* ai puri di cuore.

Anche *Malia* di Capuana traeva origine dalla lucida ricognizione del labirinto dei sentimenti dominati da un eros trasgressivo e incestuoso. *Jana*, che riverbera in parte la luce magica della *Lupa* sul piano della consapevole ansia sensuale, soggiogata dalle barriere dei vincoli familiari respinge nella mistificazione dell'autoinganno l'insano sentimento per Cola, sigillato da un ritegno estraneo all'eroina verghiana[21]. Vicina a *'A figghia di Joriu* per l'ancestrale patologia dell'esistere, ancorata al *milieu* eterogeneo, fatalmente superstizioso, religiosamente pagano, socialmente arretrato, del mondo contadino. La pulsione erotica domina la *Lupa* che irrompe in una sfera in cui la morte costituisce «il momento dell'estrema gioia e dell'estasi ineffabile ma meravigliosa»[22]. Quell'«estrema gioia» e quell'«estasi ineffabile ma meravigliosa» con cui *Mila*, rivendicando per sé il marchio infamante di maga, attesta tra le fiamme l'unicità del suo amore per *Aligi*. «Eros e distruzione, sia per il nome che per le funzioni sono gli equivalenti di *philìa* e *neîkos*: i principi fondamentali che Empedocle pone a governo del cosmo»[23], entrambi scandiscono i tempi delle passioni, l'irriducibile

20. Cfr. al riguardo: Giovanni Verga, *La Lupa*. Novella, dramma, tragedia lirica, a cura di Sarah Zappulla Muscarà, Palermo, Novecento, 1991.

21. Si veda: Luigi Capuana, *Malia*, a cura di Sarah Zappulla Muscarà, Mineo, Centro Nazionale di Sudi «Luigi Capuana», 1997.

22. Georges Bataille, *L'erotismo*, Milano, Studio Editoriale, 1986, traduzione di Adriana Dell'Orto, p. 247.

23. Marco Danesi, *Freud e l'enigma del piacere*, Bologna, Il Mulino, 1989, p. 128.

conflitto tra il privato e il sociale, la miseria ostinata della quotidiana esistenza delle tre dolorose figure femminili.

* * *

Nel 1927 viene costituita la «Compagnia dannunziana» che fa capo all'«Istituto Nazionale per la rappresentazione dei drammi di Gabriele d'Annunzio», sotto l'alto patronato di S.E. Benito Mussolini, Presidente: Sen. Vincenzo Morello, Direttore Generale: Tommaso Monicelli. Composta da oltre sessanta attori, tecnici e personale di segreteria, la Compagnia viene affidata alla «direzione artistica» del commediografo Gioacchino Forzano; in programma cinque drammi dannunziani (*La figlia di Iorio, Francesca da Rimini, Parisina, La fiaccola sotto il moggio, La gloria*) per una lunga *tournée*. D'Annunzio ha così l'occasione di dare vita a un sogno lungamente accarezzato, una spettacolare messa in scena de *La figlia di Iorio* nei giardini del Vittoriale dove Giancarlo Maroni, architetto del Vittoriale, e Antonio Rovescalli, «giornalmente sorvegliati dal Comandante», sono impegnati nell'allestimento di un grande spazio teatrale all'aperto, situato in un punto tra la collina e il lago, appositamente scelto da d'Annunzio in accordo con Forzano e Maroni, in modo che il primo e terzo atto si svolgano nello sfondo verso il monte e l'atto secondo — gli spettatori nell'intervallo dovranno cambiare direzione alla loro visuale voltando i sedili dalla parte opposta — nello sfondo verso il lago. Straordinario e infaticabile promotore di se stesso e delle sue opere, il poeta, come già in occasione della prima, trasforma la rappresentazione in un evento cultural-mondano di notevole risonanza. La stessa data del debutto, domenica 11 settembre, ottavo anniversario della marcia di Ronchi, suona come un richiamo irresistibile.

La stampa con accortezza e minuziosità diffonde quotidiane notizie sui febbrili preparativi dell'eccezionale manifestazione, sull'*élite* intellettuale e sociale che non vorrà mancare lo storico appuntamento, sulla grandiosità della messa in scena, sulla vigile presenza del poeta.

Intanto la Compagnia si è riunita a Viareggio: le parti sono così distribuite: Maria Melato *Mila di Codra*, Annibale Ninchi *Aligi*, Camillo Pilotto *Lazaro di Roio*, Emilia Varini *Candia della Leonessa* e Giulietta De Riso *Ornella*.

Alla rappresentazione potrà assistere un numero limitato di spettatori — solo cinquecento — e i biglietti sono messi in vendita presso le agenzie della Società Italiana degli Autori al prezzo notevole di lire 1.000 ciascuno. Il ricavato è destinato alla costruzione di un teatro di pietra sulla collina del Vittoriale[24].

Alla fine di agosto la Compagnia si sposta per le ultime prove al «Teatro Sociale» di Brescia. Ne approfitta Gioacchino Forzano per recarsi al Vittoriale, informare d'Annunzio del risultato delle prove e

24. ——, *Per lo spettacolo al Vittoriale*, «Giornale d'Italia», Roma, 30 agosto 1927.

vedere «la singolare costruzione del palcoscenico all'aperto preparato dagli artisti»[25]. Il giorno dopo è d'Annunzio che si reca a Brescia, accolto avanti al «Teatro Sociale» dal Prefetto e dalle altre autorità cittadine, per assistere alla prova delle sue opere (si prova anche il primo atto della *Francesca da Rimini*).

Al Vittoriale si lavora senza sosta anche di notte; d'Annunzio mette a punto, meticolosamente, i particolari della serata.

> Ci saranno in quel pomeriggio al Vittoriale le varie rappresentanze de' suoi compagni d'arme della grande guerra e di Fiume: i fanti del Carso, gli eroi del mare e del cielo, un drappello de' suoi bianchi lancieri «Navarra» — «non a cavallo, però!» — e i suoi più fidi intrepidi legionari[26].

Lo spettacolo, che specie all'ultimo atto avrà del fantastico, nella luce tarda del tramonto ed ai bagliori sanguigni delle torce che accompagneranno la processione del supplizio pei fianchi del monte, comincerà dopo le quindici, sarà preceduto dalla "Preghiera ai cittadini", appositamente composta dal poeta, e detta da Mario Pelosini, e sarà annunziato da un colpo di cannone sparato dalla nave *Puglia*. Alla fine dello spettacolo il poeta offrirà ai suoi ospiti una cerimonia intima: «riunirà tutti i presenti intorno alla nave *Puglia* e quale primo atto farà loro firmare un albo, firma questa che implicherà un obbligo assoluto di presenza ad ogni suo richiamo. Poscia a gran voce da tutti gli intervenuti farà cantare l'"Inno al Vittoriale" da lui stesso composto e musicato dal maestro Malipiero che lo sta ritoccando secondo i suggerimenti del Poeta»[27].

Finalmente ha luogo il debutto. D'Annunzio, accompagnato dalla moglie, principessa Maria di Montenevoso, assiste allo spettacolo seduto a fianco del Duca d'Aosta su una delle «tre poltrone rosse, di damasco, ad alta spalliera, poste nel mezzo della platea rivolte verso la casa di Lazaro»[28].

Ma sulla «platea erbosa» non tutti condividevano l'impostazione «troppo realistica»[29] della pastorale, pur nell'unanime riconoscimento dell'arduo compito affidato agli interpreti[30]. Anche Silvio d'Amico lodava l'impegno degli attori ma avanzava riserve sull'opportunità di

---

25. ——, *La Compagnia dannunziana a Brescia*, «La Tribuna», Roma, 1 settembre 1927.
26. Mario Corsi, *Con d'Annunzio al Teatro del Vittoriale*, «Il Giornale d'Italia», Roma, 4 settembre 1927.
27. ——, *«La figlia di Iorio», il «Siluro alato» e l' «Inno»*, «Il Piccolo della Sera», Roma, 10 settembre 1927.
28. Umberto Fracchia, *La figlia di Iorio*, «Il Secolo della Sera», Roma, 13 settembre 1927.
29. Eugenio Bertuetti, *«La figlia di Iorio» al Vittoriale*, «Gazzetta del Popolo», Torino, 13 settembre 1927.
30. Udalrigo de Vita, *«La figlia di Iorio» al Vittoriale*, «Il Mattino», Napoli, 13-14 settembre 1927.

«trasportare sullo sfondo del cielo vero e sotto i raggi del sole vero, i tre atti originariamente concepiti per le aggraziate scene di Michetti» e, definendo «un fulgido tradimento» quello di Forzano, sottolineava come «all'aperto si può recitare soltanto quello che fu concepito per il teatro all'aperto (teatro greco-romano, sacre rappresentazioni medioevali, ecc.)»[31].

Secondo Fausto Maria Martini la messa in scena di Forzano non andava esaminata secondo i criteri consueti. Malgrado la scelta realistica imposta dal teatro all'aperto che non consentiva lusinghe di musicalità e l'allestimento scenico di stile addirittura verghiano, l'elemento lirico sovrastava di gran lunga l'elemento reale pur non impedendo alla tragedia di risultare «espressiva e viva».

Di suggestione «mesta e perfetta» parla Renato Simoni.[32]

> «Invenzione stupenda» viene ritenuta quella del poeta di togliere il dramma pastorale — «con la commedia dell'arte il nostro apporto più originale al teatro del mondo» — «dalla sua leggiadra falsità e dalla sua indeterminatezza convenzionale di luogo e di costume, a una luminosa e più poetica verità regionale, di dargli una patria».

Unanime l'apprezzamento per gli attori, il costumista, lo scenografo, il *régisseur.*

***

A distanza di sette anni dallo spettacolare evento del Vittoriale si registra un'altra storica messa in scena de *La figlia di Iorio.*

Nell'aula Giulio Cesare, in Campidoglio, l'8 ottobre 1934, prende il via il IV Convegno Volta, presieduto da Luigi Pirandello, che si protrarrà fino al 14 ottobre, dedicato alla drammaturgia, promosso alla Reale Accademia d'Italia, presieduta da Guglielmo Marconi. Il convegno, al quale prendono parte le più importanti personalità del mondo teatrale europeo contemporaneo ha, sottolinea Pirandello nelle numerose interviste, per la prima volta indirizzo «essenzialmente estetico spirituale e culturale»[33].

Come i recensori contemporanei ravvisarono, emerge dagli studiosi del Volta la ferma volontà d'istituire un sistema di più efficiente comunicazione teatrale ampiamente testimoniata sia dalle diverse relazioni e dai numerosi interventi sia dalla riflessione condotta a *côté* del fenomeno drammaturgico, mescidata di voci nuove quali quelle della complessa e a volte avveniristica elaborazione di progetti architettonici.

31. Silvio d'Amico, *«La figlia di Iorio» al Vittoriale*, «La Tribuna», Roma, 13 settembre 1927.
32. R.S. [Renato Simoni], *«La figlia di Iorio» al Vittoriale*, «Corriere della Sera», Milano,13 settembre 1927.
33. Cfr. al riguardo: Sarah Zappulla Muscarà, *Il Convegno Volta e la regia pirandelliana de «La figlia di Iorio»*, in AA.VV., *Pirandello e D'Annunzio*, Palermo, Palumbo, 1989.

Non mancarono, naturalmente, le polemiche: Bontempelli, per esempio, sostenne la necessità sociale di un teatro di massa, semplice e popolare, suscitando la reazione di Marinetti, fautore di un teatro d'avanguardia.

In occasione del Convegno Volta i rapporti tra Pirandello e d'Annunzio, che si erano mossi su posizioni ideologiche tanto differenti da escludere una loro possibile conciliazione, trovano un momentaneo punto d'incontro nella messa in scena, l'11 ottobre del 1934 (lo spettacolo è stato differito di un giorno in segno di lutto per la morte di Alessandro di Jugoslavia e del ministro Barthou), al «Teatro Argentina» di Roma, de *La figlia di Iorio* per la regia dello scrittore agrigentino.

Il percorso verso l'allestimento della tragedia è siglato da una breve corrispondenza:

> 9 settembre 1934
>
> Mio caro Luigi Pirandello,
>
> sono molto contento che in tanta lontananza tu mi dia d'improvviso questa prova fraterna nell'allestire e ispirare una nuova rappresentazione della *Figlia di Iorio*, che non è se non una grande canzone popolare per dialoghi. E non serbi nell'orecchio gli accenti e le cadenze delle stupende canzoni di Sicilia?
>
> Dico che nessuno saprà intonare il verso del mio dramma come tu solo saprai e insegnerai agli attori. Anche penso che tu vorrai ridurre l'allestimento scenico a pochi rilievi essenziali, ad una semplicità potente, accordata con le forze ignude del contrasto scenico.
>
> Ho chiesto ad Antonio Bruers se io posso attendermi una visita in questo Vittoriale ove talvolta fosti atteso invano. Gioverebbe ad entrambi un colloquio quasi direi tecnico, poiché tu sei «o teknikos» come io sono.
>
> Ottimo a me ogni giorno che ti convenga e piaccia. Ti offro un bel sasso da porre sulle tue carte scritte, con un bellissimo rilievo dell'animaliere parmense Renato Brozzi. Ti prego di abbracciare per me, con l'affetto e l'ammirazione che egli di me conosce, il grande nostro Guglielmo Marconi. Gli scriverò domani. Ti abbraccio, Gabriele d'Annunzio.

E alcuni giorni dopo:

> Roma, 18.IX.1934
> Via Antonio Bosio, 15
>
> Mio caro Comandante,
>
> mi promettevo il piacere di ringraziarti a voce della tua lettera e del graditissimo dono: ma Antonio Bruers mi fece sapere della tua indisposizione proprio nell'unico giorno che mi sarebbe stato possibile

visitarti, dato il mio lavoro per la preparazione scenica della tua *Figlia di Iorio* e del prossimo Convegno Volta.

Sono lietissimo che quanto tu mi dici della tua mirabile opera concorda con la mia interpretazione. Sento anch'io *La figlia di Iorio* come una grande canzone da accentare popolarescamente, con ardore potente e in toni schietti. Farò di tutto perché gli attori sotto la mia guida si guardino da quella preziosità letteraria di cui altre volte si sono compiaciuti. Ho intanto ottenuto dal pittore Giorgio de Chirico bozzetti di scene e costumi, in questo senso, perfetti.

Se tu avessi consigli e suggerimenti da darmi, mancando ormai il tempo di parlarne di persona prima della rappresentazione, potresti darmeli per lettera, io te ne sarei gratissimo.

Ti abbraccio con la gioia che mi si sia offerta l'occasione per darti questa prova di fraternità artistica. Luigi Pirandello.

Questa la risposta di d'Annunzio:

A Luigi Pirandello
Reale Accademia d'Italia
nella Farnesina
Roma

La meschina infermità che perdura m'impedì di accoglierti nel Vittoriale non tanto per parlare della *Figlia di Iorio* quanto per discorrere di molte altre cose in un incontro che desidero da troppo tempo. Forse tu non sai che ti sono vicino fin da quando tu eri un giovinetto e il buon Ugo Fleres mi parlava di te. La tua lettera mi conferma il nostro perfetto accordo nell'allestimento scenico della *Figlia*. Confido pienamente in te e negli attori da te scelti. Oso pregarti di mandarmene la lista perché io possa a ciascuno offrire un segno e un ricordo di me. La tua maniera di trattare l'anima umana mi dimostra che sei una specie di mago penetrante. Se per magia tu potessi celare la mia presenza, io saprei dominare i miei mali e la mia infelicità per assistere alla prima interpretazione geniale della mia tragedia, alatamente compiuta dall'emulo ammirato. Ti abbraccio. Gabriele d'Annunzio[34].

E ancora:

A Gabriele d'Annunzio
8 ottobre '34

Con l'augurio più cordiale che la tua preziosa salute ti consenta d'accogliermi per un colloquio sulle cose più vive per te e per me che anch'io desidero da tanto tempo, ho la gioia d'assicurarti che la tua prodigiosa tragedia vibra di tutta la sua potente vita non solo in

34. Emilio Mariano, *Luigi Pirandello e «La figlia di Iorio»*, «Quaderni dannunziani», Gardone Riviera, VIII-IX, 1958.

Marta Abba e Ruggero Ruggeri, ma anche nel complesso degli attori chiamati a interpretarla di cui ti mando i nomi secondo il tuo desiderio [...].

Nessuna opera di magia potrebbe celare la tua corporale presenza, e io comprendo che tu te ne dolga. Purtroppo la mia magia di devoto e fervido interprete del tuo genio può valere a farti sentire a tutto il pubblico ammirato più presente che mai nella tua opera immortale. Stop. Ti abbraccio, Luigi Pirandello.

Della corrispondenza tra Pirandello e d'Annunzio si conservano inoltre tre telegrammi:

Roma, 10 ottobre 1934
A Gabriele d'Annunzio
Gardone Riviera

Accolgo col più profondo sentimento la tua lettera assicurandoti che la mia devozione spirituale e artistica è stata pari alla generosa fiducia che nuovamente mi esprimi. Stop. Ho distribuito ai miei cari collaboratori le tue lettere i tuoi doni preziosi e ti assicuro che tutti porteranno alla tua grande opera un contributo che viene dall'anima. Stop. Ti abbraccio mio grande amico - tuo Luigi Pirandello.

Roma 11 ottobre 1934
A Gabriele d'Annunzio
Gardone Riviera

Il magnifico successo di ieri sera si deve soprattutto alla magia del tuo canto al fervore alla piena dedizione in tutti i miei collaboratori. Stop. Tu mi hai sorretto nella difficile prova con una profonda generosa fraternità che non dimenticherò mai. Stop. Ti abbraccio riconoscente Luigi Pirandello.

Roma , 4 ottobre 1934
A Gabriele d'Annunzio
Gardone Riviera

Partecipanti italiani e stranieri Convegno Volta sul teatro riuniti per l'ultima seduta inviano al Poeta Gabriele d'Annunzio un fervido e riverente saluto come a colui che è stato presente ai lavori con spirito animatore e con l'arte sovrana del suo capolavoro. Stop. Pirandello presidente Convegno.

La scelta di d'Annunzio costituisce per Pirandello un atto di omaggio al regime, a colui che era ritenuto il più grande poeta vivente, e in quest'ottica trova giustificazione anche la preferenza accordata alla *Figlia di Iorio*, in quanto canto della stirpe, «grande canzone popolare per dialoghi» — specchio delle fiere origini contadine e pastorali del popolo italiano[35].

Riserve non lievi sulla poesia e sull'estetica di d'Annunzio e sul dannunzianesimo in genere aveva espresso anche Giorgio de Chirico, autore delle scene e dei costumi, che in uno scritto del 1919 su Carrà e la pittura metafisica aveva scagliato i suoi strali contro il futurismo e la pittura cosiddetta 'ufficiale' di Giulio Aristide Sartorio e Ettore Tito accusati di farsi suggestionare dal vate abruzzese definito «falso e ibrido».

Le concessioni al fascismo non escludono però la presenza di una *ratio* ispirativa nata ora da un più armonico rapporto con il teatro di poesia che costituisce, quasi nomadismo memoriale, il felice porto dei miti.

È questo anche il crinale da seguire per rintracciare le sotterranee ragioni di una scelta da non attribuire meramente ad un generico e formale ossequio.

Superando ogni preconcetto d'età, Pirandello scelse, per il ruolo di *Aligi*, quello stesso Ruggero Ruggeri che lo aveva messo in scena trent'anni prima e per quello di *Mila* Marta Abba, l'attrice prediletta.

Solo le insistenze del suo autore preferito, Pirandello, che puntava sulla preziosità di un'interpretazione affinata dall'esperienza e dalla pratica della scena, del vate d'Annunzio e del fascismo convinsero il sessantacinquenne Ruggeri a superare il timore del ridicolo e ad accettare il ruolo del giovane pastore travolto dalla passione.

Serata memorabile quella del 10 ottobre 1934 al «Teatro Argentina» di Roma, puntualmente registrata dalle cronache:

> Canzone dialogata, come una tenzone dei tempi primitivi, un contrasto semplice e tremendo: tessuto a molte trame: religione, amore, delitto, purificazione[36].
>
> Al finale del terzo atto, quando il clima scenico si leva all'empireo, la platea, soggiogata, ha dato un grido potente d'entusiasmo[37].

Assente d'Annunzio, appartato nel suo aureo Vittoriale, sempre più intristito dalla vecchiaia inesorabile, che aveva confidato soprattutto nel potere e nella suggestione del verso per un allestimento scenico ridotto «a pochi rilievi essenziali». Ma Pirandello aveva puntato sugli elementi mistici del dramma, su un paesaggio da favola, scevro da folclore,

---

35. Gianni Oliva, *Pirandello tra d'Annunzio e Antonelli*, «Ariel», a.I, n.3, settembre-ottobre 1986.

36. Giovanni Artieri, *«La figlia di Iorio» rappresentata a Roma nella realizzazione scenica di Luigi Pirandello*, «Il Mattino», Napoli, 13 ottobre 1934.

37. Luigi Antonelli, *Il grande successo de «La figlia di Iorio» rappresentata in onore dei congressisti*, «Il Giornale d'Italia», Roma, 13 ottobre 1934.

accentrando, con la metafisica complicità di de Chirico, il tema di un mondo preda delle passioni, della magia, senza tempo né spazio.

Francesco Bernardelli sottolinea

> i segni della singolare intelligenza interpretativa e scenica del Pirandello che si sono rivelati subito dal primo atto. Segni forti, acerbe sottolineature: un accumularsi, un prorompere delle passioni, delle superstizioni, del terrore popolare, fra le vaste plaghe estatiche del canto di Aligi, un addensarsi di sensi oscuri e fatali che comunicava allo spettacolo improvvisi brividi, misterioso tumulto. Il poema decisamente caratterizzato acquistava in evidenza e in comunicatività: senza che per questo ne svanisse l'indimenticabile atmosfera di sogno[38].

Non mancano tuttavia le riserve.

«Esperimento d'arte interessante e ardito» secondo Antonio Valente ma priva di coesione stilistica la recitazione per i toni lirici di Ruggeri, prosastici della Abba, leggeri della Franchini, dialettali del Donadio:

> L'unica interprete che tentò di costruire il suo personaggio con una nuova ricetta fu la Abba: ella cercò di adattare il personaggio al suo metro: ne venne una Mila ragionata e ragionevole, chiusa in una gesticolazione sincopata e scattante. Invece Ruggeri, è naturale, fu fedele a se stesso, a quel suo Aligi trasognato, morbidamente cantante, armoniosamente plastico, ch'egli creò trent'anni or sono e che ha sempre portato in giro pei palcoscenici[39].

E il severo Luigi Antonelli:

> Ieri sera ho avuto l'impressione, talvolta, di essere in mezzo a un balletto in costume d'Alsazia, sul basso Reno[40].

In questa dimensione oppositiva che sembra assicurare, al di là degli esiti rappresentativi, la funzione intrigante delle lacerazioni contemporanee, il perseguimento di un teatro capace di fissare il respiro della poesia e del mito si scontra con le difficoltà delle procedure teatrali ancora chiuse in un problematico modulo verista.

Le scena e i costumi di de Chirico, che ripetutamente in passato aveva definito il teatro luogo d'irrealtà e di magia, fantasmagoria di colori e di luci, si distendono con levità sulla fisionomia registica pirandelliana con gli attributi più del simbolismo che dell'aderenza al vero: *Aligi* è tratteggiato con linee essenziali che lo riconducono ad

---

38. Francesco Bernardelli, *La rappresentazione de «La figlia di Iorio»*, «La Stampa», Torino, 12 ottobre 1934.

39. Antonio Valente, *Il Convegno Volta per il teatro drammatico*, «Comoedia», Milano, ottobre 1934, pp. 8-9.

40. Luigi Antonelli, *Il grande successo de «La figlia di Iorio» rappresentata in onore dei congressisti*, cit.

un'atmosfera di leggenda, «or è molt'anni», *Mila* non è più una contadina abruzzese ma l'espressione della libertà del vento, della fiamma; *Lazaro* è invece fedelmente vestito di pelli caprine, secondo la didascalia dannunziana, con vistosi segni mistici superstiziosamente ostentati sul petto.

Sottili inarcature dialettiche sfuggite ai cronisti del tempo:

> Il de Chirico ha dipinto - è vero - le scene abbastanza fedeli alle didascalie del poema e ricalcate sui modelli indimenticati di Francesco Paolo Michetti, della prima edizione della *Figlia di Iorio*; ma senza dovizia d'aria, di luce, di sole, senza realistica consistenza. I costumi, poi, ricavati — dicono — da pupazzi e fantocci di antichi presepi abruzzesi, di strane fogge e di così piatti colori, hanno contribuito a rendere più grigio, monotono e senza rilievo il quadro[41].

In genere, comunque, le scene e i costumi di de Chirico furono giudicati troppo metafisici, non veristi come quelli di Michetti, ancora fortemente vivi nel ricordo degli spettatori.

Ma Pirandello, osserva ancora d'Amico in altra sede, ha interpretato la tragedia dannunziana con criteri d'una fedeltà soprattutto *spirituale*:

> Per lui l'Abruzzo della *Figlia di Iorio* non è quello delle guide, delle monografie, o d'un particolare folclore; è, genericamente, una terra di passioni e di estasi, tra favola e mito non meno che fra montagna e mare; un dramma in cui, nel conflitto tra carnalità barbara e terrore superstizioso, s'apre la via, e nel sacrificio trionfa, il grido della purificazione[42].

Quello stesso bisogno di purezza che coglie il giovane principe della *Favola* pirandelliana, dove la simulazione e la dissimulazione della realtà si associano alla restaurazione metafisica della legalità che redime. La coscienza della degenerazione che coinvolge, per una sorta di autoinganno, l'eroina dannunziana e il personaggio pirandelliano e che dà vita alla dialettica della violenza e della rinuncia costituisce in entrambi i lavori momento insostituibile per il superamento del dramma eroico-esistenziale che investe la più smagata diagnosi della realtà.

***

«Sono riuscito ad abolire il tempo e a chiudere nello stesso cerchio le anime che vivono oggi e quelle che vissero nei millenni remoti»: così

---

41. Mario Corsi, «*La figlia di Iorio*», «Radiocorriere», Roma, 21-27 ottobre 1934.
42. Silvio d'Amico, *Un passo indietro*, «Scenario», Roma, novembre 1934, p. 589. Di Silvio d'Amico cfr. pure: «*La figlia di Iorio*» *di d'Annunzio messa in scena da Pirandello all'Argentina*, «La Tribuna», Roma, 13 ottobre 1934.

scrive Gabriele d'Annunzio ad Angelo Conti il 13 maggio 1896 annunciandogli di aver ripreso la stesura della *Città morta,* primo esempio di quella drammaturgia della parola, elaborata talvolta fino al virtuosismo, in prosa o in versi, preziosa, musicale, ritmica, che irrompe sulla scena sprovincializzando il teatro italiano ancora arroccato sulle forme del naturalismo e su quelle della ormai vieta commedia borghese. Nel poeta la consapevolezza di aver dato vita ad un teatro nuovo, non claustralmente chiuso nelle forme della tragedia ellenica ma modernamente proteso verso soluzioni di avanguardismo europeo. Alla sua articolata sperimentazione drammaturgica sono ascrivibili gli esiti più significativi del Novecento, dal simbolismo all'espressionismo, al futurismo, al grottesco via via fino a Eliot, Pirandello, Lorca, Pasolini. Una linea di continuità che corre dalla parola declamata a quella franta, dal ritualismo mitico all'umorismo corrosivo.

A d'Annunzio, attento a tutti gli aspetti dello spettacolo, scene, costumi, luci, musica, coreografia, effetti acustici, visivi, coloristici, si deve l'avvento della regia intesa in senso moderno e di un nuovo stile di recitazione. Non è un caso che lo stesso Pirandello si sia cimentato ne *La figlia di Iorio* e che due grandi attori dannunziani, Ruggero Ruggeri (un modello inimitabile costituì per molti anni il suo *Aligi,* frutto, fra l'altro, di una voce particolare e dei suggerimenti direttoriali di Virgilio Talli) e Salvo Randone, siano divenuti eccellenti interpreti pirandelliani.

E tuttavia, se si esclude qualche evento di tipo celebrativo, l'opera di Gabriele d'Annunzio dal 1945 in poi attraversa una lunga fase d'oblio culminata negli anni cinquanta.

Determinanti le riserve della cultura neorealistica, la censura della critica crociana e gramsciana, le implicazioni di natura politica del poeta della stirpe. Vale la pena pertanto accennare, seppur brevemente, alle messe in scena che, riproponendo nel profondamente mutato panorama del teatro italiano del dopoguerra *La figlia di Iorio,* più hanno fatto discutere. Ardua impresa costituisce infatti la messa in scena de *La figlia di Iorio,* percorsa com'è, in un magico equilibrio, da due filoni, quello mitico, arcaico, fuori del tempo, e quello storico, reale, collegato ad un preciso contesto geografico e culturale; quasi per un'intima necessità di sostanziare di realtà il mito e di mito la realtà. Talora si rimprovera, pertanto, alle scelte registiche un'impostazione eccessivamente lirica, onirica, mitica, talaltra eccessivamente realistica, nel tentativo di ancorare il «mistero» dannunziano ad un contesto reale che renda credibili personaggi e azione ed insieme, con la sua arcaicità, li trasporti nella terra del sogno, del non *déjà vu.* Un realismo a cui forse non è estranea l'influenza di canoni recitativi che in qualche modo sono riconducibili, se pur indirettamente, al grande modello di Giovanni Grasso.

Il 26 luglio 1957 la Compagnia Proclemer-Albertazzi, diretta da Lucio Ardenzi, regista Luigi Squarzina, diede vita al «Teatro del

Vittoriale» ad uno spettacolo apprezzato dalla critica per la potenza espressiva dei suoi interpreti. Non sempre unanime, invece, il consenso sulla linea registica che, a giudizio di alcuni critici, mortificava il lirismo onirico della tragedia pastorale. Squarzina invero in quegli anni privilegiava un forte, anche se talora allucinato, realismo.

E se la *Mila* della Proclemer ricordava la tumultuosa passionalità de *La Lupa* verghiana, verso cui si indirizzavano pure le musiche di Angelo Musco *jr*, la interpretazione di Giorgio Albertazzi dava vita, in un'aura fiabesca, ad un *Aligi* tutto suo, passivo e dolorante.

Sempre al «Teatro del Vittoriale» un altro allestimento de *La figlia di Iorio* ebbe luogo il 14 luglio 1972, protagonisti Valentina Fortunato e Luigi Vannucchi, con la regia di Paolo Giuranna che impresse alla *pièce* un taglio decisamente junghiano ammiccando alla teoria degli archetipi mitici di Mircea Eliade. E la lettura della tragedia pastorale alla luce dei maggiori teorici degli archetipi mitici (e fra gli altri vanno ricordati pure almeno Károly Kerényi e Erich Neumann), già anticipata da Emilio Mariano, è stata ora approfondita da Anna Meda.

Giuranna intendeva rappresentare, come scrisse nel programma di sala: «la tragica iniziazione all'autocoscienza individuale di tre figure umane (*Mila, Aligi, Ornella*) che tentano di distaccarsi dal grembo dell'inconscio collettivo superando i legami del sangue e della tradizione (...) in nome di una *pietas* consapevole che non deriva dal sangue e che non è iscritta nell'usanza».

In *Mila* (Valentina Fortunato) tutta vestita di bianco, *Aligi* (Luigi Vannucchi) scorge, è ancora il regista a parlare, «la precisazione del suo Sé Superiore (l'Angelo Muto)». Nel terzo atto, dopo aver bevuto il vino dell'oblio, *Aligi* assume una posizione prenatale, come raggomitolandosi nel grembo della madre, ritornando nell'inconscio collettivo, e *Mila* si ricongiunge, mediante il fuoco, al suo Sé Superiore. Ma gli esiti non furono pari alle aspettative.

Nell'aprile 1973 l'irriverente regia di Giancarlo Cobelli, per *La figlia di Iorio* proposta dal «Teatro Stabile dell'Aquila», protagonisti Piera degli Esposti e Aldo Reggiani, sostituiva all'ambiente contadino e regionale quello borghese in un contesto di commedia di *boulevard* con gli uomini in frac e le donne in lungo. Una *Figlia di Iorio* che richiamava *La Signora dalle Camelie* di Dumas (ma già nel '30 l'accostamento era stato fatto da Silvio d'Amico). Tuttavia il gioco, l'ironia, la satira non realizzavano appieno le intenzioni teoriche del regista, evidenziare lo scontro tra morale di gruppo e libertà individuale, tra una realtà tranquilla e fiduciosa di sé, convinta delle proprie certezze, mai messe veramente alla prova, e un elemento estraneo che stravolge, rivelandone l'inconsistenza, l'ordine quotidiano, tale solo in apparenza. La scenografia era ridotta all'essenziale, con un palcoscenico quasi nudo dove la caducità del mondo rappresentato era sottolineata dalla straripante presenza di una materia duttile e incoerente come la stoffa.

Il 16 marzo 1982, *La figlia di Iorio* è messa in scena al «Teatro Metastasio» di Prato, con la regia di Roberto De Simone, protagonisti Edmonda Aldini e Michele Placido. Una messa in scena tesa a liberare il testo da parentele veristiche con *La Lupa* o *Cavalleria rusticana* di verghiana memoria, per immergerlo negli studi antropologici, etnografici, folclorici, nelle culture arcaiche del sud, nelle interpretazioni che dei miti e dei sogni hanno dato Freud e Jung. Negli *Appunti di regia* per il programma di sala, lo stesso De Simone a proposito di questa tragedia dell'«antico sangue» i cui segnali affondano nel tessuto profondo dei linguaggi universali osserva che essa è «la visione delirante di una cultura contadina nei suoi miti archetipici letta ed esposta dalla crisi della stessa cultura dannunziana. In tal senso è protagonista un visionarismo delirante, contrapposto ad un ideale di "fantastico" irraggiungibile». In d'Annunzio infatti «c'è un'intima aderenza ad una radice, con la coscienza del peso del peccato di un'arte senza funzione religiosa, tesa alla "prostituzione", al conflitto tra edonismo estetico, forma e contenuto».

A quasi un secolo dalla prima rappresentazione da parte della «Compagnia Drammatica Siciliana» di Giovanni Grasso, il 5 luglio 1997, *'A figghia di Joriu*, con la regia di Melo Freni, protagonisti Emma Di Martino e Giampiero Cicciò (altri interpreti furono: Turi Scalia, Fioretta Mari), ha inaugurato nello splendido scenario del «Teatro Greco» di Taormina le manifestazioni di «TaoArte '97». Con i molti elementi della pastorale, dal ritualismo arcaico all'onirismo mitico, la prorompente forza emotiva del dialetto ha esaltato in particolare uno degli aspetti più inquietanti del capolavoro dannunziano che può essere ricondotto alla hegeliana formula generale della follia. Tangibile in quei personaggi nei quali il destino si compie non come sviluppo dialettico dell'essere ma come stasi dell'essere stesso in una sua delirante identificazione ideale. Da qui l'esclusione, l'emarginazione dell'estraneo, del diverso, la violenza del singolo, del gruppo, del mondo contro chi appare destabilizzante le leggi sociali e morali. Sulla follia di *Aligi, Mila, Cannia di la Liunissa, Lazzaru di Roju,* si staglia però l'innocenza dei puri di cuore (*Ornella*) che avranno il compito di testimoniare la verità.

Certo nella quasi secolare avventura de *La figlia di Iorio*, che ha visto cimentarsi con la tragedia dannunziana le personalità di maggiore spicco del teatro italiano, molte altre messe in scena, oltre quelle delle quali si è già detto, meriterebbero, se lo spazio lo consentisse, di essere sia pur cursoriamente ricordate.

La figlia di Iorio di Gabriele d'Annunzio fra lingua e dialetto

Sarah Zappulla Muscarà

Università di Catania

«Schiacciato ammalato per le impressioni provate», ancora in preda all'«affanno che sale e fa soffrire veramente, chiudendo la gola», l'autore di *Persuasione*, il filosofo e poeta Carlo Michelstaedter, goriziano di nazionalità austriaca, di formazione mitteleuropea e di estrazione ebraica, dopo avere assistito alla messa in scena de *'A figghia di Joriu* da parte della «Compagnia Drammatica Siciliana», al «Teatro Niccolini» di Firenze, nella «notte tra il 6-7 novembre 1906» comunicando ai familiari la forte emozione così conclude:

> Quando l'atto si chiudeva dovevo fare uno sforzo quasi per ricordarmi che sono artisti e che fingono e poter cominciare ad ammirarli. Grasso è poderoso in ogni suo gesto e in ogni accento. Ha quella voce calda intensa che dà le vertigini. Specialmente il racconto che fa al santo nel 2° atto dove non c'è niente di lirico, dove tutta la bellezza poetica è tolta dalla versione in Siciliano, è un capolavoro. Pareva di rivivere le scene precedenti in tutta la loro intensità. [...] Fa l'impressione che la tragedia così in siciliano sia l'originale, l'italiana la traduzione, e certo d'Annunzio l'ha concepita così come noi la sentiamo da Grasso.[1]

Il giovane intellettuale aveva colto nel segno, giacché nella genesi de *La figlia di Iorio* fondamentali erano stati la suggestione di un attore straordinario quale Giovanni Grasso e il fascino del dialetto. A proposito di Grasso d'Annunzio aveva scritto al suo capocomico Nino Martoglio:

> In verità, la gioia di questa improvvisa rivelazione è in me commista di malinconia; perché invidio agli scrittori siciliani uno strumento

1. Carlo Michelstaedter, *Epistolario*, a cura di Sergio Campailla, Milano Adelphi, 1983, p. 139.

> d'arte meraviglioso qual è Giovanni Grasso, e mi rammarico di non poterlo adoperare e d'essere costretto a reprimere il mio lungo desiderio di tentare la tragedia agreste. Ieri sera, nella profonda commozione che mi travagliava, fui anche morso dalla nostalgia della mia vecchia terra d'Abruzzi. Grazie a voi, al grande e candido Giovanni Grasso e ai suoi compagni d'arte, in cui si esprime con tanta potenza l'anima della stirpe.[2]

È proprio la felice sintesi tra fiera passionalità ed innata teatralità a decretare il successo di Grasso e ad attrarre d'Annunzio che, seppur nei toni di una poetica fascinazione, avverte pungente *ananke* di passioni, *nostalghia* di umori mitico-pastorali. Dietro la suggestione esercitata su di lui da *La zolfara* di Giuseppe Giusti Sinopoli, a cui aveva assistito nell'aprile del 1903 al «Teatro Manzoni» di Milano, «scene sociali dal vero» che poggiavano su due grandi temi, quello economico, delle rivendicazioni sociali, della roba, del duro lavoro nelle zolfare, e quello passionale, dell'amore e della gelosia, e dal suo interprete, il poeta abruzzese promette di scrivere per quel «meraviglioso strumento d'arte, candido e grande», un dramma che abbia «anima nuova».[3] Alcuni mesi dopo, il 18 luglio 1903, d'Annunzio dà avvio alla stesura de *La figlia di Iorio*, ritornando, pur con più acceso lirismo, in quell'aura mistico-sensuale della sua prima stagione da cui sono scaturiti *Canto novo*, *Terra vergine* e *San Pantaleone*.

Il grande tragico — dal vate abruzzese battezzato «figlio della terra» (e Marinella Bragaglia «la piccola Duse») —, con la sua umanità istintiva e primordiale, ora dolente, ora disperata, partecipa così alla nascita de *La figlia di Iorio* unitamente al diaristico momento dell' 'incanata', evocato più tardi dal poeta, e al dipinto di Francesco Paolo Michetti.[4]

Stesa di getto in sole cinque settimane, nella serenità di Villa Borghese a Nettuno, dove soggiorna insieme a Eleonora Duse, la figlia

---

2. ——, *L'omaggio di Gabriele d'Annunzio alla Compagnia Siciliana*, «La Perseveranza», Milano, 30 aprile 1903 (riportato poi in: —, *Giovanni Grasso giudicato da Gabriele d'Annunzio*, «Corriere di Catania», Catania, 8 maggio 1903; —, *Giovanni Grasso e Gabriele d'Annunzio*, «Gazzetta di Messina», Messina, 12 maggio 1903).

3. Domenico Oliva, *Intorno alla nuova «Figlia di Iorio»*, «Il Giornale d'Italia», Roma, 13 settembre 1904.

4. Nell'intervista a Filippo Surico del giugno 1921 d'Annunzio, smentendo la funzione ispiratrice della tela di Michetti, preferisce ricordare l'episodio dell''incanata', accaduto a Tocco Casauria, nell'Abruzzo, a cui sarebbe stato presente insieme all'amico pittore, l'inseguimento cioè di una donna scarmigliata e urlante da parte di mietitori infoiati dal sole e dalla lussuria (Filippo Surico, *Ora luminosa. Le mie conversazioni letterarie con Gabriele d'Annunzio*, Roma, Urbs, 1939, pp.39-40). Sui dubbi avanzati al riguardo per incongruenze cronologiche che documenterebbero una presa di distanza dall'opera michettiana cfr. Ivanos Ciani, *Sulla genesi della «Figlia di Iorio»*, in AA.VV., *La figlia di Iorio*, Atti del VII Convegno internazionale di studi dannunziani [Pescara 24-26 ottobre 1985], Pescara, Centro nazionale di studi dannunziani, 1986.

Cicciuzza e l'amico Annibale Tenneroni, l'opera è siglata nell'agosto 1903 e subito d'Annunzio pensa alla pubblicazione e alla messa in scena sicché a Michetti il 31 agosto scrive:

> Per rappresentare una tale tragedia sono necessari attori vergini, pieni di vita raccolta, con gesti sobri ed eloquenti, con una voce retta dalle leggi del canto interiore. Perché qui tutto è canto e mimica.[5]

Sul finire di settembre ha luogo la prima lettura ufficiale, alla quale assistono Adolfo de Carolis e il giovane Giuseppe Antonio Borgese, invitato dal poeta a tradurre in siciliano *La figlia di Iorio* perché sia messa in scena dalla compagnia di Giovanni Grasso. È ancora viva dunque la memoria della rappresentazione milanese se il primo pensiero di d'Annunzio è la trasposizione linguistica della tragedia pastorale nei modi e nei toni richiesti da attori che parlano «il linguaggio delle passioni elementari», la cui funzione maieutica è documentata da quanto il poeta scrive a Francesco Paolo Michetti: «Quest'opera viveva dentro di me da anni, oscura». Ma lo scioglimento della Compagnia Siciliana per la romantica fuga della prima attrice, Marinella Bragaglia, con l'amministratore Vittorio Marazzi Diligenti impone a d'Annunzio la ricerca di una nuova compagnia che possa soddisfare la sua ansia di tempestiva rappresentazione. L'impegno maggiore sembra rivolto alla ricerca del materiale occorrente per la messa in scena. Per tale incombenza il poeta conta molto sull'aiuto di Michetti, ormai conquistato alla causa della messa in scena de *La figlia di Iorio*. La prima in assoluto sarà pertanto quella della versione in lingua, da parte della «Compagnia Talli-Gramatica-Calabresi», al «Teatro Lirico» di Milano, il 2 maggio 1904. Il ruolo di Mila di Codra, in un primo momento promesso a Eleonora Duse, raffreddatosi ormai il 'vate' nei confronti della 'divina', sarà assunto da Irma Gramatica. La versione siciliana sarà di pochi mesi successiva, appena il tempo per Grasso di sostituire la prima attrice.

Così Borgese, rievocando l'impressione riportata durante la lettura de *La figlia di Iorio* a Nettuno, scrive:

> Era cosa fresca e bellissima, un Aminta davvero agreste, un melodramma tutto pieno di musica senza bisogno di strumenti musicali; a me parve miracolosa; e meraviglioso dono mi parve l'invito del poeta a tradurre il poema per la compagnia siciliana nel mio dialetto nativo, e dargli la «seconda vita», com'egli troppo benevolmente mi lodò d'aver fatto dedicandomi il libro.[6]

---

5. Tommaso Sillani, *F. P. Michetti*, Milano-Roma, Treves-Treccani-Tumminelli, 1932, p. 113.
6. Giuseppe Antonio Borgese, *Grasso allo zenit*, "Corriere dela sera", Milano, 19 ottobre 1930.

E ancora molti anni dopo, sempre a proposito della famosa lettura:

> È cosa molto bella anche oggi, e il primo atto è mirabile. A me parve tutta sovrumana, un Parsifal maggiore. Quand'ebbe finito mi chiese di colpo se volessi tradurla in siciliano per la compagnia di Giovanni Grasso. Così divenivo scudiero, se non cavaliere, del santo Graal. M'invitava a una devozione.[7]

Il ventunenne siciliano, giovane intellettuale di singolare precocità, — direttore della rivista fiorentina «Hermes», autore dell'ampio saggio, molto apprezzato dal d'Annunzio, *L'opera poetica di Gabriele d'Annunzio* e di quello riccamente informato sugli studi di folclore *Giganti e Serpenti* — si accosta all'opera con entusiasmo stendendola

> in siciliano illustre e letterario, ricalcata sull'originale perfino nel numero dei versi e nelle assonanze.[8]

---

7. Giuseppe Antonio Borgese, *Con D'Annunzio a quei tempi*, in *Da Dante a Thomas Mann*, Milano, 1958, pp. 286-87.

8. Giuseppe Antonio Borgese, *Grasso allo zenit*, cit. Il trasloco linguistico deve risultare naturale a Borgese se nel maggio del 1902 alla sorella Marietta che gli rimprovera «l'influenza perniciosa» esercitata da d'Annunzio sulle sue «giovani facoltà artistiche» risponde che la forma dell'abruzzese «è troppo bella perché non incateni un artista giovine» (Leonardo Sciascia, *Per un ritratto dello scrittore da giovane*, Palermo, Sellerio, 1985, pp. 35-36). In una lettera di Grasso al «Maestro che è il vero Angelo Gabriele del buon Annunzio», come lo definisce, datata Palermo, 16 aprile 1904, troviamo come traduttore, accanto al nome di Borgese, anche quello di Giuseppe Pitrè, di cui il giovane di Polizzi Generosa era stato allievo all'Università di Palermo nell'anno accademico 1899-1900. Grasso scrive infatti a d'Annunzio: «Illustre Maestro / È qui, con me, Roberto Lombardo, venuto appositamente, come Lei sa a Catania, anche [a] organizzare la compagnia siciliana e ad annunziarmi la lieta novella della benevola concessione della Sua *Figlia di Iorio*, tradotta in siciliano dal Borgese e dal Pitrè. Per la fiducia ch'Ella ha riposto in me, la mia anima è commossa, ed ho pianto di gioia vicino a mia madre: e non trovo parole e sentimenti per restituire la mia gigante riconoscenza a Lei o Maestro che è il vero Angelo Gabriele del buon Annunzio. Lombardo torna a Roma ed Ella potrà mettersi d'accordo con lui che è l'unica persona a cui ho dato la mia fiducia e il mio affetto. Un secreto sentimento dice al mio cuore che Ella non rimarrà scontento del Suo devoto ed ubbidiente Giovanni Grasso» (uno stralcio della lettera si legge in Sarah Zappulla Muscarà e Enzo Zappulla, *Sicilia: Dialetto e Teatro. Materiali per una storia del teatro dialettale siciliano*, Agrigento, Edizioni del Centro Nazionale di Studi Pirandelliani, 1982, 2ª ed. aggiornata 1985, p. 180). Oltre alla lettera di Grasso a d'Annunzio abbiamo rintracciato un'altra testimonianza in cui figura come traduttore anche il Pitrè: «Si era annunziato che la *Figlia di Iorio* sarebbe stata eseguita prossimamente a Roma, dalla risorta compagnia siciliana di Giovanni Grasso, nella traduzione che ne hanno fatto i signori Borgese e Pitrè. La notizia non è esatta: — l'incarnazione siciliana della tragedia di d'Annunzio non potrà comparire in pubblico che nell'autunno prossimo, quando sarà in tutto compiuta la *tournée* della compagnia "Talli-Gramatica-Calabresi"» (—, *«La figlia di Iorio» in siciliano*, «La Tribuna», Roma, 8 aprile 1904).

Riscrittura di passioni elementari, in un codice intimamente riconosciuto primario, legato alla più segreta sostanza delle emozioni, la trasposizione dialettale riprende con sorprendente incisività caratteri ed ambienti del mitico borgo agreste e, conformandosi alle qualità esemplari del testo, pur nella sostanziale fedeltà, ne acuisce i sentimenti primitivi che dislagano.

Intorno alla metà di maggio del 1904, Borgese legge il testo siciliano alla compagnia di Nino Martoglio, riunita al «Teatro Adriano» di Roma, alla presenza di d'Annunzio, che approva la versione dialettale in «bellissimi versi», e dello scenografo Adolfo de Carolis.

Ne *'A figghia di Joriu* l'accorto Martoglio introduce, d'accordo con d'Annunzio, motivi musicali siciliani, opera del maestro Alberto Favara, anticipando in tal modo la raffinata operazione culturale della «Compagnia Drammatica del Teatro Mediterraneo» (1918-'19) che abilmente coniugherà dialetto e musica, secondo la lezione del teatro greco.

Il successo della prima della «Compagnia Drammatica Siciliana», al «Teatro Costanzi» di Roma, il 17 settembre 1904, è trionfale, anche se accanto a cronache entusiaste si registrano dissensi più o meno vistosi. Se Martoglio assicura che Borgese «ha usato vocaboli delle varie parlate siciliane che più si avvicinano alla lingua comune» e definisce la traduzione «ottima per colorito e per fedeltà»,[9] a Giustino Luigi Ferri il nuovo codice appare «eletto e decadente»[10] e Domenico Oliva tesse l'elogio della traduzione «fedelissima», dei versi «dolci e musicali», sottolineando nel contempo «il realismo scenico della ben congegnata tragedia pastorale».

«Incontrastata» l'ammirazione del commediografo Alessandro Varaldo:

> Fortunato chi ebbe l'idea di tradurre in siciliano il dramma di Gabriele d'Annunzio! Lo passò come in un crogiolo: tutto quanto — tutto poco — sapeva di convenzionale, quel crescere di immagini, che l'attenzione stanca e la suggestione sminuisce, dileguò: non rimase che la vita [...] in una armonia, in un insieme, in una fusione così veramente, semplicemente, supremamente meravigliosa. [...] nella veste più consona alla sua primitiva rozzezza d'immaginazione, chiusa nel siciliano aspro anche nella dolcezza, dà una copia di sensazioni veementi come nel nostro bello e piano eloquio non si credeva possibile.[11]

9. Domenico Oliva, *Intorno alla nuova «Figlia di Iorio»*, cit.

10. Leandro [Giustino Luigi Ferri], *Sul carro di Tespi. Autunno teatrale*, «Capitan Fracassa», Roma, 12 settembre 1904.

11. Alessandro Varaldo, *«La figlia di Iorio» al Politeama Regina Margherita*, «Il Corriere di Genova», 3 febbraio 1905 (poi in *Profili di attrici e di attori*, Firenze, Barbera, 1926, pp. 3-20). Cfr. inoltre: Elvi, *La figlia di Iorio*, «La Scena di Prosa», Roma, 23 settembre e 17 novembre 1904.

Il capolavoro dannunziano, comunque, in genere, appare più vicino alla sua origine.

La perizia del Borgese è consistita nel non aver depauperato i versi di d'Annunzio «della loro bellezza scultorea e soprattutto del loro carattere unico»[12] e nell'aver rinnovato nel dialetto siculo «in modo mirabile, il verso, il ritmo, la musicalità del testo originale, serbandone tutta l'alta e poetica efficacia»; nell'aver mantenuto il prezioso organismo poetico della pastorale arricchendolo nel nuovo codice linguistico, un siciliano aulico e illustre, d'immagini di grande suggestione.

Del repertorio di Grasso la tragedia pastorale di d'Annunzio costituirà sempre il fiore all'occhiello, unitamente a *Cavalleria rusticana*, *La Lupa*, *Dal tuo al mio* di Giovanni Verga, *Malia* di Luigi Capuana, *Morte civile* di Paolo Giacometti, *Zolfara* di Giuseppe Giusti Sinopoli, *I mafiusi della vicaria di Palermo* di Gaspare Mosca e Giuseppe Rizzotto.

Ma quali intime corrispondenze dialettiche fra il testo in lingua e quello in dialetto furono colte e perché la nuova veste si addice tanto a *La figlia di Iorio*?

Al dialetto, infatti, che è il marchio linguistico dell'impressionismo semantico, della realtà popolare, della passione, della memoria, della nostalgia, del mito, compete il mondo evocato, quello stesso da d'Annunzio consegnato ad una lingua che è flusso ininterrotto di preziosità ascrivibili all'intero arco della nostra storia letteraria ma pure recupero alto dell'oralità: laudari, canti popolari, rituali, nenie, malefizi, dove gli arcaici lemmi sono usati come volgarizzamenti, come dialetto, a dar corpo a sogni, concetti, sentimenti. Una sorta di umanizzazione del divino, una sua restituzione alla terra, giacché «il canto dell'antico sangue» non poteva essere intonato da una lingua lontana dai parlari del popolo. Esso doveva essere ricondotto agli idiomi di quella realtà, ai suoi sedimenti terragni, biologici e antropologici, ad una tradizione mediterranea autoctona. E Borgese, distillando segreti e fragranti umori e convertendoli in succhi e musica, faceva risorgere alla memoria l'antico.

Pochi nella fedele traduzione gli elementi di diversità fra i due testi. Ma è proprio in virtù della loro esiguità che essi si caricano di senso. Spie della più spontanea forza di emozioni, che la lingua raffrena, tali elementi investono la scelta lessicale, le figure del discorso, i modi grammaticali, la punteggiatura, sempre tuttavia nel rispetto dello stile dannunziano. Da qui perizia metrica, misura classica, accensioni liriche, cadenze musicali, aulicismi, arcaismi. Dai federiciani ai melici, il dialetto, la cui consolidata tradizione letteraria asseconda i «versi sovrumani», esibisce uno spessore più profondo per il quale le immagini, che d'Annunzio tesse come fregio dell'anima, si avviluppano in strettissimo nodo e si rapprendono. Talora basta una variante, un minimo spostamento di luogo, una *reduplicatio*, perché la pregnanza del

12. Fausto Mandalari, *D'Annunzio in siciliano*, «La Sicilia», Catania, 29-30 settembre 1904.

dialetto si dissemini in limpide sonorità e la densità lirica acquisti connotati espressionistici.

Si tratta di cambiamenti intesi ad avvicinare a più concreti veicoli di percezione l'indeterminato poetico. Per fare soltanto qualche esempio si confrontino i versi del 1° atto:

> ***CANDIA***
> *Àlzati, figlio. Come strano parli!*
> *La tua parola cangia di colore,*
> *come quando l'ulivo è sotto il vento.*
>
> ***CANNIA***
> *Sùsiti, figghiu. Parri curiusu!*
> *La to' palora cancia di culuri*
> *comu 'i pampini d'alivi pi lu ventu.*

Dalla traduzione borgesiana scompare il *come* che in lingua introduce l'interrogativa-esclamativa retorica. Ciò consente di focalizzare l'attenzione sulla partecipata consapevolezza della madre senza smorzarne il sentimento di angoscioso stupore. Nell'ultimo verso i cambiamenti investono il piano lessicale e sintattico. Allargando la base di comparazione e catturando la percezione visiva, la figura analogica d'insieme, *l'ulivo*, si parcellizza distribuendosi con valore rafforzativo a *'i pampini d'alivi*. Inoltre, realizzando un particolare tipo di sinergismo sintattico, la modale, sottratta ad ogni riferimento di tempo e di luogo (*quando, sotto* non vengono tradotti), si carica di valenze causali fortemente impressive (*pi lu ventu*).

Un altro esempio significativo della capacità del dialetto di esaltare i dettagli è nella scena d'amore del 2° atto:

> ***ALIGI***
> (appressandosi ancora)
> *Su la tua faccia il pianto non s'asciuga,*
> *creatura. Una lacrima ti resta*
> *nei cigli; trema, se parli; e non cade.*
>
> ***ALIGGI***
> (appressandosi ancora)
> *'Nta l'occhi toi lu chiantu nun s'asciuca,*
> *criatura. 'Na lagrima ti resta*
> *'nta li gigghia, ca luci e nun ti cadi.*

Per quanto in apparenza minime, le modifiche (*Su la tua faccia* → *'Nta l'occhi toi; trema* → *ca luci*) investono il campo semantico determinando il passaggio da un circuito dialogico di superficie a uno più profondo.

L'occhi, topos lirico di grande suggestione, ancorati alla più luminosa immagine del pianto (*ca luci*), attivando un processo d'identificazione empatica, catturano tenere ma tenaci emozioni. Non tradotto l'ipotetico *se parli* sostituito dal *ti* rafforzativo.

E ancora a riprova della maggiore caratterizzazione del dialetto, si confrontino i versi del 3° atto:

CANDIA
Ecco e la Madre si mette in cammino,
viene alla vista del suo dolce figlio.
— O madre, madre, perché sei venuta?
Tra la gente giudea non v'è salute.
— Portato un braccio t'ho di pannolino
per ricuoprirti il tuo corpo ferito.

CANNIA
Eccu e la Matri si metti 'ncaminu,
veni a la vista di la so' criatura.
— O matri, matri, pirchì si' vinuta?
'Ntra li genti judei nun c'è saluti.
— E purtai pi tia un parmu di tila,
figghiu, ca la to' chiaja sangunìa.

Nel 2° verso scompare l'attributo *dolce* riferito a *figlio*, tradotto col più intenso e motivato *criatura*. Il 5° verso si apre con la *E* in uso assoluto che stabilisce, in un'aura di allucinato stordimento, segrete relazioni. Al complemento di termine si sostituisce quello più incisivo di vantaggio (*pi tia*). Il cambiamento lessicale *braccio* → *parmu*, pur ruotando intorno alla stessa area semantica, tende a restringere il campo visivo recuperando sul piano connotativo la struggente memoria di un figlio bambino. L'introduzione del vocativo *figghiu*, assente in italiano, riconduce infatti l'estraniata nenia di *Cannia* alle sue sofferenze di madre, la finale *per ricuoprirti* è sostituita con la causale introdotta dalla particella *ca*, mentre *il tuo corpo ferito* diviene *la to' chiaja*, più cruenta e pertanto più toccante al pari della predicazione *sangunìa*.

S'infittiscono i diminutivi, le sfumature metaforiche, al fine di potenziare la carica affettiva della dimensione domestica; il nome proprio dei personaggi cede talora il passo a quello parentale esaltando i legami familiari (*Vienda* → *cugnatuzza*); di gran lunga più frequenti gli esclamativi che se attenuano la solennità dei versi dannunziani ne accentuano la passionalità.

Borgese ricorre quindi a tutte le seduzioni del dialetto discostandosi dal positivo in vari momenti: nell'impiego dei tempi verbali, nell'uso della metatesi, nel ricorso ad una fitta presenza di sostantivi alterati (diminutivi, vezzeggiativi, accrescitivi, peggiorativi) che assicurano alla frase ora una carica di affettività, di tenerezza, ora un senso di limitatezza o di disprezzo, nell'uso di alcuni costrutti tipici che conferiscono al dettato precisione e pregnanza. Un dialetto eterogeneo, non vistosamente caratterizzato e pertanto non riconducibile ad una ben precisa area geografica giacché abbraccia insieme parlate riscontrabili nel palermitano, nel catanese e in altre zone dell'isola. Una poliparlata, dunque, una sorta di siciliano ecumenico, vario e ricco, da cui scaturisce la suggestiva molecola stilistica che fa de *'A figghia di Joriu* un capolavoro nel capolavoro.

Espressioni, lessemi, frasi, modi di dire donano alla traduzione dialettale quel particolare sapore e colore locale che definiscono e connotano una regione differenziandola da un'altra, nel caso in specie la Sicilia dall'Abruzzo. La traduzione di Borgese quindi non solo mantiene tutto il carisma della pastorale dannunziana, ma in taluni luoghi lo potenzia arricchendolo di suggestioni liriche.

'A figghia di Joriu non può non avvalersi, oltre che dei numerosi modelli femminili della classicità, dell'esperienza teatrica siciliana, percorrendo la pastorale, fra gli innumerevoli altri, itinerari omologhi e sovrapponibili a quelli di Verga e di Capuana.

Sottili e tenaci precorrimenti della tragedia si colgono ne *La Lupa*, creatura primordiale e ferina, esemplare sinossi dell'eros che diviene consapevole volizione, drammatica rinuncia, totale annientamento. Approdata ad una dimensione archetipa, fuori da qualsiasi tempo storico, cristallizzata nella forma di un demoniaco maleficio da esorcizzare, la *Lupa* supera nella fame di sacrificio lo scarto impietoso tra istinto e ragione, tra passione e pentimento. Il lavacro di sangue accomuna la *Lupa* verghiana e la *Mila* dannunziana, entrambe incarnazione della *mavaria* ed elemento di deflagrazione dell'istituto familiare. È attraverso il loro annichilimento che la tribale società arcaica difende la propria integrità. Ma se per la *gnà Pina*, trasgressiva fino in fondo, con la carne bruciante e l'anima piagata, l'amore è essenzialmente passione erotica, per *Mila* diviene riscatto mediante la rinuncia e l'abnegazione eroica. Con la castità e la morte *'a figghia di Joriu* monderà l'infamante passato, offrendo una nuova immagine di sé giacché la verità potrà essere testimoniata da *Ornella* ai puri di cuore.

Anche *Malia* di Capuana traeva origine dalla lucida ricognizione del labirinto dei sentimenti dominati da un eros trasgressivo e incestuoso. *Jana*, che riverbera in parte la luce magica della *Lupa* sul piano della consapevole ansia sensuale, soggiogata dalle barriere dei vincoli familiari respinge nella mistificazione dell'autoinganno l'insano sentimento per *Cola*, sigillato da un ritegno estraneo all'eroina verghiana. Vicina a *'A figghia di Joriu* per l'ancestrale patologia dell'esistere, ancorata al *milieu* eterogeneo, fatalmente superstizioso, religiosamente pagano, socialmente arretrato, del mondo contadino.

Ma d'Annunzio non ha pensato subito solo alla traduzione in siciliano, ha pensato pure subito, com'è naturale, all'abruzzese. Sicché legge tempestivamente la sua tragedia pastorale ai cugini Filippo e Cesare de Titta ma poi sarà il solo Cesare a portarla a termine.

Dopo aver letto il suo dramma pastorale all'amico, d'Annunzio gli dice: «Senti? È il canto dell'antico sangue nostro. E tu e Cesare ne farete la traduzione in abruzzese, riportando *La figlia di Iorio* alla legittima dizione materna».[13] Un'unica raccomandazione aveva rivolto d'Annunzio nella lettera del 20 marzo 1910: «mondare la traduzione dalle forme troppo locali».

Il de Titta utilizzò, per la sua traduzione, condotta anch'essa con «grande fedeltà al testo originale e perizia tecnica»,[14] la parlata abruzzese dell'antica «Monteclum», piccolo comune del chietino, «semplice, rude e armoniosa» come è stata definita, quella stessa evocata nella veste italiana.

Per quel ritorno al nietzschiano «mitico grembo materno» di un'opera in cui d'Annunzio aveva voluto ricreare con cura ambienti, usi, costumi, credenze del suo Abruzzo, presente, con l'inserimento di dialettismi, anche in una lingua che ricrea il toscano antico, *La fijje di Iorie*, senza tradire il modello originale, acquista un gusto tutto locale, fortemente folclorico.

Ancora una volta, la veste dialettale «si rivela non un meccanico trasporto lemmatico, ma una "legittima rincarnazione" di favola fantasiosa in un "parlare più autentico"».[15]

Alla 'parodia', destino di tutti i capolavori letterari e teatrali, non poteva sfuggire neppure *La figlia di Iorio*.

«'A fava è bella! 'A fava è bella!»: così Eduardo Scarpetta conclude la 'commedia presepiana' in due atti *Il figlio di Iorio*, e il capovolgimento comico è già evidente dal titolo, parodiando in napoletano la celebre pastorale dannunziana alla cui prima nella versione in siciliano, il 17 settembre 1904, al «Teatro Costanzi» di Roma, egli era presente: «Appena ebbi divorati quei tre atti in una notte [...] non sognai altro che parodiare quella tragedia».[16]

---

13. Filippo de Titta, *Un capolavoro di G. d'Annunzio*, «La Fiaccola», Ortona, 25 dicembre 1914.

14. Umberto Russo, *La traduzione in abruzzese della «Figlia di Iorio»*, in AA. VV., *La figlia di Iorio*, Atti del VII Convegno internazionale di studi dannunziani, cit., pp. 272-273.

15. Vittore Verratti (a cura di), Gabriele d'Annunzio, *«La figlia di Iorio» con a fronte la traduzione in dialetto abruzzese di Cesare de Titta*, cit., p. 7. Va ricordato inoltre che si deve a Georges Hérelle la traduzione francese *La fille de Iorio.* Tragédie pastorale de Gabriele d'Annunzio, Paris, Calmann-Lévy, 1905; e che d'Annunzio stesso curò la trascrizione librettistica della sua tragedia per il compositore Alberto Franchetti, che la musicò: *La figlia di Iorio*. Tragedia pastorale di Gabriele d'Annunzio, musica di Alberto Franchetti, Milano, Ricordi, 1906. L'opera fu messa in scena al «Teatro La Scala» di Milano il 29 marzo 1906.

16. Eduardo Scarpetta, *Cinquant'anni di palcoscenico*, Napoli, tip. Gennarelli, 1922, pp. 357-358 (ristampa, con l'aggiunta di nuovi capitoli, del volume di memorie dell'attore

Il comico napoletano (non nuovo per altro alle parodie, si pensi a quella della *Bohème* di Puccini), alle rimostranze epistolari del Vate, ribatte argutamente di non credere «che egli abbia l'assoluto dominio di tutta la famiglia di Iorio», nondimeno, anche in considerazione delle gravose spese per l'allestimento scenico a cui andrà incontro, desidera ottenerne il consenso esplicito. Accompagnato dal comune amico Gaetano Miranda si spinge, pertanto, a far visita a d'Annunzio.

L'incontro, improntato a un reciproco scambio di complimenti e cortesie, è talmente cordiale da indurre Scarpetta a partire senza aver ricevuto il tanto agognato consenso scritto, ulteriormente rinfrancato dalle rassicurazioni del professor Annibale Tenneroni sulla totale benevolenza del poeta.[17]

La *première* ha luogo la sera del 3 dicembre 1904 al «Real Teatro Mercadante» di Napoli. Ma già all'annuncio della rappresentazione erano pervenute alla Prefettura proteste e pressioni per impedirne la messa in scena, che è comunque autorizzata ma che si svolge fra contrasti e non giunge alla fine.

Marco Praga, direttore generale della «Società italiana degli Autori», a nome del socio d'Annunzio e della stessa Società, sporge querela contro Scarpetta per contraffazione della tragedia dannunziana e riproduzione abusiva sulle scene. Il processo suscita notevole interesse per l'esilarante e scoppiettante comportamento dell'imputato e il calibro delle personalità che vi sono coinvolte: per Scarpetta, periti Benedetto Croce e Giorgio Arcoleo; per d'Annunzio, periti Roberto Bracco e Salvatore Di Giacomo. La perizia Croce-Arcoleo precisa che

> la contraffazione — che per le forme ingannevoli che assume, non sempre può essere colpita dalla legge — consiste nel mutare, se questo giova, lingua e particolari, serbando lo spirito dell'opera. La parodia, invece, può serbare moltissimi particolari e perfino quasi integro il linguaggio dell'opera parodiata; ma ne muta sempre lo spirito animatore.[18]

Croce e Arcoleo dichiarano che

> nel caso della Figlia di Iorio lo Scarpetta aveva innanzi un'opera di argomento e forma rara e ricercata, che si svolge in un ambiente di usi,

---

intitolato *Da San Carlino ai Fiorentini*, Napoli, tip. del Pungolo parlamentare, 1899, entrambe con prefazione di Benedetto Croce). Tutta la vicenda è rievocata nel XXI capitolo, *Il mio processo*, pp. 357-394.

17. L'episodio è reso noto, assieme ad alcuni brani della parodia, da Aniello Falcone, *«Il figlio di Iorio» di Eduardo Scarpetta. Scarpetta a... Canossa! - La pace con d'Annunzio*, «La Tribuna», Roma, 15 settembre 1904. Cfr. anche: —, *«Il figlio di Iorio» di Eduardo Scarpetta*, cit.

18. *Appendice alla Memoria nella causa per «Il figlio di Iorio» contro Eduardo Scarpetta*, depositata il 24 aprile 1908, p. 5.

> sentimenti e tradizioni recondite o ignote, con parole e nomi non facili e nuovi, e perciò si è sentito costretto a riprodurne i punti salienti perché fosse possibile allo spettatore che ride, il richiamo del dramma, che aveva destato, invece, terrore e pietà. La seconda ragione di errore è stata nello scambio tra il giudizio sull'indole di un lavoro e quello sulla sua bellezza o bruttezza; ossia nell'aver perduto di vista la questione giuridica per la questione letteraria.[19]

Le stesse argomentazioni vengono ribadite da Arcoleo nel corso del pubblico dibattimento:

> Lo Scarpetta forse avrà ingiuriato l'arte facendo un'opera sbagliata ma non ha offeso il diritto del d'Annunzio, facendogli sleale concorrenza. Qui siamo innanzi ad un Collegio che amministra giustizia, non dianzi ad una commissione che debba concedere un premio artistico.[20]

Lo Scarpetta, concludono pertanto i periti dell'attore,

> dovrebbe essere condannato se avesse commesso una contraffazione, il che non è. Ma non può essere condannato per avere eseguito un lavoro letterario sbagliato.[21]

Giudizio accolto dalla sentenza di non luogo a procedere per inesistenza di reato, il cui estensore, dopo aver stabilito che «d'Annunzio vuol destare sentimenti di dolore e di terrore; Scarpetta giovialità e riso», riferendosi alle doti comiche di Scarpetta, aggiunge: «eziandio una lagrima, cadendo dal suo viso, diventerebbe ridicola».[22] A d'Annunzio verrà rimproverata da «Le Figaro» una certa mancanza *d'esprit* poiché «i capolavori son per l'appunto le uniche opere d'arte che invitano alla parodia» sicché «più d'un autore pagherebbe ben cara la gloria d'esser messo in caricatura!», anzi la parodia «penetra sempre laddove è elemento di vitalità».[23]

Ed è proprio questa duttilità, questa disponibilità ad essere trasferita in altri codici a documentare la grandezza del capolavoro dannunziano.[24]

---

19. Ivi, p. 9. Anche in: Eduardo Scarpetta, *Cinquant'anni di palcoscenico*, cit., p. 371.
20. Eduardo Scarpetta, *Cinquant'anni di palcoscenico*, cit., p. 373.
21. *Appendice alla Memoria nella causa per «Il figlio di Iorio» contro Eduardo Scarpetta*, cit., p. 10.
22. Eduardo Scarpetta, *Cinquant'anni di palcoscenico*, cit., p. 381.
23. Il Capitan Spavento, *L'amante onorario - La famiglia di Iorio*, «Il Tirso», Roma, 3 dicembre 1905.
24. La stesura italiana de *La figlia di Iorio* del 1904, la versione in siciliano di Giuseppe Antonio Borgese, quella in abruzzese di Cesare de Titta e la parodia in napoletano di Eduardo Scarpetta si trovano ora riunite nel volume, riccamente illustrato, che ripercorre un secolo di messe in scena della tragedia pastorale: Sarah Zappulla Muscarà e Enzo Zappulla, *Gabriele d'Annunzio. «La figlia di Iorio» tra lingua e dialetti*, Catania, la Cantinella, 1998, pp. 354.

APPENDICE BIBLIOGRAFICA

Della ricca bibliografia sull'opera teatrale più felice di d'Annunzio, oltre a quella già citata nel saggio introduttivo, ci limitiamo a ricordare la più recente e significativa:

Ettore Paratore, *Naturalismo e decadentismo in Gabriele d'Annunzio*, in *Studi dannunziani*, Napoli, Morano, 1966.

Idem, *Le due tragedie abruzzesi*, in AA. VV., *L'arte di Gabriele d'Annunzio*, Milano, Mondadori, 1968.

Mario Pomilio, *D'Annunzio e l'Abruzzo*, in *L'arte di Gabriele d'Annunzio*, Milano, Mondadori, 1968.

AA. VV., *Pagine abruzzesi*, L'Aquila, 1970.

Eurialo De Michelis, *Una lettera di d'Annunzio*, in *Novecento e dintorni. Dal Carducci al neorealismo*, Milano, 1976.

Riccardo Scrivano, *Decadentismo e teatro. Note dannunziane*, «Critica letteraria», Napoli, 10, 1976.

Emilio Mariano, *Due schede teatrali. I riti della «Figlia di Iorio»* in AA. VV., *Il teatro di d'Annunzio*, «Quaderni del Vittoriale», settembre-ottobre 1978.

Anna Barsotti, *Il «teatro di poesia»*, «Rivista italiana di drammaturgia», III, dicembre 1978.

AA. VV., *Il teatro di d'Annunzio oggi*, Atti del convegno di studi, «Quaderni del Vittoriale», 24, 1980.

Luigi Scorrano, *Fonti manzoniane per «La figlia di Iorio»*, «Critica letteraria», Napoli, a.VIII, fasc.IV, 1980.

Roberto De Monticelli, *Le rappresentazioni dannunziane dopo il 1945 in Italia*, «Quaderni del Vittoriale», novembre-dicembre 1980.

Emilio Mariano, *La religiosità nella «Figlia di Iorio»*, «Quaderni del Vittoriale», luglio-agosto1981.

Raffaella Bertazzoli, *L'elaborazione della «Figlia di Iorio» dal «naturale» al «mitico»*, «Otto/Novecento», Varese, 5-6, settembre-dicembre 1981.

Paolo Puppa, *«La figlia di Iorio» tra Michetti e d'Annunzio*, «Quaderni del Vittoriale», 29, 1981 (poi in *La parola alta. Sul teatro di Pirandello e d'Annunzio*, Bari, Laterza, 1993).

Ruggero Jacobbi, *Note sul teatro dannunziano*, «Rassegna dannunziana», I, 1, 1982.

Franco Di Tizio, *Lettere di d'Annunzio a Paolo De Cecco*, «Quaderni del Vittoriale», n.37, gennaio-febbraio 1983.

Luigi Ravasi Bellocchio, *Appunti di lettura del profondo su «La figlia di Iorio»*, «Quaderni di teatro», febbraio 1983.

Alfredo Barbina, *La mantellina di Santuzza*, Roma, Bulzoni, 1983.

L. M. Gunzberg, *D'Annunzio naïf: primitivismo e arcaismo nella «Figlia di Iorio»*, «Lettere italiane», 4, 1984.

Roberto Alonge, *«La figlia di Iorio» ovvero la religione delle madri*, in AA.VV., *L'arte dell'interpretare. Studi critici offerti a Giovanni Getto*, Cuneo, L'Arciere, 1984.

Ugo Ronfani, *La bella fiamma di Edmonda Aldini*, in *Il teatro in Italia*, Milano, Spirali, 1984.

Raffaella Bertazzoli, *Percorso creativo e approdo mitico nella «Figlia di Iorio»*, «Quaderni di lingua e letteratura», Istituto di Lingue e letterature straniere, Università di Verona, 10, 1985.

Ivanos Ciani, *Lettere a Giselda Zucconi*, Pescara, 1985.

AA.VV., *La figlia di Iorio*, Atti del VII Convegno internazionale di studi dannunziani, Pescara, Centro nazionale di studi dannunziani, 1986.

Gabriele d'Annunzio, *«La figlia di Iorio» come tragedia di identità*, introduzione di Eurialo De Michelis, «Otto/Novecento», Varese, 3-4, maggio-agosto 1986.

Raffaella Bertazzoli, *«La figlia di Iorio» da Michetti a d'Annunzio*, «Annali d'Italianistica», a cura di D. S. Cervigni, vol 5, Fascicolo monografico, *D'Annunzio*, 1987.

Franca Angelini, *Teatro e spettacolo nel primo novecento*, Bari, Laterza, 1988.

Guido Nicastro, *«La figlia di Iorio» tra mito e realtà*, in *Il poeta e la scena*, Catania, Edizione del Prisma, 1988.

Riccardo Scrivano, *La figlia di Iorio, La fiaccola sotto il moggio*, in AA.VV. *D'Annunzio a cinquant'anni dalla morte*, Atti dell'XI Convegno internazionale di studi dannunziani, Pescara, Centro nazionale di studi dannunziani, 1988, vol. II.

Ottaviano Giannangeli, *D'Annunzio e l'Abruzzo. Storia di un rapporto esistenziale e letterario*, Chieti, Marino Solfanelli, 1988.

Valentina Valentini, *«La figlia di Iorio», una tragedia di popolo*, «Biblioteca Teatrale», nn.9-10,1988.

Raffaella Bertazzoli, *Il mito raggiunto. Preistoria creativa e vicenda testuale nella «Figlia di Iorio»*, Milano, Franco Angeli, 1989.

Gigi Livio, *Talli-d'Annunzio: «La figlia di Iorio»*, in *La scena italiana. Materiali per una storia dello spettacolo dell'Otto e Novecento*, Milano, Mursia, 1989.

Gabriele d'Annunzio, *La figlia di Iorio*, a cura di Vito Moretti, introduzione di Dacia Maraini, Pescara, D'Incecco, 1990.

Andrea Bisicchia, *D'Annunzio e il teatro. Tra cronaca e letteratura drammatica*, Milano, Mursia, 1991.

I. Benfante, *Mito e rito nel teatro dannunziano*, in *D'Annunzio e la giovane critica*, Pescara, Centro nazionale di studi dannunziani, 1992.

Gianni Oliva, *D'Annunzio e la poetica dell' invenzione*, Milano, Mursia, 1992.

M. A. Balducci, *Un grido lacerante. Strutture simboliche ne «La figlia di Iorio»*, «Rassegna dannunziana», XI, 23, 1993.

Laura Granatella, *Arrestate l'autore!*, Roma, Bulzoni, 1993.

Giovanni Isgrò, *D'Annunzio e la mise en scène*, Palermo, Palumbo, 1993.

L'invenzione dei luoghi nella «Figlia di Iorio» e *«La figlia di Iorio» e il teatro "en plein air"*, in Anna Meda, *Bianche statue contro il nero abisso. Il teatro dei miti in d'Annunzio e Pirandello*, Ravenna, Longo, 1993.

Valentina Valentini, *Il poema visibile. Le prime messe in scena delle tragedie di Gabriele d'Annunzio*, Roma, Bulzoni, 1993.

Gabriele d'Annunzio, *Lettere a Georges Hérelle*, a cura di M. G. Sanjust, Bari, Laterza, 1994.

Gabriele d'Annunzio, *La figlia di Iorio*, introduzione di Pietro Gibellini, prefazione e note di Raffaella Bertazzoli, Milano, Garzanti, 1995.

Gabriele d'Annunzio, *La figlia di Iorio*, a cura di Milva Maria Cappellini, Milano, Mondadori, 1995.

Gabriele d'Annunzio, *La figlia di Iorio*, introduzione di Giovanni Antonucci, Roma, Newton & Compton, 1995.

Gabriele d'Annunzio, *La figlia di Iorio*, a cura di Gabriella Giaccone, introduzione di Giorgio Bàrberi Squarotti, Milano, Mursia, 1995.

Silvana Sinisi, *L'ora, i luoghi, le stagioni nella «Figlia di Iorio»*, «Il castello di Elsinore», Torino, a.IX, 25, 1996.

Angela Falco, *A proposito della prima rappresentazione della «Figlia di Iorio», ibidem.*

Gabriele d'Annunzio, *La hija de Iorio*, introducción y traducción de Joaquín Espinosa Carbonell, Valencia, Universitat, 1998.

La figlia di Iorio between Michetti and D'Annunzio

Paolo Puppa

University of Venice

The painting *La figlia di Iorio* by Francesco Paolo Michetti was exhibited at the first Biennale of Venice in 1895. D'Annunzio's pastoral tragedy was performed at the Lirico theatre of Milan on 2 March 1904. Not only did nine years intervene between the two works, the figurative and the theatrical, but also a thick dossier of reciprocal exchanges occurred. Although a complex link existed between these two artistic personalities (who were apparently so different, the painter being satisfied with his Abruzzian *Kultur* and the poet *déraçiné* from the Roman culture of the Hubertine/Pre-Raphaelite period) this cannot be considered the only basis for their dialogue.

D'Annunzio, twelve years junior of the already renowned Michetti, had been his friend's guest in the ex-convent of Francavilla Marina, which Michetti had turned into an artistic coterie. Here, in this "semplice e serena casa," in the "sede dell'arte severa," (as stated in his two introductions), the restless and promising adolescent penned his first novels, *Il piacere* and *Il trionfo della morte*, describing exotic perversions of aimless, neurotic heroes. Paradoxically, they were dedicated to Michetti, the illustrator of country idylls and village feasts. If these early novels are dedicated to the painter with a mixture of nostalgia, feelings of guilt and of proclaimed emancipation, and if at the painter's death in 1929, the poet launches into a heartfelt epitaph, "mi sembra che una metà di me sia morta e che mi venga meno il coraggio di vivere così menomato. [...] Egli era il fratello vero della mia anima;..."[1] during the last fifteen years of the century, D'Annunzio had sought out Michetti's paintings in earnest regarding them as privileged canvasses to be transferred to a page.

1. T. Rosina, *Mezzo secolo de 'La Figlia di Iorio'* (Principato: Messina, 1955) 278.

Just before *Il Voto*, Michetti's other celebrated painting, was exhibited in Rome in 1893 and later, transferred by his friend into the *Novelle della Pescara* (the short stories "Gli Idolatri" and "L'eroe") and into the description of the procession to the Casalbordino's Sanctuary in *Il trionfo della morte*, the writer had confessed: "Ogni volta che mi metto al tavolino col proponimento di scrivere di lui, tremo, tremo come una foglia. Ho qui in mente un barbaglio di colori, una prosa guizzante e scintillante [...]. Per scrivere di Michetti, bisogna alzar la chiave dello stile."[2]

In describing his friend's paintings, D'Annunzio does not spare his superlatives. In the Epilogue to *La Chimera*, he calls Michetti the "signor del pennello,"[3] and later even ranks him first among model painters, in spite of his heterogeneity and constant revisions: "Non è soltanto il più possente e il più felice organismo pittorico apparso in questo secolo; ma è anche la più acuta intelligenza che sia penetrata nel pieno spirito dell'arte moderna."[4]

When Michetti was working on the portrait of King Umberto and Queen Margherita, peculiarly parallel to the latest of Carducci's writings on Francesco Crispi, D'Annunzio was quick to define Titian's *Francesco I* and Raphael's *Giulio II* as being its renowned forerunners! The writer, however, is not alone in this over-estimation, as in those years Michetti's artistic development was compared to that of Virgil and Pascoli: the early pastoral topics corresponding to Virgil's *Bucolics* and *Georgics* on the one hand and to Pascoli's *Myricae* on the other, just as the ensuing feast cycles, from the 1877 *Corpus Domini* to the 1900 *Le Serpi* and *Gli Storpi* would constitute the exact *pendant* of the *Aeneid* and the *Poemi Conviviali*![5]

Time has inevitably extinguished such enthusiasm and seems to have had a parallel cooling effect upon the theatrical version of the painting. D'Annunzio's *La figlia di Iorio* is performed less and less frequently, excepting special occasions, and without the ritualistic thrust promoted by Stelio Effrena for his marble theater[6] on the hills of the Gianicolo. On the contrary, in 1904 the whole of Italy had been overrun, in a surprising and dizzying out-break from one region to another, by different stage versions of the tragedy: the polished version staged by the Virgilio Talli-Ruggeri-Irma Gramatica Company (the latter having replaced, after many trials and tribulations, Eleonora Duse in the role of Mila), and the lesser versions in dialect (from the Sicilian,

---

2. M. Vecchioni. *Artisti abruzzesi contemporanei* (Pescara: Edizioni Aternine, 1956) 25.
3. G. D'Annunzio, *La Chimera*, in *Versi d'amore e di gloria*, ed. A. Andreoli and N. Lorenzini, *I Meridiani*, vol. I (Milano: Mondadori, 1982) 583.
4. B. Tamassia Mazzarotto, *Le arti figurative nell'arte di Gabriele D'Annunzio* (Milano: Bocca, 1949) 510-11.
5. M. Biancale, *Le Serpi e gli Storpi di F. P. Michetti* (Milano: Bestetti-Tumminelli, 1933) 16.

edited by Borgese for the Grasso-Musco Company to the one in Abruzzese, supervised by Antonelli).

Similar parodistic adaptations by Novelli and Scarpetta, for example, despite legal consequences after-affects, were in reality only reminders of the initial triumph. The same can be said of the many rapidly successive adaptations of the play in various European stagings (from the Parisian *Oeuvre* of Lugné-Pöe to the South-American *tournées*), the translations into various languages, the music Franchetti wrote for it (a Wagnerian-Veristic piece performed at La Scala in 1906), and the film adaptation for Casa Ambrosio in 1911. The unanimous consensus and the dithyrambic manner of reports in the newspapers (Rosina 156), from in-depth reviews to general reactions of the public for the first time completely in tune with D'Annunzio's dramatic art, evidence a taste historically confined to the beginning of the century and peculiar to that period. Moreover, these various elements provide a key for reconstructing one of the ideological underground movements that later flowed into Fascism: the *nazional-populismo rurale*, which rose out of the learned classes.

In this way the painting and the tragedy, with their many links, are emerging emblems, mythic iconic constellations, figures and fables emerging from the frustrations, the ambitions and the hardships of the lower provincial middle class, from Adua to Caporetto.

Let us return to the painting. Michetti had studied for a few years at the Naples Accademia, with Domenico Morelli, before reluctantly returning to his native Abruzzi around 1870. He had had the time to absorb the various streams of that school: Giacinto Pezzana's use of light and shade, the Palizzi brothers' detailed analysis and tranquil idyllism, Michele Cammarano's small and slightly manneristic sketches, and Moretti's theatrical organization and research for emotional effect.[7] The many techniques borrowed from the romantic-realistic tradition were soon directed into a personal thematic vision: his fixation with ethnic subjects, with regional communities celebrating their local religion through village festivals, rituals of affliction, devotional pilgrimages — a kind of monumental and at the same time humble assemblage, contemporary with the inventories Giuseppe Pitrè recorded in that same period.

6. G. D'Annunzio, *Il Fuoco*, in *Prose di romanzi*, ed. N. Lorenzini, *I Meridiani*, vol. II (Milano: Mondadori, 1989) 286. For the iconography of this novel, see P. Puppa, "D'Annunzio mette a fuoco Tintoretto," in *Jacopo Tintoretto nel quarto centenario della morte*, ed. P. Rossi and L. Puppi (Padova: Il Poligrafo, 1996) 37-45.

7. About Michetti's work, see T. Sillani, *F. P. Michetti* (Milano: Treves, Treccani-Tumminelli, 1933) and U. Oietti, "F. P. Michetti," Commemoration read at the Reale Accademia d'Italia, on 11 December 1934, in *R. A. d'Italia, Celebrazioni*, year XII. Or, more generally, see P. Lecaldano, *I grandi maestri della pittura italiana dell' 800* (Milano: Rizzoli, 1958) and V. Guzzi, *Il ritratto nella pittura italiana dell'800* (Milano: Fabbri, 1967).

In *La figlia di Iorio*, on the contrary, Michetti effected a rigorous selection of styles as opposed to former serial groups, from *Corpus Domini* to *Il Voto* and from *Domenica delle Palme* and *Venerdì Santo* to *I Morticelli* and the final *Gli Storpi* and *Le Serpi*, implementing radically new criteria. This time the scene is not festive and has a limited number of characters involved in a rustic *tranche de vie*: a prostitute is walking among sleeping reapers with the Maiella mountain in the background. It is an everyday, prosaic event, but pervaded with a dream-like atmosphere that conveys allegorical overtones as the provisional titles reveal: *The Outcast* or *Prejudice* or *Passion* (Sillani 83). D'Annunzio immediately senses this change: "Il linguaggio di cui ora dispone è uguale alla grandezza del suo sogno interiore" (Sillani 70). On the other hand, Oietti sees in it a majestic quality, like that of stage-sculptures, which seemed so eccentric in the 1895 Biennale, dominated as it was by Impressionism and Divisionism (Oietti 21).[8]

In fact, all of Michetti's large canvases with folk-liturgical subjects were executed with a perspective style developed without a central axis, through parades crossing the mansions of a theatrical Mystery.[9]

So, in our painting, the characters are limited to the female protagonist in profile, covered by a red mantle, and to five peasants in various postures with varying expressions. Two of the peasants lie in a catatonic stupor and are divided by an old and severe man from the other two, who are represented with a malicious and laughing attitude. There are also a male figure whose head is hidden by the frame, while a woman carrying an amphora stands by his side. The neutral and opposing tints are very different from the strong and hot colours of the expressionist writing of D'Annunzio, his contemporary.

For this "interior dream," Michetti used many life studies, hundreds of attempts at sketching in close contact with his *d'en bas* subjects, preserved in the hermitage-laboratory of Francavilla. D'Annunzio baptized these portraits, with a well-chosen metaphor, Michetti's 'second cranium' (Biancale 13). In order to defend himself from accusations of 'Arcadian narrowness,' Michetti had combined the direct observation of naturalistic data with the use of a camera, thus becoming a catalyst of the eventual union, by the end of the century, of figurative mimesis and the technological and scientific experimentation possible with this new device.[10] In his commentaries on the paintings, the obsession with faces and the passionate examination of physiognomic

8. By the same author, see "Tre secoli di pittura napoletana," in *Nuova Antologia*, I-IV, 1938, issue 1585.

9. L. Zorzi, "Figurazione pittorica e figurazione teatrale," in *Storia dell'Arte italiana*, vol. I (Torino: Einaudi, 1979) 429.

10. M. Miraglia, "Note per una storia della fotografia italiana (1839-1911)," in L. Zorzi, *Storia dell'Arte italiana*, vol. III, 1981. 448-49; 514-15.

details, recurring elements in Michetti's works, are irrevocably shifted by D'Annunzio into an esoteric, magic, and ancestral atmosphere. This results also thanks to the revival of the Da Vincian archetype, chosen as a mythical symbol by the *estetizzanti* and neo-platonic currents orbiting around Angelo Conti.[11] The latter, a scholar of Schopenhauer, Wagner and Pater, in 1894 authored an essay on Giorgione in which he wished that all the arts would aim to serve music. He not only influenced D'Annunzio's taste by directing it towards the decorative style of Sartorio, De Carolis, Cambellotti, between Jugendstil and Sezession, but was also himself pushed towards the majestic, the Michelangiolesque and the simplified neo-classical style, as exemplified by De Carolis's engravings for the first edition of *La figlia di Iorio*, and Cambellotti's scenography for Siracusa, after World War I. As proof of this we have the character of Daniele Glauro in *Il Fuoco*, which had actually been drawn from Angelo Conti; everything depends on the meeting between the "vero abruzzese" and the "gelida virgo preraffaellita". In any case, even if D'Annunzio interprets Michetti through Conti and Conti through Michetti, his peculiar inclination to wear out and transfigure the external reference surely caused him to view the process of observation as a projection from his inner consciousness. Before a female figure such as *The Votive Offering*, which reminds him of a 15th century sculpture, D'Annunzio polemically asserts that: "non poteva essere presa dal vero. Perché l'artista non poteva chiedere ad un modello quell'ardore di fede. Egli dunque ha dovuto sentirla" (Vecchioni 35). One has to feel, then, more than observe, and do so only after having accurately suspended one's relation with the world, replacing it with diaphragms and manneristic associations, because D'Annunzio catches nature *in picturas*, as if it were disclosing an aesthetic approach.

Thus, on the one hand we find in D'Annunzio the maniacal reconstruction of rustic objects, the overflowing commentaries describing the country-pastoral setting of his tragedy (enough to fill a kind of poor pre-Vittoriale), the *horror vacui*, following perhaps the scenographic style of Meininger. In his effort to rebuild the *milieu* with scrupulous precision and to give acting and singing an archaic quality, he avails himself very freely of the material collected by Antonio De Nino[12] in his handbooks on ethnic oral poetry. On the other hand this search for

11. F. Ulivi, "D'Annunzio e le arti," in AA.VV., ed. E. Mariano, *D'Annunzio e il simbolismo europeo* (Milano: Saggiatore, 1976) 119. See also R. Ricorda, *Dalla parte di Ariele. Angelo Conti nella cultura di fine secolo* (Roma: Bulzoni, 1993).

12. G. Crocioni, *Problemi fondamentali del folklore, con due lezioni su il folklore e il D'Annunzio* (Bologna: Zanichelli, 1928) and B. Mosca, "Un amico abruzzese del D'Annunzio e Michetti," in *Il libro italiano* (Roma: Ulpiano, 1939) no. 4, 203-16. See also the recent S. Zappulla Muscarà and E. Zappulla, *G. D'Annunzio. "La figlia di Iorio" tra lingua e dialetti* (Acireale: La Cantinella, 1997).

realism did not prevent D'Annunzio from rebuking Michetti, to whom he had recourse for the staging of his premiere: "a noi bisognano invenzioni [...] La tragedia è quasi leggendaria [...] giova allontanarsi dalla terra di Mila e di Aligi" (Rosina 126).

In D'Annunzio's opinion Michetti was able to know by intuition the "invisible groups" and so to represent the "obscured thought of Nature,"[13] according to Shelling's philosophy: hence, the prostitute running among the reapers would be a primal scene, a fragment of a dream yet to be consummated. As the image of a dream tends, however, to be fixed and to dissolve itself at the same time, to impose itself as a figure and to undergo change through unremitting metamorphosis, so the tragedy would use Michetti's icon, now centralizing it (specifically the woman strutting and the male group's desire), now displacing and condensing it in a net built around the guiding metaphor. On the other hand, D'Annunzio's poetics, even when approaching theatre, are always torn by unresolved ambivalences and dualisms, between the force pushing towards form and then towards strength, between an idea of the creative act as elaboration, device, *ars*, and an idea of it as enlightenment, *ingenium*, between a conception of the author as sculptor and another as musician.[14]

This swing in poetics accounts for the writer's adaptability in dealing with the many different scenographic sets prepared successively for the tragedy, his difficulty in choosing between the call of truth (against falsity and artifice) and the appeal of the veil of dreams. Michetti had been asked, as previously stated, to collaborate in the first staging of the tragedy, in 1904, and, although he had great aspirations for systematic research in the field, in the end because of time limitations he got the actors to wear the same costumes he had painted. D'Annunzio had always maintained this flexibility regarding the images of *La figlia di Iorio,* swinging between truthful and recognizable pictures and a kind of dreamlike quality (we could call it *unheimlich*). He approves both the solutions suggested by Giovacchino Forzano on the occasion of the 1927 *en plein air* staging at the Vittoriale (which came after the important ones by Marco Praga at the Manzoni, in Milan, in 1915, and by Dario Niccodemi at the Argentina, in Rome, in 1922), and the opposite inventions by De Chirico for the Pirandellian 1934 edition, again at the Argentina. Forzano relies on the effects of *luce-*

13. E. Raimondi, "Dal simbolo al segno: il D'Annunzio e il simbolismo," in *Strumenti critici,* no. 28 (1975): 311-12.

14. B. Tamassia Mazzarotto, "Introduzione a uno studio su D'Annunzio e le arti figurative," in *Civiltà Moderne,* year XI, no. 6 (XVIII): 9-13. See also S. Jacomuzzi, "D'Annunzio e il Simbolismo - Il linguaggio liturgico sacramentale," in E. Mariano, 192-96 (which draws an interesting parallel between Dannunzian form and Marxist fetishism about goods).

natura, using hundreds of extras, with *Massenspiel* rhetoric, and he asks the actress in the role of Mila, Maria Melato, for a prosaic and natural delivery, both of which D'Annunzio approves enthusiastically: "Niente carta, niente tela, niente gesso. Natura, soltanto natura, coi suoi prati, i suoi boschi [...] ed una casa di pastori abruzzesi vera, ed una vera grotta" (Rosina 254).[15] Yet, seven years later, presented with the suppression of all the regional *décor* and the almost abstract and undoubtedly unnaturalistic stylization conceived by De Chirico, D'Annunzio seemed equally pleased, describing his tragedy in a letter to Pirandello as a "grande canzone popolare per dialoghi"[16] that seemed to have found a universal significance.

This mingling of dream and reality is also to be found in the text's structure and in its cultural models, which have elements taken from medieval mysteries, rustic comedies, pastoral fables, romantic dramas and symbolist theater. Even the choices of vocabulary and syntax and the visual language of the plot, increase the general ambivalence of the work. In fact the play is divided between a religious psychology, primitive but nevertheless socially and geographically well determined, and a mystical barbarian exoticism, with the result that it is brought alternately close to and far from the audience. Exoticism, for instance, as the dominant tone, is not only the inevitable *topos* of a sublime eroticism and of the sacred/profane stereotypes typical of *fin de siècle* decadence (following in the footsteps of Huysmans and Gautier) with its luxurious Oriental overtones and exhaustive mystical practice, but also creeps inside the domestic *tranches de vie*. D'Annunzio started from a painting about peasants, shepherds, fields and mountains, at the same time complementary to but very different from Pellizza da Volpedo's *Il Quarto Stato*, and made the characters *sing* in a manneristic, archaic language, at times monodic, at times contrapuntal, like a Péladian *melopoeia*. This was indeed a direct challenge, in 1904, to both the bourgeois theatre/drawing-room (in Becque's manner, at best, or Bernstein/Bataille's in boulevard cases), and the Naturalistic-Veristic strategies. We are talking about an authentic mirroring of the *milieux d'en bas*, with social references provided by the link with Michetti's painting, in spite of the removal of all the mimetic devices that would have reproduced the real common reality.

---

15. For the ambiguous relationships between D'Annunzio and the most important actress in the contemporary Italian stage, Eleonora Duse, see M. Schino, *Il teatro di Eleonora Duse* (Bologna: il Mulino, 1992) 249-97.

16. C. Sofia, "Conversando con Pirandello," in *Quadrivio* (1 October 1934). About the history of D'Annunzio's productions, see G. Isgrò, *D'Annunzio e la mise en scène* (Palermo: Palumbo,1993) and V. Valentini, *Il poema visibile. Le prime messe in scena delle tragedie di Gabriele d'Annunzio* (Roma: Bulzoni, 1993).

Recently, some have sought to explain the tragedy's extraordinary success in 1904, pointing out its perfect adherence, behind the archaic and rural appearance, to the operatic canon of the 19th century and the *Dame aux camélias* archetype. Concealed in the rural antiquities would therefore be the drama and well-tested mechanism of classic passion, a dialectical counterpart to the stock exchange values.[17] The critics who have retrenched the supposed lyricism of the text, underlining its effective and irresistible *coups de théâtre*, strengthen these suspicions.[18]

Let us analyze, then, the sets prepared for the key parts of the text. The first act takes place in the cool shade of the matriarchal house, a reassuring *demeure* filled with objects manufactured locally. Before the shocking appearance from the little backdrop's windows, of the excited reapers' hairy arms, the *potlàc* ceremony was just celebrated with its symbolic gift and the initiatory offers for Aligi and Vienda's wedding. The slow procession of relatives is filtered by the *ianua*, the scarlet woolen scarf, the *bidente*, the *conocchia*, that like protective amulets control the relationship with the external world: so, little by little, an Arcadian *bozzettismo* is formed, among hieratic hugs and New Testament salutations. If the first act enhances intimacy, subsequently putting it in crisis, the second act places itself in an even more profound space: the mountain cavern, the "inside" of Maiella (the same mountain dominating Michetti's painting), with its usual *bric-à-brac*, now not pastoral but rural. Here too there is an opening towards the outside, in the large mouth from where one can catch a glimpse of the slope "che verde è come i pascoli dei monti,"[19] and from where Aligi's father Lazaro appears, intending to take Mila back. In the dimly light of the cave, badly lit by the "lampadetta d'olio d'olivo," Aligi and Mila, terrified of being left in darkness, consummate their odd Platonic relationship, as if descended (metaphorically ascended) into the bowels of the earth, into an intimate hollow that mimics the archeological one of *La città morta*. Here Leonardo, bringing to light the Argive gold, lets the obscure recesses of the primordial roots, of the mysterious elements of his being, where the incestuous attraction towards his sister finds its origin, come to the surface. In this wild alcove is an ascetic sanctuary where the dividing line between transgression and sublimation is unclear, the fabulous holders of magic power sleep squatting or lying down on sheep skins: Malde the treasure finder, Anna Onna the medicine woman, and Cosma the seer, each of them an agent of

17. Cobelli's provocative but not parodic staging of 1972 belongs to this trend. See E. Groppali, *Il teatro di Trionfo, Missiroli, Cobelli* (Venezia: Marsilio, 1977) 174-81.

18. G. Getto, *Tre studi sul teatro* (Caltanisetta: Sciascia, 1976) 168; the devaluation of *La figlia di Iorio* coincides with the exaltation of *La città morta*.

19. G. D'Annunzio, *I pastori*, in *Alcyone*, in *Versi d'amore e di gloria*, vol. II, (Milano: Mondadori, 1980) 815.

enigmatic dealings with Nature, old Jungian-Proppian characters, perfect metaphors of the place's *unheimlich.* The cavern also acts as a Vulcanic forge, an aesthetic laboratory, where Aligi the mystic sculptor and humble artisan feverishly searches for the vision of the weeping Angel (the ghost that had stopped him from assaulting Mila, in the first act), carving it out of a walnut-tree log, just as Michelangelo released his statues from their marble prison.

In this regard, one notices that in the sculpture the motif of Aligi's hand raised to kill his father and destined to be cut off as a punishment for parricide almost coincides with —but seen from another angle— Silvia Settala's squashed limb: in *La Gioconda* she sacrifices herself to save the statue of her unfaithful husband. In the third act the scene opens wide onto the large threshing-floor, with the ancient oak-tree as the emblem of the return to normality after the traumatic revolt. The house that in the first Act was juxtaposed with the external world now fuses in perfect harmony with the road and is shown from the outside, in this way changing the perspective. Lazaro's body lies in front of the house, his head resting on a sheaf of ears, surrounded by his female relatives, who sadly strike up the *corrotto,* the funeral dirge, attempting to console Aligi's mother, Candia, who stands petrified, her lips sealed.[20] Here the new procession, symmetrical to that of Act I, will arrive, preceded by the black standard, with the parricide come to receive the "consòlo," before being thrown in the whirlpool, his wrist cut, inside a sack with a mastiff. Here eventually, the noble substitution will occur with Mila accusing herself as she exaltedly approaches the bonfire. These are then, the settings for the *fabula.*

Let us now consider the two main characters. We immediately see that D'Annunzio's stage directions, which are so abundant when listing props, are in this case oddly elliptical, hastily introducing the characters and seemingly taking for granted the audience's knowledge of them. In fact the characters avail themselves of a mythical horizon, as in Michetti's painting, that unleashes for their benefit a kind of charismatic aura, an iconographic memory, strengthened also by some prior appearances (at least in the eponyms) in the pages of D'Annunzio the novelist. These characters are recognizable ethnic types, for those who have seen the painting, read the *Novelle della Pescara* or *Il trionfo della morte.* They echo the majestic figures of Michetti's canvases, and at the same time are musical ingredients, reciting voices, emblematic counterpoints of a never- ending poem, in the metaphorical magma of the writing, always animated by the dialectical relationship between Form and Strength we have mentioned in the beginning. The *dramatis*

20. G. D'Annunzio, *La figlia di Iorio,* in *Tragedie - Sogni - Misteri,* vol. I (Milano: Mondadori,1949) 907.

personae are therefore clearly differentiated one from the other, but nevertheless coalesce together: all are images from afar, complete in themselves and in their own world. This world is remote, and exists at an epic distance in relation to time/space and author/audience.[21] Yet, if these icons do not offer points of contact with the everyday world, with the unfinished, with that which is temporary, together they nevertheless still form our symbolic 'past,' a kind of anthropological cycle of foundation, that precedes the birth of the modern individual entity before the division of the ethnocentric cell and the formation of conscious lonely entities. For instance Ornella, Aligi's sister, who intercedes for the prostitute and eventually senses her sacrifice, is an example of Christian charity that frees itself from the ties of the archaic-tribal *mens,* the first example of interjection of moral law. Mila, moreover, exemplifies an ethical metamorphosis, a radical shift of identity from prostitute to saint, and as such, an enrichment and stratification of her interior life. In Aligi as well, who pits himself against the power of his symbolic father, who would like to "passargli sopra con l'erpice" (*Figlia di Iorio* 891), we see a change, both in his attitude towards the family code and in the loosening of the strict patriarchal taboos. These at least were D'Annunzio's intentions.

In fact Aligi coming to life, as if after 700 years of dreaming, with the ecstatic features of Michetti's reaper, is also reminiscent of other characters, cultural variants of D'Annunzio's world. Behind his rustic style emerges the shadow of Andrea Sperelli, and also that of Tullio Hermil, of Giovanni Aurispa, with their visionary temperaments, their regressive tendencies and their pathologies. Amongst these, it becomes evident with Giorgio Aurispa, the main character of *Il trionfo della morte,* created just after Michetti's *Il Voto* in 1894, that Aligi weaves a delicate net of secret connections. First of all, the successful parricide satisfies, at a distance, the unconfessed impulses of Aligi's socially higher colleague, who is blocked in the novel by his Hamlet-like indecisiveness.[22] Moreover if Aligi, with his dreamy drowsiness, motivates the theatrical course of the tragedy with its refrains of major dreamlike scenes (the crowd's aggression and later its exorcism in Act I, the hallucinating cohabitation in the cavern and then the parricide in Act II, the final apotheosis of Mila's martyrdom in Act III), it is Giorgio who in the novel determines the crisis of the plot's progression, of the tendency to interrupt, to go back to past experiences, to conform itself to the character's mental events.[23]

21. M. Bachtin, "Epos e romanzo," in *Problemi di teoria del romanzo,* ed. V. Strada, (Torino: Einaudi, 1976) 191.

22. M. David, *Letteratura e psicoanalisi* (Milano: Mursia, 1967) 158-60.

23. M. Guglielminetti, *Struttura e sintassi del romanzo italiano del primo Novecento* (Milano: Silva, 1964) 37.

A fresh-faced youth who fosters a morbid affection for the women of his clan, particularly his sisters, Aligi addresses Ornella with meaningful passion: "le mie foglie di menta / in bocca, le mie foglie odorose / che mi davan freschezza e piacenza / fino al cuore del mio pasturare" (*Figlia* 862). He certainly has something in common with the many restless Dannunzian brothers, from Leonardo in *La città morta* to Simonetto in *La fiaccola sotto il moggio*. Further, in his domination by Mila's sorcery, he is near to Swinburne's iconographic model, that is, to one of the complex archetypes of the Anglo-French Byzantine culture: the surrendered youth, "the powerless victim of the furious rage of a beautiful woman,"[24] together with the Wagnerian pure madman, between Tannhauser[25] and Parsifal subdued by Kundry. [26]

Now, what are Aligi's favourite gestural and verbal attitudes? Following the model of Michetti's stupefied shepherds who watch the woman pass by, the theatrical shepherd Aligi is always immersed in a state of half-sleep, between brief moments of paroxysm and relapses into torpor, suspended and constantly alternating between binding and loosening. In Act I, as soon as he tears Mila's mantle and unveils her face (which in the painting is covered and in profile) he is immediately exposed to the enchantress's *fascinus*. After vacillating between the demand that he chase her (coming from his mother and his kin) and the contrary demand that he integrate her (from his sister Ornella), he is going to strike her with his shepherd's staff when she bewitches him, so that behind her back he sees the mute crying Angel she had just then mentioned. As a result, he kneels down in a mystic position with outstretched arms and, while before he had been watching helplessly the excited crowd of male reapers from behind the door, now he is able to face them, tame them, and make them kneel in an attitude reminiscent of Christ or Saint Francis in a hagiographic *epos*.

The whole of Act II, as far as Aligi is concerned, swings around the axis of tying and loosening, giving rise to whirling refractions: while wishing to free himself from the unconsummated wedding contract with Vienda (and to achieve this aim he is even willing to go to Rome and ask the Pope's permission), he at the same time tenaciously works the log of walnut wood to free the figure of the Angel. He is present at the release of the epileptic Salvestro, who has appeared in the cavern "magro e verdastro come una locusta [...] le braccia constrette contro i fianchi da più giri di corda passati intorno al tronco seminudo" (*Figlia* 862), but soon thereafter he is immobilized by his father, who has come

24. M. Praz, *La carne, la morte e il diavolo nella letteratura romantica* (Firenze: Sansoni, 1966) 202. By the same author, see also *Il patto col serpente* (Milano: Mondadori, 1972) 323-421.

25. A. Caraccio, *D'Annunzio dramaturge* (Grenoble: P.U.F., 1950) 112.

26. E. Paratore, *Studi dannunziani* (Napoli: Morano, 1966) 291.

into the cavern to fetch Mila back, looking like "un bifolco che abbia sciolto il bue" (*Figlia* 885). After being freed by Ornella, as if she were an involuntary Electra, and having committed the parricide, Aligi parades in Act III with wooden bonds around his wrists. In a certain sense, the enigmatic sentence that Cosma the seer has whispered in his sleep, "Non lo sciogliere! No, no! Non lo sciogliere!" (*Figlia* 885), seems to cover this complex semantic net. Sentenced to death, followed by his staff, the death-dealing axe, and the Angel covered by a drape (all objects carried by the judicial procession, devices of the event now elevated to become a *historiola allegorica* and a memorable commentary), Aligi will come to receive from his mother the "consòlo," the drink supposed to render his death less atrocious: in this way, incredulous, confused and again bewitched by the potion, he can listen to Mila's fake confession and can fall again into Candia's arms, the *Mater Matuta*, who catches him, now safe, with a "fremito quasi di belva" (*Figlia* 928). Mila also takes from the painting a distinctive feature: her walk. She brings back to life the Parnassian-Alexandrian *topos* of Maddalena/Thaïs, of the redeemed prostitute, the endless iconographic motif of the *femme fatale*, who exercises a Medusian[27] influence over the inexperienced and passive youth, but who at the same time is able to move from *eros* to *agapè*. Priestess of *algolagnia* (mixture of lust and pain), key element in the cross-pollinations between sacred and profane, provoker of mourning and metamorphosis, contemporary to the boulevard heroines (to Bataille's *La lépreuse*[28] and to Sardou's *La sorcière*[29]), Mila is herself a variant of D'Annunzio's strong feminine model. Pamphila, of the *Poema paradisiaco*, "da tutti posseduta, dal mendico / e dal sire, coperta di carezze / immemorabili,"[30] Comnema of *La gloria*, Basiliola of *La nave*, Pantea of *Sogno d'un tramonto d'autunno*, just to mention D'Annunzio's poetic-theatrical works, are all present in Mila and are married in her to their opposites: Isabella of *Sogno di un mattino di primavera*, "Viviana May de Penuele / gelida virgo preraffaellita" (D'Annunzio *Chimera* 464). In Mila, however, the ethnocentric tradition also reappears. In her position as the center of male desire, the "mala brama," we recognize the ancient "incanata," with the symbolic passage of a female stranger and of the scapegoat during the reaping working cycle: in short the cultural whole connected with the Spirit of the Wheat that Michetti secularized and turned into an enigmatic and

27. About the medusian aspects of D'Annunzio's work, as well as Praz, see also F. Masini, "Lo sguardo della Medusa," in A. Mariano, *D'Annunzio e il simbolismo*, 283-299.

28. A. Mariano, "Appunti sulla Figlia di Iorio," in *Quaderni dannunziani* (1958): 47-50.

29. Rosina 55-56; here see P. Puppa, "D'Annunzio e la scena francese tra boulevard e simbolismo," in *La parola alta. Sul teatro di Pirandello e D'Annunzio*, (Bari: laterza, 1993) 173-84.

30. G. D'Annunzio, *Poema paradisiaco*, in *Versi d'amore e di gloria*, vol. I, 662.

unrecognizable event, and that D'Annunzio traced back to its mythical foundation.[31] The archaic mythical kernel is therefore brought into focus by Mila, humanized *pharmakos*, who has taken shelter near the *focus sacer*, in its double meaning of purity and abjection, in Candia's *demeure*. These are her words that transform and reduce the myth into a story: "Passavo. Ero sola per via. / Allora le grida, gli insulti, / le zolle scagliate, la corsa... / Ah, son come cani furenti. / Mi vogliono prendere. Strazio / faranno di me sventurata [...] / Sono pazzi di sole e di vino, / cani furenti" (*Figlia* 820-21, 824). At the centre of a fantasy of violence, between the *grand guignol* and the *boulevard du crime*, in the *feuilleton*'s low tones, Mila is the victim that suddenly denies herself to her symbolic persecutors and in so doing brings upon herself the resentful contempt of the group: "Vattene ai cani! [...] cagna randagia [...] bagascia di fratta e di bosco / putta di fienile e di stabbio [...]/ sotto di te mille volte / è bruciata la stoppia, magalda!" (*Figlia* 836, 829-30). The ritual has been broken and consequently the woman seems destined to flee, to walk in perpetuity. In the cave where she tempts Aligi with sublime incestuous invitations: "Siamo soli, fratello, siamo soli" (*Figlia* 866), she describes herself to her companion at the climax of their amorous moment: "Io son la creatura / che trovasti seduta su la pietra / che veniva chi sa da quali strade" (*Figlia* 866).

The dialectics of ethnocentric culture, from Cosmos to Chaos and back again to Cosmos, through Mila and her surprising act of taking shelter in the honest *demeure*, reveals itself also as an Oedipal ritual, as a primary Freudian scene. Mila in fact slips inside the family as a transgressive spirit who first destroys and then, when she destroys herself as well, strengthens the unity/stability of the culturally warranted kinships. Inside the dark cave, Mila lives with Aligi as if she were his mother and sister: when she kisses him, a pagan animism seems involved in this apocalyptic act, and Maiella seems to collapse with a dark rumble. Right after that, Ornella, covered by the same black drape that in the beginning veiled the "magalda," arrives, officially to beg Mila to release her brother, but in reality to seal with her an exchange of roles, a kind of transfer. Now it is the Mother's turn to be evoked, the other complementary female ghost raised by the arrival of the ravenous Lazzaro, who claims his rights to Mila and is caught by his son in the act of raping her. Finally, in Act III, Mila defiantly faces the crowd that no longer desires her but now condemns her, and while she offers herself to the martyrdom of fire, her constituent element, in a fever of self-destruction, her double, Ornella, salutes her. The latter is the only one who has intuited her perfect integration with the group, at

31. About the antropological aspects of the culture of the sheaf, see E. de Martino, *Morte e pianto rituale* (Boringhieri, 1975) 236-88. See also A. Meda, *Bianche statue contro il nero abisso. Il teatro dei miti in D'Annunzio e Pirandello* (Ravenna: Longo,1993).

the very moment in which everyone clamours for her final banishment, and she gives another gloss to the scene: "Io ti bacio i tuoi piedi che vanno" (*Figlia* 933).

In his relationship with Mila, Aligi both reaffirms and deeply changes the stereotypes of D'Annunzio's characters. It is well known that in his works the character is usually only a projected mask, fixed in an affected narcissism and incapable of emerging from his own obsessive world. He is the refined and sensitive artist who is constantly deformed by an hypertrophic self-analysis.[32] He is the *déraçiné*, troubled by an ambiguous lust for life, for instinctive self-expression, and he often falls in a state of impotence in the face of concrete action.

Thus, the thrust towards the *Übermensch* actually passes through the virginal pallor of Aligi the shepherd. Without his presence in Michetti's painting, D'Annunzio's hero would be condemned to replay the endless ambitions of Claudio Cantelmo in *Le Vergini delle Rocce*, the aesthetic narrations of Stelio Effrena, who is the "*miles gloriosus* dell'arte" (Paratore 112) for the aristocratic audience of Palazzo Ducale in *Il Fuoco*, the ideological frustrations of Corrado Brando who can only crave for distant Africa in *Più che l'amore*, since the colonial adventure is possible only in a dream or a memory.[33]

The energy, which cannot be fruitfully directed and which in the case of Giorgio Aurispa turns into a *cupio dissolvi*, finds the possibility of freeing itself through the influence of one of Michetti's typical characters. It is here that we find the passage from lustful to dominating heroes, as has already been noticed,[34] from the heroes of *Zivilisation* to the ones of *Kultur* (of whom Marco Gratico in *La nave* is a model prototype).

During his Parisian period, just before the First World War, at the time of the Ballets Russes and of Ida Rubinstein, D'Annunzio wrote about the feeble Sebastian's martyrdom and Pisanella's death by roses. This was just a momentary return to *Zivilisation*, dictated also by financial difficulties, before the ideological turnabout that led him to Quarto and to Fiume. The new hero, as Claudio Cantelmo used to prophesy a little too generally, will build himself up through mystical practices and extreme self-determination, through "vita ascendente,"[35] but especially through his communion with the crowd.

The gestural word, the ritual of theatre-oratory, the mythical soliloquy, shift in this way from the page and from the scene to the

32. S. Battaglia, "L'estetica dannunziana dell'indefinito," in *Occasioni critiche* (Napoli: Liguori, 1964) 74.

33. G. Barberi Squarotti, *Il gesto improbabile* (Palermo: Flaccovio, 1971) 110-12.

34. L. Tonelli, *La tragedia di G. D'Annunzio* (Milano/Roma: Sandron, 1914) 119-31.

35. J. Goudet, *D'Annunzio romanziere* (Firenze: Olschki, 1976) 174-76.

reality of piazzas, of balconies occupied by the writer who turns himself into the Hero. Similar to Paolo Tarsis in *Forse che sì forse che no*, the new protagonist is "un Ulisse che osa sfuggire al dominio di Circe,"[36] since he has exorcised the woman, radically transforming her from *femme fatale* into Santa, holy creature. If Aligi in Act I and Act II spared Mila from having sexual intercourse with a crowd of reapers first, and then with his father, now, in Act III, he lets her sacrifice herself and in this way allows her to be sublimated from perverted lover to symbolic Mother who saved Aligi as pastoral leader.

At this point the Crowd is the clamorous emblem of this ideological-anthropological renewal. Let us go back for a moment to the *Novelle della Pescara*, which is closer to Michetti's *The Votive Offering*. D'Annunzio's crowd, initially, is *grimace*, a gruesome deformation, a humiliating and menacing antithesis of the Ego, more influenced by the romantic paroxysms in the style of Géricault and Delacroix, or by Zola's frenetic pilgrimages,[37] than by Michetti's composed and humble processions. In the vicissitudes of "Gli idolatri" and of "L'eroe," the presence of the feud between the two villages that launch themselves into a mutual massacre to take possession of the statue of the Patron Saint of the other, allowed D'Annunzio to barbarize and to dramatically transfigure the affable situation of the groups of Michetti's canvases, shifting from *sermo cotidianus* to *sermo elatus/plebeius*, if we want to quote the aesthetic rules of the horrific. The similitudes used to describe the peasant crowd are fished out from a zoomorphic vocabulary, from degrading bestiaries, in which the species regress to pre-individual evolutionary stages. The negativity of the plebs corresponds to this lack of specificity: collectivity is the home of savagery, of the radically different, of what is not recognizable to a city-dweller, to an aristocrat and/or a middle-class point of view.

The rural and lower-class crowd is described in gothic or thriller "black novel" style and has a hallucinatory anonymity, a confused heap of sketched synecdoches, swift zooms from which elementary, merely external and biological gestures emerge. In Saussurian terms, the *parole* is completely non-existent, all summarized in an obscene, bodily *langue*, in a kind of sad carnival. The only legitimate hero is the simulacrum of the Saint, with its indifference to the desperate movements of the crowd, the foaming vortex that opens and shuts to support it, which could lead to a personal sacrifice on behalf of the bearers, of the peasant that places "il membro informe e sanguinante" next to the head of the Patron Saint that "scintillava dall'alto come un faro."[38] During the

36. E. Giachery, *Verga e D'Annunzio* (Milano: Silva, 1968) 216.

37. For a detailed comparison between D'Annunzio and Zola, see E. Paratore, 100-103.

38. G. D'Annunzio, *Le Novelle della Pescara*, in *Tutte le novelle*, ed. A. Andreoli and M. De Marco (Milano: Mondadori, 1992) 195, 179.

clashes between the opposite factions, the pagan-Christian idol "barcollava come ebbro sul brulicame del sangue iroso [...] traballava, dava tintinni sonori agli urti dei rami, s'illuminava di lampi vivissimi ad ogni accenno di precipizio" (*Novelle* 195).

These beastly crowds fight to the death not for bloody and merciless totems only. Hordes of rebels do not assault the rural basilica alone. In "La Morte del Duca d'Ofena," for instance, violence seems to become historic, to fill itself with social significance, and is directed against the Palace of the local squire, suspected of possible sexual perversions. Scythes and billhooks then, uncaring for the saint's "orbite vuote" (*Novelle* 195), dash against Authority, indulging in deliberate sadism. But this is a rare occurrence: the primitive, the pre-logical, usually coincides with collective erotic instincts that naturalize the social protest, censoring it through transference and condensation. In his work during the years of Fasci Siciliani (1894 is the year of Crispi's counter-action in Sicily, as well as the year of *Il trionfo della morte*) and of the first organised protest by the peasants, D'Annunzio moved away from the topic of rebellions, parallel at that time to the police repression on one hand and the conservative demonization of the rebels on the other in Gustave Le Bon's book, *Psychologie des foules*.[39]

The crowd from fields and mountains, from little squares and sanctuaries, manifests itself as a noise, "ululato continuo [...] uragano imminente [...] mareggiamento confuso di tempesta" (*Novelle* 180, 178, 185); but when the metaphors from naturalistic become anthropomorphic, there arise disquieting references to social negritudes. The writer then refers to the tumultuous massess as "una tribù di negri ammutinati", and as "mulatti, sanguinari" (*Novelle* 183, 187). Is it the phantom of the street protests that appears in much nationalistic and futuristic writing as a terroristic *topos*? D'Annunzio's political positions of those years, fluctuating quite radically, advise caution when answering this question.[40]

Going back to D'Annunzio's specific criticism about Michetti's *Il Voto*, we can find the evidence of his initial degrading attitude towards the lower classes. With regard to the peasant that at the right hand-side of the canvas humbly bows to the ground, at the foot of the Patron Saint's silver head, waiting for his turn to rapidly kiss it, the writer reconstructs the scene with a feverish commentary in which he describes the monstruous embrace by the convulsive old man who yearns and "s'avvinghia al simulacro [...] e gli attacca alla bocca la bocca

39. P. Puppa, "Scena e Tribuna da Dreyfus a Pétain," in AA.VV., *Eroi e massa* (Bologna: Patron, 1979) 149-281.

40. N. Valeri, *D'Annunzio davanti al fascismo* (Firenze: Le Monnier, 1963) and M. A. Ledeen, *Il Divo*, in AA.VV., ed. N. Merola, *D'Annunzio e la poesia di massa* (Bari: Laterza, 1978) 73-99.

sanguinante"(Vecchioni 32). When, in the same review of the painting, he mentions the social reference, he explicitly reveals his own perspective: "Noi abbiamo visti quei volti tante volte nelle casupole basse e fetenti della campagna, in mezzo al vapore grasso delle stalle [...]. La fede l'acceca e l'inferocisce [...] si appaga in quei tremendi baci insanguinati su una maschera d'argento, sognando il paradiso"(Vecchioni 36).

The grand scene of the procession to Castelbordino, in the novel *Il trionfo della morte*, turns the preliminary sonata of the *Novelle* into a symphony, exaggerating the Rembrandtian *tranches*, the baroque slaughters, the *synesthesiae* by which the sublime matter of the Crowd is perceived. The image emits the same perverted *fascinus* made up of attraction/repulsion to which Giorgio and Ippolita are drawn back. These are the famous pages, full of hypotyposis, meaning the "monstrous" (that is "to be shown") combination of words, the *oratio perpetua* that dwells on endless details which add one to the other in a feverish, paratactic, syntax and are scanned by iterative imperfect tenses. All this variety of language causes a kind of centrifugal push that D'Annunzio intended to be an emulation, using clauses of rhythmical prose, as in Wagnerian music. The pilgrimage, with its gloomy atmosphere of chthonic ritual in which a miserable magma is swarming (looking like a Lombrosian-Brueghelian parade), not conscious of being observed by an outsider, is very far from the affable faith-abiding humanity that fills the nave in Michetti's painting, so innocent that it does not even menace the code of the middle-class *décor*.

The community that populates this, as other, festive canvases is composed of protagonists of the cult, not by its mere objects. The painter depicts these types without any exaggeration or, least of all, degradation, and presents them as something different from the world of the city, autonomously and spontaneously organizing themselves, but only in religious moments, thus revealing his precise ideological choices. Michetti's removal of all the political and social aspects, from his position as an observer in the field, of sympathetic closeness and of moral solidarity *à la* Verga, paradoxically goes deeper than D'Annunzio's poetic emphasis and his demonisations, which chiefly give rise to the menace mentioned previously. Michetti's Abruzzian people are first of all beautiful, proud and majestic; the church that in the *Novelle della Pescara* was placed in the scene as a *battle ground,* is made by Michetti the centre of a tranquil and rhythmical dance, where the child —who possibly is reminiscent of the naked cupids, crowned with vine-leaves as in the *Corpus Domini*— the old man and the mother are the privileged characters with faces full of faith and *pietas*. Even in the later works, which are Michetti's answer to D'Annunzio's *Il trionfo della morte*, the potentially depressing theme undergoes an exorcism by means of reassuring presences. In the first painting, in fact, the serpents become shabby bunches hanging like toy strings in the chubby hands of blossoming young girls, while the atrophied stumps of the second painting are neutralized by the attentive and protective majesty of buxom matrons and of placid bulls dominating from the top of a hill, majestic and fertile. In short, Poverty is always accompanied by its opposite correlatives, Health and Religion, which defuse and evangelically exalt it.

We have already stated that *La Figlia di Iorio* is the only work by Michetti that is open to non-ritualistic content, relying instead upon Mila's tempting, prosaic, non-processional strut. In Michetti the first signs of individuality, that dialectically clash with the collective spaces in the pages of D'Annunzio, are equally kept at an everyday level, preventing the potentially explosive situation from going beyond allusive hints.

D'Annunzio's bestially excited crowd, in Michetti's sketches, limits itself to some playful sneers, to the sly glimpses of the two conscious reapers, controlled, moreover, by the severe and frowning attitude of the old man at the center. In a sense Michetti's crowds, satisfied by a perennial rural feast, are the companions of Gauguin's contemporary depiction of an oceanic culture. Both painters portray the humble and meek exoticism of a fabulous people, expressed through naturalistic symbolism, dealing with distant times as opposed to distant places, and with the metaphysical translation of everyday life which speaks about a peaceful pre-history.

It is also thanks to Michetti, and to his patient iconological excavation, that D'Annunzio's crowd becomes gradually more composed, aesthetically reorganizing itself, finally becoming an allegory of people, of nationality, in which the hero, as a modern Anteo, rediscovers his trutly authentic roots. On the other hand, already in *Il trionfo della morte* the expressionistic scene of the climb to the Sanctuary was preceded by the return to the mother, an exhausting and unsuccessful return for Giorgio Aurispa (the *demeure* there underwent the tribulations caused by the father who had run away with the beautiful kept woman, who could be considered an unrepentant Mila). However, this action in that particular moment of the plot, the meeting of the mother and then of the crowd on the mountain, brought to light the internal links between the two poles.

The narrative itinerary that arches from *Il trionfo* to the tragedy, also shows D'Annunzio's altered ideological attitude towards the common people through *Le Vergini delle rocce* and *Il fuoco*, where they are no longer different but complementary. This alteration is contemporary to the appearance of women subdued by the hero, sacrificed for him, beginning with the Leonardesque trio in *Vergini* to Foscarina in *Il fuoco* and ending with Mila. This is the passage, following in the footsteps of

Barrès, from the cult of the self to the national energy, from aestheticism to the fighting tribune's dynamism. Theater with its direct impact on the audience (the *Figlia di Iorio*'s triumph in Milan accelerates this process) favors this kind of thematic-mythological shift (Caraccio 24).

In the tragedy, the crowd exhibits its entire typological range, allowing different interpretations, the diverse faces, repellent and decent, the sublime d'*en haut* and the sublime d'*en bas,* to co-exist, comparable to Mila's metamorphosis in which she becomes the Mother most pure. At the beginning of the work, the Crowd is sexual noise, brute panting at the door that sweeps away the nuptials, a horde that announces itself as "clamore selvaggio" (*Figlia* 810), and with its noisy movements provokes the *angst* of Aligi and of his naive sisters. Addressing his mother, the astonished youth asks: "Madre, e chi è che grida così forte?"[41] Soon after that the human flow with its emblematic hairy hands groping around and beastly expressions will rise up to the window's grill, while all around we can imagine a Waste Land setting, with the arid sultriness and the cicadas, the wine and the "demonio di mezzodì."

Aligi's hieratic gesture, inviting the masses, as in a liturgy, to bow down and then to leave for the burning country, as if they were deluded and tamed beasts, prepares the final apotheosis. The crowd does not appear in Act II, which is entirely set in the mountain's bowels where the only hybris allowed in the Umbertian Italy was being consummated —specifically the incestuous fantasy— but it comes back in Act III, entering the courtyard, standing in front of Lazaro's corpse (the murdered and beatified father) and finally becoming People by reorganizing itself for the sacred ceremonies of the dirge and of the tribunal.

In the end the crowd parading in an austere procession, seals the passage from Chaos to Chronos (anticipating parades no longer only rural or theatrical), and preludes the homogenization and removal of hierarchies characteristic of the Fascist Feast.

41. *Figlia* 810. About this see R. Alonge, "La Figlia di Iorio ovvero la religione delle madri," in AA.VV., *L'arte dell'interpretazione. Studi critici offerti a Giovanni Getto* (Cuneo: L'Arciere, 1984) 665-682.

Visual Arts and *Riders to the Sea*

Claude Evans

University of Toronto at Mississauga

One of the most striking achievements of the Irish Literary Renaissance of the late nineteenth and early twentieth centuries is the creation of an Irish theater. As Anatole Le Braz remarked in his thesis on the Celtic theater, it is an anomaly that, even though Ancient Irish literature is so wonderfully full of all the elements of drama, there are no Medieval Irish plays (Le Braz *Le Théâtre* 1-46).

As part of his efforts to stimulate the development of a national literature, William Butler Yeats felt it was essential to develop an Irish dramatic movement. His 1898 Manifesto explains how literary ideals backed up his conception of an Irish theater: "We propose to have performed in Dublin in the spring of every year certain Celtic and Irish plays… We will show that Ireland is not the home of buffoonery or easy sentiment, as it has been represented, but the home of ancient idealism." (Hunt 18). Critical of such playwrights as John Farquar and Richard Steele and inspired by Matthew Arnold (*On the Study of Celtic Literature*) and even more by Ernest Renan (*Poetry of the Celtic Race*), Yeats idealized the Celts as a people longing for the infinite and who were consequently doomed to suffering in this life (Yeats *Essays* 173). He called for plays that would give the Irish a sense of their identity. His own dramatic works, based on the ancient sagas, were not very successful in achieving his purpose. But *Riders to the Sea*, the first of Synge's plays to be written —in 1902— and the second to be performed by the Irish National Theater —in 1904—, is a brilliant illustration of the Yeatsian myth (Williams 82).

Riders to the Sea is a one act tragedy in the course of which the old mother, Maurya, sees her sixth son, Bartley, taken from her by the sea, as the other five and her husband have been. With her are her two daughters, Cathleen and Nora. The setting —a poor cottage in "an island off the West of Ireland"— is obviously inspired by the strong visual impression the Aran Islands made on Synge.

It is Yeats who is credited with suggesting to Synge a visit to Aran —the three islands of Inishmore, Inishmaan and Inishere, situated thirty miles from Galway, out into the Atlantic— where a primitive form of Irish life was preserved well into the twentieth century.[1] Yeats urged Synge to "give up Paris and go to the Aran Islands to live there as one of the people themselves" so that he would "express a life that has never found expression" (Grene 19). Synge visited Aran five times and altogether spent a little more than four and a half months there (Greene and Stephens 85). Up to this point in his life, Synge had not had much success as a writer (Greene and Stephens 83). He had devoted several years to a musical career which he had to give up. However, he had traveled extensively in Germany and France and was a man of vast culture having spent many years reading in Hebrew, Irish, Latin, Greek, French and German (Synge *The Autobiography* 15). It seems that it is indeed his visits to the Aran Islands which triggered his creativity and that his first achievement was in the area of visual arts through the medium of black and white photography.

Lilo Stephens has suggested that Synge's purpose in taking the photographs was "to increase his knowledge and understanding of the people. The camera was used to produce a visual record of the types of people he brought to life in his literary and dramatic works" (*My Wallet* vii). This might be true, but the interaction between the photographs taken in the Aran Islands and *Riders to the Sea* also takes place at a deeper level.

During his first visit to Inishmore in 1898 Synge bought a camera from a fellow visitor at the inn where he was staying (Greene and Stephens 89). In 1903, when he first got to know John Masefield, he had about fifty photographs of Irish landscapes to show his new friend (Masefield 13). Most of them —including twenty-three on Aran— were published in 1971 under the title *My Wallet of Photographs*. Fourteen have been used as illustrations for the 1979 edition of *The Aran Islands*, first published in 1907, but on which Synge began work in 1901, a year before he wrote *Riders to the Sea*. The black and white photos are very evocative of the life described in the play, the harsh life of fishermen in a hostile environment.

Synge's stage directions for his play are succinct and precise: "Cottage kitchen with nets, oilskins, spinning wheel, some new boards standing by the wall etc." (*Riders to the Sea* 85). In other words, Maurya's

1. Aspects of this life are preserved on film thanks to John Flaherty's *Man of Aran*. A few pictures from the film illustrate Pat Mullen's *Man of Aran* which is an account of the filming.

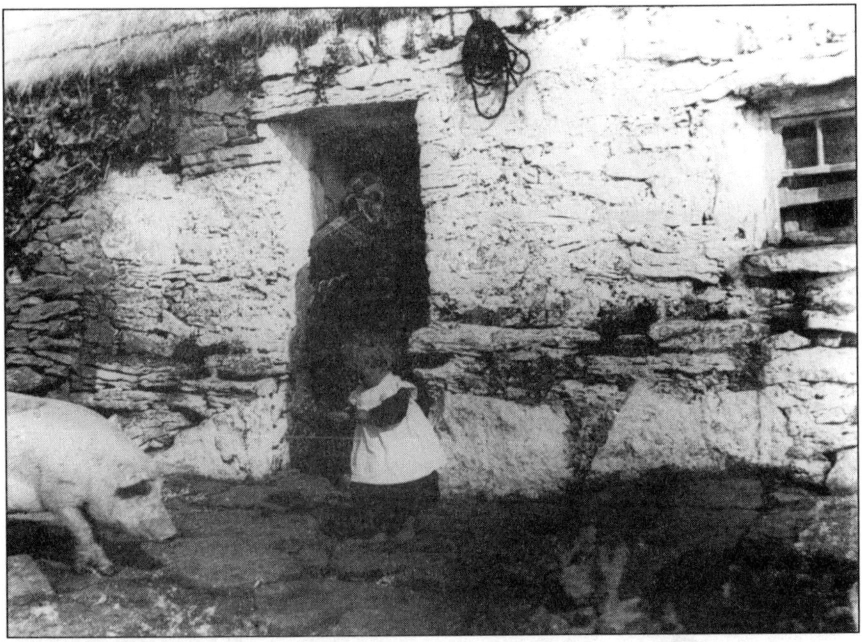

Figure 1 from *My Wallet* # 37

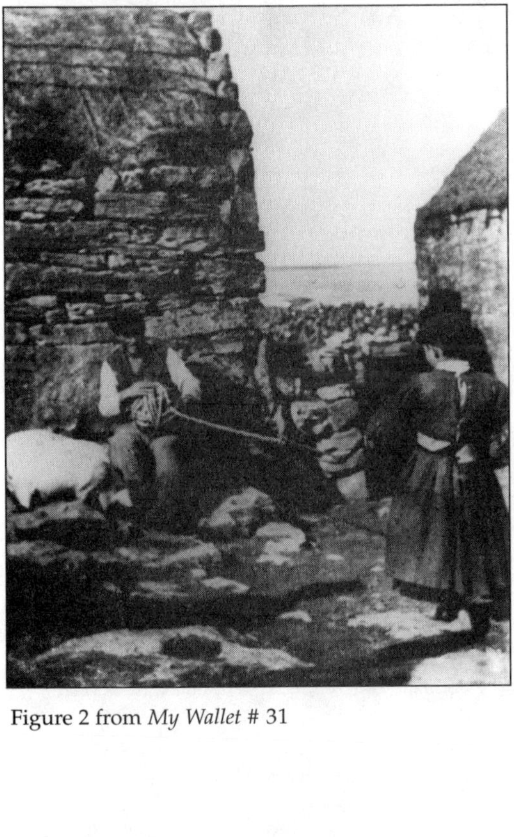

Figure 2 from *My Wallet* # 31

cottage resembles the typical island dwellings photographed by Synge (Figure 1. *My Wallet* plate #37). In one of the pictures a bundle of rope hangs at the front of the cottage and elsewhere local rope-making is documented (Figure 2. *My Wallet* plate #31). This is the "new rope" that Bartley needed to make a halter for riding the horses into the sea (*Riders to the Sea* 87). In the left-hand corner of the same photo a pig is roaming by, reminiscent of the "pig with the black feet" who has been eating the new rope (*Riders to the Sea* 87). A prototype of the pony who knocks Bartley over and appears in his mother's vision is part of the collection (*My Wallet* plate #32) and the most beautiful composition of all, taken against the light, shows a man of Aran "watching the currach on its way to collect turf from a Galway hooker" (Figure 3. *My Wallet* plate #44) echoing Maurya's question "Isn't it turf enough you have for this day and evening" and Nora's mention of "the hooker tacking in from the east" (*Riders to the Sea* 87).

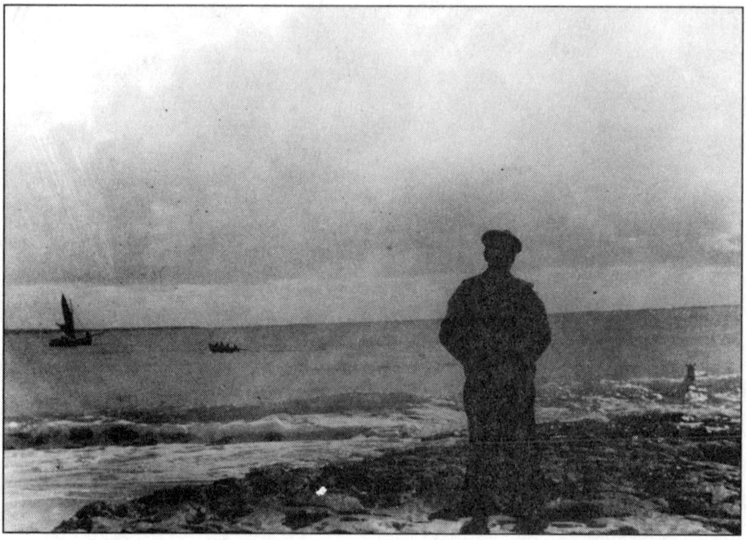

Figure 3 from *My Wallet* # 44

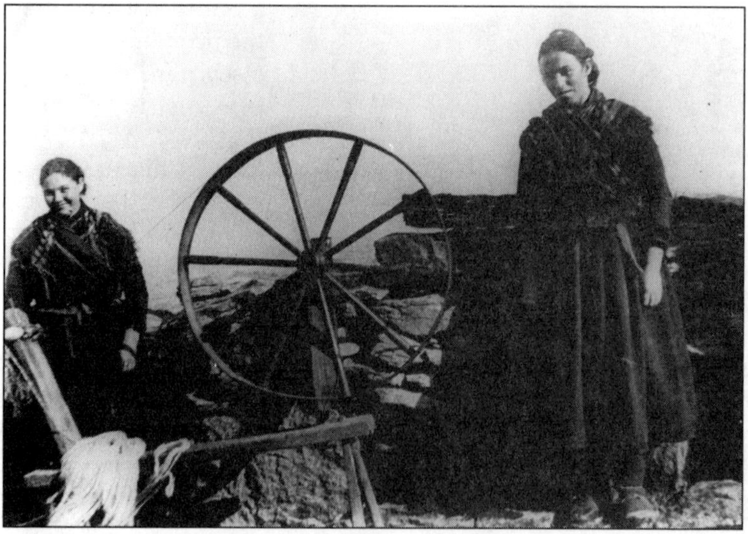

Figure 4 from *My Wallet* # 33

It is well documented that, when the play went into rehearsal, Synge was very insistent that all the props and costumes should be authentic. Particular care was taken over the spinning wheel. Lady Gregory had one sent from Galway which had been in a family for a hundred years and Synge himself instructed a girl on how to use it. He even insisted on having it carried to London for the opening in March 1904 (Roberts 5; Kopper 41). An excellent photograph of an Aran spinning wheel has been preserved in the collection (Figure 4. *My Wallet* plate #33).

The costumes worn by the actresses in a 1906 performance (de Breffny 211) are exactly those of island women as photographed by Synge (Figure 5. *My Wallet* plate #43). Lady Gregory, ever resourceful, had discovered in Galway a man who could dye flannels in "madder" to obtain the right shade of crimson. The petticoats were made according to Synge's directions, "with a broad strip of calico at the top" (Roberts 19-20) so that the white waistband would be visible (*Riders to the Sea* 96). The pampooties, cowhide moccasins worn by islanders, represented another hurdle (Figure 6. *My Wallet* plate #28). Traditionally they were constantly kept wet but the actors became squeamish and resorted to a dry skin. Synge brought a pair he had used himself to help create a pattern (Roberts 19).

In his quest for authenticity, Synge was also most anxious about the exactitude of the keening scene. "Keening" is a chanting for the dead peculiar to Ireland which involves clapping of hands and swaying of the body. Once more, a native of Galway came to the rescue: a Galway

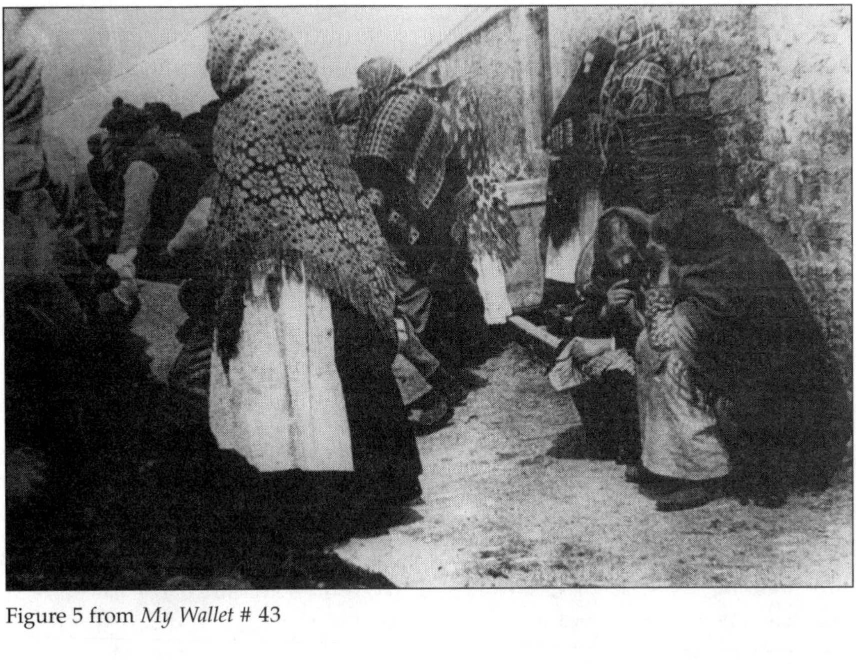

Figure 5 from *My Wallet* # 43

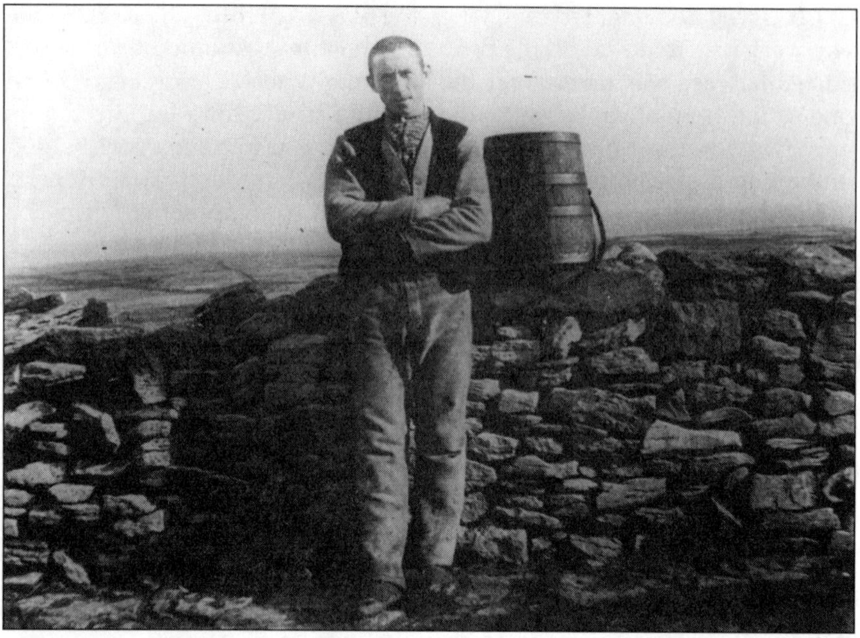

Figure 6 from *My Wallet* # 28

woman living in the suburbs of Dublin agreed to give instruction to the actresses. However, it soon became evident that she was unable to perform the rite without a corpse so George Roberts was required to play the part of the dead body! (Roberts 19)

Altogether, the black and white photographs give a rather stark impression of life on the Aran Islands. On the contrary, the famous Irish painter, Paul Henry, who, for about seven years in the 1910s, painted on Achill Island —an island off the coast of Co Mayo where lifestyle and landscape were similar to Aran's— was dazzled by the "colourful barbaric clothes" of the women (Henry 51) and by the beautiful hues of the sea and skies which are glorified in his paintings: *The Potato Diggers* (1912) (Kennedy plate); *Achill Head, County Mayo; A Sunny Day, Connemara* (Henry plates). In *The Aran Islands* —a factual account of his stay on Aran— Synge also dwells on the intensity of colors: "the unusual depth of blue of the mountains of Connemara" (27), "the sun passing like a lozenge of gold flame into the sea" (48), "the red dresses of the women" (27) whom he finds "as beautiful as tropical sea-birds" (40).

None of this exultation is apparent in *Riders to the Sea*. In fact, in the fifteen pages of the text, there are six occurrences of the adjective "black," six of "dark," three of "gray" (sic) and six of "white" whereas there are few touches of color, with "green" and "red" being used three times each. These choices are certainly deliberate since the adjectives are often repeated for effect rather than for meaning —as in the three occurrences of the "gray pony" (sic) and the two of "the pig with the black feet" (*Riders to the Sea* 94, 95, 97; 87, 88)— or else they belong to a somewhat unusual usage as in "the dark word will be broken" (90) and "there is a black knot on it (on the bundle) you would not loosen in a week" (92). A somber atmosphere —attuned to the black, white and grey of the photographs— is created and it is very likely that there is a connection between the visual and the literary production.

Synge wanted total accuracy in his representation of Aran life but his interest went much beyond the surface. Because of his thorough knowledge of Irish and Celtic literature and folklore he could grasp the deeper meaning of what he observed. He had taken Irish at Trinity College, Dublin (Greene and Stephens 38), and Celtic Studies at the Sorbonne with d'Arbois de Jubainville (Greene and Stephens 131). He was also familiar with Anatole Le Braz' work on Breton folklore (Greene and Stephens 73, 102-103). There are echoes of Ancient Celtic themes in his play and this is what gives the words "gray" and "dark" their deep resonance. "There is something not right about a grey horse" says one of the narrators in Lady Gregory's collection, *Visions and Beliefs in the West of Ireland* (136). This is because the grey horse, according to Yeats, is probably a púca, "an animal spirit" "of the race of nightmare" (Yeats *Fairy* 87; Kiberd 164). Also, in Ancient Ireland, the year ended at the festival of Samhain —November 1st— which marked the beginning of the dark half of the year while the light half would begin at Beltine, May 1st (Cunliffe 110-111). So, when Maurya talks of "the dark nights after Samhain" (*Riders to the Sea* 98), she is referring back to a tradition already recorded in the Gaulish Coligny Calendar of the 1st c. BC. The "black hags that do be flying on the sea" (93) are not merely witches, as some authors have said, but lost souls who are heard crying at night among the roaring waves. Anatole Le Braz relates that, at the turn of the century, a colleague of his, whose boat was overturned at sea was not rescued by the coastal people of Northern Brittany because they mistook his calls for help for the howling of lost souls (*La Légende* vol. 1, lxix-lxx).

The Celtic Otherworld, the Irish *Síde*, is often associated with islands and the sea, as illustrated by the Irish Voyage Tales, the *immrama* (Dillon and Chadwick 328-332), and by the Breton legends describing souls wandering over the sea waiting to be transported by boat to the Otherworld (Sébillot 191). The mention of ominous birds also brings to mind the "battle crow" or "battle raven," one of the incarnations of the Irish war goddess, the Morrigán, who appeared on the battle-fields to prophesy death and disaster (Greene *Dictionary* 69).

Indeed, the title *Riders to the Sea* clearly alludes to Ancient Celtic culture and the sense of doom which pervades the play is strongly reminiscent of an Early Irish saga, *The Destruction of Da Derga's Hostel*

(Gantz 60-106), which relates how King Conaire, who has broken all the *geissa* or taboos which were placed upon him from birth, rides through Ireland with his entourage on a course inevitably leading to his destruction (Rees 327- 333). On his voyage he meets several forebodings of death. For instance, three horsemen dressed in red tunics and mantles and riding red horses. Maurya's vision at the well, when she sees Bartley riding a red mare followed by her dead son Michael, on the grey pony, "with fine clothes on him (95)" presents obvious similarities with this scene. In *The Destruction of Da Derga's Hostel*, one of the *Deirgs* —the Red Horsemen— explains: "We ride the horses of Dond Tétscorach of the Sìde. Although we are alive we are dead" (Gantz 69-71). Donn is the Irish god of the Dead (MacCana 36-38) and horses were revered among the Celts as shown by the prevalence and splendour of the horse motif in Celtic art. Examples in point are the huge Bronze Age Uffington Horse carved into the chalk of a hill in southern England (Greene *The Horse;* Cunliffe 50), the elaborate horse-trappings from the Polden Hill hoard (Megaw plate #1: 17; plate #365: 218; plate #366: 219) or the stunning bronze head from Yorkshire, perhaps an ornament on a war chariot (Duval 26).

Maurya and her family, like Conaire, unwittingly break all the taboos (Kopper 43-44): they wear Michael's shirt and carry his walking stick although it was thought dangerous in their society to use what belongs to a person who has just died; Maurya does not give her blessing to Bartley when he leaves, the words choke in her throat when she tries to do it later, and that too is a very bad omen. It has also been suggested that not killing the pig for St Martin's day —November 11— goes against the established custom of the European peasantry[2] (Kopper 43). Such a breach of tradition would not have been lost on Synge who, after studying with Petit de Julleville at the Sorbonne (Greene and Stephens, 58; O'Brien Johnson 137), was so conversant with Medieval French culture that he borrowed the theme of a later play, *The Well of the Saints,* from a fifteenth century Burgundian farce by Andrieu de la Vigne, "Moralité de l'Aveugle et du Boiteux"(Greene and Stephens 139).

The immediacy of death when Bartley's corpse is brought in on stage and left on the table (*Riders to the Sea* 97) shocked quite a few of Synge's contemporaries. Willie Fay, who played Bartley in the première, wanted to increase the shock effect by stretching his head over the edge of the table (Saddlemeyer 43). Fifty years later, George Roberts recalled that "some of the audience were horrified at the sight of a corpse on stage, [and that] a few of them left the hall while the performance was going on" (Roberts 21). The newspaper critics also reacted strongly: the *Irish Times* found the episode repulsive arguing that realism should not

2. On this tradition, see Verdier plate #1.

be equated with art and the *Leader* called the play "the most ghastly production ... ever seen on the stage" (Kopper 42; *File on Synge* 20-21).

Yet jarring descriptions of the realities of death were commonplace in the Middle Ages. As in the fifteenth century Breton Dances of Death, in which skeletons go hand in hand with the living (Lascaux 16-17), there is in Synge's play a physical proximity to a corpse which is shunned by modern society. When she lays her hands together on Bartley's feet (*Riders to the Sea* 99), Maurya —"Mary of the seventimes wounded heart," as David Clarke calls her (*Sunshine* 44)— resembles a medieval Pietà, like Pietro Perugino's, which was painted c. 1500 and bought by the National Gallery of Ireland in 1896, during Synge's lifetime (Keaveney 17). The allusions to Medieval Christian culture tinge Maurya's tragedy with an atmosphere of naïve piety. Maurya is truly a universal picture of suffering motherhood but the references are not only Christian since the three women on stage recall the triple mother-goddesses of Gallo-Roman Europe (Greene *Dictionary* 155-156).

However, the most striking resemblance with a tripartite mythological figure is with the Fates of Greek tradition because of the prevalent sense of doom in the play and, most of all, because of Cathleen's spinning, and of her cutting the knot on the bundle which contains Michael's clothes (*Riders to the Sea* 85, 92; Gerstenberger 37). In Antiquity and the Middle Ages the three sisters, Clotho, Lachesis and Atropos, daughters of Zeus and Themis, were traditionally represented spinning human destiny which was symbolized by a thread (Grimal 110; Aguion 222-223). For instance, in the twelfth century *Anticlaudianus of Pommersfeld*, Clotho is drawing from the distaff, Lachesis is holding the thread, Atropos the spindle. Clotho is represented as an older woman, whose head is covered, like Maurya's on the Irish stage (Blisniewski 8-12 and Illustration #3).

When he refers to "Fate," Homer does not use the plural form "Moire" for the three sisters, but the singular "Moira" (Blisniewski 9). Is the resemblance to the Irish Maurya purely coincidental? Synge liked to underplay his extensive scholarship (Kiberd 155), so this might be another example of the hidden meaning and cross-reference of which this complex playwright was fond.

In Synge's work, images and symbols are constantly superimposed. For instance, the theme of riders and horses which is central to the play has its roots in Celtic antiquity, as discussed earlier, but it is also reminiscent of biblical verses which carry a sense of doom and sacredness (Kopper 43): "And I looked, and beheld a pale horse: and his name that sat on him was Death" (Revelation 6:8); "the horse and his rider hath he thrown into the sea" (Exodus 15:1).

The superposition of imagery, beginning with *A Wallet of Photographs,* but echoing into Celtic and Greek mythology and

Medieval Christian tradition gives *Riders to the Sea* its extraordinary density and makes it a very powerful drama which, with a very simple story line, reaches deep into the human heart and psyche. This is what Frank Fay recognized when, on tour in the United States while John Synge lay dying prematurely at the age of thirty-seven, he wrote to a friend: "I hear that Synge has had an operation and I am quite prepared to hear that he is no more. Well, if he has gone, I envy him. It is not every one who leaves a Riders to the Sea behind" (Hogan and Kilroy 211-212).

ACKNOWLEDGEMENT

The use of the Synge's photographs was made possible by the "John Millington Synge Trustees" and the "Board of Trinity College Dublin".

WORKS CITED

Aguion, Irène, Claire Barbillon, François Lissarague. *Héros et dieux de l'Antiquité, guide iconographique*. Paris: Flammarion, 1994.

Arnold, Matthew. *On the Study of Celtic Literature*. New York-London: Everyman's Library, 1916.

Blisniewski, Thomas. *"Kinder der dunkelen Nacht," Die Ikonographie der Parzen vom späten Mittelalter bis zu späten XVIII. Jahrhundert*. Berlin: Wasmuth, 1992.

Clarke, David R. "Synge's Perpetual 'Last Day' Remarks on Riders to the Sea," *Sunshine and the Moon's Delight, a Centenary Tribute to John Millington Synge, 1871-1909*. Ed. Suheil Badi Bushrui. Gerrards Cross, Bucks: Colin Smythe, American University of Beirut, 1972. 41-51

Cunliffe, Barry. *The Celtic World*. New York: Greenwich House, 1979.

De Breffny, Brian ed. *The Irish World*. New York: Harrison House/Harry N. Abrams, 1986.

De Vries, Jan. *La Religion des Celtes*. Trans. L. Jospin of *Keltische Religion*. 1961. Paris: Payot, 1984.

Dillon, Myles, and Nora Chadwick. *Celtic Realms*. London: Sphere Books, 1973.

Duval, Paul-Marie. "Celtic Art." *The Celts*. Eds. Sabatino Moscati et al. New York: Rizzoli, 1991. 25-27.

File on Synge. Ed. Nesta Jones. London: Methuen Drama Books, 1994.

Gantz, Jeffrey ed. and transl. *Early Irish Myths and Sagas*. London: Penguin Books, 1981. Reprint 1988.

Gerstenberger, Donna. *J. M. Synge*. Revised ed. Boston: Twayne Publishers, 1990.

Goldman, Arnold. *Synge, The Aran Islands: A World of Grey*. Gerrards Cross: Colin Smythe, 1991.

Greene, David H., and Edward M. Stephens. *J. M. Synge, 1871-1909*. New York, 1959. Revised edition. New York: New York UP, 1989.

Greene, Miranda A. "The Symbolic Horse in Pagan Celtic Europe," *The Horse in Celtic Culture, Medieval Welsh Perspective*. Eds. Sioned Davies and Nerys Jones. Cardiff: University of Wales Press, 1977. 1-22.

——. *Dictionary of Celtic Myth and Legend*. London: Thames and Hudson, 1992.

Gregory, Lady. *Visions and Beliefs in the West of Ireland*. Gerrards Cross, Bucks: Colin Smythe, 1970.

Grene, Nicholas. *Synge, A Critical Study of the Plays*. London and Basingstoke: Macmillan Press, 1975.

Grimal, Pierre. "Greece: Myth and Logic." *Larousse World Mythology*. Trans. from the French: Patricia Beardsworth. London: Hamlyn, 1989. 97-175

Henry, Paul. *An Irish Portrait*. London, New York, Toronto, Sydney, 1951.

Hogan, Robert and James Kilroy. *The Abbey Theatre, The Years of Synge, 1905-1909*. Dublin: The Dolmen Press, 1978.

Hunt, Hugh. *The Abbey, Ireland's National Theatre, 1904-1979*. Dublin: Gill and Macmillan, 1979.

Keaveney, Raymond, Michael Wynne, Adrian Le Harivel and Fionnula Croke. *National Gallery of Ireland*. London: Scala Books, 1990.

Kennedy, S. B. *Paul Henry, 1876-1958*. Dublin: Town House, 1991.

Kiberd, Declan. *Synge and the Irish Language*. London: Macmillan, 1979.

Kopper, Edward A. Jr. "Riders to the Sea." *A. J. M. Synge Literary Companion*. Ed. Edward A. Kopper Jr. New York: Greenwood Press, 1988. 39-49.

Lascaux, M. *Légendes et Traditions de la Mort en Bretagne*. Châteaulin: Editions Jos, 1983.

Le Braz, Anatole. *Le Théâtre Celtique*. 1905. Genève-Paris: Slatkine, 1981.

——. Introduction. *La Légende de la Mort chez les Bretons armoricains*. 1893. 3d ed. Paris: Champion, 19120. Vol. 1: v-lxxv.

MacCana, Proinsias. *Celtic Mythology*. Feltham, Middlesex: Newnes Books, 1984.

Man of Aran. Dir. John Flaherty. Perf. Colman (King) Tiger and Maggie Oirrane, 1934. Videocassette. Morningstar Entertainment Inc., 1960.

Masefield, John. *John M. Synge. A Few Personal Recollections with Biographical Notes*. Letchworth: Garden City Press, 1916.

Megaw, Ruth and Vincent. *Celtic Art*. London: Thames and Hudson, 1990.

Mullen, Pat. *Man of Aran*. New York: E. P. Dutton, 1945.

O'Brien Johnson, Toni. *Synge: the Medieval and the Grotesque*. New Jersey: Barnes and Noble, 1982.

Pocock, P. J. "Synge and the Photography of His Time," *The Autobiography of J. M. Synge*. Dublin: Dolmen Press, 1965. 41-46.

Rees, Alwyn, and Brinkley Rees. *Celtic Heritage*. London: Thames and Hudson, 1989.

Renan, Ernest. *Poetry of the Celtic Races and Other Essays*. Trans. of "La poésie des races celtiques", *Revue des Deux Mondes,* Feb. 1, 1854. London and Felling-on- Tyne, New York: The Walter Scott Publishing Co, 1916.

Roberts, George. "The Plays of Synge". *Irish Times* (Dublin, 2 Aug. 1955): 5, *File on Synge*. Ed. Nesta Jones. London: Methuen Drama Book, 1994. 19-20.

Sébillot, Paul. *Le Paganisme Contemporain chez les Peuples Celto-latins*. Paris: Octave Douin, 1908.

Stephens, Lilo. Introduction. *My Wallet of Photographs: The Collected Photographs of J. M. Synge.* Arranged and introduced by Lilo Stephens. Dublin: Dolmen Editions, 1971. vii-xv.

Synge, J. M. (John Millington). *The Aran Islands*. 1907. Ed. Robert Skelton. Oxford: Oxford UP, 1986.

——. *The Autobiography of J. M. Synge, from the Manuscripts of Alan Price*. Dublin: The Dolmen Press; London: Oxford UP, 1965.

——. *Playboy of the Western World and Riders to the Sea*. Ed. William E. Hart. Arlington Heights, Illinois: Crofts Classics, 1966.

——. *My Wallet of Photographs: The Collected Photographs of J. M. Synge*. Arranged and introduced by Lilo Stephens. Dublin: Dolmen Editions, 1971.

Williams, Simon. "John Millington Synge: Transforming the Myths of Ireland." *Facets of European Modernism, Essays in Honour of James McFarland*. Ed. Janet Garton. Norwich: University of East Anglia, 1985. 79-98.

Yeats, W.B. "The Celtic Element in Literature." *Essays and Introductions*. London: Macmillan, 1961.

——, ed. *Fairy and Folk Tales of Ireland*. New York: Collier Books, 1973.

Cinematographic Techniques and Stereotypes in the Stories of Annie Vivanti

Anne Urbancic

University of Toronto

It is well known that in 1890, when Annie Vivanti at the age of twenty-one audaciously asked Giosuè Carducci for a preface to her first anthology of verses, the poet, recognizing the immaturity of the work at hand and perhaps the possibilities of her further developed talent, gave her some advice. He wrote that although he was of the opinion that women and clergy should not try their hand at poetry, hers was nevertheless worthy of being published for what he termed the "immediatezza della rappresentazione," the "immediacy of representation." At the same time, however, he warned her that a book like *Lirica* was unique and that she should try to write other different types of books. Vivanti took his advice.

In 1898, in a letter to author Matilde Serao, Carducci again praised another of Vivanti's works. This time it was a play entitled *La Rosa azzurra*. Despite his words, the play was critically a failure. Nevertheless, it was evidence of Annie Vivanti's ability to translate the "immediatezza della rappresentazione" for which Carducci had praised her poetry, into another genre.

Nor was he the only critic to have observed the immediacy of representation. Writing in the *Fortnightly Review* about Vivanti's first novel *The Devourers* (1910), Georg Brandes refers to *Rosa azzurra* as "a work marked by lively movement and animated dialogue, which Sarah Bernhardt once thought of producing." Later in the same review, he described the novel in almost theatrical terms. He noted that Vivanti was "a writer of great lyrical facility and undoubted dramatic gifts.... Annie Vivanti Chartres is a mistress of the art of suggesting a *milieu*,

1. Vivanti's acquaintance with Brandes is remembered in the character of Dr. Brandes in her *L'Invasore*.

with the atmosphere and illumination" (Brandes 172-3).[1] Ruth Shepard Phelps, writing in *Forum* of Vivanti's first collection of short stories, *Zingaresca* (1918), was also struck by the element of immediacy:

> [Vivanti writes with] "such verve, such *brio*, such gaiety and humor that those little ripples of laughter sweep over the reader who sits enjoying them alone by his fire which are usually the tribute only to spoken wit. They are familiar and incidental enough to be journalism, their constant inclination toward a daintily reckless exaggeration perhaps is journalism...." (Shepard Phelps 89)

Today, we are fascinated not so much by Vivanti's expertise and excellence in the theatrical genre but by the fact that she was able to apply even to her prose the immediacy that is such a fundamental characteristic of the theater. Some of Vivanti's prose creates the sensation that the events narrated are unfolding before our very eyes. Pietro Pancrazi has expressed this most clearly in his re-evaluation of Vivanti's works in 1946, four years after her death. He laments the silence to which Annie was relegated by the anti-Semitic laws in force in Italy at the time of her passing, and insists that she had given to Italian literature "a most singular gift":

> This writer always felt a need to prepare herself as if for a recitation or a part; or to move props or scenery around herself. It was understood that eventually Vivanti would offer us fragrant flowers, either from the fields or from a greenhouse, still covered with dew; but she wanted to offer them to us as if from a small stage. And since not only did she not hide this desire, but rather (at times with impunity at times mischievously) she even revealed to us the stage, reader and critics alike were charmed by her and by the novelty of her game. (Pancrazi 187)

As the century turns, it is opportune to stop for a moment and reconsider the "novelty" of Vivanti's approach. We have seen that critics have already associated novelty with "immediacy" in her case. This study will consider the period when Vivanti was publishing her prose works. It is clear that at the time she was very much aware of the effects on an audience of another genre that offered both theatrical immediacy and novelty. That genre is film.

Cinematography and Annie Vivanti made their first public appearance at about the same time in the 1890s. Because her marriage to John Chartres ensured her relative financial security, and because she had traveled so much both as a young girl and later as a married woman, Vivanti was in the enviable position of being able to experience first-hand such new inventions as the telephone, the car and the movies, especially American movies. These experiences she then brought into her narrative prose. For many of her less privileged Italian readers, her descriptions of these novelties were likely their vicarious introduction to them. It is no surprise then, that Annie should "appropriate" cinematographic techniques and make features of this genre part of her own literary production, both thematically and stylistically. In fact, by 1910-11, the period in which Vivanti's writing career re-established itself with the publication of *The Devourers* (*I divoratori*), the cinema was firmly entrenched and acclaimed as an industry and an art. Gladys Smith had already become Mary Pickford and had been starring in pictures since 1908. Sarah Bernhardt, who, as we recall, had once considered performing Vivanti's script for *Rosa azzurra*, had been presented to the American public in 1912 in the movie *Queen Elizabeth*. More interesting still, the years in which Vivanti's works were sometimes published serially in magazines for women, saw the advent of serial movies like *What Happened to Mary* (1912-13) and *The Million Dollar Mystery*. The former was presented on screen and simultaneously had monthly episodes published in *The Ladies World*, while the latter had originally been released as a news item and was then serialized in the *Chicago Tribune* even as it was being shown in theatres.

In 1915 David Wark Griffith released *The Birth of a Nation* with its stunning new cinematographic techniques of last-minute rescues, iris dissolves, close-up shots, fade outs, soft focus close-ups, back lighting and cut back shots. The most widely publicized film to date, it was seen by millions who appreciated it for its realism and excitement.

In Italy too, cinema had firmly established itself. The 1910 film *La caduta di Troia* had soon been followed by *La sposa del Nilo* (1911) and *Quo vadis?* (1912). The latter was seen both in America and England. It was followed by the acclaimed *Cabiria* (1914) with a screenplay by D'Annunzio and direction by Pastrone. By the time that *Zingaresca* was published both Febo Mari and Eleonora Duse had made their transfer from stage to film. Soon after, in 1919, Italy even had its own vamp in the figure of Francesca Bertini. Cinema historian Vittorio Martinelli has been able to trace hundreds of titles of Italian silent movies filmed in the years of the First World War, years that coincide with Vivanti's second "debut" as a writer.[2]

Vivanti was particularly sensitive to and aware of the importance and impact of the cinema on contemporary society. A close examination of two of her short stories will demonstrate how Vivanti felt the influence of the genre and how she incorporated in her writing the attitudes, the stereotypes (even as seen in stills taken from movies for publicity purposes) and the stylistics of this genre. This is not to say, however, that there occurred a distinct stylistic change in Vivanti's

2. The excellent overview is published in the several volumes by Martinelli and Bernardini.

writings directly attributable to the growing popularity of movies. Yet some recent criticism draws certain linkages between the advent of cinema and earlier novels. Barbara Korte's observations in her study *Body Language in Literature* are in some measure applicable to Vivanti's writing. Korte writes that, after the advent of film, "the body language of characters in the novel occasionally has a distincly cinematic effect.... [C]haracters exhibit non verbal behaviour that seems more familiar from film than from real life." John L. Fell has made similar observations in his study of film and the narrative tradition. He has further elaborations on the passive co-opting and manipulation of the audience by movies. "Motion Pictures impose our perceptions onto tangible, rather than once-removed, realities," he writes. "They endow everything with meaning, bypassing the value orderings which are implicit in language." Annie Vivanti endowed her prose with similar meanings that enabled her to turn cinematic tropes into narrative, film-like stereotypes.

The first story for our consideration is titled "Il Cinematografo" ("The Movie Theatre") and is found in her first collection of short stories, *Zingaresca*, published in 1918.[3] It represents the world of the movies from both sides of the screen, so to speak, while meticulously avoiding what unfolds on the screen itself. In the story, the narrator Annie describes how the contemporary audience has been enchanted by movies: willingly, viewers arrived to the point of losing critical acuity for the sake of being entertained by the silver screen. She then turns her attention to the travails of a screenwriter who is forced to forego artistic integrity and commitment to excellence and verisimilitude for the sake of providing entertainment. As an interesting twist to the story, Annie Vivanti's "I," who is the narrating voice, is implicated in both perspectives.

The story is structured along two easily discernible lines. In the first, Vivanti deals with audience participation at the movies and the viewers' reaction to them. The story proceeds through narrative description. In the second part, however, Vivanti's "I" allows us to see the frustrations of the screenwriter/narrator. We slowly become aware that we are, in fact, reading a quasi-script or screenplay. In the first part, the reader is directly addressed (and the reader is quite specifically female), while in the second, the reader merely observes the exchanges and the interaction between the screenwriter and the actress. Narration in the second part is kept at a minimum.

3. "Il Cinematografo" was also the title of a short story written by Vivanti's contemporary, Ada Negri, and published in the *Corriere della sera*, 22 November 1928. Annie Vivanti was well known for her English versions of her own work. She never translated the short stories presented here, however. Translations are mine; quotations are from this edition.

Vivanti's narrating "I" in Part One is a busy socialite with many obligations. But she envies her young daughter, a violin prodigy, who rather than perform before an adoring public, claims that she prefers to go to the movies. Annie confesses that to be her preference also. She bids us, her dear readers, to examine our consciences and exhorts us to admit that surely, we too, would prefer the movies. Once she has involved us in this confidence on our part, she proposes a satirical stereotype of the moviegoer:

> Seated in a movie theater, we find total intellectual rest.... We are placid and inert, sunk deep into the theater seat, under the charitable shadow of our cloche hats, and we do not converse, we do not sparkle [with intelligence], we are not, nor can be, witty or caustic, sharp or biting. No; at most we read half aloud, in a chorus with all our seat mates the bits of literature that precede each scene....
>
> Having thus contributed to the subdued collective murmur, we abandon ourselves passively without agitation for the artists, without discussions or arguments, to the tempered fascination of the movies. (176-177)

Once she has established the stereotypical figure of the placid female spectator whose critical ability is being manipulated by the movie she watches, Vivanti invites us behind the scenes to observe her while she shows us how bereft of critical acumen the actress can be. In this case, the latter is a demanding American star, "with a huge bunch of violets at her waist and under her arm a ruffled Skye-terrier [named Phébus]... both flowers and dog are strongly perfumed with ylang-ylang" (**Figure 1**). The actress shakes the blonde curls above her clear eyes.

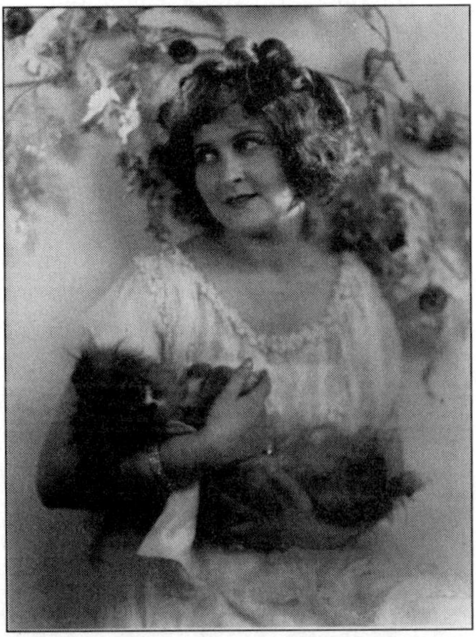

Figure 1: "with a huge bunch of violets at her waist and under her arm a ruffled Skye-terrier..." Hope Hampton around 1920 from Kobal, John. *Hollywood. The Years of Innocence*, p. 141.

As stated earlier, this second part of the short story is, in effect, a script for a series of scenes about a future screenplay. But, the screenwriter/narrator actually has no control over the material she is to write, even as the moviegoers have no say over what they are to watch. Instead, it is the actress who determines the interaction. The actress thus compromises the screen writer's artistic credibility with her movie star whims. Unfortunately, the actress is never satisfied with the script, and asks for major changes even though the scriptwriter has allowed the star's every request. In the following passage we can see the incorporation of cinematographic elements into narrative discourse. This is typical of this second part of the story with predominant dialogue. The minimal "stage" directions would require a close-up, impossible to show in a traditional stage setting, but which had become, already at that time, a convention in film:

> "Dear God. I forgot to tell you that I must be inaccessible to love. Passions will burn all around me, and I shall pass, cold and untouchable, in the midst of the flames set alight by me."
>
> "Yes, madame."
>
> "And then, this is important, there has to be a scene...."
>
> "For Phébus [the dog]?"
>
> "No. A strange scene... that cannot be understood.... And I shall be immobile... like this.... "And the beautiful creature slowly lowered her made-up eyelids over her clouded pupils. **[Figure 2]** "And then ... all of a sudden... in my look you see everything!! Like this!... "And she opened wide her luminous yellow-green eyes. **[Figure 3]** "So the public understands that I have come to a ter-r-rible decision." **[Figure 4]** (182)

The emphasis on the eyes, reminiscent of actresses in silent films, is an element that Barabara Korte also considers as textual derivation from films. She has noted that while, until the 20th century, looks or glances "almost always have an emotional and/or interpersonal significance" (237), after the advent of films, eye behavior is incorporated right into dialogue passages, as it is here. Here, of course, it is used almost as gestural hyperbole with overt intertextual reference to cinematic techniques, but in other stories by Vivanti it is used, as Korte has suggested, in an unconscious phatic function to establish human contact.

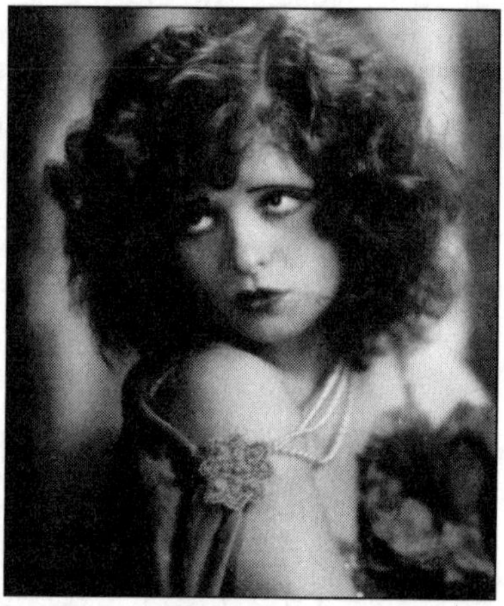

Figure 2: "And the beautiful creature slowly lowered her made-up eyelids over her clouded pupils" Clara Bow in Lloyd, Ann, ...*Silent Years*, front cover

"The Movie Theater" reveals other cinematographic strategies as well. The "script" part of the story is

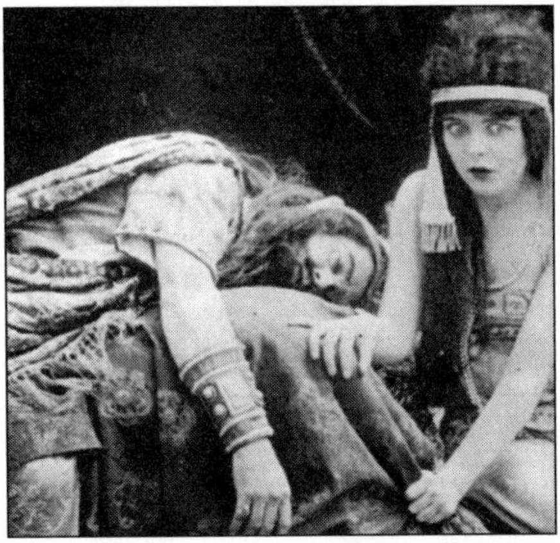

Figure 3: "She opened wide her luminous yellow-green eyes" Blanche Sweet in Lloyd Ann, ...*Silent Years*, p. 26.

clearly divided into scenes that are textually marked by asterisks separating one from another. In each scene, the famous actress changes her mind once again about the screenplay. Each scene gives Vivanti another opportunity to cleverly "visualize" traditional narrative discourse. In the following passage, for example, the actress has demanded that the screenwriter portray her, no longer as the Parisian *femme fatale* with an Apache lover as she had insisted previously, but as a Swiss mountain girl with an alpine guide for a lover. The screenwriter comments using language that is as literally appropriate to the new scene as it is metaphorically appropriate to the screenwriter's reaction:

> In order to imbue myself with alpine inspiration, I departed for Vall'Anzasca and there, at the foot of Monte Rosa, I transformed my heroine of the Bal Bullier into a mountain Venus.
>
> The whole script was already shimmering white [*biancheggiava*] and glistening, snowy and adamantine on my paper, when there arrived an urgent telegram from Biarritz [demanding changes]....
>
> Swept away by the avalanche of cinematographic requirements, I descended precipitously from Macugnaga to Bordeau. (183)

Nor is this the only example of where metaphoric self-referentiality is employed to juxtapose a visualized script with the activities of the increasingly frustrated scriptwriter. In fact, references to film are also made more explicit in the reactions of the scriptwriter. For example, in response to still another request for a scenographic change, the scriptwriter confesses that she requires "a moment of silence in which I try to put my ideas 'in focus'." The words 'in focus' are emphasized by quotation marks. (185).

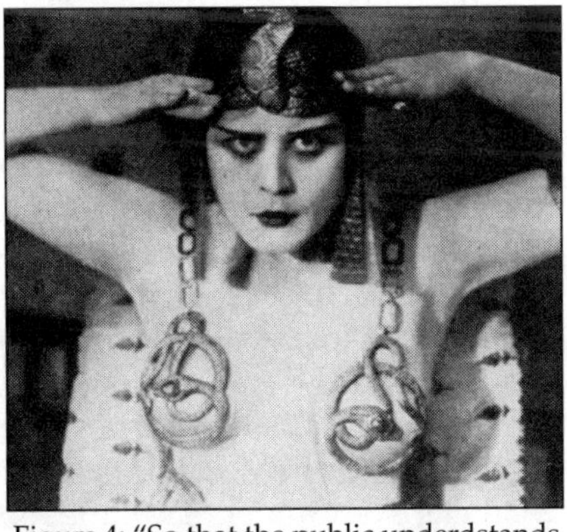

Figure 4: "So that the public underdstands I have come to a ter-r-rible decision" Theda Bara in Taylor, Deems et al., *Pictorial History....*, p. 34.

The use of the present tense in places where a traditional narrative reading would expect past tenses also emphasizes the cinematographic characteristics of this short story. The events unfold as we read, as they do while viewing a movie.

Similar techniques are found also in the story titled "The Beauty Contest," from Vivanti's collection *Perdonate Eglantina*.

Around 1911, Francis X. Bushman had won the "Most Handsome Man" contest sponsored by *The Ladies World* magazine. Not long after, he became a star with Essanay Studies, thereby establishing the ever more popular trend of equating physical beauty with movie stardom. Soon contests focusing on female pulchritude also became ubiquitous. Winning ensured certain entry into the world of American films and eventual stardom. In this short story, Annie Vivanti has proposed a slightly distorted version of a beauty contest. It is not the usual beautiful girl wins beauty contest, is courted by movie studios, accepts their offer and becomes a star. Instead, its plot runs more along the lines of: rather plain girl doesn't really win the beauty contest she is purported to have won, is courted by movie studios, refuses their offer, and becomes a star. This story too, is divided into "scenes," with indicators to show where one scene ends and the next begins. Scene I is told in the present tense, with a predominance of dialogue and minimal descriptive "interference," much of which could easily be transferred to directions for camera shots. For example, the story opens with an iris shot: the two interlocutors are surrounded by a veil of steam in a sauna; around them in the mist are other groups of people. As readers we are immediately drawn to, and focus on the secret that one of the two reveals to the other. The same scene later includes a close-up shot ("Alda Colli is here?" The big eyes open wide. "But who is Alda Colli?" *Perdonate* (33) (**Figure 5**) and ends with a dissolve shot that leads the narrator protagonist to the next scene. In "Beauty Contest," Vivanti adds yet another twist, which in fact, confirms that, at least she is consciously manipulating filmic techniques and conventions while remaining within the narrative frame of the short story. The "screenplay" characteristics and possibilities of the scenes are re-emphasized ingeniously at the end of the story when the famous American movie director, D. W. Kay —

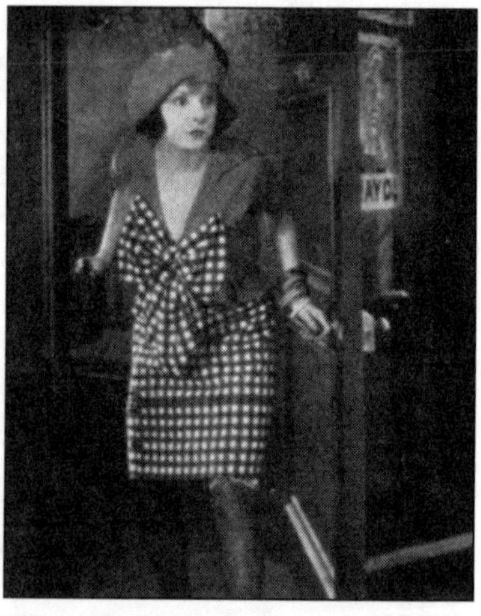

Figure 5: "Alda Colli is here?" The big eyes open wide. "But who is Alda Colli?" Norma Talmadge in Deems et al., *Pictorial History...*, p. 173.

though aware that the girl Alda Colli is not the girl whose photograph had appeared in the newspaper with Alda's name in the caption–has her just the same sign a contract for a film. Miss Colli will star as a plain young woman whose name was mistakenly used to identify the winner of a beauty contest. Thus the main story about the beauty contest has actually been a storyboard for the future screenplay of the beauty contest movie.

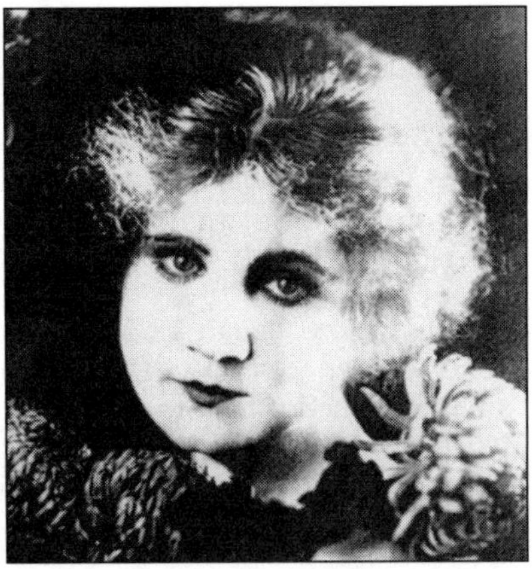

Figure 6: "[Mme Angèle] dusted [Alda's] face with pink powder... Florence Lawrence in Karney Robin, *Chronicle....* p. 81.

In "The Beauty Contest" frequent references are made to the movies. As in the previous piece, Vivanti's many uses of techniques derived from cinematography are also employed to poke fun at the genre. For example, the omnipotent movie producer is parodied in the figure of the American Film King, D. W. Kay, as is the rivalry between studios competing for stars. The star-making-machinery is parodied in the tabloid titles that Mr. Kay invents for the purposes of introducing his newly discovered star to the public. Among them he includes the "rags to riches" stereotype (*Perdonate* 45). Nor is the importance of costuming and make-up for cinematography overlooked. As Alda is being prepared by the local beautician for her meeting with Kay, each detail of her facial make-up is revealed, as is the effect it creates:

> [Mme Angèle] dusted [Alda's] face with pink powder and powder Rachel; she applied a touch of cinnabar in the center of her mouth to make it smaller, and two lines of black pencil at the corners of her eyes to make them bigger. Then she curled her short blond hair, making it sweep around the thin face as if it were soft foam; the irregularities of her features were minimized by the halo of those blond shades." (*Perdonate* 47-48) **(Figure 6)**

Vivanti also points out how lighting affects a scene: she has one of the characters improvise red lampshades for the specific purpose of creating a backlit scene, and she then places the action of the story in the foreground

> [Mr. Kay and his assistant] sat and waited in silence in the suggestive rosy shadows.
>
> Finally the door opened and on the threshold there appeared, vivid and extravagant under her huge black hat, the tiny figure of Alda. As

> if to make her stand out more, the two older women [the mother and the beautician] stood off to the side. (*Perdonate* 49)

And in the scene depicting the meeting between Mr. Kay and Alda, we, as readers accustomed to filmic techniques, can certainly visualize the camera shots that could potentially capture the ensuing conversation on celluloid:

> Alda, who began to feel a bit reassured, shook her head under the brim of the great hat and repeated capriciously and stubbornly:
>
> "I don't accept."
>
> And the King of Film stood up: he was very tall and imposing. **[Figure 7]**
>
> "But do you know, Miss, that you are refusing a six figure amount?"

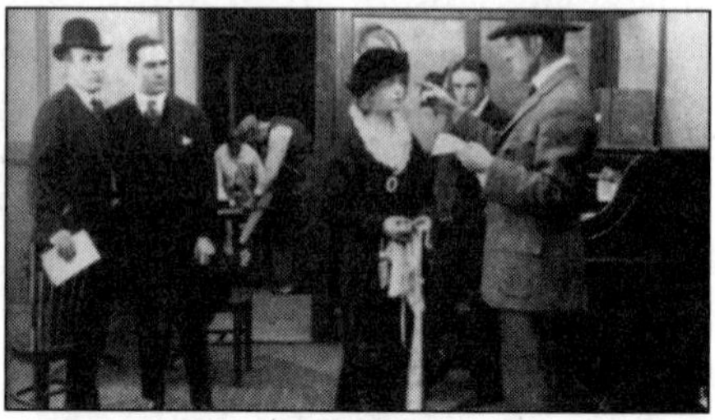

Figure 7: And the King of film stood up: he was very tall and imposing. D.W. Griffith and Lilian Gish in Shipman, David, *Story of Cinema*, p. 116

> A six figure amount!... Her mother and Mme Angèle looked at each other. Then they looked at Alda....
>
> Mme Angèle shook. The mother gasped.
>
> But Alda, swaying back and forth in her showy multicoloured shawl, repeated obstinately:
>
> "I don't accept. No, I don't accept." (*Perdonate* 50)

And finally, Vivanti uses the ending of this short story to parody the stereotypical romantic ending of many films of the day. She writes:

> In only one aspect does the movie story [about Alda] depart from reality. On the screen the winner of the beauty contest marries an Australian billionaire, while Alda....
>
> But hush! The event has not yet been officially announced. (*Perdonate* 53)

Annie Vivanti was no stranger to the world of movies. Vittorio Martinelli indicates three verifiable Vivanti contributions to Italian cinema, as well as one uncertain one; in each of the four cases she is credited with providing the subject matter for a silent movie. There is no indication whether or not she actually prepared the script.[4]

4. See Martinelli and Bernardini. In 1916 the film *Amor di barbaro* (Augusta Film, Roma) appeared. Its subtitle *Vae victis*, imitated the title of Vivanti's novel (1917), which itself was a reworking of the play *L'Invasore*. The names of the characters differ from those of the play and novel but the subject matter is the same. Vivanti denied any

Nevertheless, she remains an acute observer and admirer of her contemporary social milieu, readily appropriating and adapting the new inventions of the early 20th century into her works. The stories described here are not the only ones in which the influence of film may be discerned, but they are the most salient examples, dealing as they do with film and the movie industry. Although it remains difficult to ascertain whether Annie Vivanti was specifically aware of visualizing her works as specific camera shots, it is nonetheless of interest to observe that there is indeed, at least in these two stories, more than a thematic affinity between her writing and cinematography. But even in other stories we can view the action as if we were watching a film. Indeed she has grasped the excitement and novelty of cinema but also its tendency to exaggerate movement, events, stories, people, life. Her particular sense of humour quickly brings her to stereotyping. We can appreciate her fascination with the movies, and we can see how she has incorporated into her prose her own definition of the genre, as expressed in the story "The Movie Theater":

> Cinematography! The triumph of movement, of rapidity, of impetus, of the dizzying speed, of the unexpected, of the unlikely, of the paroxysmal. The victory of movement over immobility, of act over word, of action over description. (*Zingaresca* 187)

It is wittily clear even in her prose that, as she had confessed, she would indeed prefer to go to the movies, and that she would want us there with her.

WORKS CITED

Brandes, Georg. "The Devourers." *Fortnightly Review* 94 (July 1910): 170-173.

Carducci, Giosuè. "Liriche di Annie Vivanti." Book review in *Nuova Antologia* (16 giugno 1890): 748-755.

Fell, John L. *Film and the Narrative Tradition*. Norman, Ok.: Oklahoma UP, 1974.

involvement in the production of this film. In 1917 the film *Astrid* (Floreal-Film, Roma) based on Vivanti's little known eponymous novel (1911), garnered critical praise and success. In 1918 production stopped of *L'Invasore* and *Le bocche inutili*, both based on Vivanti's plays. According to Martinelli, the Minister of War Propaganda felt the works would be of little interest since the was about to end. But the star of *L'Invasore*, Mary-Cleo Tarlarini, decided to present it to the office of the Censor just the same, and despite its brevity.

Finler, Joel W. *Silent Cinema*. London: BT Batsford, 1997.

Karney, Robyn, ed. *Chronicle of the Cinema*. London: Dorling Kindersley, 1985.

Kobal, John. Hollywood. *The Years of Innocence*. London: Thames & Hudson, 1985.

Korte, Barbara. *Body Language in Literature* . Toronto: U Toronto P, 1997.

Lloyd, Ann. *Movies of the Silent Years*. London: Orbis, 1984.

Martinelli, Vittorio and Bernardini, Aldo. *Il Cinema muto italiano. I film dei primi anni. 1910.* Torino: Nuova ERI, Rivista del centro sperimentale cinematografica [RCSC], 1996; *I film degli anni d'oro. 1911.* Torino: Nuova ERI, RCSC, 1995; *I film degli anni d'oro. 1912.* 2 vols. Torino: Nuova ERI, RCSC, 1994; *I film degli anni d'oro. 1913.* Torino: Nuova ERI, RCSC, 1994. Vittorio Martinelli. *Il Cinema muto italiano. I film degli anni d'oro. 1914.* 2 vols. Torino: Nuova ERI, RCSC, 1993); *I film della grande guerra. 1915.* 2 vols. Torino: Nuova ERI, RCSC, 1992; *I film della grande guerra. 1916.* 2 vols. Torino: Nuova ERI, RCSC, 1991; *I film della grande guerra. 1917.* Torino: Nuova ERI: RCSC, 1991; *I film della grande guerra*. 1918. Torino: Nuova ERI, RCSC, 1991.

Pancrazi, Pietro. *Italiani e stranieri*. Milano: Mondadori, 1957.

Rhode, Eric. *A History of the Cinema from Its Origins to 1970*. New York: Hill & Wang, 1976.

Shepard Phelps, Ruth. "Annie Vivanti," *The Forum* 71 (January 1924): 83-90.

Shipman, David. *The Story of Cinema. An Illustrated History*. London: Hodder & Stoughton, 1982.

Taylor, Deems, Marceline Peterson and Bryant Hale. *A Pictorial History of the Movies*. New York: Simon & Shuster, 1943.

Trent, Paul. *The Image Makers. Sixty Years of Hollywood Glamour*. New York: McGraw-Hill, 1972.

Vivanti, Annie. *Perdonate Eglantina*. Milano: Mondadori, 1926.

Vivanti, Annie. *Zingaresca*. Milano: Quintieri, 1918.

Staging the Self: Giorgio de Chirico and the Theatricality of Self-Portraiture

Jennifer Hirsh

BRYN MAWR COLLEGE

Memory installs remembrance within the sacred;
history, always prosaic, releases it again.
Pierre NORA, "Between Memory and History: *Les Lieux de Mémoire*"

BEST KNOWN for his metaphysical paintings packed with enigmatic images, Giorgio de Chirico remains one of the most influential Italian artists of the twentieth century.[1] De Chirico's *arte metafisica*, frequently figuring hauntingly nostalgic *piazze* and faceless mannequins replete with odd combinations of unrelated subject matter, established him as the most notable painter of oneiric visions and as a role model for the surrealist movement (Hollier, Rosenstock).[2] The metaphysical paintings completed between 1910 and 1918, such as his *Enigma of a day* of 1914 (Fig. 1), have defined de Chirico's contribution to Italian art in most critical appraisals of his work (Baldacci *De Chirico: The*

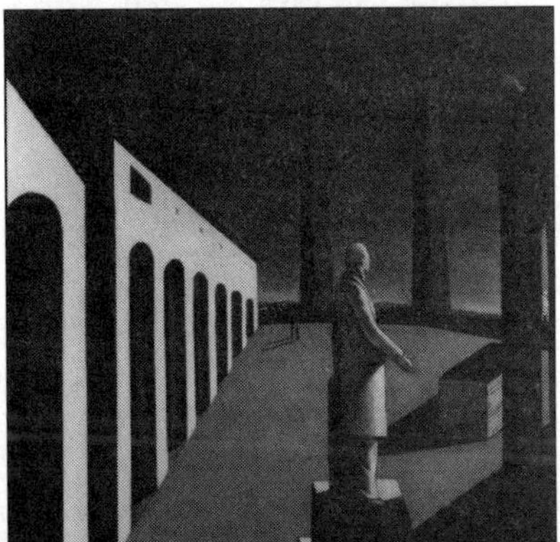

1. Giorgio de Chirico, *Enigma of a Day*, 1914. Museum of Modern Art, New York.

1. While I refer to de Chirico as Italian here, the question of his national identity will be discussed in depth later in this essay.
2. In his discussion of the distinction between artistic works that create their own shadows and those that *represent* unreal shadows, Hollier includes de Chirico in his survey of surrealist images that figure artificial shadows within compositions Sloane links de Chirico's *arte metafisica* to "later fantasies of the Surrealists" (3).

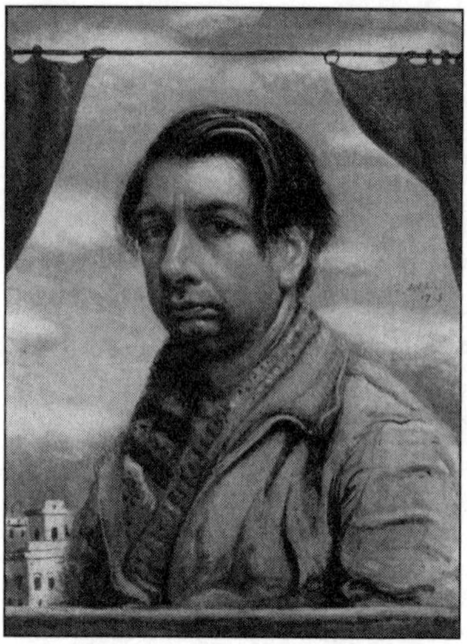

2. Giorgio de Chirico, *Self-Portrait*, 1925. Galleria Nazionale d'Arte Moderna, Rome.

Metaphysical Period, 1888-1919, Rubin, Soby). What remain relatively understudied, however, are the artist's later and less typical works, and especially his self-portraiture, a massive body of work that spans the early years of his career until his death in 1978.[3] Given that de Chirico was so prolific throughout his entire career, it remains puzzling that so high a percentage of his work, that is the majority of works executed after 1918, has received little critical attention, with the exception of their being dismissed as the late, bad de Chirico.[4] Focusing on this undervalued aspect of de Chirico's *œuvre*, this essay investigates the artist's construction of the self insofar as de Chirico delineates his identity explicitly and implicitly in both painted and written self-portraits. This reconsideration of de Chirico's visual and verbal self-portraits elucidates the ways in which they manifest a common set of artistic and philosophical concerns through self-consciously performative means.

That notions of "performativity" and "theatricality" will play a significant role in my interpretation of de Chirico's work follows from the artist's own extensive experience in the world of theatre. Indeed, one self-portrait from 1925, complete with the drawn-back curtains signaling his performance as painter, makes this connection in a rather literal fashion (Fig. 2). While de Chirico's formal style shifted greatly in both his self-portraits and other canvases from the 1920s onward, he maintained certain theoretical and thematic aspects in his works as he continued his metaphysical project.[5] De Chirico, however, was active

3. Baldacci notes the split amongst scholars who do and do not acknowledge the value of his later works (*Italian Art in the Twentieth Century*). For a positive analysis of de Chirico's works executed at the end of his career, see Calvesi and Ursino.

4. See Emily Braun's introduction to the exhibition catalog *De Chirico and America* for a review of the current De Chirico literature and the ways in which post- war criticism has wrongly shaped the impression of the contemporary reception of post-1918 works, especially those of the 1920s and 1930s in America (13-24).

5. Speranza notes the shift in de Chirico's iconography from the metaphysical to an interest in museum works and old masters, specifically documenting paintings by Renaissance artists including Raphael, Michelangelo, and Carpaccio, as well as works by Watteau, Rubens, Veronese and Fragonard (89-90).

not only as a metaphysical painter, but also as a writer, set and costume designer for theatrical and operatic productions, and sculptor for most of his life. During his career, de Chirico participated in 26 theatrical productions both in Italy and other parts of Europe, including Luigi Pirandello's *La giara* at the Théâtre of Champs Elyséés in Paris in 1924, a 1929 production of Diaghilev's ballet *Le Bal*, and costumes and scenes for Vincenzo Bellini's *I Puritani* in 1933, to name a few (Gigli 188-203). Many exhibitions on the relationship between painting and theatre have included de Chirico as a key artistic figure, such as the 1997 *Sipario/Staged Art* held at the Museum of Contemporary Art in Castello di Rivoli (Gigli 70-107; Fagiolo dell'Arco *Sipario/Staged Art*). While exhibitions such as this one (and their accompanying literature) have made accessible de Chirico's fantastic stage sets and costume designs, they make only limited comparisons between his theatrical accomplishments and his canvas paintings insofar as his early metaphysical mannequins and haunting *piazze* resurface on the stage. Marianne Martin has effectively opened the discussion about de Chirico's work in the theatre, considering the ways in which de Chirico and his brother Alberto Savinio's paintings and writings provide stage-like and cinematic images and texts (343). How de Chirico's extensive periods of work in the theatre proper may have influenced his representation of the self is an area still rich for exploration. Rather than delineating one-to-one correspondences between the artist's activities as a painter inside and outside of the theatre, this essay returns to de Chirico's self-portraits in order to examine their theatrical strategies and motifs. Just as the painted self-portraits illustrate the roles de Chirico performed as he constructed his various identities and immortalized his image in paint, so too do his written self-portraits incorporate many similar dramatic techniques.

De Chirico's painted self-portraits allowed the artist to explore self-representation as he inhabits canvases in which he masquerades as both modern and classical hero in various guises. De Chirico included classical symbols in the form of literary characters, architecture and inscriptions featuring Latin texts that bear a theatrical role, much like stage sets and other props. This essay maintains that de Chirico's involvement in theatrical productions informs the stylistic shifts in his self-representations. His choice of objects, as well as his placement of them, replicates theatrical settings, thereby imparting a performative quality to his works as they communicate with the viewer as audience.

An itinerant artist born in Greece of Italian heritage, who relocated regularly from country to country, settling in Rome only in the second half of his 90-year lifetime, de Chirico lacked a single national and cultural identity. These representations of the self included and depended upon certain theatrical strategies in order to present and represent the artist as a character within his own theatrical visual productions that themselves cross cultural, historical and temporal constructs. De Chirico's image of the self is unstable, ranging from ancient playwright to modern Italian hero to mother, as he plays various roles within his modern (or perhaps post-modern) theatre of memory, history and death.

Crucial to de Chirico's staging of the self is the problem of memory. De Chirico himself cited memory as an integral component of sanity, noting that "Schopenhauer defines the madman as a person who has lost his memory.... [I]n fact, that which constitutes the logic of our normal acts and our normal life is a continuous rosary of recollections of relationships between things and ourselves and vice versa" (de Chirico in Chipp 450). Within his project of constructing an artistic identity, de Chirico also relied upon the representation of memory, be it personal or cultural, in both figural and verbal self-portraits. This essay thus takes as its focus two aspects upon which I believe de Chirico's literary and pictorial project depends: (1) the insistent presence of his personal experiences in his written and painted works (thus, his personal memory) and (2) historical references from the *Risorgimento* and classical antiquity (a gesture of cultural memory). Just as in his more than 50 painted images of the self, in his autobiography, *Le memorie della mia vita*, and his surrealist novel, *Hebdomeros*, both of which offered him more subtle forms of self-representation alternative to painting, de Chirico combined the personal with the historical without abandoning the metaphysical, and to a certain extent "uncanny," aspect of his earlier work (Freud).

One of the central problems of the modern condition has been a need to reconcile the past with the present in an effort to pin down the fragmentary, unstable and unpredictable nature of the present within the stability and predictability of the past. Thus history, or a reconstruction of the past, is called in through active memory, or the living tradition in which the history is being worked out. In his overview of a monumental study on the national memory and identity of France entitled *Les Lieux de mémoire*, Pierre Nora has considered some of the differences between history and memory:

> Memory and history, far from being synonymous, appear now to be in fundamental opposition. Memory is life, borne by living societies founded in its name. It remains in permanent evolution, open to the dialectic of remembering and forgetting, unconscious of its successive deformations, vulnerable to manipulation and appropriation, susceptible to being long dormant and periodically revived. History, on the other hand, is the reconstruction, always problematic and incomplete, of what is no longer. Memory is a perpetually actual

phenomenon, a bond tying us to the eternal present, history is a representation of the past (8).

In juxtaposing the classical past with his own present, de Chirico activates the past through his painting and writing by *reviving* what has expired and *euthanizing* the present in order to seal its own mortality. Inscribing the present (that is, *his* present) in a visual language that replicates the form of monumental objects, de Chirico ensures that they too will gain the status of the historical icons that accompany them; moreover, he deceptively adds his art and himself to a well-established art-historical canon as if his art-making and artistic reputation warranted similar adoration and emulation. By alluding to studied objects such as the *Apollo Belvedere* and authors as renowned as Euripides, Dante and Homer, de Chirico underlines the necessary loss of immediacy and therefore an inability to comprehend intended meaning in artworks which survive the test of time. Thus, de Chirico's centralization of isolated elements that seem to neither communicate with nor explain one another can be read as self-consciously indecipherable; moreover, his resulting conception of a present that cannot make sense of its collection of remnants from the past seems to prefigure the postmodern condition. Baldacci, relying on Vernant's explanation of Orphic religion, connects de Chirico's construction of time to "Orphic doctrines and the Greek concept of Mnemosyne, the persona of Memory," stating that "[I]n Orphic religion, Memory redeemed man from his individual destiny through an anamnesis that reunited the soul with its divine principle and removed it from the temporal cycle of life" (*Italian Art in the Twentieth Century* 65). With carefully selected icons of history and the past, however, de Chirico subtly inserts clues to his own memory. For example, in his painting, *The Song of Love*, of 1914 (Fig. 3), we see one such odd configuration of unrelated items, including a painted representation of the Apollo Belvedere head with more mundane objects, including a pink glove and ball. The sense of irrationality in the composition is heightened by an antiquated railway train on the left and empty arcade on the right that frame these items. The

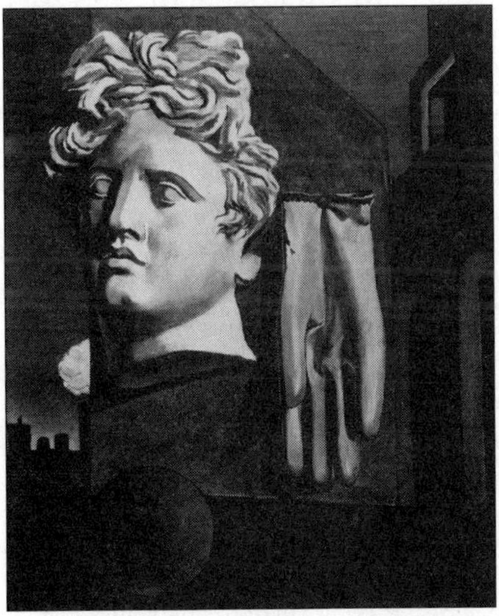

3. Giorgio de Chirico, *Song of Love*, 1914. Museum of Modern Art, New York.

inclusion of these more personal items perhaps relates to the artists' father, who was an engineer working in Greece on the design of the railway system, while the more haunting cardboard-like arcades recall the Italian *piazza* architecture known to have fascinated the artist.[6]

Further consideration of Nora's theory of memory and history leads to that author's more tangible application of this theory to actual monuments and counter-monuments that inspire remembering as a means of gaining access to history. He shows that "[m]emory takes root in the concrete, in spaces, gestures, images and objects; history binds itself strictly to temporal continuities, to progressions and to relations between things. Memory is absolute, while history can only conceive the relative" (9). With a unique pictorial and verbal rhetoric that has labeled him a "one-man movement" (Kundig 97), de Chirico presents historical traces as though they are pieces of his own memory, thus fusing his personal profile with history that indeed, if only fleetingly, functioned as a memory for a now-past society that he reclaims as his own. A problematic tension ensues within his insistent exploration of this paradox that requires the past to make sense of the present, yet simultaneously denies linear temporality by rupturing the logical sense of historical progression. As Denis Hollier has pointed out, de Chirico literally ruptures logical time by confusing the times of day staged in his images with what he defines as "orphan shadows"; he includes time pieces which give one hour, frequently midday, yet includes long shadows which imply dusk and a quality of light that occurs in the late afternoon (119-121). De Chirico mythologizes the modern world by repeatedly intersecting his living personal memory with dead history. Once appropriated though, these historical elements devoid of their own meaning pique the viewer's desire to make sense of them. They function like Nora's *lieux de mémoire*, spaces which map the intersection of history with memory "created by a play of memory and history, an interaction of two factors that results in their reciprocal overdetermination" as "[m]emory attaches itself to sites, whereas history attaches itself to events" (19, 22). I would argue that a similar model of memory is at work in de Chirico's compositions in which monumental historical figures (indices of events or historical moments) such as Garibaldi or even Homer's Hector and Andromache trigger events within the modern stage sets of de Chirico's empty *piazze* and rooms.

6. In his discussion of the "Metaphysical Aesthetic," de Chirico explores the fascination of arcades "Nell'arco v'è qualche cosa di incompiuto, che ha bisogno ed è capace di compimento — *esso lascia ancora presentire*. Perciò, anche l'anello è sempre simbolo di qualcosa di non morale o antimorale". (Questo pensiero chiarì per me l'impressione eminentemente metafisica che mi hanno sempre fatto i portici ed in genere le aperture arcuate). Si sono spesso veduti, nelle figure geometriche, dei simboli di una realtà superiore ("Sull'arte metafisica" 17).

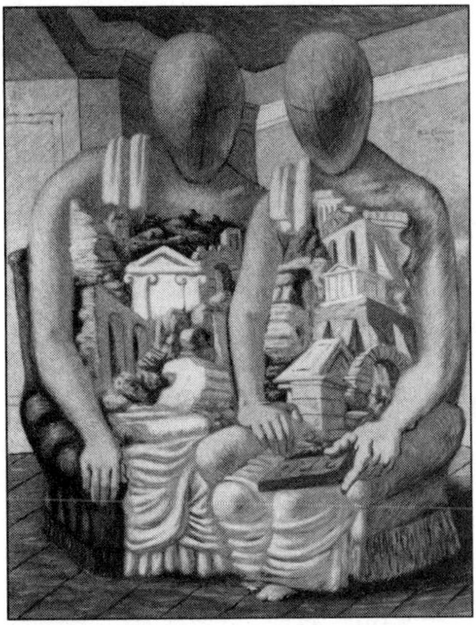

4. Giorgio de Chirico, *Archaeologists*, 1927. Galleria Nazionale d'Arte Moderna, Rome.

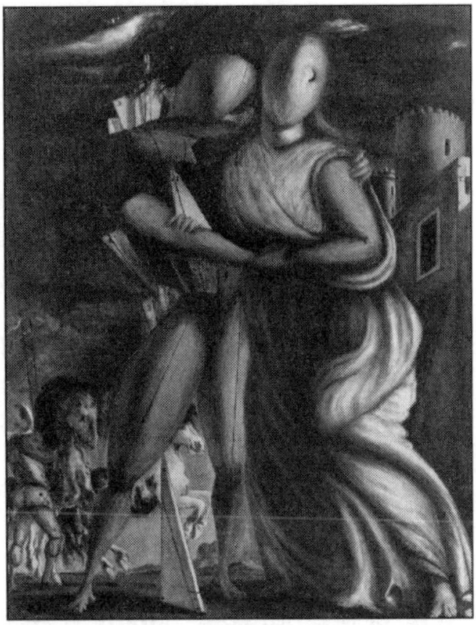

5. Giorgio de Chirico, *Hector and Andromache*, 1924. Galleria Nazionale d'Arte Moderna, Rome.

De Chirico's iconographical choices in the post-metaphysical period center on architectural and sculptural fragments. His *œuvre* is defined by images filled with detached pieces of Classical architecture such as those found in his series of paintings entitled *Archaeologists* (Fig. 4), which he makes as both paintings and sculptures from the 1920s onward. De Chirico peppered his nonsensical landscape paintings with Renaissance *palazzi*, antique statues and modernly dressed figures (such as his *Roman Villa* of 1922), while his many self-portraits that include self-referential Latin inscriptions label him a *pictor classicus*.[7] In addition, he employs literary characters derived from classical mythology, as in his many paintings featuring Homer's tragic figures *Hector and Andromache* (Fig. 5), or in his classical *Gladiators and Lion* of 1927 (Fig. 6).

De Chirico's family history should be considered in an examination of his crisis of identity and temporality. The artist spends more than 60 pages of his autobiography on his youth, underlining the importance

7. Cowling and Mundy provide an overview of the Italian, French and Spanish painters who, in the early twentieth century, return to classical figuration In particular, they point to the "melancholy" aspect that "pervades the work of some of the new classicists — Derain, Picasso and de Chirico especially" (12-13). They note also that "de Chirico employed the same style in theatrically disposed scenes of Renaissance buildings set in hilly landscapes, animated by classical statues and figures in modern dress..." (13). They note that the "writings as well as the paintings of de Chirico and Carrà during these years reflect their close study of Italian Renaissance traditions. De Chirico who had received an intensive academic training, now demanded the most rigorous classical standards, made a number of close copies of old master paintings" (15).

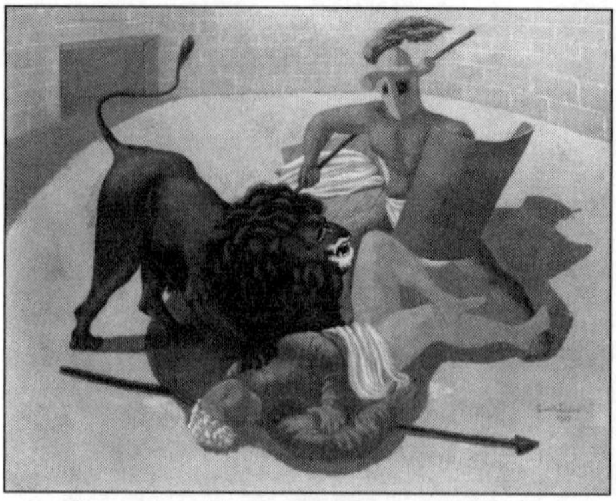

6. Giorgio de Chirico, *Gladiators and Lion*, 1927. The Detroit Institute of Arts, Detroit.

of this period in his life. While the father dies when de Chirico is only seventeen, he remains close by his mother well into his adulthood. Hal Foster provides a psychoanalytic reading of the artist's production which links the nostalgia of his disjunctive historical elements with "uncanny" sentiments relating to his dead father (67-71). This essay, however, will examine the presence of the mother, insofar as it is de Chirico's ongoing relationship with his mother (and his two wives) that locates the artist's complicated identity issues which recur in both his painting and writing. De Chirico opens and frames his *Memorie* with a description of his fascination with his mother's scarf and constantly refers to her essential caretaking of him whenever and wherever he would fall ill (9). He repeatedly notes his travels with his mother, as well as the onsets of illness that befell him inevitably during separations from her, and especially his haunting dream signaling her death (148-9). I suggest that his obsession with his mother, as we shall see in his relationship to his wives as well, provided him with an immediate personal context in which to anchor his sense of "modern" chronology which he interspersed with his sense of a more historicized past in order to forge his diachronic present.

Were de Chirico an Italian citizen born and raised within the geographical boundaries of the peninsula, an examination of his national identity might not seem relevant. However, born to Italian parents living in Greece, de Chirico did not remain for long in any one place as a child or as an adult, moving from Greece to Italy, then through Germany and France, and even to North America.[8] This nomadic pattern continues throughout the artist's life including countless migrations from Florence to Paris and back to Rome, in addition to an eighteen-month sojourn in Manhattan from August 1936 to January 1938 (de Chirico *Le Memorie* 143-8; Braun *De Chirico and America* 235-9). As a result, de Chirico regularly experienced from an early age great shifts in both language and culture.

8. Martin discusses de Chirico's sojourns in Milan and Florence (342), while Baldacci notes that on his way to Paris in 1911, de Chirico stopped in Turin, where he made a "visit of seminal importance" during which he experiences the "long rows of porticoes; the monuments to bourgeois political figures and conquering kings; the mythic heroes of the Risorgimento; trains hidden by walls..." (*Italian Art in the Twentieth Century* 63).

In several instances in his *Memorie*, de Chirico distinguishes between individuals with hybrid national identities and migrant existences, and others who have a more homogeneous nationality commensurate with long-term residency. When describing his friend the painter Nino Bertoletti in his autobiography, de Chirico notes with admiration the stable and static nature of that painter's life.

> Da più di venticinque anni che lo conosco egli ha cambiato casa solo due volte mentre nello stesso periodo io ho cambiato casa ventun volte, senza contare i soggiorni più o meno prolungati negli alberghi, nelle pensioni, negli appartamenti ammobiliati, nelle camere mobiliate, da amici e da parenti e senza contare i cambiamenti di città, di regione, di paese e perfino di continente. Bertoletti ha sempre abitato la stessa città, ha conservato i suoi mobili, libri ed oggetti (18).

De Chirico announces that he too would have liked such a "vita tranquilla e regolata, in mezzo alle mie cose" (18). Even the mundane aspects of de Chirico's life were affected by his itinerant nature.

> "Poi mi è spesso capitato che quando, dopo molti mesi, a volte anni, che ho dovuto lavorare per fare capire al barbiere il mio desiderio e che sono finalmente riuscito a farmi tagliare i capelli senza, alla fine, la proposta della frizione, devo partire, cambiare casa o città, o addirittura Paese, e così, nella nuova residenza, mi tocca ricominciare tutto da capo" (37).

Indeed, de Chirico notes that "si cambiava spesso casa in Grecia, ogni due anni circa avveniva lo sgombero; è una fatalità della mia vita quella di cambiare sempre abitazione" (32-33). In describing the fate of his friend Guillaume Apollinaire, he returns to the issue of identity:

> Egli anelava quindi ad appartenere ad un Paese, ad una razza, ad avere un passaporto in regola. Molti provano questa specie di pudore e di vergogna di essere nati in un Paese, mentre hanno la nazionalità di un altro Paese (79).

While it is clear that by calling attention to his own internationality, de Chirico flaunts his flavorful past, his position is a defensive one. He further emphasizes his homelessness when he mentions other literary celebrities with experiences similar to his own:

> [O]gni qualvolta io dico che sono nato in Grecia, c'è sempre qualcuno che aggiunge:'Ma allora lei è greco!' Ed a nulla vale che io protesti e citi i casi di Ugo Foscolo, di Matilde Serao, di Arturo Graf ed aggiunga persino che il poeta francese André Chénier, benché fosse nato a Costantinopoli, nessuno lo ha mai creduto un poeta turco (79).

Thus, in rejecting non-Italian status, de Chirico aligns himself with other acclaimed artists from recent centuries. Destined to move throughout his life, de Chirico brought with him a sense of homelessness and homesickness wherever he went; moreover, he internalized this void of "home," negotiating his identity through the representation of otherness.

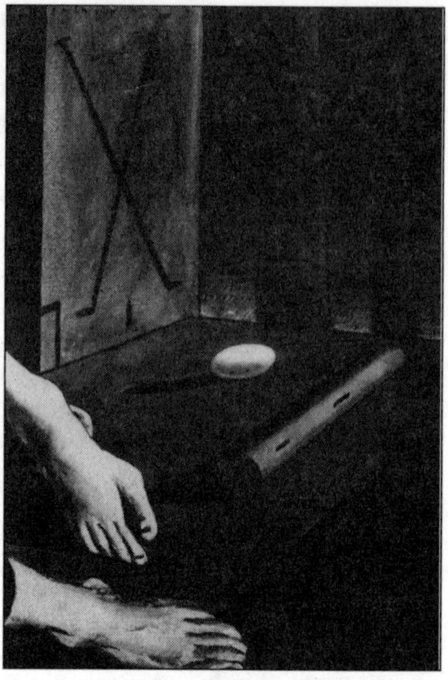

7. Giorgio de Chirico, *Metaphysical Composition*, 1913. The Alex Hillman Family Foundation, New York.

This tension between past and present, as well as history and memory, can be seen in many of de Chirico's pictorial self-portraits. For example, a *Metaphysical Composition* of 1913 referred to as a self-portrait while still in the collection of Paul Éluard (Braun, ed. 50-53; Baldacci *De Chirico* 236-240), prefigures the problems inherent in later self-representations by staging smoke-stacks, an egg, a scroll and other seemingly random objects in an unidentifiable space (Fig. 7). Dramatically detached stone feet haunt the lower left section of the composition. Braun has corrected the formerly accepted mistitling of the work from *Self-Portrait* to *Metaphysical Composition*, showing how the polemical relationship between de Chirico and the Surrealists in the 1920s led to criticism of even his metaphysical style. Interestingly, however, it is such a mistitling that allows us to see that certain aspects of de Chirico's metaphysical pictorial strategy reappear in the painted self-portraits that come under analysis in this essay. In other words, although I turn to this specific metaphysical composition because of the irony of its mistitling as self-portrait, it also prompts me to locate the temporal crisis native to such metaphysical compositions in many of the artist's self-portraits as well. In this image, dramatically detached feet haunt the lower left section of the composition: one foot is a statuary fragment, while the other foot creeps into the image from the edge, thus extending out of the picture into a space inaccessible to the viewer. Joseph Sloane has identified these feet as a quotation of drawings of Giuseppe Garibaldi's feet, thus marking them a symbol of the *Risorgimento* (15). Rather than identifying the artist with this political hero, I would argue instead that the self resides in the very discontinuity reified by the presence of such a historical index in its surrounding space, or his own theatre of modernity. Kenneth Bendiner argues that de Chirico further embeds the *Risorgimento* into his

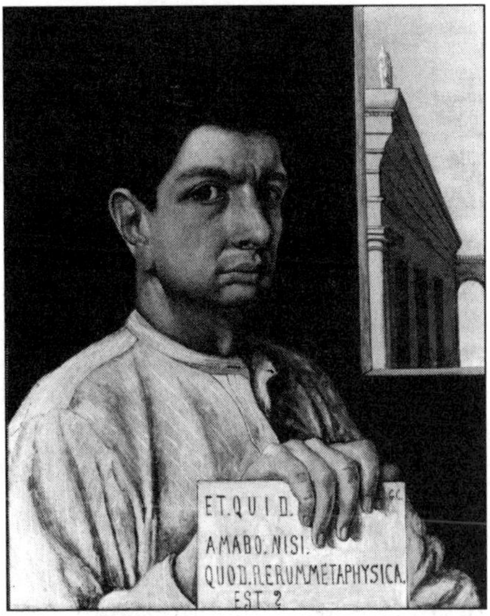

8. Giorgio de Chirico, *Self-Portrait*, 1920. Staatsgalerie Moderner Kunst, Munich.

paintings featuring arcades, a well-established feature in the paintings of the Macchiaioli, the group of Tuscan artists based in Florence in the mid- to late nineteenth century, contemporary with the developments leading up to and continuing with the *Risorgimento*.

The inclusion of classical text within de Chirico's self-portraits not only historicizes the artist's view of himself, but also imparts provenance to the character depicted and the object which is the portrait. One such painting of 1920 (Fig. 8) asks the question, "Et quid amabo, nisi quod rerum metaphysica est? or "What would I love if not that which is metaphysical?", while a detail of classical architecture lurks behind the artist, providing a theatrical setting for the displaced classical artist. A *Self-Portrait* from 1924 declares, "Mihi fama perennis quaeritur in toto semper ut orbe canar," or "My everlasting renown is sought as I will be sung of throughout the whole world." Speaking in an ancient tongue, de Chirico here finds himself within the studio engaged as the modern painter. I would argue that these Latin texts also evoke associations with the epigraphs found on classical tombs, thereby projecting a sense of death, or a future passing, onto the depiction of the *then* present artist. Maurizio Fagiolo dell'Arco relates these inscriptions in self-portraits to similar practices by the German painters Holbein and Dürer studied by de Chirico during the early 1920s (*de Chirico. Gli anni venti* 40).

As noted by Fagiolo dell'Arco in his exhibition catalog of de Chirico's work from *Gli anni venti*, the artist frequently relies on a technique of doubling whereby he repeatedly paints himself in the company of "altri" (36). In a *Self-Portrait* completed in 1923, de Chirico depicts himself before the god Mercury, mimicking the stance of this divine character whose arms wrap around him. Both the dead statue and the living artist arrest the spectator's gaze with their hand gestures. Though Mercury's winged sandals propel him from place to place in order to deliver urgent messages, in this composition he remains mute, his message spoken through the facial expression of the artist who urges the spectator to stop and contemplate the image. Thus, de Chirico associates himself with the classical identity of Mercury not only through the god's winged helmet and lyre, but also through the laurel leaves forming a halo around the artist's head. Similarly, in 1922-1923, de Chirico paints his self-portrait with the bust of the classical Greek playwright Euripides, bearing the message, "Nulla sine tragedia gloria," or "There is no honor without tragedy." *The Self-Portrait with the bust of Euripides* presents the artist looking out anxiously, while the immortal portrait of the now dead dramatist is the figure whose glance of approval seems to validate the painter's ambiguous status as part-classical, part-modern. The portrait of Euripides, a memorial to the past, bears the power of sight, yet Euripides' empty eyes are fixed on the subject, who is the artist's self, also frozen into the time of the image. The active looking of the dead portrait bust underscores the imminent mortality of the sitter, or the artist who looks out to the viewer who occupies the present in the same way that he does in the moment of painting himself with Euripides' gaze pinned to him.[9] Crediting Baldacci, Fagiolo dell'Arco accounts for de Chirico's choice of Euripides by noting that "la tragedia come arte comincia con Euripide," whereas "Eschilo rappresenta direttamente il tragico universale, mentre Sofocle dà voce al tragico umano" (*Gli anni venti* 46). These classically inscribed canvases are merely examples culled from many such images that contain similar prose messages that case de Chirico as modern actor of classical drama, a classical painter in a different time and place. Yet it is in the very collapse of the space between the two temporalities that de Chirico underlines the problem inherent in his own rhetorical gesture.

De Chirico struggles with a similar problem in figuring the intersection of past and present as located in the mortality of the artist in two other self-portraits from 1922 and 1924. In his *Self-Portrait* of 1922, the artist turns out toward the viewer, as though moving out of the world of representation into the viewer's space, yet he is held back by what seems to be a process of gradual petrifaction. Seen best in his hands as well as his clothing, the dead coldness of immortal and inorganic stone has washed over his body, although his head still retains natural, skin-tone color since the process is not complete. De Chirico's countenance is both serious and focused, suggesting his awareness of what is happening. The juxtaposition of the flesh-tones of his face with the harsh, stone-like material of the body locates de Chirico's conflict between his present condition and his knowledge of necessarily slipping into the past. Indeed, this painting is a visual analog for the passage of time, a literal representation of the artist's mortification. Signaling his awareness of the complex dynamic between

9. Roos has written a stimulating essay that takes the *Self-Portrait with Euripides* as an example of the double-portraits common in de Chirico's works of the 1920s.

past and present, de Chirico petrifies himself, suggesting that he is already partially eternalized, though not yet a relic of history.

In a particularly dramatic *Self-Portrait* of 1924 from the Toledo Museum of Art, de Chirico re-stages a similar problem, this time creating two versions of himself: one the completely dead, frozen monumental bust and the other, a realistic portrait of himself that seems caught in a troubled gaze that again confronts the paradox of having one's own effigy gaze actively through inanimate eyes at the subject which is the same figure still living and therefore confronting the disturbing condition of historicizing one's own memory.[10] This image splits apart past and present to create two perfectly discrete temporal realities, while the previous image of 1922 discussed above makes two chronological points continuous and imperfect. De Chirico seems to dissociate himself from his bust in order to show that aspect of him residing in antiquity rather than in modernity. He is neither modern nor classical; rather, he seems to function within a dialectic that can be read rather literally into this split sense of self where the past seems to mirror the future. Does de Chirico suggest that his two versions of the "self," petrified and real, should be equated since the present is predestined to become the past? The bright color and central position of the detail of the lemon underscores it as a focal point in the image. This piece of *natura morta*, or still life, seems to gesture toward the juxtaposition of dead life in the bust and living death in the figure underscore the mortality inherent in the portraiture of the living. The lemon stands before what could be the absence or cancellation of the palette no longer accessible to the artist paralyzed by the passage of time. This "palette" does not interact with the artist's hands and does not draw the attention of either the stone or flesh figures; instead, the palette provides another paradox in its present, yet inaccessible position. These spectral traces of the artist, living and dead, gain force as viewed under the folds of a theatrical curtain that signals their performative roles. Resting in the space of the statue, the corporeal de Chirico is wedded to and contained by his already dead self, while his connection to the present is barred by the frame of the image and, more pointedly, by the act of representation itself.

In a later painting of 1934, entitled *Self-Portrait in the Paris Studio*, the now mature de Chirico engages again in the discourse of the living dead, provoking a polemical reaction with his figure clad in casual

10. De Chirico paraphrases Arthur Schopenhauer's commentary on the distinction between eye-level busts and elevated statues "Schopenhauer, che la sapeva lunga in tali faccende, consigliava ai suoi conterranei di non porre le statue dei loro uomini illustri sopra colonne e piedestalli troppo alti ma di posarle invece su zoccoli bassi, 'come si usa in Italia, diceva, ove alcuni uomini di marmo sembrano trovarsi al livello dei passanti e camminare con essi" ("Sull'arte metafisica" XI).

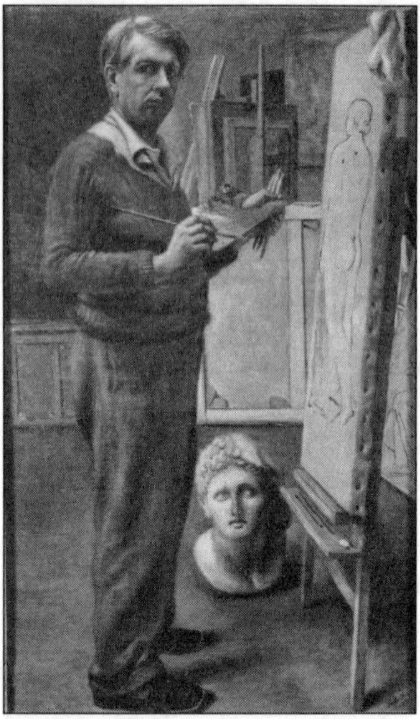

9. Giorgio de Chirico, *Self-Portrait in the Studio*, 1934. Galleria Nazionale d'Arte Moderna, Rome.

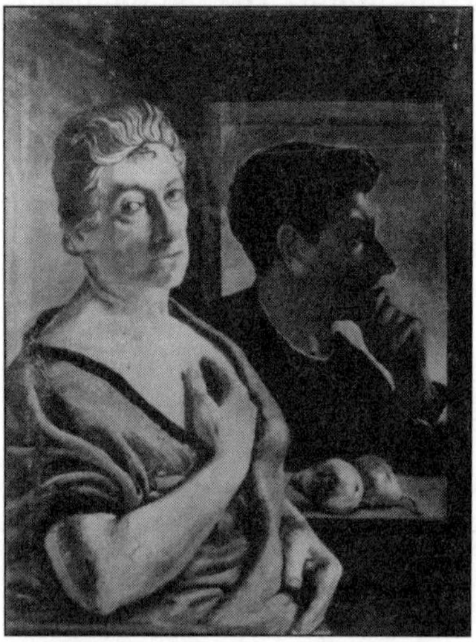

10. Giorgio de Chirico, *Self-Portrait with Mother*, 1919. Centre Georges Pompidou, Paris.

dress and slippers (Fig. 9) (Fagiolo dell'Arco *de Chirico. Gli anni trenta* 29-30). Both the artist and the piece of antique statuary at his feet stare actively, but the objects receiving their gazes are not the same. While the body of the artist turns to the spectator, what should be a frozen, sculpted head of stone instead turns her eyes onto the canvas, as though to critique its contents. Her lively eyes look at the not yet completed painting resting on the easel, as the unnerved artist pauses from his brushstrokes. Endowing the dead with the powers of the living, the artist confuses the spectator as he casts the object as subject. Thus, the statue fragment becomes a living actor in his theatre of the self where temporal, historical and cultural boundaries collapse. By pitting himself against this icon of antiquity, de Chirico challenges the tradition of portraiture as he inverts the expected roles of artist and object. Strangely this canvas contains *two* signatures of the artist, suggesting that perhaps one signature is part of the self-representation itself, while the second serves as the actual signature, which authenticates the work.

Though de Chirico depicted his mother on numerous occasions, his 1919 *Self-Portrait with Mother* locates a particularly haunting connection of the artist's likeness to that of his mother (Fig. 10). Here, the effaced artist appears behind his mother, framed by a window. The pronounced features of the artist's mother substitute themselves for those missing from the artist's effigy. The window resembles a mirror, suggesting that the artist is a reflection of his mother, implying that his self resides in her. The paint of the 1919 self-portrait looks more like fresco effect than the oil (which is its actual material), offering the cracks and muted tones characteristic of great Renaissance works. Monumental and masculine, de Chirico's mother's body recalls images such as Michelangelo's sybils from the Sistine ceiling, figures also labeled female, who instead bear the physique of men.[11] The banality of still life objects like the two centrally-placed pears introduces a sense of cynicism to this self-portrait that is really the stone-like and overbearing portrait of the artist's mother. Simultaneously, although not literally, they mirror one another, promoting de Chirico and his mother as mutual reflections. By making a modern painting in the tradition of a Renaissance one, de Chirico places his work in that genre of painting.

Like his mother, de Chirico's wives also provide a constant source of subject matter for his painting and writing, as is perhaps clear from the persistent archaeological fragments which index his first marriage to Raissa Krol, a trained classical archaeologist.[12] Turning to his marriage of nearly 50 years to Isabella Far, we find that de Chirico transfers much of his maternal obsession to Isabella, describing his relationship with her in terms very similar to those he had used to qualify his affection for his mother.[13] Much like his mother, Isabella determined the success or failure of the artist physically, mentally and professionally, as de Chirico's enterprise of painting was mediated by his relationships with and representations of himself with others. When describing his first meeting with Isabella, de Chirico makes clear his admiration for her. "In quel periodo di marasma e di costernazione generale mi capitò però una grande fortuna ed una grande felicità: quella di conoscere Isabella Far, la persona più profondamente intelligente che io abbia incontrato nella mia vita" (*Le Memorie della mia vita* 137). He compares her with two other mentors in his life, the Greek architect Pikionis and his brother Alberto Savinio, yet it was "nella intelligenza di Isabella Far ho trovato qualcosa di più profondo e di più positivo" (*Le Memorie della mia vita* 138). It is as though the artist's sense

11. Indeed, Braun has noted that much of de Chirico's art was, after all, "*transvestitio* in the style of others" in her discussion of the ways in which de Chirico's "slippages of identity" include his crossing and blurring of gender lines, whether in his reversal of the male gaze with his many nude male bathers and gladiators alike. I extend her arguments here to include de Chirico's gender blurring in his depiction of his mother, where the artist himself seems effeminized as well (*De Chirico and America*).

12. Fagiolo dell'Arco describes how de Chirico met Raissa Krol in the theatre of Pirandello, where she worked as a dancer prior to returning to the university to pursue her career in classical archaeology (*La Vita di Giorgio de Chirico* 136).

13. Baldacci notes that de Chirico's relationships with his wives were not of a sexual nature, though he relies on Luisa Spagnoli's rather sketchy biography (Baldacci *De Chirico*, Spagnoli 169).

of security depends on the leading ladies in his life; "home" is not a geographical distinction, but instead an emotional dynamic.

De Chirico hints at his literary epic status in both his fictional and non-fictional prose, as made clear by the photograph he staged with Irving Penn in 1944. Not surprisingly, it was de Chirico who broke off the laurel sprigs during a stroll in the Roman Forum, placed them on his head and requested his photo to be taken as such, "as a Roman conqueror" (Braun, *De Chirico and America* 232, citing Penn 18). In describing one of his many gastrointestinal disorders (usually coincidental with his separations from his mother) in his autobiography, de Chirico compares his own cure with that of Julius Caesar in describing the treatment prescribed by his doctor: "...la cura di quelle acque, tanto salutari, dette dai romani *aquae calidae*, ove circa duemila anni prima Giulio Cesare curò la sua dyspepsia...mi fecero molto bene" (*Le Memorie della mia vita* 70). A nearly identical incident occurs during the adventurous and unstable travels of Hebdomeros, the protagonist of de Chirico's 1929 surrealist novel of the same title (61). While written as a narrative novel, *Hebdomeros* denies the progression of linear time as well as the dynamism traditionally generated by cause-and-effect relations; instead, it describes associations and analogies to what is "seen." As Renée Riese Hubert states "Comparisons do not establish similarities of appearance, but by moving, visually from object to impression, and chronologically, from modern to prehistoric times, his writing expresses a refusal to delimit, to circumscribe" (157). Hubert also notes that de Chirico grants Homeric proportions to his novel not only via the Ulysses-like character whose primary mission is to move forward, but also through his name, a hybrid of the Greek adjective seventh (hebdomos) and the poet Homer. Hebdomeros is always moving, yet he never reaches a concrete destination or home. The urgency inherent in his travels echoes the epic proportions of the Homeric odyssey, yet the proportions granted to journeys across rivers and mountains are not dissimilar to those assigned to brief excursions down a short corridor or up a flight of stairs. The narrator often describes figures in comparison with classical figures. "Nor did he remind one of gladiators lay, or warriors wounded or dying. This strange man looked more as though he were petrified, which is why he brought to mind the corpses uncovered at Pompeii" (16). Such descriptions run rampant throughout the novel that describes the irrational wanderings of an artist lacking a concrete destination and a traditional sense of space, arguably much like the artist who authored this cryptic tale. [14]

As both painter and writer, de Chirico disseminates traces of the past which allow his viewers to access the role he plays anachronistically

14. De Chirico presents a semi-autobiographical account of himself as an artist in *Il Signor Dudron* as well, but this will be the subject of my work in a future project.

within the space between antiquity and modernity. In his paintings filled with disconnected historical icons, de Chirico injects instances of history into his own modern conception of classical identity creating dreamlike visions, or memories, which in their very impossibility defy a perfected aspect and become imperfect as they show the past that leads up to the present, rather than allowing the past to exist in its completion. De Chirico's paintings make a similar gesture with their hauntingly empty spaces replete with symbols of the past: classical statues, arcades and mythological figures. By relying on such a vocabulary, de Chirico appropriates the other in varied guises and recasts them with a diachronic aspect that functions as a language whose tense we can neither identify nor access directly; moreover, he foreshadows his own passing, gesturing toward a future perfection. In the last lines of his senseless wanderings, *Hebdomeros* meets a woman "with the eyes of his father." She tells him, "Hebdomeros, I am Immortality. Nouns have their gender, or rather their sex, and the verbs, alas, decline" (117). Painting in a language which defies discreet tenses and disrupts the logic of traditional visual syntax, de Chirico transcends representational limits to ensure the continual performance of his pictorial and verbal eulogy; moreover, he underlines his immortality by problematizing what he defines as the monumental project of constructing his identity through his unique *pre-* rather than *post mortem* memorial gestures.

WORKS CITED

Baldacci, Paolo. *De Chirico: The Metaphysical Period, 1888-1919*. Trans. Jeffrey Jennings. Boston: Little, Brown, 1997.

——. "De Chirico and Savinio: The Theory and Iconography of Metaphysical Painting," in *Italian Art in the Twentieth Century. Painting and Sculpture 1900-1988*. Ed. Emily Braun. Munich & London: Prestel Verlag, 1989. 61-70.

Bendiner, Kenneth. "De Chirico and the Macchiaioli." *Source: Notes on the History of Art* 1:4 (Summer 1982): 24-27.

Braun, Emily, ed. *The Hillman Family Collection: Manet to Matisse*. New York: Alex Hillman Family Foundation in association with U of Washington Press, Seattle, 1994.

——. *De Chirico and America*. Turin: Allemandi, 1996.

Calvesi, Maurizio and Mario Ursino. *De Chirico—The New Metaphysics*. Buffalo: Craftsman House/G&B Arts International, 1996.

Chipp, Herschel. *Theories of Modern Art: a source book by artists and critics*. Berkeley: U of California Press, 1968.

Cowling, Elizabeth and Jennifer Mundy. *On Classic Ground: Picasso, Léger, de Chirico and the New Classicism 1910-1930*. London: Tate Gallery, 1990.

De Chirico, Giorgio. *Le memorie della mia vita*. Milano: Rizzoli, 1962.

——. *Hebdomeros*. Trans. unidentified. Cambridge: Exact Change, 1992.

——. "Sull'arte metafisica." *Valori Plastici* I: 4-5 (April-May 1919). Reprinted as *Valori Plastici*. Rivista d'arte. Roma 1918-1921. Riproduzione anastatica conforme all'originale. Archivi d'arte del XX secolo, Roma. Milano: Gabriele Mazzotta, 1969. 15-18.

Fagiolo dell'Arco, Maurizio, ed. *de Chirico. Gli anni trenta*. Milano: Mazzotta, 1999.

——. *de Chirico. Gli anni venti*. Milano: Mazzotta, 1986.

——. "La Scena è un quadro che si muove e parla," *Sipario/Staged Art*. Milano: Charta, 1997. 12-45.

——. *La vita di Giorgio de Chirico*. Torino: Allemandi, 1988.

Foster, Hal. "Convulsive Identity," in *Compulsive Beauty*. Cambridge: MIT Press, 1993. 57-98.

Freud, Sigmund. "The Uncanny," in *Studies in Parapsychology*. Vol. X. Ed. Philip Reiff. New York: Collier Books, 1963.

Gigli, Elena. "De Chirico e lo spettacolo," *Sipario/Staged Art*. Milano: Charta, 1997. 70-107; 188-203.

Hollier, Denis. "Surrealist Precipitates: Shadows Don't Cast Shadows." *October* 69 (Summer 1994): 110-132.

Hubert, Renée Riese. "The Fabulous Fiction of Two Surrealist Artists: Giorgio de Chirico and Max Ernst." *New Literary History* 4 (1972): 151-166.

Kundig, Karen. "Giorgio de Chirico, Surrealism, and Neoromanticism." *De Chirico and America*. Ed. Emily Braun. Turin: Allemandi, 1996. 97-110.

Martin, Marianne. "Reflections on De Chirico and *Arte Metafisica*." *Art Bulletin* (June 1978): 342-353.

Nora, Pierre. "Between Memory and History: *Les Lieux de Mémoire*." *Representations* 26 (Spring 1989): 7-25.

Penn, Irving. *Passage: A Work Record* I. New York: Knopf, 1991.

Roos, Gerd. "*Nulla sine tragoedia gloria*. The Self-Portrait with Euripides (1922-23) by Giorgio de Chirico" in *De Chirico and the Mediterranean*. Ed. by Jole de Sanna. New York: Rizzoli, 1998. 51-58.

Rosenstock, Laura. "De Chirico's Influence on the Surrealists," in *De Chirico*. New York: The Museum of Modern Art, 1982. 111-129.

Rubin, William, ed. *De Chirico*. New York: Museum of Modern Art, 1982.

Sloane, Joseph. "Giorgio de Chirico and Italy." *The Art Quarterly* 21:1 (Spring 1958): 3-22.

Soby, James Thrall. *Giorgio de Chirico*. New York: Museum of Modern Art, 1955.

Spagnoli, Luisa. *Lunga vita di Giorgio de Chirico*. Milano: Longanesi, 1971.

Speranza, Maria Grazie Tolomeo. "L'immortalità come ultimo fine," in *Giorgio de Chirico. Pictor Optimus: Pittura Disegno Teatro*. Rome: Carte Segrete/Data Arte s.r.l., 1993.

Vernant, J. P. "Aspects mythiques de la mémoire," *Journal de Psychologie* (1959): 1-29.

Theatre and Its "Truth": A Reading of Alberto Savinio's *Il Suo nome*

Luca Somigli

UNIVERSITY OF TORONTO

ALBERTO SAVINIO, born Andrea de Chirico and brother of the painter Giorgio, is a unique figure in the landscape of European culture in the first half of the twentieth century. While his brother may have enjoyed more success, both critical and popular, during his lifetime, Savinio's many-sided genius has made of him an archetypal avant-garde artist, an intellectual and actual wanderer equally at home in Paris as in Milan, and before a canvas as before a piano. He once wrote about himself: "My interest for all forms of expression is not limited to any specific one. I go from one to the other like, in olden days, one changed horses at every post-stage" (*Palchetti* 18).[1] A musician, painter, writer and critic formed in the school of the German and Parisian avant-garde, and later heralded by Breton as one of the spiritual fathers of Surrealism,[2] Savinio displayed an interdisciplinary vocation which seemed to find an almost natural home in the theatre, in spite of his discontinuous relationship with it. Savinio's forays into the theatre involved all of its aspects, with the exception of acting: in addition to several plays, he also wrote ballets (*La morte di Niobe* 1925 and *Vita dell'Uomo* 1951) and an opera, *Orfeo vedovo* (1950), and he drafted the stage and costume design for several performances, including a famous

1. "L'interesse che io porto alle varie forme dell'espressione, non è esclusivo per nessuna di esse. Passo da una all'altra come una volta, di posta in posta, si cambiavano i cavalli." All translations are mine.

2. See Breton's introduction to his selection from Savinio's *Introduction à la vie de Mercure* in *Anthologie de l'humour noir*, which begins with the famous assertion: "Tout le mythe moderne encore en formation s'appuie à son origine sur les deux œuvres dans leur esprit presque indiscernable, d'Alberto Savinio et de son frère Giorgio de Chirico" (1122). Notice how Breton reverses the usual hierarchical relationship between the two brothers, and defines Giorgio as brother of Alberto Savinio, rather than vice versa.

edition of Rossini's *Armida* for the Maggio Musicale Fiorentino in 1952, which, for good measure, he also directed.[3]

Though Savinio's relationship with the theatre dates back to his collaboration with Pirandello's "Teatro d'Arte" in 1925 (and perhaps even further back, since certain sections of his first major works, *Les Chants de la Mi-Mort* and *Hermaphrodito*, have a distinctly dramatic structure),[4] it was in the years immediately before and after World War II that he engaged in a sustained confrontation with the stage. In particular, the late thirties (Savinio was the theatre reviewer for the weekly *Omnibus*, published between 1937 and 1939) and early forties were times of intense meditation on the possibilities of the theatre and on its current state, and it is in the short and often occasional pieces from this period that we can trace the foundations of Savinio's dramatic theory.[5] In a short 1943 piece on theatre which was later included in

3. On Savinio's critical fortune (or lack thereof) from the earliest reviews of his works to the end of the '80s, see Marcello Carlino's well-balanced and appropriately ironic bibliographical essay (67-183). Savinio's theatre has been the object of a double repression, as a minor activity of an author on the margin of the literary canon. Between the late '80s and early '90s, with the re-publication by Adelphi, and under the able editorship of Alessandro Tinterri, of his five theatrical *pièces* in two volumes (*Capitano Ulisse* in 1989 and *Alceste di Samuele e atti unici* in 1991; the latter also includes *Il suo nome*, *La famiglia Mastinu*, and *Emma B. vedova Giocasta*), there has been a resurgence of interest in Savinio's theatre, prompting the staging of *Capitano Ulisse* (1990; directed by Mario Missiroli), *Il suo nome* (1989, directed by Luca Valentino, and 1991, directed by Egisto Marcucci), and *La famiglia Mastinu* (1990, directed by Marcucci), and in the publication of Tinterri's and Valentino's monographic studies of Savinio's theatre. For a production history of the plays and of the other works for the stage, see Tinterri 265-270 and Valentino 253-255. On Savinio's theatre, in addition to the studies referred to here and in the other notes, see also Lanuzza 89-99 (although he does not specifically discuss *Il suo nome*, Lanuzza is especially interesting on the ambiguous relationship between the stage and the text), Piscopo 231-254, and Gutiérrez, *Alberto Savinio* 3-7. Two beautiful exhibitions, complemented by critical catalogues, have documented Savinio's activity as scenographer and costume designer: see Bossagli and Barbero.

4. On the theatrical structure of *Les Chants de la Mi-Mort*, see Lapini, who notices how in Savinio's first major work, "The theatre does not become an expressive means upon which to dwell, but rather a place of transit from the predominant interests of the musician to those of the writer and then of the painter" (32). In other words, the *Chants* confirm the interdisciplinary nature of Savinio's inspiration before it becomes fully explicit in his actual works. Valentino also argues convincingly for the importance of the *Chants* for Savinio's later theatrical production (see especially ch. 2).

5. Savinio's theatre reviews were collected in *Palchetti romani*, also (with occasional variations) the title of the column in where they appeared in *Omnibus*. A selection had already been reprinted in 1977 in the *Rivista italiana di drammaturgia*, with an introductory note by Edo Bellingeri. It should be noted that "Il Teatro è fantasia" discussed below, is one of two pieces in *Palchetti romani* which did not originally appear in *Omnibus*. It was first published in the September 1938 issue of *Scenario*. For a detailed discussion of the principles underlying Savinio's theatre criticism, see Antonucci. On Savinio's collaboration to periodicals, see Buttier.

Nuova enciclopedia,[6] he vehemently defended the experience of the historical avant-garde, which had been fundamental to the formative years of his career, against a generalized "return to order" which aimed at undoing the break with realist theatre that had marked the experimental theatre of the early twentieth century:

> THEATRE: One often hears people say: "these things are *passé*." This statement refers in particular to what was done in that period of great research, great renewal, and great achievements which roughly goes from 1910 to 1930. [...] Everything that has been done since then was a "minor" consequence of that period. In the meantime, much has been given up, and there has been a retreat which, out of decency, we have agreed to define as return to reason, return to order, rebirth of fundamental values. (355)[7]

In a kind of pre-emptive critical strike against what would become the dominant mode of post-war literature, Savinio returned to and expanded on his fierce and scathing critique of any form of artistic production which falls under the province of realism — an attack which he had already articulated in the essay "Il teatro è fantasia" (1938), his first major reflection on the subject. In "Il teatro è fantasia" he writes:

> In the theatre better than anywhere else one can see the damages wrought by *verismo* —this misunderstanding on which real or self-styled authors, directors, public, critics play— this refuge for imbeciles.
>
> *Verismo* has infected our Theatre to such an extent, our actors are so besmeared with *verismo*, that they are now *ashamed* to disguise or mask themselves, to return to their "truth" as actors. (*Palchetti* 19-20)[8]

And a few paragraphs later, he further clarifies: "In order to achieve a supposed 'truth,' the actor is no longer an actor: he has been emptied

---

6. Savinio had intended to collect in *Nuova enciclopedia* several of his short pieces published in magazines and newspapers (specifically *Domus*, *La Stampa* and *Il Corriere della Sera*) between 1941 and 1948, along with other unpublished material and the 1932 article "Giovanna D'Arco." The volume was first published posthumously in 1977.

7. "TEATRO. Si sente dire molto spesso: «Sono cose superate». Questa frase si riferisce in modo particolare a quanto è stato fatto in quel periodo di grandi ricerche, di grande rinnovamento, di grandi conquiste che a un dipresso va dal 1910 al 1930. [...] Tutto quanto è stato fatto di poi è una conseguenza 'minore' di quel periodo. Ci sono state nel frattempo molte rinunce e un ripiegamento che per decenza ci si accorda a chiamare rinsavimento, ritorno all'ordine, rinascita dei valori."

8. "Nel Teatro meglio che altrove si misurano i danni del «verismo»: questo equivoco sul quale giocano autori, direttori di teatro, attori, pubblico, critici o sedicenti tali: questo rifugio degli imbecilli.

   Il verismo ha talmente infettato il nostro Teatro, i nostri attori sono talmente lordi di verismo, che di travestirsi, mascherarsi, rientrare nella loro «verità» di attori, ormai *si vergognano*."

out into a ghost, a grey shadow which does not walk, does not speak, does not gesticulate" (20).[9]

The "truth," then, is the stake of bourgeois realist theatre, the theatre positing as its centre the question which, in a review of Pirandello's *I giganti della montagna*, Savinio described as contrary to the "galateo superiore" that governs the approach to a work of poetry, namely the question "What does it mean?" But, with his characteristic eye for the hermaphroditic, contradictory nature of things, Savinio suggests that in asking that "improper" question realist theatre becomes the paradoxical locus in which the truth of the theatre is annihilated, in which the frame between "reality" and "art" is collapsed. In a realist work, what is on stage signifies itself, the signs of reality proliferate, and the "reality effect" signaled by Roland Barthes as the identifying feature of realism governs the fictional universe.

By telescoping reality and its representation, by eliding the constructed nature of the spectacle, *verismo* hypostatizes *its* truth as *the* truth, following a procedure which in the entry on "Verità" in *Nuova enciclopedia* —an entry published a year after Mussolini's fall from power— Savinio ascribes to absolutist regimes:

> The greatest defect and the most profound immorality of absolutist regimes, as of any absolutist condition, is the principle of the one "truth." Whereas it is well known that human truth, our truth, the true truth, is made up of truth and falsehood: more falsehood than truth. (387)[10]

This perspective gives rise in "Il teatro è fantasia" to Savinio's distinction between the actor's truth and the "supposed truth," "una supposta «verità»" (20) —with the significantly indefinite article— of theatrical *verismo*: the latter denies the more profound truth of the theatre, that is, the opening up of a space of difference in which the plurivocity of truth is performed by actors whose "truth" is precisely that of being deprived of a firm identity, of a true and univocal self. The "impurity" of the theatre is also this: its instability, its "mettersi in gioco" with every new performance. *Verismo*, on the other hand, rejects

9. "Per aver voluto raggiungere una supposta «verità», l'attore ha cessato di essere attore: si è svuotato in fantasma, in larva grigia che non cammina, non parla, non gestisce."

10. "Il difetto maggiore e la profonda immoralità dei regimi assolutisti come di ogni condizione assolutista, è il principio della 'verità' unica. Mentre si sa che la verità umana, la verità nostra, la verità 'vera' è fatta di vero e di falso: più di falso che di vero." See also Walter Pedullà's observation that Savinio "is concerned with reminding us that behind every choice, culture, faith, language and behavior are the interests of the one or of the many, of a group, or perhaps of a class" (34), and Silvana Cirillo's discussion of the notion of truth in Savinio in her monograph on the author (14-15).

the instability of the stage for the solidity of the world and in so doing reduces the fantastic and plurivocal to the familiar and univocal. Another quote, from a review of the "rivista satirica in 2 parti e 25 quadri" *S.O.S.* should further clarify Savinio's position:

> How many reasons justify the existence of the theatre?
>
> First and foremost illusion — the main reason, in our opinion.
>
> There is furthermore the masochistic satisfaction for those spectators —and they are the majority— who, as a result of a kind of upside-down narcissism, enjoy seeing reproduced upon the stage, and thus exalted by the light of art, the most miserable, depressing, and shameful events of their daily little lives. (*Palchetti* 140)[11]

In place of a theatre that dwells on the minute and the sordid, Savinio advocates a theatre which is worthy of its name of "thing *deserving to be watched*" ("cosa *degna di essere veduta,*" *Nuova enciclopedia* 362), free of any limitations and restrictions, a theatre which eschews the commonplace to give voice to what has heretofore been silenced.

The one-act play *Il suo nome*, written in 1945 and published in the same year in the journal *Maschere*, marks Savinio's return to writing for the theatre after the critical debacle of *Capitano Ulisse.*[12] For his return to the theatre, the artist chose to adapt for the stage a 1943 short story entitled, like the play, "Il suo nome," later anthologized in the volume *Tutta la vita* (1945). While the plot of the play faithfully follows that of its source —the protagonist is assigned almost *verbatim* large portions of the narrative— the structure of the play can be read as an exercise in the kind of "impure theatre" which had been the central concern of Savinio's journalistic writing.

The play opens in a theatre. The stage is empty, and the action first begins with the arrival of the protagonist, Lodovico, from the main door into the auditorium, pursued by two "Maschere," that is, two ushers, because he is apparently without a ticket.[13] After a heated exchange,

11. "Quante le ragioni che giustificano l'esistenza del teatro?

    L'illusione anzitutto: per noi ragione principale.

    Viene quindi la soddisfazione masochista di quegli spettator i —e sono in maggioranza— i quali, per una sorta di narcisismo rovesciato, godono di vedere riprodotti sulla scena, ed esaltati dunque nella luce dell'arte, i fatti più miseri, più avvilenti, più vergognosi della loro piccola vita quotidiana."

12. Originally written in 1925 for Pirandello's "Teatro d'Arte", *Capitano Ulisse* was only produced in 1938 by Anton Giulio Bragaglia's "Teatro delle Arti." Tinterri notes that the critics "dismissed the text as the anachronistic exhumation of a theatrical fashion buried with the avant-garde" (90), a reception which provoked Savinio's defense of that experience discussed above.

13. While I do not address this issue here, the polisemy in Italian of the term "maschera," whose primary meaning is that of "mask," is important, as it links the play to a complex genealogy in modern Italian theatre (especially between the two world

Lodovico argues that, unlike the other spectators, he is not in the theatre "to amuse himself" ("per divertirsi") but rather for the strange necessity to "confess" publicly the story of his greatest missed opportunity, and thereby attempt to give the experience order and meaning. He then climbs onto the stage, a space forbidden to the two ushers, who are left to sit on the steps to wait for him. This division, an invisible and yet unbridgeable gap between the space of the actors and that of the audience, or between the locus of representation and that of reality, is remarked by the ushers themselves, whose dialogues will punctuate Lodovico's story throughout the rest of the performance. Lodovico then begins to tell his story. While living in an unidentified foreign country, Lodovico had consented to the death-bed request of his friend and fellow emigrant Enrico to return to his fiancée, an older, lame spinster, the letters she had sent him during their separation. Realizing that Enrico's fiancée is a woman of some means, Lodovico weaves a complex plan to replace his dead friend in her affections: he will first praise Enrico as a faithful lover and a selfless worker only to reveal the truth that he had in fact led a dissolute life and had taken advantage of her generosity and devotion. But Lodovico's plan comes to a disastrous end when he embellishes his story with a detail that brings down his house of cards. Betrayed by his own words, and by the truth they speak in spite of his intentions, Lodovico is forced to leave the woman's house, and yet remains haunted by the bizarre details of his defeat.

As Lodovico reminisces, certain episodes of the story are performed in a series of "*scenarietti*" which occupy the previously empty stage. Here, following the disordered and fragmented flux of memory, are represented the station of Fàbara, the city where Enrico's fiancée lives, Enrico's death, and some key moments in Lodovico's encounter with the woman. The action of the play thus takes place in three physically separate places, corresponding to three diegetic levels: that of the ushers in the auditorium, that of Lodovico, who sits on a chair on the stage, "his back to the audience, and who looks towards the back of the stage" (205; "le spalle voltate al pubblico, e guarda il fondo della scena"), and that of the "*scenarietti*" in which the memories evoked by Lodovico are redoubled and given form (in the stage directions Savinio distinguishes between the Lodovico narrator and the character in the "*scenarietti*" by calling them Lodovico I and II, respectively). But Lodovico's initial tone of almost analytical detachment eventually gives

wars) which includes the recurrence of the trope of the mask in the *teatro grottesco* (one of whose foundational texts is Luigi Chiarelli's *La maschera e il volto* 1916), the ironic identification of identity with one's external guise in Massimo Bontempelli's *Nostra Dea* (1925), and, of course, the theme of self-identity as an empty locus filled by the constructions of others which is at the core of the theatre of Luigi Pirandello, who entitled his theatrical œuvre *Maschere nude*.

way to an ever-increasing intervention on the actions of his double in the "*scenarietti.*" Thus Lodovico, initially located in a liminal space on the border or at the crossing between the reproduction of his narrative and the reality of the auditorium —in other words between the two universes whose continuous flux of oppositions structures the play—becomes also the go-between that links these two universes.

The antinomy between stage and auditorium is initially oriented along the traditional axis of fiction and reality, but this orientation is immediately disturbed. The opening of the play in the auditorium, though a clear indication that the action cannot be contained and safely bracketed in the "other," enclosed space of the stage and that representation threatens to spill onto reality, is not in itself a new conceit. Not only had Savinio already used it in *Capitano Ulisse,* but by 1945 the gesture itself had a long genealogy going back to the provocations of the "serate futuriste" and to Pirandello's metatheatre.[14] What is most remarkable, in fact, is not what happens in the auditorium at the beginning, but what happens on stage — *nothing.*

> The curtain is drawn, the stage is empty. The back wall with the signs "No smoking," "Silence," etc. is visible. (199)[15]

"Reality," the actual, unadulterated materiality of an empty stage has taken the place of the representation, and gives itself to the viewer in all its nakedness. In *Capitano Ulisse* or its most immediate predecessor, Pirandello's *Six Characters in Search of an Author,* from the beginning the space of representation and that of reality are contaminated in a vertiginous *mise-en-abîme* — actors, for instance, play actors playing parts given them by people who are themselves characters. In Savinio's *Il suo nome* however, the stage is the space of authenticity because untainted by the "virus" of representation. But, like the actors in "Il teatro è fantasia," the truth of the stage *as* stage, to which its bareness alludes, is the fact that it fulfills its proper function only at the moment in which its "emptiness" is filled by the play of representation.[16]

Likewise, the distance between representation and reality is called into question by the actions of the ushers in the auditorium. When

14. On Savinio and Pirandello, see in particular Tinterri ch. II, in which the critic documents the difficult gestation of *Capitano Ulisse,* and Puppa, who provides a careful comparative analysis of the poetics of the two playwrights.

15. "Il sipario è aperto, il palcoscenico vuoto. Si vede il muro di fondo con le scritte «Vietato fumare», «Silenzio» ecc."

16. The opening of Peter Brook's beautiful essay *The Empty Space* points to this "truth," which precedes and grounds any possible kind of theatre, including the varieties he then goes to describe in the volume: "I can take any empty space and call it a bare stage. A man walks across this empty space whilst someone else is watching him, and this is all that is needed for an act of theatre to be engaged" (11).

Lodovico on the stage calls for a prop, the ushers, who are unable to see or hear him, become nevertheless mysteriously aware of his request and proceed to answer to it.

> LODOVICO: There's nowhere to sit, here.... A chair!
>
> SECOND USHER (to the First Usher, as if he were awakening from a dream) A chair! Go fetch a chair!
>
> FIRST USHER: What are you saying?
>
> SECOND USHER: A chair!... Can't you *feel* that a chair is needed?
>
> FIRST USHER: I... can't feel anything.
>
> *In spite of his declared insensitivity, the First Usher gets up, [...] pretends to pick up a chair, and to place it in the middle of the forestage [...]. At the same time, and with perfect synchronicity, an Usher identical to the First Usher, but in a white uniform like a plaster statue (a white "reproduction" of the First Usher) comes in from stage left carrying a chair which he goes to place in the middle of the stage [...]; in other words he carries out "truly" what the First Usher "pretends" to carry out.* (204)[17]

Luca Valentino has already pointed out that the "allusive meanings" of the scene are a further homage to Pirandello's theatre, and that Savinio seems to be almost indulging in "the 'pirandellismo' of this contrivance" (124). Indeed, as Valentino seems to suggest, the Second Usher's line "In any case, down here we can only imitate" (*Il suo nome* 219; "Tanto quaggiù noi non possiamo fare che delle imitazioni") can be read as an all-too-obvious and unmediated reference to the metatheatrical subtext. Nevertheless, it serves to emphasize the constant overturning of the two poles of reality and fiction, and, more importantly, the permeability of the two states. The real chair, the one which Lodovico can actually use to sit on, is the one which is brought by the unreal, fictional ushers, who are allowed to traverse the gap between reality and representation. Through this device, Savinio gives form to the critique of *verismo* discussed above: the weaving between

---

17. "LODOVICO Qui non c'è da sedere... una sedia!

II MASCHERA (*alla I Maschera, come svegliandosi da un sonno*) Una sedia!... Vai a prendere una sedia!

I MASCHERA Che dici?

II MASCHERA Una sedia! ... Non *senti* che c'è bisogno di una sedia?

I MASCHERA Io ... non sento niente.

Malgrado la sua dichiarata insensibilità, la I Maschera si alza [...] finge di prendere una sedia e di venire a collocarla in mezzo all'iposcenio [...]. Contemporaneamente e con sincronia perfetta, una Maschera del tutto identica alla I Maschera ma vestita di una uniforme bianca come una statua di gesso (replica «bianca» della I Maschera) entra in scena da sinistra reggendo una sedia che va a deporre in mezzo al palcoscenico [...] ossia esegue «al vero» ciò che la I Maschera esegue «per finta»."

the two states, the shuttling back and forth of the white ushers between the tangible world of props and the intangible world of memories and projections of theatrical representation serves to distance and distinguish their respective and different status, their peculiar truth, which theatrical realism denies by constructing the space of fiction as contiguous and superimposable to that of reality through the identification of their respective truths with a single, transcendental "Truth." In this sense, the mechanism of *verismo* is like that attributed to the first "pertinent feature" of the locution "the truth in painting" in Jacques Derrida's volume of the same title: art (painting, theatre) is ascribed "the power of direct reproduction, of restitution, of adequation or transparency," and therefore its "truth" is "truth itself restored, in person without mediation, make-up, mask or veil" (5). But this "truth," as Derrida argues, is already doubled and divided, as it entails the play of resemblance, and the power to produce itself "in accordance with the two genitives: truth of truth and truth of truth" (5). Against this truth as closure, Savinio multiplies the levels of representation, making them collide with one another, and placing Lodovico at the centre (as narrator) and on the margin (as character) of the representation because, as Marcello Carlino has noted, "God condemned man to duality or discrepancy between yes and no, and to the ensuing irriducibility of language to the *unicum*" (*Alberto Savinio* 5).

Lodovico is thus both bearer and victim of this double vision, of this capacity to see simultaneously a truth and its other — the peculiar sickness which he calls "eccesso d'intelligenza:"

> This sickness to which I hope you will always be immune. This sickness which leaves no space for illusion, no door closed for defense, no wall against which to lean; which suddenly uncovers all aspects of things, shows them inside and out, and not just as they are, but as they were and as they will be; it chops them up, it breaks them down, it annihilates them.... (202)[18]

But it is a truth which is also mobile, always in the process of reconstituting itself in new configurations. Lodovico compares his story-telling to the work of a mosaicist whose tesserae are made of memories and reminiscences; the final aim of his compulsion is to keep boredom at bay, "this ineffable leprosy which spreads over me in larger and larger patches so that I could burn without feeling any pain, and little by little, it covers me with emptiness" (202).[19] In the short story

18. "Questa malattia di cui le auguro di rimanere sempre immune. Questa malattia che non lascia ombre all'illusione, non porta chiusa alla difesa, non muro sul quale appoggiarsi; ma in un baleno ti scopre tutti gli aspetti delle cose, te le fa vedere e dentro e fuori, e non solo come sono ma come erano e come saranno; te le sminuzza, te le frantuma, te le annienta... "

from which the play was adapted, the narrator further suggests that through this process of elaboration of memories Lodovico is able not only to regain possession of the facts, "but also the secrets which emerge from the dark depth of facts" (*Tutta la vita* 13; "ma anche i segreti emersi dall'oscuro fondo dei fatti"). The possibility of new interpretations, of discovering new false bottoms beneath the apparent surface stability of facts is what drives Lodovico. Boredom and death are the inevitable result of the slow process of consumption of these hidden truths, of the schlerotization of the interpretative process in the single truth about Lodovico's missed opportunity. Lodovico's speech about boredom and memory is followed by the first dialogue between the two ushers, which clearly serves as a commentary to the scene. Of the two ushers, the first is without personal ideas and opinions and believes fully and blindly in the regulations of his job, while the second is capable of independent thought and action. When the former, disturbed by Lodovico's disappearance in the "hole" of the stage, expresses his concern, the second responds: "Provisional things are not frightful. You who are unchanging, you certainly are frightful" (203).[20]

The "*scenarietti*" which provide a visual correlative to Lodovico's memory serve as doubles of both the events that the protagonist relates and the materializations of his psychic mechanisms. Thus, upon his arrival to Fàbara, Lodovico finds himself irrationally disappointed not to find Enrico's fiancée at the station. The only human being present on the scene is a young woman at the window of the station, "dressed in black and [with] her face 'neutralized' by a veil or a film which obliterates her features"[21] (205; the station master is mentioned and heard, but not seen). The subject of this "*scenarietto*," a woman waiting for the return of her spouse, is a familiar one for Savinio, who had already used it in at least two pictures painted ten years apart, namely *La fidèle épouse* and *Penelope* (1930 and 1940, respectively).[22] In both paintings, the central figure is set against a window surrounded by a curtain, framing the scene like the wing of a stage opening onto a view of the backdrop. While the bodies of the women are slightly distorted

19. "Questa lebbra ineffabile che mi spande addosso le sue macchie sempre più larghe, che io potrei bruciare senza sentir dolore, e a poco a poco mi rivestono di vuoto."

20. "Le cose provvisorie non fanno paura. Tu che sei definitivo, tu, sì, fai paura."

21. "[V]estita di nero e [con] la faccia «neutralizzata» da un velo o pelle aderente che annulla i tratti."

22. Reproduced in Fagiolo dell'Arco 163 and 199, respectively. See also the c. 1940 tempera work *Penelope* (164). The "theatrical tension" of *La fidèle epouse* is noted by Pia Vivarelli in her note to the painting in *Alberto Savinio. Paintings and Drawings* (78). The theme of Ulysses and Penelope is a recurrent one in Savinio's figurative works. See for instance *Il ritorno di Ulisse* (c. 1928; Fagiolo dell'Arco 137), in which a female figure (Penelope?) is represented with a kind of blank mask which recalls the "film" worn by the characters of the woman at the station and of the fiancée in *Il suo nome*, and

but fundamentally realistic, their heads, following a strategy often employed by Savinio in his visual *œuvre*, are metamorphosed into those of a bird. If, as Pia Vivarelli has suggested, "[i]n Savinio, the metamorphoses always come about through either specific or implicit appeals for a recovery of the mythological capabilities for interpreting the world" (22), it is clear that here the myth is in fact "de-mythicized" or, to use Paolo Puppa's term, "de-heroicized" (57), according to the strategy which Savinio himself ascribes to the artists of the avant-garde:

> [W]e who were protagonists of that time, imagined God descended from his throne, the gods descended from their pedestals, walking upon the earth, in a friendly relationship with human beings, at our own level. (*Nuova antologia* 359)[23]

Thus, the faithful spouse Penelope is transformed into a bourgeois matron whose dim-eyed ostrich head suggests that her heroic waiting is perhaps only a form of indolence (the representation of human beings with animal heads is for Savinio "the quest for their character, beyond the euphemisms of nature, beyond the corrections of civilization, beyond the embellishments of art"[24]). Like the faceless woman at the station, also featureless, the fiancée appears in Lodovico's words, "even more dead than my friend Enrico, who had become a corpse and buried down there, on the bank of the great river" (*Il suo nome* 208).[25] The parallel drawn between the woman at the station and the fiancée, and the intertextual references to the paintings of the Penelope series make it possible to read the figure of the former as another link in this series of examples of sterile and deferred love. In like manner, Lodovico becomes a debased Ulysses, an adventurer who upon his return to the shores of his homeland feels ready to find a haven in which to end his journey.[26]

As the flow of memories defies the strictures of chronology, the first scene evoked by Lodovico which also involves the woman is not that of

---

Penelope e Ulisse (1945; Fagiolo dell'Arco 213), in which the two characters are metamorphosed into pieces of furniture, a frequent trope in Savinio's fiction and paintings, for the stifling comforts of bourgeois life.

23. "[N]oi che di quel periodo fummo attori, abbiamo figurato Dio disceso dal suo trono, gli dei discesi dai loro piedistalli, a passeggio sulla terra, in rapporti confidenziali con gli uomini, alla stessa nostra statura." The theme of the debasement of myth is a *locus classicus* of Savinio criticism. See for example Sanguineti 407-409, Piscopo 231-236, Castelli, and Gutiérrez, "Il mito in pantofole."

24. "*Uomini con teste bestiali:* È la ricerca del carattere, di là degli eufemismi della natura, di là dalle correzioni della civiltà, di là dagli abbellimenti dell'arte." In *Bollettino della Galleria del Milione* no. 66, 1940; quoted in Fagiolo dell'Arco 162.

25. "[A]nche più morta del mio amico Enrico, trasformato in cadavere e seppellito laggiù in riva al grande fiume"

26. The parallel between Lodovico's story and Savinio's re-writing of the Homeric myth was also noted by Valentino 137.

their first encounter, but rather one in which she explains her repairs to her house in expectation of her fiancé's return:

> LODOVICO II: How beautiful! How serene! How austere! It seems as if it could protect those who live there... like a mother protects her children.
>
> LODOVICO II (with a jerk): Listen to the stupid things I had to say! I wouldn't have lived in that house for all the gold in the world.

But Lodovico quickly reconsiders his statement:

> LODOVICO I: Because that wretch, apparently so lifeless and sterile, was the woman-mother in all her implacable fury.
>
> But wasn't that what I wanted, after all? To find everything in a woman, even the mother I have never known. The nest! What do I want? What have I always wanted? The nest! [...] A prison for me! The sweetness, the safety of a prison. (213-214)[27]

---

27. "LODOVICO II Com'è bella! Com'è serena! Com'è austera! Sembra che debba proteggere chi ci abita... come una madre protegge i figlioli.

LODOVICO I (*scattando*) Senti le sciocchezze che mi toccava dire! Io in quella casa [...] non ci avrei abitato per tutto l'oro del mondo. [...]

LODOVICO I Perché quella sciagurata, così spenta in apparenza e sterile, era la donna-madre in tutto il suo tremendo e implacabile furore. [...]

Ma dopo tutto non era proprio questo ciò che io volevo? Trovare in una donna tutto, anche la madre che io non ho mai conosciuto. Il nido! Che voglio io? Che ho sempre desiderato? Il nido! [...] Una prigione per me! La dolcezza, la sicurezza di una prigione!"

The theme of the "moglie-madre," in its two aspects of the erotic dimension of the relationship between mother and son on the one hand, and of the desire for maternal security in the relationship between husband and wife on the other, is a recurrent one in Savinio's works. As he writes in "Visita di K...," "A 'complete' wife brings together wife and mother" ("Una moglie 'completa' associa in sè moglie e madre;" *Il signor Dido* 12). But in Savinio's peculiar re-working of the Freudian model, the "moglie-madre" also constitutes a kind of castrating super-ego whose task is to circumscribe the freedom of the individual. The passage in "Visita di K..." continues with a comment which links the figure of the "moglie-madre" to several of the themes we have seen at work in *Il suo nome*, and in particular to the question of absolute truth and to the mechanisms of power and repression which underlie it:

"Until the very end, when I was a forty-six year old child, my mother never consulted me before she made me do what, in her judgment, she had decided what was right for me to do. She confronted me, in Hitlerian fashion, with the *fait accompli*. For those who bestow absolute good, freedom of judgement means freedom to make mistakes. And wives, mothers, dictators, are so many bestowers of absolute good. Their example, after all, comes from on high" (12).

("Mia madre, fino all'ultimo, e quando io ero già un bambino di quarantasei anni, non mi consultò mai prima di farmi fare quello che essa, nel suo giudizio, aveva stabilito che era bene che io facessi. Mi metteva hitlerianamente davanti al fatto compiuto. Per i dispensatori di bene assoluto, libertà di giudicare equivale a libertà di sbagliare. E

The play between the different diegetic levels makes it possible for Lodovico to present the multiple truths of his actions. In this case, there is the "truth" he shows Enrico's fiancée, a lie, the truth he tells himself, a kind of self-deception, and then a third truth, which does not in itself cancel the second. It is true both that Lodovico loathes everything the woman in mourning stands for —the narrow and utilitarian logic of the provincial petit bourgeois, the cloying and sterile sensibility of the spinster, the blind and self-deceiving trust of the simple-minded idealist — *and* that he is undeniably attracted by precisely those characteristics that repulse him, by the woman's disarming openness and by her promise of an uncomplicated and sheltered future: "I managed to find her lack of seductiveness seductive, I was moved by certain strange ideas that crossed my mind" (228).[28]

As a whole, the account of Enrico's life overseas, in which the false story told by the Lodovico in the "*scenarietto*" is counterpointed by the true story told by Lodovico the narrator is a dizzying virtuoso performance, almost a game that the protagonist plays for his own benefit, rather than the woman's:

> So I started to tell her Enrico's false story, but always keeping the true story in mind, as in a dangerous exercise, out of some risky bravery, the danger which I closely skirted in that narration, the threat of an oversight which might suddenly make me say what I thought, shattering that very frail fiction. (226)[29]

Lodovico's lies are effective because they are a kind of truth, the truth the woman wants to hear and believe, and which she attributes to the dead man. However, Valentino has warned against too strict a "Pirandellian" reading of *Il suo nome*. In discussing Lodovico's difficulty in understanding the name of the town upon arriving at the station (believing it to be Fabàra instead of Fàbara, he was unable to interpret the conductor's call of the stop "A'-ba-a!"), Valentino writes that "the 'pirandellismo' of the contrast between truth and fiction is mischievously solved by a simple change of accent" (129). In the case of Lodovico's story, too, the collapse of the woman's truth is simply the result of a badly played move in the game between her and Lodovico.

---

mogli, madri, dittatori, sono altrettanti dispensatori di bene assoluto. L'esempio, del resto, viene dall'alto.")

28. "Riuscii a trovare seducente la mancanza di seduzione di colei, mi commossi a certe strane idee che mi traversavano la mente."

29. "Io allora cominciai a narrare la falsa storia di Enrico, ma senza mai staccare la mente dalla storia vera, come per un esercizio pericoloso, per una rischiosa spavalderia, assaporando il pericolo che rasentavo filo filo in quella narrazione, la minaccia di una dimenticanza che d'improvviso mi poteva far pronunciare quello che pensavo, mandando a soqquadro quella fragilissima finzione."

When she asks him what Enrico's last words were, Lodovico —out of, as he says, "goodness" (236; "per *bontà*—perché sono buono, sono buono, è questa la mia colpa")— fatefully answers "your name" ("Il suo nome") only to realize that he only knows her grotesque and vulgar last name, Chiappadoro. Thus, the "Truth" exposes Lodovico, and shows him in a new light: "I could feel, I could 'see' her, grown gigantic like an avenging goddess, like Justice, driving away the horrible, frightful, incredible Truth" (233).[30] But the nature of this new truth is in itself not clear: which illusion is shattered here, the one about Enrico's life or the other about Lodovico's trustworthiness? Is the woman losing Enrico for the second time because she realizes that he was not what he pretended to be, or because she realizes that she cannot find solace and even a kind of replacement in Lodovico? Certainly when she asks him to repeat Enrico's last words, the woman is in effect turning him into a simulacrum of her dead love: "My name… . Look, I'll close my eyes, and you who were near him… . Say it! say it! As if you were him …" (231).[31] And yet the motivation for Lodovico's final lie, his thoughtfulness, reproduces the intention of Enrico's dying words, which were indeed dedicated to his fiancée, as the play had already showed in the "*scenarietto*" of Enrico's death:

> ENRICO: Her letters are in this packet. I'm giving them to you […] The address is on the packet.
>
> LODOVICO II: […] To Miss…
>
> ENRICO (he interrupts him): No, forget that name, don't say it. I may be a scoundrel…. Poor woman! Can I trust your discretion?
>
> LODOVICO: I assured Enrico of my greatest discretion. A few minutes later, he died. (218- 219)[32]

So, Enrico did die with his fiancée's name on his mind, if not on his lips, and with a gesture of pity and even sympathy which recalls the motivation of Lodovico's disastrous, or, as he calls it, "pious" lie ("pia menzogna;" 231). The identification between the two characters,

30. "[S]entivo, «vedevo» lei che scacciava da sé, ingigantita, come una dea vendicatrice, come la Giustizia, l'orribile, la spaventosa, l'incredibile Verità."

31. "Il mio nome... Ecco: io chiudo gli occhi, e lei che gli era vicino… . […] Lo dica! Lo dica! Come se fosse lui… ." For a similar argument, see Valentino 141-142.

32. "ENRICO In questo pacchetto sono le lettere di lei. Le consegno a te […] Sul pacco c'è l'indirizzo.

LODOVICO II […] Alla gentilissima signorina… .

ENRICO (*interrompendolo*) No, lascia stare quel nome, non lo pronunciare. Per quanto io sia un mascalzone… . Disgraziata! Posso fidarmi della tua discrezione? […]

LODOVICO Promisi la massima discrezione a Enrico, il quale dopo pochi momenti morì."

visually emphasized by the fact that Enrico is described as "in every way like Lodovico, as if he were a third simulacrum of Lodovico" ("del tutto simile a Lodovico, come se fosse una terza replica di Lodovico;" 216), and desperately wanted by Lodovico, falls apart at the moment when their behavior made them indeed most alike.[33]

Savinio himself gives the best clue for the interpretation of *Il suo nome*. In *Alcesti di Samuele*, his most sustained engagement with theatrical writing, Savinio gives his stage *persona*, the character of the author, the task of formulating his own definition of the purpose of the theatre. The theatre is "the place where what is wrong is corrected, what is incomplete is completed. The theatre is like dreams. Dreams enact what we can't enact when we are awake. This, at least, is what Freud says" (78).[34] Like the dreamwork, Lodovico's monologue and the "*scenarietti*" it evokes destabilize and rearrange the linearity of time and the solidity of the subject according to the principles of condensation and displacement. Thus, separate figures, the woman at the station and the fiancée; Enrico and Lodovico himself, are identified in Lodovico's hallucinated tale, while Lodovico projects his own fears of solitude and boredom onto the other characters he evokes: the woman in the first "*scenarietto*," the station master, the priest on the train. In the process, the stage becomes the place where Lodovico is confronted with the

33. It has been noted (Tinterri 144-146) that the play recalls, in a parodic way but also with precise inter-textual references, the closing scene of Joseph Conrad's *Heart of Darkness*, in which the narrator, Marlow, visits Kurtz's "intended" and lies to her by telling her that Kurtz's last words, the famous cry: "The horror! The horror!" (Conrad 85) had instead been the woman's name, "The last word he pronounced was — your name" (93). The results, however, are quite the opposite: in Marlow's case, his lie both denies Kurtz "that justice which was his due" (94), and works as an effective means of repressing the darkness at the heart of the European colonial enterprise. The validation of the intended's system of beliefs ["I knew it — I was sure!" is her response, to which Marlow can only reply "She knew. She was sure" (93)], makes its continuation possible. Lodovico's lie, on the contrary, shakes from the very foundations the world of Enrico's fiancée and casts Lodovico himself back into the world of instability which he had sought to evade. Here the echoes between the two texts are certainly not the result of chance. The world around Marlow does not change, in spite of his expectations, as a result of his lie: "It seemed to me that the house would collapse before I could escape, that the heavens would fall upon my head. But nothing happened. The heavens do not fall for such a trifle" (94). On the contrary, Lodovico flees surrounded by the metaphoric destruction of the house of cards of the woman's illusions: "I *saw* the great fiction collapse within her, upon her, around her, and her faith rend like a rag, and the dream turn into a tiny puff of smoke, and finally disappear" (233) ("*vedevo* crollare in lei, su lei, intorno a lei la grande finzione, e la fede squarciarsi come uno straccio, e il sogno ridursi a un piccolissimo globo di fumo, e anche questo alla fine dissiparsi").

34. "Il luogo che corregge quello che è sbagliato, completa quello che è incompleto. Il teatro è come i sogni. I sogni attuano quello che da svegli non possiamo attuare. Così almeno dice Freud."

different and conflicting truths about himself and his actions. In attempting to stitch them together into a narrative, he remains capable of avoiding the death by boredom which would result from identifying once and for all with a univocal self — with a transcendental truth about himself. In the introduction to *Casa «La Vita»* Savinio writes that "All the meanness, all the cowardliness of the world comes from this: from our wanting to feel always 'at home,' from this horror for everything which is not 'ours'" (6).[35] Lodovico's story is finally that of a narrow escape from this "wanting to feel 'at home'," from a surrender to the stability and immobility of the bourgeois life promised by Enrico's fiancée, and yet it is also the story of a "paradise" desired and lost. Lodovico is condemned to freedom, and to the "excess of intelligence" which forces him to examine obsessively his own motives and actions: "This rumination of memories is awful... ." Lodovico says at the end of his performance. "To find them alive, ready to pounce on you..." (235).[36] If, to use one last Savinian definition, "Art carries within itself the memory of the paradise lost, and the promise of the paradise regained" (*Nuova enciclopedia* 356),[37] in its translation for the stage Lodovico's torment for the loss of his petty bourgeois paradise in Fàbara becomes an illustration of the possibilities of the "multicolored adventure" to speak the truth about the openness of art, about its power to point the way to the paradise found of a world free of the shackles of Truth.[38]

WORKS CITED

Antonucci, Giovanni. "Alberto Savinio e l'invenzione della critica drammatica." *Studi romani* 31.2 (1983): 173-185.

Barbero, Luca, ed. *Alberto Savinio. Pittore di teatro/Peintre de Théâtre*. Milano: Fabbri, 1991.

Barthes, Roland. "The Reality Effect." *The Rustle of Language*. Trans. Richard Howard. New York: Hill & Wang, 1986. 141-148.

---

35. "Nasce da qui tutta la meschinità, tutta la pusillanimità del mondo: da questo volersi sentire sempre 'in famiglia', da questo orrore di quello che non è 'nostro'."

36. "Terribile è questo ruminare i ricordi ...;" "Ritrovarseli vivi e che ti saltano addosso..."

37. "L'arte porta il ricordo in sé del paradiso perduto ma insieme porta la promessa del paradiso ritrovato." See also Tinterri 9.

38. I thank Rocco Capozzi, Manuela Gieri, Mario Moroni, and Max Statkiewicz for their critical readings of previous drafts of this paper and for their insightful comments. I gratefully acknowledge the support of the Social Sciences and Humanities Research Council of Canada and of the Connaught Fund for this project.

Bellingeri, Edo. "Alberto Savinio, il piacere della critica." *Rivista italiana di drammaturgia* 2.5 (1977): 111-114.

Bossaglia, Rossana, ed. *I De Chirico e i Savinio del Teatro della Scala*. Milano: Amici della Scala, 1988.

Breton, André. *Anthologie de l'humour noir*. 1940. Rev. ed. 1966. *Œuvres complètes*. Ed. Marguerite Bonnet *et al.* Vol. 2. Paris: Gallimard, 1992. 863-1176.

Brook, Peter. *The Empty Space*. London: Penguin, 1968.

Buttier, Rosanna, ed. *Savinio giornalista: itinerario bibliografico*. Roma: Bulzoni, 1987.

Carlino, Marcello. *Savinio*. Lecce: Milella, 1988.

Castelli, Silvana. "L'occhio di Andromeda." *Azzardo. Landolfi, Savinio, Delfini*. Milano: Spirali, 1982. 49-87.

Cirillo, Silvana. *Alberto Savinio. Le molte facce di un artista di genio*. Milano: Mondadori, 1997.

Conrad, Joseph. *Heart of Darkness*. Ed. Ross C. Murfin. New York: St. Martin's, 1989.

Derrida, Jacques. *The Truth in Painting*. Trans. Geoff Bennington and Ian McLeod. Chicago and London: U Chicago P, 1987.

Fagiolo dell'Arco, Maurizio. *Alberto Savinio*. Milano: Fabbri, 1989.

Gutiérrez, María Elena. *Alberto Savinio: lo psichismo delle forme*. Firenze: Cadmo, 1999.

____. "Il mito in pantofole: Le muse domestiche di Alberto Savinio." *Italian Quarterly* 35.135-136 (1998): 47-55.

Lanuzza, Stefano. *Savinio*. Firenze: La Nuova Italia, 1979.

Lapini, Lia. "Alberto Savinio e il teatro: da 'Les Chants de la Mi-Mort' a 'Capitano Ulisse'." *Quaderni di Teatro* 2:6 (1979): 29-37.

Pedullà, Walter. *Alberto Savinio*. 1979. Rev. ed. Milano: Bompiani, 1991.

Piscopo, Ugo. *Alberto Savinio*. Milano: Mursia, 1973.

Puppa, Paolo. "Savinio versus Pirandello." *The Yearbook of the Society for Pirandello Studies*, 15-16 (1995-1996): 54-70.

Sanguineti, Edoardo. "Alberto Savinio." *Studi sul surrealismo*. Roma: Officina, 1977. 405-431.

Savinio, Alberto. *Alcesti di Samuele e atti unici*. Ed. Alessandro Tinterri. Milano: Adelphi, 1991.

____. *Il signor Dido*. Milano: Adelphi, 1978.

____. *Nuova enciclopedia*. Milano: Adelphi, 1977.

____. *Palchetti romani*. Milano: Adelphi, 1982.

____. *Tutta la vita*. Milano: Bompiani, 1969.

Tinterri, Alessandro. *Savinio e lo spettacolo*. Bologna: Il Mulino, 1993.

Valentino, Luca. *L'arte impura: percorsi e tematiche del teatro di Alberto Savino*. Roma: Bulzoni, 1991.

Vivarelli, Pia. *Alberto Savinio. Paintings and Drawings 1925-1952*. Milano: Electa, 1992.

Man, Man as Dancer, Art Figure: Oskar Schlemmer's Experiments on the Bauhaus Stage

Deborah Tihanyi

University of Toronto

Hard on the heels of a surge of artistic movements that existed in Europe in the early part of the century leading up to the horrors of the first World War, architect Walter Gropius merged two institutions for the study of art in Weimar (one for the fine arts, and one for the study of crafts) to found the Bauhaus (literally 'to build a house') in March of 1919. Best remembered, perhaps, for its unique industrial designs for chairs and teapots, the Bauhaus represented far more than any one aesthetic theory. Gropius intended the Bauhaus to be a place where the study and practice of the arts and crafts —including such diverse areas as painting, sculpture, woodworking, metal crafts and weaving— could be brought together under the aegis of architecture, an effort that (he hoped) would "culminate finally in a new cultural equilibrium of [the] visual environment" (Gropius 7). The faculty of the Bauhaus school changed over the fourteen years of its existence, and included painters and sculptors, master craftsmen and architects, all with widely different notions on the teaching and practice of art. For Gropius, however, these differences would only add to the richness of the Bauhaus experience, making the school a nexus of creative freedom. Students at the Bauhaus were not moulded to fit the aesthetic principles of their teachers; instead, the medieval constructs of apprentices, journeymen and masters were applied, with faculty taking up a position of mentorship.[1]

1. Several of the original Bauhaus students did eventually become masters themselves — of a sort. Unofficially known as the "Young Masters," six former students of the Bauhaus took over responsibility for several of the workshops: Josef Albers (preliminary course), Herbert Bayer (printing), Marcel Breuer (carpentry and cabinet-making), Hinnerk Scheper (mural painting) and Joost Schmidt (sculpture); Gunta Stölzl assisted Georg Muche with the weaving workshop until he left the Bauhaus in 1926, at which point she took over. Although they performed the same duties as the

It was to this environment of artistic experimentation that Oskar Schlemmer came in 1920. Schlemmer was trained as a painter, but, by this time, had also begun his stage experiments and worked as a set and costume designer in a number of Germany's theatres. Gropius had already established the stage workshop as an integral part of the Bauhaus curriculum, feeling that the theatre, like architecture —which combined various kinds of artistic practice, and is, first and foremost, a "public art" (Whitford 1984, 83)— would promote the kind of collective work that the school sought to establish (Whitford 1984, 83). Schlemmer was initially hired to teach mural-painting, and shortly thereafter, he became the head of the sculpture workshop; in 1923, he took over as head of the stage workshop, where his most important work at the Bauhaus took place.[2]

Schlemmer's interest in the theatre seemed to spring directly from his work as a painter and sculptor — a natural progression for his experiments with form and colour. He, too, understood the theatre's inherent importance to the Bauhaus:

> It is natural that the aims of the Bauhaus —to seek the union of the artistic-ideal with the craftsmanlike-practical by thoroughly investigating the creative elements, and to understand in all its ramifications the essence of *der Bau*, creative construction— have valid application to the field of the theater. For, like the concept of *Bau* itself, the stage is an orchestral complex which comes about only through the cooperation of many different forces. It is the union of the most heterogeneous assortment of creative elements. *Not the least of its functions is to serve the metaphysical needs of man by constructing a world of illusion and by creating the transcendental on the basis of the rational* [my emphasis]. (Schlemmer in Gropius 81)

Furthermore, Schlemmer saw the stage workshop as providing an outlet for the grand objectives of the Bauhaus that often could not be realized due to economic constraints. In a letter dated 14 June 1921, he says, "We must be content with surrogates, create out of wood and cardboard what we cannot build in stone and steel" (Schlemmer 1972, 107).

The attempt of the Bauhaus to join the "artistic-ideal" and the "craftsmanlike-practical" was an endeavour with which Schlemmer was very familiar. His letters and diaries show that he spent a great deal of time trying to reconcile seemingly conflicting dualities, which caused

---

'old' masters, these students-turned-teachers earned only two-thirds' the salary; promises of promotion went unfulfilled (Whitford 1984, 166).

2. Lothar Schreyer was originally in charge of the stage workshop. Like Schlemmer, he was a painter who had strong ties to the theatre community (Gropius first saw his work at an avant garde theatre in Hamburg). Schreyer was, however, a little too avant garde — even for the Bauhaus; he left in 1923 after a production of his own play was deemed too obscure by his colleagues (Whitford 1984, 85).

him no end of "inner torments" (Schlemmer 1972, 9): idea and form, the ethical and the aesthetic, the classical and the modern, the organic and the constructed. In April 1913, Schlemmer wrote of painter and friend Willi Baumeister:

> a wild hodgepodge of influences, skilfully assimilated in his painting.... He absorbs all the influences of modern art, many of them undigested. The entire process, complete with undigested or purely instinctual elements, enters right into the paintings. Even the upset stomach helps shape his pictures. But he has more of what it takes to produce a work of art than I. "The drop of folly" which I lack. I know too much.
>
> I feel that objective representation of nature would be the way to capture a more profound form of mysticism. The mysticism that is crucial to the painter's vision.
>
> The symbolic force and import of the dot, the line, the triangle, the square, the circle... (Schlemmer 1972, 10)

Here, Schlemmer implies that a kind of aesthetic innocence is required on the part of the artist if the work of art is to achieve the necessary transcendent quality — an innocence which he feels he lacks. Yet, at the same time, he hints at a way for the 'worldly' artist to enter into the realm of the mystical — through an "objective representation of nature," where nature is broken down into its most basic constituents ("the dot, the line, the triangle, the square, the circle").

It is here that the ideas of the nineteenth-century playwright Heinrich von Kleist begin to resonate in Schlemmer's own theories of art.[3] In "On the Marionette Theatre," the stories exchanged by Kleist's narrator and Herr C- seem similar to Schlemmer's account of Baumeister's approach to painting. Both the narrator's story of the young man who loses his natural grace when he becomes self-conscious, and Herr C-'s tale of his encounter with the naturally-talented fencing bear, illustrate the true beauty —in whatever form— that is possible through unfettered innocence (Kleist in Sidnell 239-40). Herr C- concludes:

> We see that in the organic world, as reflection grows darker and weaker, grace emerges more radiant and powerful. But just as two lines intersecting on one side of a point, after their passage through infinity, suddenly reappear on the other side, or just as the image in a concave mirror, after moving out into the infinite, suddenly becomes visible again, so too grace returns, when knowledge has, as it were, gone through an infinity; thus grace appears most purely in that

3. Schlemmer does not mention Kleist by name in his diaries until September 1922, in an entry in which he discusses the renewal of ballet through the recognition of the artificiality of the theatrical medium (Schlemmer 1972, 126).

> human form which has either no consciousness at all or an infinite one —that is, in a puppet or in a god. (Kleist in Sidnell 240)

The narrator confirms that "'we would have to eat once more of the tree of knowledge in order to fall back into the state of innocence" (Kleist in Sidnell 240). In a similar vein, Schlemmer —in 1913— realizes that only an intensive study of the elements of nature ("knowledge") will lead him to the mystical ("state of innocence").

Schlemmer attempted to reach the ideal through an intensive study of form. Unlike many of his contemporaries, he did not reject outright the classical forms (the Greeks, the Italian Renaissance artists like Da Vinci) in favour of modern ones (Cubism, Expressionism). Instead, he embraced all forms that tended to further his artistic productivity. For Schlemmer, the "idea" and "form" were linked through art, as form "provides a sort of framework and the tools with which to capture an idea as it wells up from the ethical realm" (Schlemmer 1972, 46). His goal was to "devote [himself] completely to pure form until [he had] it at the beck and call of the idea.... Form is by nature aesthetic, related to the realm of beauty and play; whereas the idea is rooted in the ethical realm" (Schlemmer 1972, 53). Here Schlemmer's notions of the ethical realm (the idea) and the aesthetic realm (that of form) lead back to Herr C-'s grace and knowledge, whereby the idea —or truth— can be revealed only by the grace of supreme consciousness of nature.

In exploring Schlemmer's stage experiments, it is natural to draw some parallels between his work and that of his contemporaries, including Appia, Craig, Piscator (with whom Schlemmer had a limited professional contact, due mostly to Piscator's insistence on politicizing his work), the Futurists (Marinetti, Depero and Prampolini), and others that are too numerous to mention here. While describing Schlemmer's theatrical explorations in the passages that follow, these artists may sometimes be mentioned, calling attention to similarities and differences between their respective works. It is important to note, however, that it is not the purpose of this study to offer up a comparative analysis of the theatre practice of the time, but rather to use these other practitioners as a kind of temporal and aesthetic framing for Schlemmer's own work, which is our primary concern.

Schlemmer's exploration of form as a means of reaching some kind of artistic truth took him "from the geometry of the one-dimensional surface to the half-plastic (relief), and thence to the fully plastic art of the human body" (Schlemmer 1972, 82) on the stage. Schlemmer's stage experiments —including his *Triadic Ballet* (which will be discussed in more detail later)— dealt with the relationship between man and space, and were inscribed by very strict, geometric constructs. He used costume to exaggerate the human form, reduce it to its most basic components—a series of cubes or of spheres and ellipses that transformed the actor into "ambulant architecture … [or] the marionette," (Schlemmer in Gropius 26) respectively. He used costume together with movement to illustrate "the laws of motion of the human body in space [to create] a technical organism" (Schlemmer in Gropius 27). And he emphasized the "metaphysical forms of expression" (Schlemmer in Gropius 27) —in effect, signs— present in the human form, such as "the star shape of the spread hand, the [infinity] sign of the folded arms, [and] the cross shape of the backbone" (Schlemmer in Gropius 27).[4]

Like Kleist before him, Schlemmer saw the ballet of his time as moribund, but also as the conduit through which a renewal of theatre could be achieved. With *The Triadic Ballet*,[5] Schlemmer realized, at least in part, the visions he expressed in the experiments with actor, costume and movement described above. Other figures in dance at the time, such as Rudolf von Laban and Jacques Dalcroze, and their disciples, Kurt Jooss and Mary Wigman, were taking the medium in new directions as well. However, while Laban and Dalcroze concentrated on the unadorned body of the dancer, moving in space, giving in to the fact of gravity that classical ballet had for so long eschewed, Schlemmer felt

> justified in reviving their opposites: the brightly colored masquerades once so popular with the people; theatrical costume dance; and also ballet, to be born in a new form. For human beings will always love bright games, disguises, any festive, eye-catching, colorful reflection of life. This speechless theatrical dance, this non-committal Muse who says nothing yet means everything, contains possibilities for expression and articulation which an opera or a play could not offer in such purity; theatrical dance, originally the form from which opera and the drama sprang, is free of constraints and thus predestined to furnish time and again the starting point for a theatrical renaissance. (Schlemmer 1972, 196)

Reconstructing *The Triadic Ballet* is no easy task; only parts of the performance have been preserved on film, as well as in still photographs, and descriptions by Schlemmer and those who witnessed and/or performed the piece. The unifying theme for Schlemmer's first

4. Here, Marinetti's "Dynamic and Synoptic Declamation Manifesto" may come to mind, in which he suggests "'an outlined and topographic gesticulation that synthetically creates cubes, cones, spirals, [and] ellipses" (Marinetti in Kirby 101), indeed a "mechanization of the actor … through geometricized movement" (Kirby 104).

5. Parts of *The Triadic Ballet* were first performed in Stuttgart for a party hosted by Schlemmer's military regiment in 1916; the piece was subsequently performed in its entirety on 30 September 1922 at the Stuttgart Landestheater, in 1923 in Weimar's German National Theatre, in 1926 at a music festival in Donaueschingen, at the Grand Bridge Revue in Frankfurt am Main and at the Metropol Theatre in Berlin, and in Paris in 1932 at the International Dance Congress, where it received a prize (Schlemmer 1972, 4, 92-3, 177, 252).

ballet, the 'triad,' was perhaps an attempt to overcome both individual ego and binary opposition with the collective. The concept of the triad also brought together fundamental elements such as form, colour and space, the three dimensions of height, width and depth, the three basic forms (the ball, the cube and the pyramid) and the corresponding primary colours (red, blue and yellow), as well as the principal constituents of his work, dance, costume and music (Schlemmer 1972, 196). Three actors —two men and one woman— donned eighteen different costumes in which they performed twelve different dances. The costumes were comprised of padded cloth and painted papier-maché. The piece itself "consist[ed] of three parts which form[ed] a structure of stylized dance scenes, developing from the humorous to the serious. The first ... a gay burlesque with lemon-yellow drop curtains[,] the second, ceremonious and solemn, ... on a rose-colored stage[,] and the third ... a mystical fantasy on a black stage" (Schlemmer in Gropius 34). The music conformed to the tone set by the costumes —colour and form— ranging from "the cheerful grotesque to full pathos," (Schlemmer 1972, 197) all performed on a player piano.

In notes on *The Triadic Ballet* written in his diary in July, 1926, Schlemmer describes the relationship between dance, costume and music in his work:

> the mechanical instrument [the player piano] corresponds to the stereotypal dance style, dictated in part by the costumes, if not set as general objective; this in contrast to the spiritual and dramatic exuberance which music is usually used to convey these days. On the other hand, this music provides a parallel to the costumes, which follow the mathematical and mechanical outlines of the body. In addition, the doll-like quality of the dances corresponds to the music-box quality of the music and this should furnish the unity implied by the concept of "style." (Schlemmer 1972, 197)

In this way, costume, dance and music form an interlocking triad, each acting on and being acted upon by the others.[6] Schlemmer, in this same entry, goes on to say that, were the resources available (both financial and technological), one could do away with the human element altogether, creating a dance with puppets as "described in Heinrich Kleist's essay on the marionette" (Schlemmer 1972, 197).

6. The symbiosis created by costume, dance and music may bring to mind various experiments in "Colour-Music" in the late nineteenth and early twentieth centuries, among them the translation of music and musical instrument into light and colour by A. Wallace Rimington; Thomas Wilfrid's emotional-metaphorical transposition of the art of music and the art of colour with his Clavilux; as well as Adrian Bernard Klein's theories of the relationship between colour-music, line and shape (which he later put into practice with a colour projector for lighting the stage) (Scholes 205-7).

In his experiments at the Bauhaus stage workshop, Schlemmer attempted to move closer to a kind of marionette theatre. This objective was achieved in a variety of ways: by portraying the human form on the stage transformed by the use of costume to take on puppet-like qualities; by creating dances whereby the actor was rendered practically invisible by light/shadow and costume and only the prop pieces could be seen, as if in motion by themselves; and by using actual puppet creations on the stage, either alone or in sharp contrast to the human actors beside them.[7]

The actor-as-puppet can be seen in *The Triadic Ballet*, where the use of costume not only transforms the actor's physical appearance, but also dictates the range of movements which he/she can accomplish. In the "Flats Dance," three stage flats —one red, one yellow, and one blue— are moved around the stage area by three actors dressed in grey. The actors also wear white masks, square in shape, with holes cut out for eyes and mouth, and a protrusion for the nose, and white gloves and slippers. The actors are initially completely hidden behind the flats, which seem to take on a life of their own on the stage. Different groupings are created with the flats: sometimes they are side by side, sometimes on top of one another, always combined in different spatial and colour relationships. Then, the flats are lined up side by side, and the actors slowly begin to appear. However, they do not appear as three separate beings; rather, they seem to create one large being behind the three flats. The head of one actor appears over the top of the flats; the arm and leg of another appear at the right; the arm and leg of yet another appear at the left. Common sense dictates that it would not be possible for an average human being to stretch his limbs to such an extent—even one with the greatest agility. After some time, the actors

7. In these descriptions, I rely upon many still photographs taken during Schlemmer's actual stage workshops. However, I have also used a reconstruction of his dances, created during the 1970s and available on video: "Man and Mask: Oskar Schlemmer and the 'Bauhaus' Stage." The use of this video as a reliable source upon which to base critical discussion of Schlemmer's work is justified, I believe, for several reasons. There is a great attention to detail in the use of costume and prop/set pieces, which so much resemble the original photographs that it is difficult to tell them apart. The movement, or dance, also closely follows what remains of Schlemmer's diagrams, illustrations and instructions; many of the photographs of his work were taken with the express purpose of capturing the actor in motion. Finally, and perhaps most importantly, Schlemmer's widow, Tut (who was responsible for selecting and editing his diaries and letters for publication, and remained a font of information about Schlemmer and his work) is listed as an "Artistic Adviser." It is true that some of the elements of the recreations might be considered suspect — particularly those 'filmic' liberties taken to speed up actors' movements, or make them disappear from one place and reappear someplace completely different in an instant. However, for the purposes of this discussion, the value of the video outweighs the uncertainties associated with theatrical reconstruction.

appear in front of the flat, and begin to interact, walking around the flats and each other. What has been created is a living being that is both man and not-man, playfully appearing and disappearing behind the flats. Schlemmer has constructed a puppet-figure out of three actors moving independent of one another, yet with a common goal.[8]

Schlemmer experimented in another way with the extension of the limbs and torso of the actor, with poles in his "Pole Dance." The actor, dressed completely in black (including a cloth mask —worn to cover the face and head— and gloves and slippers) is almost indistinguishable from the black background behind him. What remains visible are the poles. Again, as with many of Schlemmer's costumes, the range of movements which the actor can perform are limited by the length and rigidity of the poles attached to his body. The actor, here, is both puppet and puppeteer; the stage image is not only of man exploring the space around him (albeit with limbs that are somewhat alien to him), but an exploration of the purely linear in motion.

In a similar vein, the "Hoop Dance" shows the actor, again in black, manipulating with each hand hoops of various sizes. The movements are slow and circular. In variations of the "Hoop Dance," the actor ceases to appear: sheets made of hoops attached to one another are lined up, one behind the other from downstage to upstage; figures (constructed of hoop shapes that vary in circumference to approximate a human form) hang from the ceiling of the stage space, in front, behind and amongst the sheets of hoops.[9] The hoop sheets and hoop figures, once set in motion, continue to swing — back and forth, side to side; in effect, they dance. As both 'actors' and set pieces, they take on a dual role: they not only explore the stage space, but help to define the nature of that space.

In the same way that Kleist's Herr C- speaks of the "center of gravity" (Kleist in Sidnell 236) as the key element in the dance of both human and puppet, so too does Schlemmer explore this concept with the swinging of the hoops — either by the actor's hand, or suspended from the ceiling. Herr C- also describes the relationship of the puppeteer to the puppet as having a mathematical precision; likewise Schlemmer believed that there was an intrinsic geometry to both the human body and the space around it, and that this relationship was precisely what was illustrated on the abstract stage (Schlemmer in Gropius 23).

The actor-as-puppet effect was also achieved in Schlemmer's "Chorus of Masks." Here, actors are dressed in black against a black background, with only the white masks and gloves visible. The masks

---

8. Once again, the similarities here between combining actor and setting may be compared to the Kinetic Stage of the Futurists, in its simplest form (Kirby 80).

9. Here, too, are echoes of "Prampolini's sketches for *The Merchant of Hearts* ... [with] hanging frames, screens, symbolic elements, and even abstract human figures that apparently moved during the performance" (Kirby 80).

are of varying shapes, sizes and styles, but all serve to exaggerate the human face in some way that renders it alternately cartoonish, grotesque, or even decidedly un-human. The dance begins with the masks lined up from the left to the right of the stage, and gradually evolves into a procession. The actors themselves are of different heights — and this effect is at times augmented by a stationary actor standing on a raised platform. The procession —even the use of the word "chorus" — alludes to the dance of ancient Greece; the masks, on the other hand, are reminiscent of Schlemmer's artistic contemporaries (notably Picasso and the Cubists): once again, he plays with "forms" from different epochs to achieve his aesthetic end. And, as with the "Pole Dance" and "Hoop Dance," the actor animates the inanimate to create the performance.

However, the actor-as-animator is not always invisible. "The Game of Bricks" shows the actor in a prominent role, constructing objects that are greater than the sum of their parts; indeed, the dance can be seen as a metaphor for the Bauhaus and the Bauhaus stage. Three actors, dressed in grey, and wearing white masks (painted with stylized eyes, eyebrows, nose and mouth), white gloves and white slippers, manipulate fifteen cubes (each with a side painted red, yellow, blue, green, white and black). Their own movements, as well as the constructions they create, follow a square with diagonals laid out on the floor. Initially, they each take their own cubes and build something on their own; each creation is different in its structure and in the colour scheme visible to the audience. Then, a change occurs, signalled by a raised hand and index finger, indicating that a new approach has been discovered (this gesture, made by one or more of the actors, becomes the sign for change in the stage environment in the rest of the piece): two of the actors combine their cubes to create a new structure. Another raised hand, and the third actor is invited to integrate his cubes into that structure. The three actors move the cubes to create various new shapes, changing them also by turning the cubes to expose different colours/sides. Their movements are precise and organized; however, their decisions are not reached without struggle, as one urges one direction while another has a different idea. Finally, a tower of cubes is erected, taller than any of the actors. The actors lie prone on three sides of the tower, gently rotating it to reveal its many facets. This rotation is interesting on a number of levels: there is the slow, almost balletic movement of the tower initiated by the actors; there is the image created of the human body lying prostrate before an (inanimate) creation; there is an element of physical danger and uncertainty created by the rotation of the tower — will it fall, crushing the human bodies lying beneath it? In the end, the actors leave the stage, never getting off the floor, but rather sliding backwards away from the object they have built; the tower stands alone.

The tension created on stage between the human body and the constructed body is perhaps the essential motif in Schlemmer's work. In his essay, "Man and Art Figure," Schlemmer describes the relationship between Man as Dancer (the Tänzermensch) and the Art Figure (Kuntsfigur). The Tänzermensch is the intermediate step between the human actor and the automaton or marionette: the figure in the "Pole Dance," the "Hoop Dance" and the "Chorus of Masks." The Tänzermensch "obeys the law of the body as well as the law of space; he follows his sense of himself as well as his sense of embracing space" (Schlemmer in Gropius 25). For Schlemmer, theatre became possible when the plastic world and the organic world (as represented by man) were combined.

The final stage in the evolution of the performer, the Kuntsfigur, relegates man to the role of master builder/puppeteer, creating the stage object and the means by which it moves. Like Kleist's marionette, Schlemmer's Kuntsfigur is not without a soul, as it were; the existence of the Kuntsfigur is possible only through the sensitivity and creativity of its human originator. According to Schlemmer, with the Kuntsfigur many things become possible on the stage. Any movement or position can be achieved and held for any length of time; the size of the figure is no longer limited by the human form; the Kuntsfigur, rather than being flesh and bone, can be made of any number of materials, each endowing it with different characteristics. However, perhaps most important to Schlemmer's concept of theatre is the idea that natural man and the Kuntsfigur can (and should) confront one another on the stage, resulting in "an intensification of their peculiar natures" (Schlemmer in Gropius 29).[10]

This confrontation between man and art figure remained largely in the realm of theory for Schlemmer (once again, due to the limits imposed upon him by the Bauhaus' resources). He did, however, create a "working drawing" on this theme, "The Two Solemn Tragedians," which he includes in "Man and Art Figure" with the following description:

> Two monumental figures, proscenium height, personifications of lofty concepts such as Power and Courage, Truth and Beauty, Law and Freedom. Their dialog: voices amplified by megaphones proportionate to the size of the figures; fluctuating in volume, at certain times with orchestral accompaniment.

10. Here, there is a resonance with Craig's Uber-Marionette, its "aim to clothe itself with a death-like beauty while exhaling a living spirit" (Craig 85). However, in the essential confrontation between Kuntsfigur and natural man, Schlemmer most definitely parts ways with Craig, and comes closer to Prampolini's notion of reconciling "'*man* (the dynamic element) and his *environment* (the static element)'" (Prampolini in Kirby 113-4) — whereby the "static element" includes the marionette.

> The figures —on wagons— are conceived as three-dimensional reliefs; cloth skirts trail behind upon entrance; masks and torsos made of papier-mâché are covered with metallic foil; arms are hinged in order to make possible sparse and significant gestures.
>
> By contrast, and to give the proper scale, there is natural man with his natural voice, moving about in the three zones of the stage (i.e., up, down, and center stage), establishing the dimensions vocally and physically. (Schlemmer in Gropius 31)

The title of the piece, as well as the illustration of the great figures, invoke an element of Greek tragedy (as with the "Chorus of Masks"). "The Two Solemn Tragedians" takes, as its starting point, the "psychical impulses [of organic man] ... which find expression in the great actor and in the mass scenes of great tragedy," (Schlemmer in Gropius 25) and transposes them to the constructed figures. The emotions of the human being are elevated, with the figures becoming the embodiment of "lofty concepts." Not only are the figures imposing in size, but their abilities to vocalize, for example, are equally amplified. As in *The Triadic Ballet*, music plays an integral part in the creation of the piece: in this case, "orchestral accompaniment" complements and emphasizes the grand scale of costume and movement (dance). The figures are also mobile, to a degree —they can be moved by means of the wagons on which they sit, and their arms have hinges that allow for "sparse and significant gestures"— large puppets that are manipulated by individuals behind the scenes. However, the figures have the ability to create meaning on the stage only in relation to the human forms that accompany them, with all their human limitations in size and sound. Schlemmer here conceives of something more than a puppet theatre: he creates both dialogue and dialectic between man and art figure.

And yet, many questions remain: exactly what kind of interaction takes place between the figures on the stage? and how is meaning created and communicated to the audience? Schlemmer's work has been described —both by Schlemmer himself and his contemporaries— as a synthesis of the Dionysian-emotional and the Apollonian-mathematical (Schlemmer 1972, 128). Meaning was created out of pure form, hinting at a kind of universal truth that was waiting to be found, if only the artist knew where to look. Schlemmer wrote in 1922, "the idea was not based on any particular 'intellectual' considerations. It grew rather out of inventive, aesthetic pleasure in mixing opposites of form, color, and movement and shaping the whole into something which conveyed significance and an underlying concept" (Schlemmer 1972, 128). Schlemmer's student, T. Lux Feininger, confirms Schlemmer's assertion, saying that "'play' with meaningful form was expected eventually to yield meaning, sense or message; ... gesture and sounds would become speech and plot" (Feininger in Gropius 9).

It is evident in Schlemmer's diaries that he felt drawn to the theatre, and derived pleasure from orchestrating and performing in his stage pieces. In a letter dated early December 1928, he writes: "I always succumb to the theater's wealth of figures and the fascination of dance, music, color, and personality. Also the stretch for a climax, performance with its joys and sorrows. Joys and sorrows, and that in the company of others, upon whose ability, enjoyment, love, loyalty, etc. success depends" (Schlemmer 1972, 237). Thus, while he speaks of an ultimate form of theatre which revolves around the presence of a Kuntsfigur, Schlemmer as master craftsman —and his "company of others"— are never entirely absent from the stage.

WORKS CITED

Carlson, Marvin. *Theories of the Theatre*. Ithaca and London: Cornell UP, 1984. Rpt. 1993.

Craig, Edward Gordon. *On the Art of the Theatre*. London and New York: Heinemann and Theatre Arts Books, 1956. Rpt. 1980.

"Dance of the Century: From Free Dance to Dance Theatre. German Expressionism." Writ. and dir. Sonia Schoonejans. La Sept/Pathe Television/Duran/Gedeon, 1992. *Performance*. Introd. Richard Ouzounian. TVO, March 1998.

Feininger, T. Lux. "The Bauhaus: Evolution of an Idea." *Criticism* II, 3 (Summer 1960): 260-77.

Gropius, Walter, ed. *The Theater of the Bauhaus*. Trans. Arthur S. Wensinger. Middletown, CT: Wesleyan UP, 1961.

Hochman, Elaine S. *Bauhaus. Crucible of Modernism*. New York: Fromm International, 1997.

Kirby, Michael. *Futurist Performance*. New York: E.P. Dutton, 1971.

"Man and Mask: Oskar Schlemmer and the 'Bauhaus' Stage." Dir. Margarete Hasting. Bavaria Atelier/GMBH, 197?.

Neumann, Eckhard, ed. *Bauhaus and bauhaus people*. New York: Van Nostrand Reinhold Company, 1970.

Scheyer, Ernst. "The Shapes of Space: The Art of Mary Wigman and Oskar Schlemmer." *Dance Perspectives* 41.

Schlemmer, Oskar. *The Letters and Diaries of Oskar Schlemmer*. ed. Tut Schlemmer. Trans. Krishna Winston. Middletown, CT: Wesleyan UP, 1972.

——. *Théâtre et abstraction (L'Espace du Bauhaus)*. trad. Eric Michaud. Série *Théâtre Années Vingt "Écrits théoriques."* Lausanne: Éditions L'Age d'Homme, 1978.

Scholes, Percy A. *The Oxford Companion to Music*. London: Oxford UP, 1970.

Sidnell, Michael J., ed. *Sources of Dramatic Theory 2: Voltaire to Hugo*. Cambridge UP, 1994.

Whitford, Frank. *Bauhaus*. London: Thames and Hudson, 1984. Rpt. 1986.

——. *The Bauhaus. Masters & Students by Themselves*. London: Conran Octopus, 1992.

Soft Dictatorship as Asylum

Ilona Fried

University of Budapest

The Performance of *The Persecution and Assassination of Jean-Paul Marat as Performed by the Inmates of the Asylum of Charenton under the Direction of the Marquis De Sade* by Peter Weiss, During the Last Decade of the Kádár regime in Hungary

In this article I shall examine the historical and political importance of a particular staging of Weiss' *Marat-Sade* play, by the theatrical company of the country town of Kaposvár, which ran from 1981 to 1989, shortly before the fall of the Kádár regime in Hungary. The incredible success of the play was due to the fact that it had been adapted to mirror and comment on the political events of the time and allowed Hungarian people to express their otherwise forbidden feelings towards their government.

Ever since the last century Hungarian theater has had the tradition of being interwoven with politics, a characteristic shared also by other European countries. After the second world war Hungary had for a few years a really flourishing theatrical life, with interesting plays, a high standard of staging and excellent actors trained during the period between the two World Wars. From 1948 onwards, following the nationalization of theaters, the state provided for them financially, creating a new population of theater-goers among working class people and peasants, social strata which had never before been interested in such activities. While in the early fifties social dogmatism was a clear obstacle for the whole of culture including theater, in the sixties cultural life opened up to new theatrical trends, directors, and guest performances.[1] These

1. Among the foreign companies there were the Royal Shakespeare Company, with *King Lear* directed by Peter Brook, and the Berliner Ensemble which brought Brecht's method and had strong impact on Hungarian theater.

new experiences led to a less strong naturalism or a less orthodox Stanislavskian way of acting.

These trends were almost exhausted by the seventies and the eighties, when there appeared a new wave of directors and actors, first mainly in the politically less controlled theaters of the provinces, then also in Budapest. These new directors introduced in their plays a new micro realism, which emphasized details with ironic and parodic effects. They created new group work and used choreography as an integral part of acting in order to criticize social and political taboos.

At the end of the fifties and in the sixties plays were written in genres not accepted in the decade before: the parable, the grotesque, and the tragicomedy. Their themes dealt with very serious topics, which included the issue of individual responsibility in history and the analysis of the past in order to see more clearly in the present (e.g. the failure of the revolution). Some of the great performances of the seventies and the eighties were everyday life-stories or popular plays of the fifties, apparently viewed seriously, but in reality treated as parodies. Cultural life could break away at last from the isolation of the fifties, and theater of the absurd found its way on the Hungarian stage. Throughout this period theater was used as a safety valve for a society which was moving towards consolidation and towards social compromises, which remained in place right until the end of the regime.

The company of Kaposvár that staged the *Marat-Sade* during the Kádár regime was perhaps the best one in Hungary at the time. The play was first performed on 4th December 1981, a few days before the military takeover in Poland on 13th December, and eight years before the fall of the Kádár regime itself, an event, which, of course, no one could foretell then. It won all three first prizes at the BITEF in Belgrade in 1982: a shared first prize, the prize for best direction, and the prize of the audience. It also won the critics' award the same year in Hungary. The play was an enormous success among students and intellectuals and appealed also to the local audiences: busloads of people used to travel to the country town of Kaposvár to see the performances. As a result the play was kept on in the following years. On 22nd April 1989, just a few months before the fall of the regime, a renewed version was presented with the same director and cast.

Looking back in time to these events, we can conclude that these performances represented the feelings and state of mind of the Hungarian people during the last decade of the socialist regime. The regime portrayed itself as a political system which cared for culture, arts and literature, but it was cautious with intellectuals and let them express themselves freely only up to a certain point. Since social criticism was almost impossible in politics, the press and mass media, literature and the performing arts (especially Hungarian cinema) served as a substitute for the lack of public life. It is not by accident that parables and grotesque situations were so widespread in the arts of the time.

The play, written in 1964 by Peter Weiss, is a pièce à thèse, based on the antagonism between the two main characters, De Sade and Marat. They represent opposite ways of seeing life and opposite ideologies: De Sade stands for extreme individuality, while Marat shows faith in the changes brought about by revolution. *Marat-Sade* takes the form of a play within a play: the patients of the asylum of Charenton stage, as part of their therapy, enact the history of the French Revolution, concentrating on Marat's murder. Weiss based himself on historical events and documents. He made use of actual speeches made by Marat, and of the fact that De Sade had been confined to the asylum of Charenton where he had staged plays.

The play is very complex and has many layers of meaning. There is a clear socio-political level where the asylum represents an intolerable social situation, with patients subjected to constant humiliations inflicted on them by the nurses and the director of the hospital who represent their oppressors. There is a metatheatrical level, where we see the relationship between the patients and their roles, and we have also a philosophical level, based mainly on the debate between the two main characters of the play within the play, concerning the importance of the revolution.

One of the key issues is power, and the possibility for private or collective freedom. The different characters stand for love or sexual aberrations and either seek private happiness, or collectivism. They are partly moved by De Sade, partly by instincts for freedom, but get repressed by power, represented by the dictators of the mental hospital. The character of De Sade, much older than Marat, has also a leading role in the plot as the 'director' of the play. As Weiss put it: "What interests me in bringing together Sade and Marat is the conflict between an individualism carried to extreme lengths and the idea of a political and social upheaval."[2] The play has a circular structure: it looks at attempts for revolution and subsequent failure, which repeat themselves. The play's feeling of doom results from this structure and the fact that the events of the revolution and the death of Marat are presented from the subsequent point of view of the Napoleonic restoration as announced several times right from the beginning.

The play was staged in 1964 by Peter Brook and a film was also made of this memorable performance. Peter Brook was fascinated by the experimental nature of the play and its conflictual elements. In his 1965 introduction to the *Marat-Sade* he wrote:

2. Peter Weiss, *Marat-Sade*. Translation by Geoffrey Skelton. Introduction by Peter Brook. New York: Atheneum, 1965, 106.

> Weiss not only uses total theatre, that time-honoured notion of getting all the elements of the stage to serve the play. His force is not only in the quantity of instruments he uses; it is above all in the jangle produced by the clash of styles. Everything is put in its place by its neighbour — the serious by the comic, the noble by the popular, the literary by the crude, the intellectual by the physical: the abstraction is vivified by the stage image, the violence illuminated by the cool flow of thought. The strands of meaning of the play pass to and fro through its structure and the result is a very complex form: like in Genet, it is a hall of mirrors or a corridor of echoes — and one must keep looking front and back all the time to reach the author's sense.[3]

A Hungarian critic aptly remarked on Peter Brook's interpretation of the play:

> The antagonistic aspirations of Artaud and Brecht, the theatre as ritual or therapy, intellectual alienation, irony, pathos, singing and motion theatre, naturalistic scenes and surrealist visions appear side by side in the performance and later on in the film.[4]

The complexity and innovation of the play's theatrical elements could be one of the reasons why directors continued to experiment with it and came up with such interesting and up to date performances. In the particular staging, which is examined in this article, the Hungarian director Ács János [5] uses the play to criticize the "soft dictatorship" of the Kádár regime. This dictatorship was not cruel and functioned with the least necessary violence in order to keep control over the subjects. The director shows us that one must rebel even against that type of dictatorship and, at the same time, foresees that this revolution is doomed to fail — he mourns over this failure as well as the failures of previous revolutions that took place in Hungary (1956, 1968) and in Poland (1981). The 'Napoleonic restoration' following the revolution during which the play takes place is a clear allusion to the Kádár regime.

In the Kaposvár staging of the *Marat-Sade* it was clear that director and actors were fully aware of the importance of their message and that this awareness helped them create a homogeneous and touching performance. As Eörsi István who translated the *Marat-Sade*'s poems observed, it was a very deeply felt performance, reflecting all the sufferings of Eastern Europe.[6]

---

3. *Ibidem*, p. vi.
4. Peter Brook, *Időfonalak*, Európa: Budapest, 1999, (*Threads of Time*, A Memoir, Methuen Drama: London, 1998), postscript by Lengyel György, p. 373. My translation.
5. In Hungarian names always have the surname first and the first name second.
6. Eörsi made this comment whern the play was broadcast on television on 15th November 1989, a few months after the political changes in Hungary.

A critic noted the differences in the reception of the play in 1981 and in 1989.[7] In 1981 there was a homogeneous public, unanimously against the regime, with a clear view of the side on which they stood, (despite the compromises depicted also in the staging). In the spring of 1989 the decadence of the socialist world was even greater and the former opposition had fallen into different groups. As a result of this the nature of power was not really clear and the audience was divided by internal misunderstandings and fights, which derived from the new political entities. However different the political situation may have been throughout these years the play did not fail to produce a strong effect when it addressed the unfulfilled hopes in social change and the impossibility of a "good revolution."

If we now look at the difference between the original text of the play and the Hungarian staging, we notice that there are several striking changes. The characters in the Hungarian staging are not dressed as patients, even though they are placed in a mental hospital, and there is little evidence of their being ill. Not only do they wear regular street clothes, but they also act as autonomous people. In fact the role of the nurses who, according to the original text, ought to move the puppet-like inmates, has changed. There are just one male nurse and one female nurse, with no nuns to help them. They both wear police uniforms, with clear reference to the political situation. At the very beginning of the performance the radio news is on, so that everything becomes very concrete and present.

This performance of *Marat-Sade* was realized as abn integration of the different theatrical traditions present in the text[8], including Brechtian alienation, obtained through the use of songs and the employment of the chorus, and elements of the theatre of cruelty, as for example, the highly abstract movements imitating executions during the revolution, or the striking of Sade by Corday, who beats him with a wet piece of cloth.[9] This beating is a ritual which has some elements of the theatre of cruelty, but is also made comic and ironic by stylization and overemphasis. There are other abstract elements in the play: for instance Marat's bath-tub has no water in it.

The play's micro-realism is evident in most of the costumes, which are normal street clothes that belong to the eighties. There are elements of micro realism also in certain situations and in the portrayal of Coulmier and his family. At the very beginning of the play some

---

7. Fenyö D. György, Marat-Sade. Manuscript.
8. See note 2
9. It is interesting to note that Corday beats Sade with the same soft material used for the curtains and for the final photo, while Sade is placed on top of Marat's bath-tub turned upside-down, with Marat lying under it. Sade apparently feels the blows but, unlike the original, he can bear them without any sign of suffering.

characters wearing street clothes (not hospital uniforms) arrive on stage: this is a realistic portrayal of the preparation for a performance. The director's suit is not a really good one, and one perceives that the person who wears it reached to a higher rank in society than he should have, and is not prepared for it. Even his gestures are typical of Coulmier, the functionary he represents, a leading figure of the 'Napoleonic' restoration. His way of reading his speech, of handling his glasses, all the details belong to this type of person. He is always ready to accept the excuses of the Narrator, when he interferes to prevent the characters from going too far. He is also typical in the way he wants to exercise his power without open violence. The social parody goes on with his family as well: the wife and the daughter are rough and ignorant nouveaux riches, who don't understand anything of what is going on around them. The daughter even looks rather frightened. They are dressed with a vulgar attempt at elegance and the wife wears a heavy make-up.

Marat and Sade, unlike Weiss's stage directions, are the same age and the same weight and their illness is not stressed. Sade wears a silken gown which is not worn out, as described in Weiss's text, but in fact appears to be "normal" and elegant.

Charlotte Corday is somewhat different from the original character, because she is an independent minded person. She is attractive as indicated in Weiss's text and there is no excess in her way of dressing. Duperret's sexual aberrations are played down or even eliminated in order to stress the speeches with which he tries to persuade Corday to save her life in order to obtain *private* happiness. Simone is dressed as a very simple housewife; she is not physically crooked and is an autonomous person, without the catatonic movements of the original role. Though she is completely at the service of Marat, she has her own dignity. In fact the "normal" and dignified appearance of the characters contributes to giving the play a more direct social and political message, in comparison to the philosophical message of the original text.

As a whole the performance is highly structured with symbols and metaphors of historical events, which makes the play less cruel and more abstract. The metaphor of the mental hospital as an image of the whole society is very straightforward.. The hospital becomes a space in which people can move about and live in a less constricted way than in the original text. There are just a few scenes in which the policemen use violence, as in the case of the priest, who has some water poured on him, or Roux, who is kicked down (he is bending over the knees of the policeman who is pouring water on him — not only does the policeman kick him, but so does the priest). The four "clowns," though they mainly follow the *commedia dell'arte* and the Brechtian traditions, also add some elements of the theatre of cruelty which bring a tone of parody to the performance.

Choreography plays a very important role. The coordinated movements of the patients, and the fact that, except for the main characters, all of the others join in the chorus (as do the protagonists in some very important moments), produce the effect of a conscious rebellion. This is underlined also by the harmony of colours: while the scenery is greyish brown, many of the inmates' costumes are white. In contrast with these sober colours the two women clowns wear red and blue. Kokol wears a blue dress with a red scarf and Rossignol has a red dress with a white and blue scarf. They occasionally use their scarves to represent the French flag and in this they are faithful to Weiss's description of Kokol as standing for the figure of Marianne. They have a key role in the movements of the group, representing the will of the "people," and are usually placed more or less in the middle of the stage, that is, in the open space.

The chorus has a very important role in so far as it creates an alienating effect in the play. Music and songs form an integral part of the play: no musicians are on stage and one can only hear the music. The rhythm of the play varies partly in accordance with the music: slow and sad scenes alternate with strong and harsh ones. Sometimes the music gests faster during moments of great tension and strong passions; at other times music and melodies contrast with the text. In this way music and songs contribute to the play's circular structure and underscore the two poles of the play, the movement for and against the theories of De Sade and Marat.

The scenery was planned by an architect — as a matter of fact, architects, artists quite often worked for the theatre. The bath hall of the mental hospital is a big open space, where the entire action takes place, and as a critic observed, practically everyone is always on stage.[10] This space can be divided by the curtains, (but they are practically never used) and by the movements of the individuals and/or the group. It is the scene of hopes and disillusions, of marches, of the highly stylized and often mocked moments of the revolution, and of oppression. There are horizontal and vertical wooden planks of geometric shape similar to the floor and the walls, which resemble the bars of a prison and give sharp contours to whatever is on stage. The hard nature of wood is contrasted to the softness of the curtains made of cloth, which remind us of the bath hall and also connect wood with the third material used, water. Underneath the wooden bars which form the "floor" of the stage there run waterpipes, which cannot be seen by the spectators. Water becomes the means of oppression and can only be handled by the policeman and the policewoman, as it is used to terrorrize the characters — a reminiscence of the water cure of the mental hospital.

10. Fenyö D. György, *op. cit.*

The two "nurses" turn on the water spray as part of their job. They do not show anger or thirst for power: they are just performing their duty. The strongest squirt of water, which hits Marat right in the middle of his monologue and causes him to fall to the ground, arrives from above, and is directed towards him by a casual 'power' — we do not see who is holding the hose. So the oppressed are not faced with a vicious power, just a neutral one, always on the alert, continually ready to manipulate them, but never more severe or more cruel than they suppose is strictly necessary.

This multi-functional space houses both the balcony for the 'public,' the outside world (the director of the hospital and his family), the shower room with the individual characters, the Narrator, the comedians and the two nurses personifying oppression. The spatial stratification of the stage changes at the very end of the performance, when the director and his family in the final song and march are attracted instinctively by the crowd. They leave their separate space on the balcony, *above* the bath hall, *above the space* where the rest of the acting takes place,and join the others, who are below. The characters singing about the people who are locked up, do not mean those who are ill, but those who are politically persecuted. The march does not become an open revolt, but a compact and unified demonstration. The characters in the Hungarian performance, unlike the original play or the memorable performance by Peter Brook, maintain their normality in the mental hospital, thus making it easier for the public to identify with them. They suffer a clearly political manipulation, and the play ends on the note of the failure of a well united and non-violent rebellion. In the final march for "victory," which is joined not only by the director and his family but also by the policemen, the oppressors and the oppressed share a common fate. All of a sudden they fall down on the ground in the open space: all the scenery of the hospital bath-hall has disappeared, but the back curtain[11] shows a clear, but *painted* historical object. So everyone becomes part of the big, inevitable machinery, and in this way the oppressors and the oppressed, get mixed up, and the go-between, the Narrator also gets involved in the action.

Whereas the characters in Brook's staging were tragic puppets due to their illness, which was caused by their rejection of destiny or society, the characters of Ács are puppets because of their historical and political fate, in fact because they are members of a certain society. At the end the oppressors and the oppressed are marching together and get defeated together. On the back cloth is *depicted* Corvin köz, a picture of one of the headquarters of the 1956 revolution (sometimes there was

11. The soft material of the back curtain is the same used for the curtains in the bath-hall, but this time it signifies final defeat.

instead Place de la Concorde) and the Narrator has in his hand a cobblestone, a poor symbol of the Paris revolt of 1968. While all the characters are lying motionless on the ground in silence, the Narrator who has been the outsider so far and is the only figure left standing, starts crying. The curtain falls.

The end of the film of Peter Brook showed the inmates climbing up the bars of their prison. Ács finishes on a note of complete failure, with the Narrator mourning over the defeated revolt and lost ideals both for the oppressors and the oppressed. The *Marat-Sade* play becomes in this case a drama which reflects the political situation of Eastern and Central Europe during the last decade of socialism.

Lepage's Psychoanalytic Interpretation of Schoenberg's *Erwartung*[1]

Giuliana Sanguinetti Katz

University of Toronto

In this article I will examine the psychoanalytic interpretation that Lepage gave of Schoenberg's *Erwartung*, in his *mise en scène* of the opera in 1993 and 1995 for the Canadian Opera Company. Schoenberg, the Austrian composer credited with inventing expressionistic (dodecaphonic) music, composed his one act, four scene monodrama *Erwartung* in 17 days (between 27 August and 12 September 1909). On this occasion he was inspired by the libretto of Marie Pappenheim, a medical student who was a member of Schoenberg's circle and wrote poetry.[2] Pappenheim had written for Schoenberg upon his request a highly poetic text, which explored the inner wanderings of a woman, who waited for her lover in a wood, looked for him anxiously among bushes and thorns, remembered their past encounters and discovered his body, murdered by her in a fit of jealousy because of his infidelities. In conclusion, the "awaiting" of the title did not lead to an encounter between lovers, a common literary and pictorial theme (Kallir 32), but to the discovery of the dead body of the treacherous man.

Pappenheim's text is a lyrical poem, written in the fragmentary style of somebody who tries to remember a series of dreams or visions. It has been suggested that Marie Pappenheim availed herself of Freud's

---

1. I am deeply indebted to Ms. Lee Milliken, stage manager of the Canadian Opera Company, who patiently explained to me the notes and drawings based on Lepage's stage directions of *Erwartung*. Without her this paper would not have been written.

I would also like also to thank Ms. Birthe Joergensen of the Canadian Opera Company, who repeatedly showed me photographs, slides and videos of the performances and helped me with the illustrations for this article.

2. For the collaboration between Pappenheim and Schoenberg see Spiel, *Vienna's Golden Autumn* 172; Stuckenschmidt, *Schoenberg, His Life, World and Work* 119-22; Kallir, *Arnold Schoenberg's Vienna* 32.

psychoanalytic writings, all the more so since she was related to Berta Pappenheim, the famous Anna O, about whom Freud and Breuer wrote their first case of hysteria (Spiel 172; Stuckenschmidt 119-20).[3]

The strong emotional content of the libretto and its expressionistic form were given a very powerful voice by Schoenberg's music. Stuchenshmidt comments that this was the ideal text for Schoenberg because of the concentration of dramatic action and asserts that "the monologues of the woman drew from him [Schoenberg] an imagination in sound beyond all the limits which he had set himself in the vocal movements in the George songs and the instrumental writing in the orchestral pieces"(120). Though Schoenberg wrote his monodrama with an amazing rapidity which prompted one critic to see in it an example of surrealist automatic writing (Griffith 5), he also gave it a clear structure with "a series of analysable events, a train of motives bound together for long stretches" (Stuckenschmidt 120-21).

Erwartung' s combination of an anguished outpouring of emotion and a recognizable musical form, may have reflected Schoenberg's desire to express and control his reaction to recent events in his relationships with family and friends. In 1908 one of Schoenberg's closest friends, the painter Richard Gerstl, having fallen in love with Schoenberg's wife Mathilde, had an affair with her and induced her to leave her husband and come to live with him. When Mathilde was persuaded by Weber to return to her husband and their two small children, Gerstl committed suicide first by trying to hang himself and then by stabbing himself through the heart. After Gerstl's death Schoenberg, who had never painted much, spent three years painting intensely and used Gerstl's expressionistic style in his portraits and landscapes, almost in an effort to identify with the dead friend, make amends for his death and bring him back to life.[4] In fact Schoenberg's personal experience of betrayal on the part of wife and friend, followed by the friend's gruesome death may have combined with Marie Pappenheim's text about longing, love, jealousy and murder in inspiring the composer to write so quickly such a heartfelt and harrowing opera.

If we now come to Lepage's interpretation of the opera, the first thing we notice is the fact that in his staging he dispenses with the realistic and very detailed descriptions in the libretto, which portray various landscapes with paths leading in and out of the wood. He also departs from the libretto's description of the woman's physical appearance and of her anxious wandering in the wood, looking for her

3. For the case of Anna O, see Sigmund Freud and Joseph Breuer, *Studies on Hysteria*, *S.E.* 2:

4. The relationships between Gerstl,Schoenberg and his wife Mathilde are discussed at length in Kallir 23-8, 40. See also the comments made on this subject by Schorske 354-5.

lover, tearing her clothes and her flesh on brambles, afraid of the trees that catch her in the night. Beside this, Lepage, besides, does not avail himself of the expressionistic sets Schoenberg had drawn for his opera, consisting of a frontal path leading into the dark wood (Kallir fig. 41).

In Scene 1 of the libretto the singer appears as a bejewelled woman, in a white dress covered with red roses, standing at the edge of a moonlit wood, with a broad path leading into it. In Scene 2 she moves gropingly along the broad path with tall trees surrounding her. In Scene 3 a band of light runs next to the path and the moon casts its light on a glade in the wood with grass, ferns and yellow toadstools. Finally, in Scene 4 a road through fields and meadows comes out of the wood and is joined by a path that leads to a house with dark shutters and a white balcony.[5]

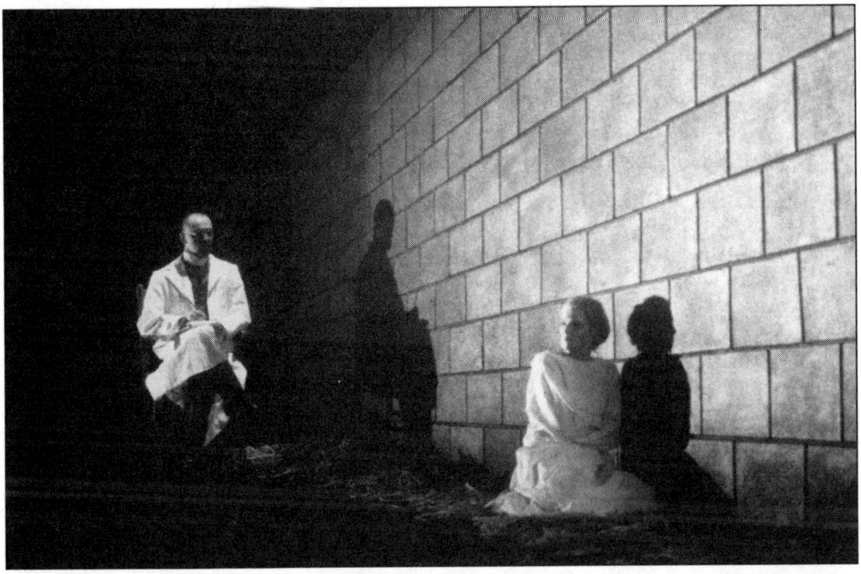

Figure 1: Michael Cooper Photographer. Courtesy of the Canadian Opera Company. 1993 production of *Erwartung*. Directed by Robert Lepage. Conducted by Richard Bradshaw. Designed by Michael Levine. Rebecca Blankenship as *The Woman* and Mark Johnson as *The Psychiatrist*.

Instead of these detailed descriptions present in the libretto, Lepage portrays the woman in a white straightjacket, crouching by the wall of a mental hospital or wandering within the confines of the institution, lost in her fantasies of love and death, while a middle aged psychiatrist is jotting down her thoughts on his pad (fig. 1). The stage is bare, apart

5. For the libretto I have used the original version of *Erwartung* with Kenneth Chalmers' translation, included in the London recording of the Wiener Philarmoniker performance, directed by Cristoph von Dohnanyi. London, CD 448 279-2, 1992.

from the long wall that traverses it and the occasional prop that appears and disappears on it (the doctor's chair, a naked branch, a sickle, a bed, a pool of blood). Though the analytic encounter is timed and limited by the presence of the doctor taking notes on the stage, it acquires nonetheless special psychic depth when the woman unties her straightjacket and abandons herself to her visions. At this point, the doctor becomes part of her fantasy and loses his objective dimension, becoming in turn a seducer, a voyeur, a conjuror.

In sum, Lepage not only changes dramatically the meaning of the libretto, turning the awaiting into an analytic session, but he also conjures up visions and situations that flash in front of us through the dark, portraying the anxious thoughts emerging from the woman's unconscious. Moreover, Lepage translates the many descriptions of the mysterious wood present in the very lyrical and allusive libretto, into repeated encounters between the woman and her lover, rendered more complex by the presence of the psychiatrist.

The most remarkable feature of Lepage's staging is the large transversal wall, mentioned above, that crosses the stage lengthwise to the right of the spectators, a wall that functions both as the enclosure of the mental hospital where the woman/singer is held in a straightjacket, and as the wall of her ego, through which break the dreams and memories of her unconscious.

In Lepage's interpretation the song of the woman does not correspond to any outside reality, but reflects only her rambling thoughts, which are fixed on paper by the omnipresent doctor, provided with pad and pencil, who is there at the very beginning and concludes the opera: the lights go down when he finishes taking his notes and shuts his pad. In fact the opera could be called "The Case of the Woman," since her story is presented as a case history taken down by a zealous analyst.

I will mention the key moments where Lepage introduces elements completely foreign to the libretto, which embody the woman's fantasies. In Scene 2, while she is groping in the dark wood and feeling her way with her hands, the woman is full of fear and anguish and sings:

> Was? lass los! *(zitternd auf, versucht, ihre Hand zu betrachten)* Eingeklemmt? Nein, es ist etwas gekrochen… *(wild, greift sich ins Gesicht)* Und hier auch…Wer rürt mich an? *(schlägt mit den Händen um sich)* Fort — nur weiter… um Gotteswillen… *(geht weiter, mit vorgestreckten Armen.)*
>
> What's that? Let go!*(straightens up, trembling she tries to see her hand)* Is it caught? No something crawled… (*clutching her face wildly*) And here too… who is touching me? (*flapping her hands around her*)
>
> Away — further… for God's sake… (*She moves onwards, with her arms held out in front of her.*) (p. 13)

At this point, in Lepage's staging, the woman is not wandering through a wood but is lying on the stage, with the psychiatrist lying down in his chair, parallel to her, still taking notes (fig. 2). At the same

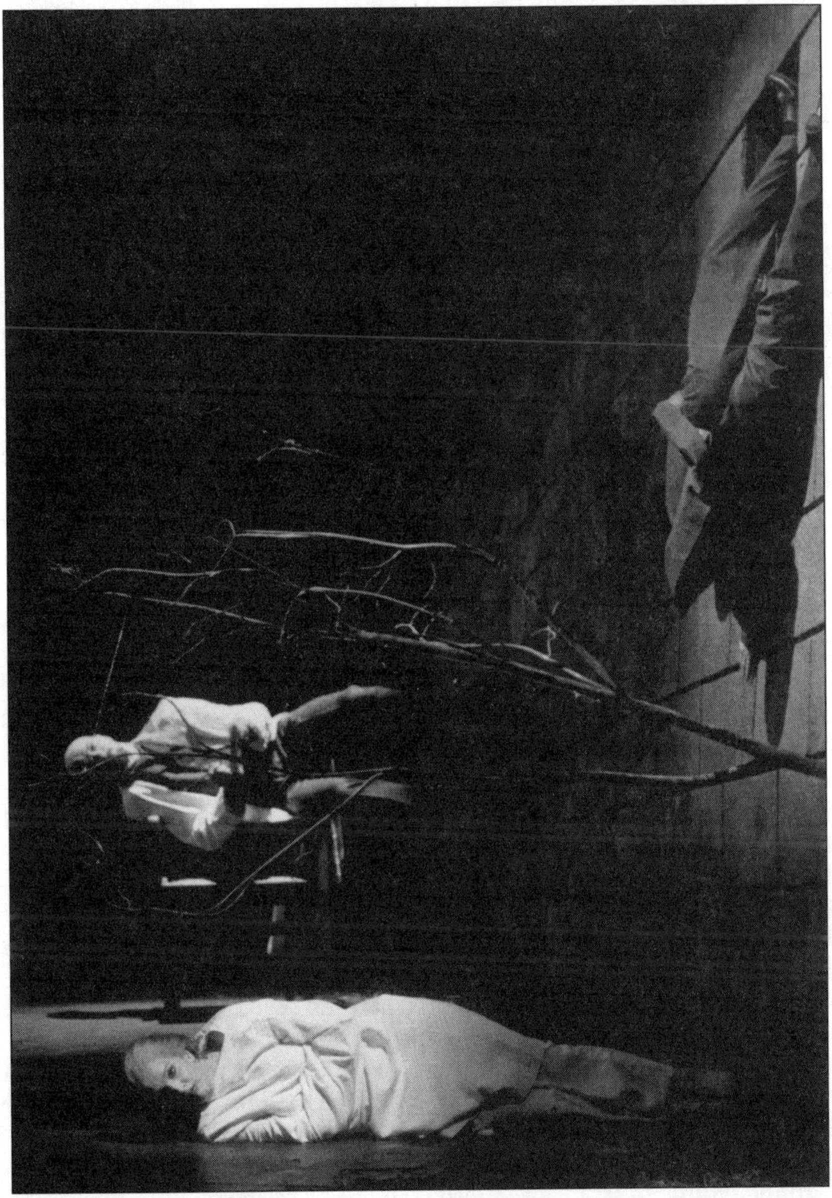

Figure 2: Michael Cooper Photographer. Courtesy of the C.O.C. 1995 production of *Erwartung*. Directed by Robert Lepage. Conducted by Richard Bradshaw. Designed by Michael Levine. Rebecca Blankenship as *The Woman*, Mark Johnson as *The Psychiatrist* and Noam Markus as *The Lover*.

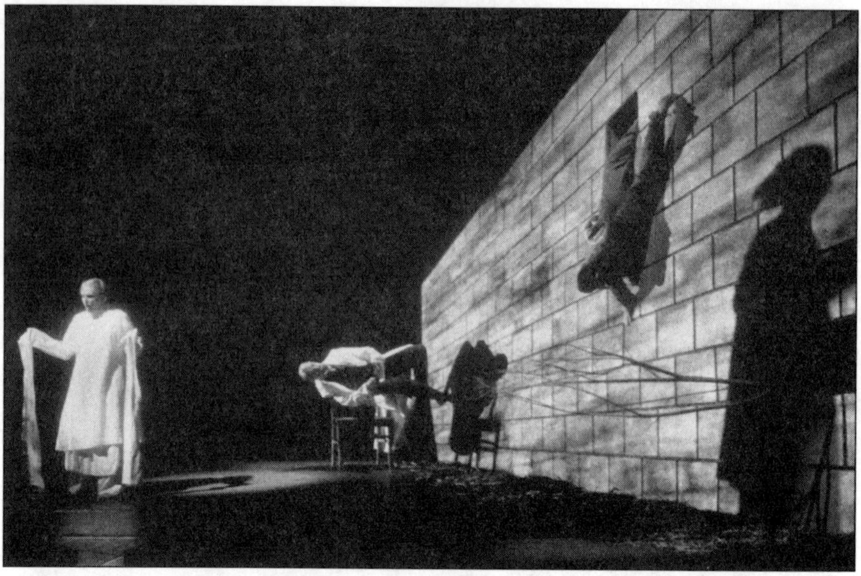

Figure 3: Michael Cooper Photographer. Courtesy of the C.O.C. 1995 production of *Erwartung*. Directed by Robert Lepage. Conducted by Richard Bradshaw. Designed by Michael Levine. Rebecca Blankenship as *The Woman*, Mark Johnson as *The Psychiatrist* and Noam Markus as *The Lover.*

time a naked branch slowly sticks out horizontally through a flap in the wall and the woman's lover crawls down another flap, further back. Then the woman, while singing "Fort — nur weiter… um Gotteswillen" (Away — further… for God's sake…), undoes her straightjacket (fig. 3). At this point the tree and the lover disappear behind the wall and the doctor takes his chair and exits.

We see the woman, here, struggling with her fantasies of love, death and sexuality that emerge from her unconscious and poke suggestively through the wall on the half lit stage. Both the lover and the branch appear as phallic symbols, the former hanging limply down the wall like a puppet and the latter sticking out in a threatening way, a premonition of death. The horror with which the woman greets them and her attempt to get rid of them make us realize that she perceives sexuality as something threatening, even deadly.

In this very rich and suggestive scene we are also made aware of the feelings of the woman towards her psychiatrist. The fact that the doctor lies on the floor when lover and branch come out of the wall and disappears when they disappear, shows that we are dealing exclusively with the woman's fantasies and that she has transferred onto her doctor the love-hate relationship she had towards her lover.

The transformation of the serious doctor into a seductive person is emphasized by the fact that the role of the doctor is played by an acrobat who, after sitting gravely on his chair, suddenly turns himself sideways and slowly falls to the ground while remaining seated. The unexpected agility of the doctor appears symbolic of his sexual prowess and his apparent middle age is belied by his youthful movements, which make him similar to the acrobatic lover who crawls down the wall.

Lepage stresses the woman's visions by making them reappear in Scene 2. As she remembers the idyllic moments when she walked with her lover down the path behind the garden wall and the sky was so transparent and distant, her memory is interrupted by the thought that in the recent past her lover did not come to meet her and she screams in anguish at something beating from branch to branch and coming towards her.

> Jetz rauscht es oben... Es schlägt von Ast zu Ast... Es kommt auf mich zu... *(voll Entsetzen seitwärts flüchtend, Schrei eines Nachtvogels)* Nicht her!... lass mich Herrgott, hilf mir...
>
> Now there's rustling above me... it's beating through the branches... coming towards me... *(She runs off to the side in horror. A night-bird screeches.)* Don't come here!... Leave me alone! God, help me... (p. 14)

At this point Lepage introduces again the lover through the wall, who this time crawls in horizontal position and embraces the woman, who first responds to his embrace, but then pushes him away in horror (fig. 4). The frightening night-bird of the libretto, which screeches and drives the woman away, is rendered by Lepage in a clearly erotic scene, with the lover reaching for the woman, who reacts with a mixture of attraction and horror.

In Scene 3 the anxiety increases and is fraught with sexual tension. When the woman sings: "Dort tanzt etwas Schwartzes.... hundert Hände..." (Something black is dancing here... a hundred hands) (p. 14), Lepage portrays the woman in bed with the lover on top of her. Then the lover disappears behind the bed and the woman remains alone on the bed. When she moves off, the bed is lifted by the psychiatrist, the lover and the lover's mistress. The lover, then, carries the bed away from the stage, while the psychiatrist remains with the woman and restrains her, as she flails about and sings in a distraught way:

> Aber der Schatten kriecht doch! Gelbe, breite Augen, so vorquellend, wie an Stielen... Wie es glotz... (Knarren im Gras) Kein Tier, lieber Gott, kein Tier... Ich habe, solche Angst... Liebster, mein Liebster, hilf mir...
>
> But the shadow is crawling! Wide yellow eyes, sticking out, as if on stalks...Staring...Not an animal, dear God, not an animal... I am so frightened... Darling, my darling, help me... (p. 15)

In this revealing scene the role of the psychiatrist, who lifts the bed and opens his coat in the process, is particularly important since it

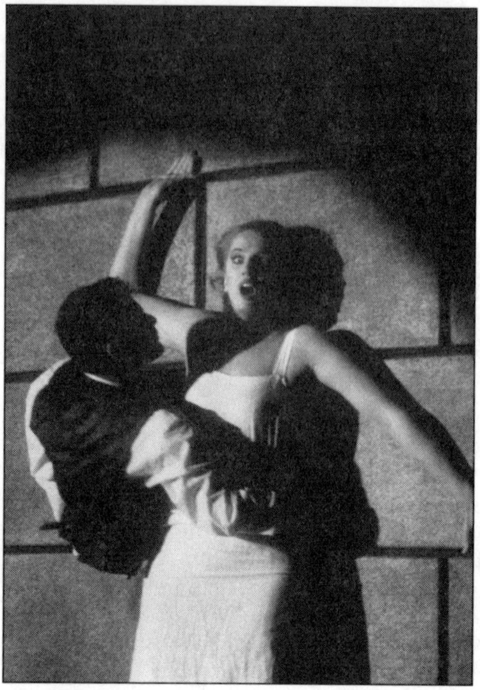

Figure 4: Michael Cooper Photographer. Courtesy of the C.O.C. 1993 production of *Erwartung*. Directed by Robert Lepage. Conducted by Richard Bradshaw. Designed by Michael Levine. Rebecca Blankenship as *The Woman* and Moam Markus as *The Lover.*

portrays the doctor not only as the person who observes and comments on the events, but also as the person who makes them happen and reveals them to the woman as well as to the spectator. In this particular instance he is in fact the double of the lover, who is concealed behind him, while he lifts the bed. In Lepage's interpretation of the opera the Woman perceives the middle aged doctor as a seductive father and the anxiety she feels about frightening visions of yellow eyes and crawling hands in the night is due, at an unconscious level, to her forbidden incestuous wishes. The mysterious and threatening creature in the wood is none other than the seductive father himself, who intervenes at the end of the scene to restrain the anguished woman. Lepage uses, in fact, Freud's cases of hysteria (in particular the case of Frau Emmy Von N.) to portray on the stage the anxious erotic fantasies of the woman, who translates into animal phobias her fear-desire of being seduced by a father figure.[6]

In the course of the opera Lepage develops further the symbolism of the branch and of the bed, while introducing other elements as well: the knife, the house and the pool of blood. In Scene 4 the woman, in her anxious wandering in search of her lover, needs to rest on a bench. In Lepage's choreography she rests in fact on the bed, on which there is blood. Then she wanders around and sings about a dead person and when, after much fear and hesitation, she bends down, she recognizes her lover. In Lepage's staging, at this point, the lover has replaced the bloodied bed and is lying face down with blood dripping from his

6. For the case of Frau Emmy von N. see Sigmund Freud, *Studies in Hysteria.* S.E. 2, 48-105. The fear of seduction on the part of a father figure is particularly evident in Freud's *Fragment of an Analysis of a Case of Hysteria* (the Dora Case), S.E.7, 3-122.

heart, and at the same time the psychiatrist has reappeared, sitting astride the wall, taking notes and looking down. The woman's murderous feelings are made evident by the fact that, while she is imploring her dead lover to wake up and not to be dead, she is in fact raising a large sickle, an important detail not present in the libretto (fig. 5). She then remembers the ecstasy of their sexual encounters and turns the lover face up, without accepting the fact that he is dead. Then she moves towards the wall. At this point the psychiatrist disappears slowly from his position on top of the wall and the woman crosses the stage over to the site of her dead lover, who is now replaced by the tree branch.

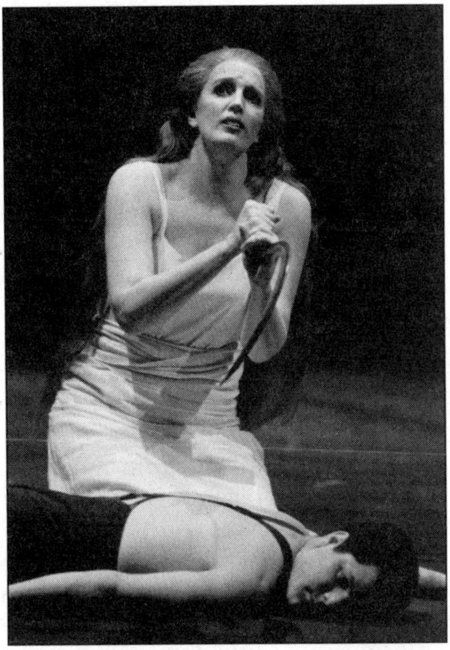

Figure 5: Michael Cooper Photographer. Courtesy of the C.O.C. 1995 production of *Erwartung*. Directed by Robert Lepage. Conducted by Richard Bradshaw. Designed by Michael Levine. Rebecca Blankenship as *The Woman* and Noam Markus as *The Lover*.

In this complex sequence the murder scene appears in broken fragments to the woman: first the bloodied bed, then the body of her lover dripping with blood, then the actual knife raised by her, finally death embodied in the naked branch we saw at the beginning, poking through the wall. What is more, the psychiatrist is an ever present, threatening figure. In vain the woman tries to deny her murderous feelings: the psychiatrist is always watching her and aware of what is happening. He is domineering and prying on the scene from the top of the wall, while the lover is the predestined victim.

The doctor is perceived as a controlling father figure, the other side of the helpless lover, who fills the woman with anguish because of the mixture of sexual attraction and murderous anger that she feels towards him. The position of the analyst on top of the wall and his slow withdrawal accentuate the dreamlike quality of his presence. Once more we are dealing exclusively with the woman's fantasies and not with her actual analysis.

There follows an intensely dramatic sequence where the woman remembers her lover's betrayal and the fact that she waited for him in vain. Lepage portrays concretely the betrayal showing us the lover who walks slowly across the stage with an arm stretched towards his mistress's arm, which comes seductively out of a flap in the wall. The lover grabs the mistress's hand and his arm starts disappearing into the wall in a way suggestive of a sexual encounter. The stage positions are then reversed. The mistress moves on the inside of the wall, which now looks like a window with curtains and wallpaper, and helps the lover inside the house. The lover and the mistress embrace, roll together on the stage, get into the bed covered with a sheet and writhe under the sheet. The woman who has watched the whole scene, and has been singing about the fact that her lover has betrayed her and she is now deserted, picks up the sickle and approaches the bed, while the psychiatrist peeks at the scene through a hole in the wall. Then the doctor withdraws his head and thrusts an arm through the hole and takes away the bed sheet, revealing the lover in bed with the mistress. The latter rolls away from the bed and there remains only the lover, naked in bed, reaching tenderly for the woman (fig. 6). The woman raises the sickle and kills the lover who rolls down in slow motion towards a pool, while the mistress tumbles off stage with the bed. While the woman is singing by the pool, remembering her love and addressing her dead lover, the latter slowly sinks into the pool along with the sickle. The actions of the psychiatrist and the presence of the sickle and of the pool of blood are all added by Lepage.

Once more the sexual encounter is relived in its full dramatic import. The psychiatrist, who sticks first his head then his arm through the wall and uncovers the lovers, like a magician performing a trick, has something devilish about him. His arm and head poking through the wall have definite phallic connotations. He is like an evil father figure, revealing to the innocent daughter the secrets of sexuality and tempting her into a forbidden sexual encounter. It is also to be noted that, while the mistress remains always dressed, like the woman, the lover is naked in bed. His nakedness represents in fact the full revelation of his seduction and therefore the threat he represents to the woman.

The fact that the mistress is dressed in white, like the woman, might indicate that, in Lepage's interpretation, she is not only the hated rival but also the sexual side of the woman's personality, the side she most dreads. The way the mistress beckons to the lover, helps him climb into the house, and rolls on the stage with him, shows her active sexuality as opposed to the woman's passive and fearful behaviour.

A final important point is the disappearance of lover and sickle into the pool, a symbol of the woman's attempt to bury her feelings in the unconscious, indicating that her thoughts are intolerable to her and that they probably go back to very painful childhood experiences (the fact that the mistress's house looks like a doll's house might allude to these childhood memories). In fact, as we have seen before, both the lover and the psychiatrist represent in her mind her ambivalent attitude towards her father, seen now as seductive, controlling and all powerful (the doctor), now as tender, loving, controlled by the mistress's wishes and victim of the woman's murderous jealousy (the lover).

In Lepage's staging, at the end of *Erwartung*, the woman recognizes her desolate condition at the break of morning, goes back by the wall, crouches down, ties on her straightjacket and resumes her initial position. At the same time the psychiatrist pirouettes on his chair and straightens himself up, resuming the position he had at the beginning. After the woman has finished singing, the doctor writes a few seconds more on his notepad and when he closes it, the light goes out and the opera is over.

At this point, in Lepage's interpretation, the woman's existence appears defined by her predicament in the mental hospital. She is the object of the psychiatrist's case history and does not have a life of her own: she is both oppressed by her fantasies about her father in her emotional life and by society and the medical establishment in real life. Her alienation and entrapment are complete.

One last comment on Lepage's use of visual motifs. As we have seen he does not resort to Schoenberg's expressionist sketches for *Erwartung* with the white way disappearing frontally into a wood. He uses instead the wall of a mental hospital, inspired, perhaps, by the expressionistic film, *The Cabinet of Dr. Calligaris* where the paranoid fantasies of a patient in a mental hospital include a strange lady in white wandering at night along a wall. He also appears influenced by the surrealist paintings of Magritte (especially *L'assassin menacé*) where clear and detailed pictures of persons and buildings, are placed in incongruous, absurd situations, with objects and people poking through and above walls, or flying through the air. In short, Lepage speaks to us the language of dreams, while reconstructing an early psychoanalytic case history and gives *Erwartung* a fascinating new dimension.

WORKS CITED

Freud, Sigmund. *Standard Edition of the Complete Psychological Works of Sigmund Freud.* Trans. James Strachey. 24 vols. London: Hogarth Press and the Institute of Psycho-analysis, 1953-1966.

Griffith, Paul."The Fervent Pursuit of Expression" in Arnold Schoenberg. *Erwartung. Brett-Lieder.* With Jessye Norman. Cond. James Levine. Metropolitan Opera Orchestra. Philips Classics, 1993, 5-6.

Kallir, Jane. *Arnold Schoenberg's Vienna.* New York: Galerie St. Etienne and Rizzoli, 1984.

Pappenheim, Marie. *Erwartung.* Trans. Kenneth Chalmers. In Arnold Schoenberg. *Verklärte Nacht. Chamber Symphony.Variations. 5 Pieces. 6 Songs. Erwartung.* With Anya Silija. Cond. Zubin Mehta and Christoph von Dohnányi. Los Angeles Philarmonic Orchestra, the Cleveland Orchestra and Wiener Philarmoniker. London,CD1 74.56,1996, 12-23.

Schorske, Carl E. *Fin-de-Siècle Vienna. Politics and Culture.* New York: Vintage Book, 1961.

Spiel, Hilde. *Vienna's Golden Autumn 1886-1938.* London: Weidenfeld and Nicholson, 1987.

Stuchenschmidt, H. H. *Schoenberg, His Life, World and Work.* London:Calder, 1977.

LIST OF CONTRIBUTORS

Salvatore Bancheri is Associate Professor at the University of Toronto. His research has been primarily in the areas of textual criticism, religious theatre, Eighteenth-Century literature, Sicilian literature, second-language teaching and learning, theatre: theory and performance, development of CALL software, and computer and research. He is the co-founder of the theatrical company *Maschere Duemondi* as well as the co-director of the Italian plays performed annually at the University of Toronto at Mississauga.

Nancy Copeland is Assistant Professor of Drama at the University of Toronto at Mississauga and the Graduate Centre for Study of Drama, University of Toronto. Her recent publications include an edition of *A Bold Stroke for a Wife*, by Susanna Centlivre (Broadview Press, 1995), "Mimicry and Hegemony: Feminist Performance Theory and Aphra Behn," in *The Performance Text*, ed. Domenico Pietropaolo (Legas, 1999), and "Reviving Aphra Behn: The Rover in the Restoration Repertoire," *Restoration and Eighteenth Century Theatre Research* (Summer 1999).

Eric Csapo is Associate Professor of Classics at the University of Toronto. He specializes in the social and institutional history of the ancient theatre. His publications include *The Context of Ancient Drama*, co-authored with William Slater.

Konrad Eisenbichler is Professor of Italian at the University of Toronto and teaches Italian Renaissance literature and culture. Past Director of the Centre for Reformation and Renaissance Studies (1990-2000), he is also a prize-winning scholar: his monograph *The Boys of the Archangel Raphael. A Youth Confraternity in Florence 1411-1785* was awarded the Howard Marraro Prize for best book of 1999 by the American Catholic Historical Association. His major area of research is Italian theatre in the fifteenth and sixteenth centuries, with special emphasis on productions mounted by confraternities.

Luba Eleen is Professor Emeritus in the Department of Fine Art at the University of Toronto. She is the author of *The Illustration of the Pauline Epistles* (Oxford, 1982) and many articles on medieval imagery. Her book on the illustrated New Testaments from Verona, incorporating some of the material in the present article, will be completed soon.

Claude Evans is a Senior Lecturer in the Department of French at the University of Toronto at Mississauga. She has co-authored a book, *A Supplement to the "Dictionnaire des Gloses en Vieux Breton"* (Toronto: Prepcorp, 1985) and written several articles in the fields of Breton philology, toponymy, onomastics and traditional peasant society, the Medieval Celtic Church history and literature. She is preparing an edition of the *Archives of Bégard Abbey* (c. 1156- 1463).

Ilona Fried is head of the Italian department at Eötvös Lóránd Tudományegyetem Tanárképzo Foiskolai Kar, Budapest. She is teaching Italian literature and performing arts, specializing on 20th century, has published among others essays on Pirandello, on contemporary theatre, and on the literature of the "frontiers". She is preparing a book on the cultural history of a multi-ethnic, multi-cultural town, Fiume.

Vera Golini is Associate Professor of Italian (PhD, University California, Berkeley) at St. Jerome's University (U. Waterloo). She has published on Italian Canadian and Italian women writers from the Renaissance to the present. Her critical studies have appeared in refereed journals, monographs, and anthologies. Since 1997 she also administers the Women's Studies Program at the University of Waterloo.

Francesco Guardiani is Professor of Italian a the University of Toronto. His area of specialization is Baroque literature (*La meravigliosa retorica dell'"Adone" di Giovan Battista Marino*, 1989; *Lectura Marini*: *"L'Adone" letto e commentato*, ed., 1989; *The Sense of Marino: Literature, Fine Arts and Music of the Italian Baroque*, ed.,1994; *Going for Baroque: Cultural Transformations 1550-1650*, ed. 1999). He researches also other areas of literature and criticism (*New Italian Fiction*, ed. 1992), and has written a volume on the history of Italian literature (*In prospettiva. Letteratura italiana dalle origini all' ultimo Novecento*, 1999).

Jennifer Hirsh is a Ph.D. candidate in the History of Art Department at Bryn Mawr College, where she specializes on twentieth-century Italian visual culture. She is currently completing a dissertation on self-representation in the painting and writing of Giorgio de Chirico.

Anna Migliarisi teaches and directs in the Theatre Studies Program at Acadia University. Her research interests include the theory and practice of play production in Renaissance and Baroque Italy, theories of acting, and contemporary Anglo-American approaches to actor training

Domenico Pietropaolo was Director of the Graduate Centre for Study of Drama and is Professor of Italian and Drama at the University of Toronto. He is also President of the Canadian Institute for Mediterranean Studies and Director of the Iacobucci Centre for Italian Canadian Studies. His current research interests include general dramaturgy, dramatic theory, and Italian literary history from the Middle Ages to the Enlightenment.

Paolo Puppa is Professor of Theatre History at the Faculty of Foreign Languages and Literatures at the University of Venice, at Ca' Foscari. He is the author of many articles and books on modern theatre. He is also a theatre director and a playwright. His playwriting credits include among many others *Svevo a Venezia* (1991), *Le parole al buio* (1993), *Mephisto, La collina di Euridice* (Pirandello prize in1998), translated in English as *Eurydice's Hill* and published with *Words in the Dark* (Legas 1998). More recently he wrote *Famiglie di notte* (Sellerio 2000) and *Venire a Venezia* (Club 2000), two series of monologue plays.

Giuliana Sanguinetti Katz is Associate Professor of Italian at the University of Toronto in Mississauga. She has published a study on *The Uses of Myth in Ippolito Nievo* (Longo, 1981) and has coedited *Pirandello and the Modern Theatre* (Canadian Society for Italian Studies, 1992), *Le fonti di Pirandello* (Palumbo, 1996) and *Natalia Ginzburg. A Voice of the Twentieth Century* (University of Toronto Press, 2000).

Luca Somigli is Assistant Professor of Italian Studies at the University of Toronto. He specializes in the study of the historical avant-garde and modernism, both within the Italian literary tradition and from a comparative perspective, and has also written on cinema and cultural studies. In addition to articles on Massimo Bontempelli, Filippo Tommaso Marinetti, Primo Conti, and Aldo Palazzeschi, he has published a volume on the satirical works of the English writer and painter Wyndham Lewis. He is currently working on a study of avant-garde manifestoes and co-editing a volume of the *Dictionary of Literary Biography on Italian Fiction between 1900 and 1945.*

Deborah Tihanyi is currently a PhD candidate in Drama at the University of Toronto; her thesis is entitled *Aspects of Developmental Dramaturgy in Canada*. Her Masters' thesis on the role of the dramaturge in Canadian play development has been used as a text in dramaturgy courses at several Canadian universities, and she has taught at the University of Alberta and the University of Toronto at Mississauga. She is a former Managing Editor of *Theatre Research in Canada*, and is a member of the *Association for Canadian Theatre Research*.

Anne Urbancic is currently Senior Lecturer in the Department of Italian Studies at the University of Toronto. She also teaches in the Program for Semiotics and Communication Theory. She has published widely, with focus on late 19th century/early 20th century Italian literature, on semiotics and on second language pedagogy.

Mary Alexandra Watt is an Assistant Professor of Italian at the University of Florida where she teaches Italian literature, cinema and language. She is currently researching the interplay between the underlying cruciform structure of Dante's Divine Comedy and the culture of pilgrimage and crusading in the Middle Ages. Most recently she has published an article on the reception of Dante in the time of Cosimo I.

Sarah Zappulla Muscarà is Professor of Italian Literature at the University of Catania, where she also teaches Film History and Criticism. Her fields of research include 19th and 20th century narrative, theatre and cinema, and editions of unpublished texts and collections of letters. Among her most recent publications and editions are *Martoglio cineasta* (Editalia), *Luigi Capuana e le carte messaggiere* (C.U.E.C.M.), *Il fiume di pietra* by Giuseppe Bonaviri (Mondadori);

Enzo Zappulla is President of the Institute of the History of Sicilian Theatre, Artistic Director of "Verga's Festival" and Member of the Administration of the National Centre of Pirandellian Studies in Agrigento. He has been the curator of various exhibitions which have circulated throughout Italy and abroad. Among his most recent works he has published, along with Sarah Zappulla Muscarà: *La figlia di Iorio tra lingua e dialetti* (la Cantinella), *Bonaviri inedito* (la Cantinella).

AGMV Marquis
MEMBER OF SCABRINI MEDIA
Quebec, Canada
2001